Research Methods in Psychology

# Research Methods in Psychology

*4th edition*

*RAJIV S. JHANGIANI, I-CHANT A. CHIANG, CARRIE CUTTLER, AND DANA C. LEIGHTON*

# Contents

Chapter I. The Science of Psychology

Chapter II. Overview of the Scientific Method

Chapter III. Research Ethics

## Chapter IV. Psychological Measurement

## Chapter V. Experimental Research

## Chapter VI. Non-Experimental Research

## Chapter VII. Survey Research

## Chapter VIII. Quasi-Experimental Research

Chapter IX. Factorial Designs

Chapter X. Single-Subject Research

Chapter XI. Presenting Your Research

Chapter XII. Descriptive Statistics

Chapter XIII. Inferential Statistics

# Acknowledgements

This textbook represents a labor of love and a deep commitment to students. Each of us had previously worked on adapting, updating, and refining successive editions of this textbook since its initial publication. In coming together to produce this fourth edition collaboratively, we were able to build on our own expertise and classroom experience as well as thoughtful feedback from several peer reviewers.

We would like to thank the Rebus Community, especially Zoe Wake Hyde and Apurva Ashok, for guiding and supporting us through the process of peer review and for building an intellectually supportive and encouraging community of authors and open educators.

We are immensely grateful to our peer reviewers Judy Grissett (Georgia Southwestern State University), Amy Nusbaum (Washington State University), and one additional anonymous reviewer, who volunteered their time and energy to provide valuable suggestions and feedback that improved the quality and consistency of the 4th edition of this book.

Finally, we are grateful to Lana Radomsky for her assistance with formatting and compiling the glossary and references.

Rajiv, Carrie, and Dana (May 2019)

*Rajiv S. Jhangiani, Carrie Cuttler, & Dana C. Leighton*

# About this Book

This textbook is an adaptation of one written by [unnamed original author] and adapted by The Saylor Foundation under a Creative Commons Attribution-NonCommercial-ShareAlike 3.0 License without attribution as requested by the work's original creator or licensee. The original text is available here: http://www.saylor.org/site/textbooks/

The first Canadian edition (published in 2013) was authored by Rajiv S. Jhangiani (Kwantlen Polytechnic University) and licensed under a Creative Commons Attribution-NonCommercial-ShareAlike 3.0 License. Revisions included the addition of a table of contents, changes to Chapter 3 (Research Ethics) to include a contemporary example of an ethical breach and to reflect Canadian ethical guidelines and privacy laws, additional information regarding online data collection in Chapter 9 (Survey Research), corrections of errors in the text and formulae, spelling changes from US to Canadian conventions, the addition of a cover page, and other necessary formatting adjustments.

The second Canadian edition (published in 2015) was co-authored by Rajiv S. Jhangiani (Kwantlen Polytechnic University) and I-Chant A. Chiang (Quest University Canada) and licensed under a Creative Commons Attribution-NonCommercial-ShareAlike 4.0 International License. Revisions included: (throughout) language revision, spelling & formatting, additional video links and website links, interactive visualizations, figures, tables, and examples; (Chapter 1) the Many Labs Replication Project; (Chapter 2) double-blind peer review, contemporary literature databases, how to read academic papers; (Chapter 3) Canadian ethics; (Chapter 4) laws, effects, theory; (Chapter 5) fuller description of the MMPI, removal of IAT, validity descriptions; (Chapter 6) validity & realism descriptions, Latin Square design; (Chapter 7) Mixed-design studies, qualitative-quantitative debate; (Chapter 8) 2 × 2 factorial exercise; (Chapter 9) Canadian Election Studies, order and open-ended questions; (Chapter 13) p-curve and BASP announcement about banning p-values; "replicability crisis" in psychology; (Glossary) added key terms.

The second U.S. edition (published in 2017) was authored by Dana C. Leighton (Southern Arkansas University) and licensed under a Creative Commons Attribution-NonCommercial-ShareAlike 4.0 International License. Revisions included reversion of spelling from Canadian English to U.S. English and the addition of a cover photo: "Great Wave off Kanagawa" after Katsushika Hokusai (葛飾北斎) is public domain.

The third U.S. edition (published in 2017) was authored by Carrie Cuttler (Washington State University) and licensed under a Creative Commons Attribution-NonCommercial-ShareAlike 4.0 International License. Revisions included general reorganization, language revision, spelling, formatting, additional video links, and examples throughout. More specifically, the overall model section was moved from Chapter 1 to Chapter 2, new sections were added to Chapter 1 on methods of knowing and goals of science, and a link on the replication crisis in psychology was added to Chapter 1. Chapter 2 was also reorganized by moving the section on reviewing the research literature to earlier in the chapter and taking sections from Chapter 4 (on theories and hypotheses), moving them to Chapter 2, and cutting the remainder of Chapter 4. Sections of Chapter 2 on correlation were also moved to Chapter 6. New sections on characteristics of good research questions, an overview of experimental vs. non-experimental research, a description of field vs. lab studies, and making conclusions were also added to Chapter 2. Chapter 3 was expanded by adding a definition of anonymity, elaborating on the Belmont Report (the principles of respect for persons and beneficence were added), and adding a link to a clip dispelling the myth that vaccines cause autism. Sections from Chapter 4 (on defining theories and hypotheses) were moved to Chapter 2 and the remainder of the previous Chapter 4 (on phenomenon, theories, and hypotheses) was cut. Chapter 5 was reorganized by moving the sections on four types of validity, manipulation checks, and placebo effects to later in the chapter. Descriptions of single factor two-level designs, single factor multi-level designs, matched-groups designs, order effects, and random counterbalancing were added to Chapter 5 and the concept of statistical validity was expanded upon. Chapter 6 was also reorganized by moving sections describing correlation coefficients from Chapters 2 and 12 to Chapter 6. The section of the book on complex correlation was also moved to Chapter 6 and the section on quasi-experiments was moved from Chapter 6 to its own chapter (Chapter 8). The categories of non-experimental research described in Chapter 6 were change to cross-sectional, correlational, and observational research. Chapter 6 was further expanded to describe cross-sectional studies, partial correlation, simple regression, the use of regression to make predictions, case studies, participant observation, disguised and undisguised observation, and structured observation. The terms independent variable and dependent variable as used in the context of regression were changed to predictor variable and outcome/criterion variable respectively. A distinction between proportionate stratified sampling and disproportionate stratified sampling was added to Chapter 7. The section on quasi-experimental designs was moved to its own chapter (Chapter 8) and was elaborated upon to include instrumentation and testing as threats to internal validity of one-group pretest-posttest designs, and to include sections describing the one-group posttest only design, pretest-posttest nonequivalent groups design, interrupted time-series with nonequivalent groups design, pretest-posttest design with switching replication, and switching replication with treatment removal designs. The section of Chapter 9 on factorial designs was split into two sections and the remainder of the chapter was moved or cut. Further, examples of everyday interactions were added and a description of simple effects was added to Chapter 9. The section on case studies that appeared in Chapter 10 was edited and moved to Chapter 6. Further, labels were added to multiple-baseline across behaviours, settings, and participants designs, and a concluding paragraph on converging evidence was added to Chapter 10. Only minor edits were made to the remaining chapters (Chapters 11, 12, and 13).

This fourth edition (published in 2019) was co-authored by Rajiv S. Jhangiani (Kwantlen Polytechnic University), Carrie Cuttler (Washington State University), and Dana C. Leighton (Texas A&M University–Texarkana) and is licensed under a Creative Commons Attribution-NonCommercial-ShareAlike 4.0 International License. Revisions throughout the current edition include changing the chapter and section numbering system to better accommodate adaptions that remove or reorder chapters; continued reversion from the Canadian edition; general grammatical edits; replacement of "he/she" to "they" and "his/her" to "their"; removal or update of dead links; embedded videos that were not embedded; moved key takeaways and exercises from the end of each chapter section to the end of each chapter; a new cover design. In addition, the following revisions were made to specific chapters:

- Chapter 1:
  - Updated list of empirically supported therapies.
- Chapter 2:
  - Added description of follow-up research by Drews, Pasupathi, and Strayer (2004) demonstrating

that cell phone conversations while driving carry a greater risk than conversations with a passenger
- ◦ Added the term meta-analysis along with a definition of this term
- ◦ Replaced terms men and women with males and females
- ◦ Updated the description of the number of records returned with different search terms to a broader description of the relative number of records (that will not change as more articles are added to PsychINFO)
- ◦ Replaced the term "operationally define" variables with a more general statement about measuring variables since the term operational definition is not formally defined until later in the text
- ◦ Added a citation for Zajonc's (1965) research
- ◦ Added a brief description of factors (i.e., small sample size, stringent alpha level) that increase the likelihood of a Type II error.
- • Chapter 3:
  - ◦ Removed titles of tables in references to tables
  - ◦ Added statement that many people, including children, have died as a result of people avoiding the MMR vaccine
  - ◦ Added a statement about self-plagiarizing being unethical and provided an example of submitting the same assignment in multiple classes
  - ◦ Explained the respect for persons principle
  - ◦ Revised the levels of IRB review to match terminology used in federal regulations
  - ◦ Footnotes for references were made actual footnotes in Pressbooks
- • Chapter 4:
  - ◦ Removed potentially offensive or stigmatizing examples
  - ◦ Clarified definition of levels of measurement
  - ◦ Added citations for the various scales described
  - ◦ Added further description of why IQ is measured on an interval scale
  - ◦ Added descriptions of the indicators of central tendency that are appropriate to compute and report for each of the scales of measure (nominal, ordinal, interval, ratio)
  - ◦ Added a paragraph on operationally defining the construct that reviews the process of transferring a conceptual definition to something that can be directly observed and measured
  - ◦ Added brief description of PsycTESTS and link to these tests
  - ◦ Removed the statement that family and friends can serve as good pilot subjects
- • Chapter 5:
  - ◦ Clarified the distinction between independent and dependent variables
  - ◦ Moved up the discussion of a control condition
  - ◦ Briefly discussed research ethics within the description of the study by Guéguen & de Gail (2003)
  - ◦ More clearly defined a power analysis and emphasized the importance of conducting one
  - ◦ Referenced confounds within the discussion of internal validity
  - ◦ Noted that within-subjects experiments require fewer participants
  - ◦ Removed duplicate reference
  - ◦ Added citations
  - ◦ Updated language

- Chapter 6:
  - Clarified when non-experimental approaches are appropriate
  - Added information about Milgram's non-experimental study of obedience to authority
  - Added a discussion of cross-sectional, longitudinal, and cross-sequential studies
  - Revised organization of non-experimental approaches
  - Removed description of experimenter-selected independent variable
  - Specified types of variables that may be measured in correlational research
  - Added an example of a correlational study that uses categorical variables
  - Added a factor analysis table
  - Listed more examples of nonstatistical data analysis techniques
  - Added a table to summarize some differences between quantitative and qualitative research
  - Described some group dynamics and personality characteristics that might influence participation in focus groups
  - Discussed Festinger's research on cognitive dissonance that used disguised participant observation
  - Described the Hawthorne effect
  - Added an example of a study that used structured observation within a laboratory environment
- Chapter 7:
  - Clarified language concerning data collection methods vs. research designs
  - Mentioned randomizing the order of presentation of questions as another way of reducing response order effects
  - Explained reverse coding
  - Described additional types of non-probability sampling
  - Reiterated the importance of conducting a power analysis
  - Added common online data collection sites
- Chapter 8:
  - Discussed how the inclusion of a control group rules out threats to internal validity within a one-group design study
- Chapter 9:
  - Clarified discussion of non-experimental factorial designs.
- Chapter 10: No substantive changes
- Chapter 11:
  - Added regional psychology association conferences to list of conferences
  - Condensed and clarified discussion of final manuscripts
  - Updated discussion of open sharing of results to acknowledge some journals that require open data
  - Added explanation of person-first language
- Chapter 12:
  - Corrected erroneous APA style recommendations and added references to specific Publication Manual sections
  - Standardized the use of the terms "figure" and "chart" to better correspond with APA style

- Minor changes to discussion of poster formatting
    - Moved list of conferences to end of discussion to not break up the material
- Chapter 13:
    - Defined p-hacking and clarified discussion of p-hacking
    - Made definition of $p$-value more technically correct

# About the Authors of the Current Edition

## Rajiv S. Jhangiani

Dr. Rajiv Jhangiani is the Associate Vice Provost, Open Education at Kwantlen Polytechnic University in British Columbia. He is an internationally known advocate for open education whose research and practice focuses on open educational resources, student-centered pedagogies, and the scholarship of teaching and learning. Rajiv is a co-founder of the Open Pedagogy Notebook, an Ambassador for the Center for Open Science, and serves on the BC Open Education Advisory Committee. He formerly served as an Open Education Advisor and Senior Open Education Research & Advocacy Fellow with BCcampus, an OER Research Fellow with the Open Education Group, a Faculty Workshop Facilitator with the Open Textbook Network, and a Faculty Fellow with the BC Open Textbook Project. A co-author of three open textbooks in Psychology, his most recent book is *Open: The Philosophy and Practices that are Revolutionizing Education and Science* (2017). You can find him online at @thatpsychprof or thatpsychprof.com

## Carrie Cuttler

Dr. Carrie Cuttler received her Ph.D. in Psychology from the University of British Columbia. She has been teaching research methods and statistics for over a decade. She is currently an Assistant Professor in the Department of Psychology at Washington State University, where she primarily studies the acute and chronic effects of cannabis on cognition, mental health, and physical health. Dr. Cuttler was also an OER Research Fellow with the Center for Open Education and she conducts research on open educational resources. She has over 50 publications including the following two published books: *A Student Guide for SPSS* (1st and 2nd edition) and *Research Methods in Psychology: Student Lab Guide*. Finally, she edited another OER entitled *Essentials of Abnormal Psychology*. In her spare time, she likes to travel, hike, bike, run, and watch movies with her husband and son. You can find her online at @carriecuttler or carriecuttler.com

# Dana C. Leighton

Dr. Dana C. Leighton is Assistant Professor of Psychology in the College of Arts, Science, and Education at Texas A&M University–Texarkana. He earned his Ph.D. from the University of Arkansas, and has 15 years experience teaching across the psychology curriculum at community colleges, liberal arts colleges, and research universities. Dr. Leighton's social psychology research lab studies intergroup relations, and routinely includes undergraduate students as researchers. He is also Chair of the university's Institutional Review Board. Recently he has been researching and writing about the use of open science research practices by undergraduate researchers to increase diversity, justice, and sustainability in psychological science. He has published on his teaching methods in eBooks from the Society for the Teaching of Psychology, presented his methods at regional and national conferences, and received grants to develop new teaching methods. His teaching interests are in undergraduate research, writing skills, and online student engagement. For more about Dr. Leighton see http://www.danaleighton.net and http://danaleighton.edublogs.org

# Preface

Psychology, like most other sciences, has its own set of tools to investigate the important research questions of its field. Unlike other sciences that are older and more mature, psychology is a relatively new field and, like an adolescent, is learning and changing rapidly. Psychology researchers are learning and changing along with the emerging science. This textbook introduces students to the fundamental principles of what it is like to think like a psychology researcher in the contemporary world of psychology research.

Historically, psychology developed practices and methods based on the established physical sciences. Unlike physical sciences, psychology had to grapple with the inherent variation among its subjects: people. To better account for this, we developed some practices and statistical methods that we (naïvely) considered to be foolproof. Over time we established a foundation of research findings that we considered solid.

In recent years, psychology's conversation has shifted to an introspective one, looking inward and re-examining the knowledge that we considered foundational. We began to find that some of that unshakable foundation was not as strong as we thought; some of the bedrock findings in psychology were being questioned and failed to be upheld in fuller scrutiny. As many introspective conversations do, this one caused a crisis of faith.

Psychologists are now questioning if we really know what we thought we knew or if we simply got lucky. We are struggling to understand how what we choose to publish and not publish, what we choose to report and not report, and how we train our students as researchers is having an effect on what we call "knowledge" in psychology. We are beginning to question whether that knowledge represents real behaviour and mental processes in human beings, or simply represents the effects of our choice of methods. This has started a firestorm among psychology researchers, but it is one that needs to play out. For a book aimed at novice psychology undergraduates, it is tempting to gloss over these issues and proclaim that our "knowledge" is "truth." That would be a disservice to our students though, who need to be critical questioners of research. Instead of shying away from this controversy, this textbook invites the reader to step right into the middle of it.

With every step of the way, the research process in psychology is fraught with decisions, trade-offs, and uncertainty. We decide to study one variable and not another; we balance the costs of research against its benefits; we are uncertain whether our results will replicate. Every step is a decision that takes us in a different direction and closer to or further from the truth. Research is not an easy route to traverse, but we hope this textbook will be a hiking map that can at least inspire the direction students can take, and provide some absolute routes to begin traveling.

As we wrote at the beginning of this preface, psychology is a young science. Like any adolescent, psychology is grappling with its identity as a science, learning to use better tools, understanding the importance of transparency, and is having more open conversations to improve its understanding of human behaviour. We will grow up and mature together. It is an exciting time to be part of that growth as psychology becomes a more mature science.

# CHAPTER I
# THE SCIENCE OF PSYCHOLOGY

Many people believe that women tend to talk more than men—with some even suggesting that this difference has a biological basis. One widely cited estimate is that women speak 20,000 words per day on average and men speak only 7,000. This claim seems plausible, but is it *true*? A group of psychologists led by Matthias Mehl decided to find out. They checked to see if anyone had actually tried to count the daily number of words spoken by women and men. No one had. So these researchers conducted a study in which female and male college students (369 in all) wore audio recorders while they went about their lives. The result? The women spoke an average of 16,215 words per day and the men spoke an average of 15,669—an extremely small difference that could easily be explained by chance. In an article in the journal *Science*, these researchers summed up their findings as follows: "We therefore conclude, on the basis of available empirical evidence, that the widespread and highly publicized stereotype about female talkativeness is unfounded" (Mehl, Vazire, Ramirez-Esparza, Slatcher, & Pennebaker, 2007, p. 82)[1].

Psychology is usually defined as the scientific study of human behavior and mental processes, and this example illustrates the features that make it scientific. In this chapter, we look closely at these features, review the goals of psychology, and address several basic questions that students often have about it. Who conducts scientific research in psychology? Why? Does scientific psychology tell us anything that common sense does not? Why should I bother to learn the scientific approach—especially if I want to be a clinical psychologist and not a researcher? These are extremely good questions, and answering them now will provide a solid foundation for learning the rest of the material in your course.

# 1. Methods of Knowing

Take a minute to ponder some of what you know and how you acquired that knowledge. Perhaps you know that you should make your bed in the morning because your mother or father told you this is what you should do, perhaps you know that swans are white because all of the swans you have seen are white, or perhaps you know that your friend is lying to you because she is acting strange and won't look you in the eye. But should we trust knowledge from these sources? The methods of acquiring knowledge can be broken down into five categories each with its own strengths and weaknesses.

## Intuition

The first method of knowing is intuition. When we use our intuition, we are relying on our guts, our emotions, and/or our instincts to guide us. Rather than examining facts or using rational thought, intuition involves believing what feels true. The problem with relying on intuition is that our intuitions can be wrong because they are driven by cognitive and motivational biases rather than logical reasoning or scientific evidence. While the strange behavior of your friend may lead you to think s/he is lying to you it may just be that s/he is holding in a bit of gas or is preoccupied with some other issue that is irrelevant to you. However, weighing alternatives and thinking of all the different possibilities can be paralyzing for some people and sometimes decisions based on intuition are actually superior to those based on analysis (people interested in this idea should read Malcolm Gladwell's book Blink)[1].

## Authority

Perhaps one of the most common methods of acquiring knowledge is through authority. This method involves accepting new ideas because some authority figure states that they are true. These authorities include parents, the media, doctors, Priests and other religious authorities, the government, and professors. While in an ideal world we should be able to trust authority figures, history has taught us otherwise and many instances of atrocities against humanity are a consequence of people unquestioningly following authority (e.g., Salem Witch Trials, Nazi War Crimes). On a more benign level, while your parents may have told you that you should make your bed in the morning, making your bed provides the warm damp environment in which mites thrive. Keeping the sheets open provides a less hospitable environment for mites. These examples illustrate that the problem with using authority to obtain knowledge is that they may be wrong, they may just be using their intuition to arrive at their conclusions, and they may have their own reasons to mislead you. Nevertheless, much of the information we acquire is through authority because we don't have time to question and independently research every piece of knowledge we learn through authority. But we can learn to evaluate the credentials of authority figures, to evaluate the methods they used to arrive at their conclusions, and evaluate whether they have any reasons to mislead us.

## Rationalism

Rationalism involves using logic and reasoning to acquire new knowledge. Using this method premises are stated and logical rules are followed to arrive at sound conclusions. For instance, if I am given the premise that all swans are white and the premise that this is a swan then I can come to the rational conclusion that this swan is white without actually seeing the swan. The problem with this method is that if the premises are wrong or there is an error in logic then the conclusion will not be valid. For instance, the premise that all swans are white is incorrect; there are black swans in Australia. Also, unless formally trained in the rules of logic it is easy to make an error. Nevertheless, if the premises are correct and logical rules are followed appropriately then this is sound means of acquiring knowledge.

## Empiricism

Empiricism involves acquiring knowledge through observation and experience. Once again many of you may have believed that all swans are white because you have only ever seen white swans. For centuries people believed the world is flat because it appears to be flat. These examples and the many visual illusions that trick our senses illustrate the problems with relying on empiricism alone to derive knowledge. We are limited in what we can experience and observe and our senses can deceive us. Moreover, our prior experiences can alter the way we perceive events. Nevertheless, empiricism is at the heart of the scientific method. Science relies on observations. But not just any observations, science relies on structured observations which is known as systematic empiricism.

## The Scientific Method

The scientific method is a process of systematically collecting and evaluating evidence to test ideas and answer questions. While scientists may use intuition, authority, rationalism, and empiricism to generate new ideas they don't stop there. Scientists go a step further by using systematic empiricism to make careful observations under various controlled conditions in order to test their ideas and they use rationalism to arrive at valid conclusions. While the scientific method is the most likely of all of the methods to produce valid knowledge, like all methods of acquiring knowledge it also has its drawbacks. One major problem is that it is not always feasible to use the scientific method; this method can require considerable time and resources. Another problem with the scientific method is that it cannot be used to answer all questions. As described in the following section, the scientific method can only be used to address empirical questions. This book and your research methods course are designed to provide you with an in-depth examination of how psychologists use the scientific method to advance our understanding of human behavior and the mind.

# Notes

1.  Gladwell, M. E. (2005). *Blink: The power of thinking without thinking.* (9th ed.). New York: Little, Brown & Co.

# 2. Understanding Science

## What Is Science?

Some people are surprised to learn that psychology is a **science**. They generally agree that astronomy, biology, and chemistry are sciences but wonder what psychology has in common with these other fields. Before answering this question, however, it is worth reflecting on what astronomy, biology, and chemistry have in common with *each other*. It is clearly not their subject matter. Astronomers study celestial bodies, biologists study living organisms, and chemists study matter and its properties. It is also not the equipment and techniques that they use. Few biologists would know what to do with a radio telescope, for example, and few chemists would know how to track a moose population in the wild. For these and other reasons, philosophers and scientists who have thought deeply about this question have concluded that what the sciences have in common is a general approach to understanding the natural world. Psychology is a science because it takes this same general approach to understanding one aspect of the natural world: human behavior.

## Features of Science

The general scientific approach has three fundamental features (Stanovich, 2010)[1]. The first is **systematic empiricism**. Empiricism refers to learning based on observation, and scientists learn about the natural world systematically, by carefully planning, making, recording, and analyzing observations of it. As we will see, logical reasoning and even creativity play important roles in science too, but scientists are unique in their insistence on checking their ideas about the way the world is against their systematic observations. Notice, for example, that Mehl and his colleagues did not trust other people's stereotypes or even their own informal observations. Instead, they systematically recorded, counted, and compared the number of words spoken by a large sample of women and men. Furthermore, when their systematic observations turned out to conflict with people's stereotypes, they trusted their systematic observations.

The second feature of the scientific approach—which follows in a straightforward way from the first—is that it is concerned with **empirical questions**. These are questions about the way the world actually is and, therefore, can be answered by systematically observing it. The question of whether women talk more than men is empirical in this way. Either women really do talk more than men or they do not, and this can be determined by systematically observing how much women and men actually talk. Having said this, there are many interesting and important questions that are not empirically testable and that science is not in a position to answer. Among these are questions about values—whether things are good or bad, just or unjust, or beautiful or ugly, and how the world *ought* to be. So although the question of whether a stereotype is accurate or inaccurate is an empirically testable one that science can answer, the question—or, rather, the value judgment—of whether it is wrong for people to hold inaccurate stereotypes is not. Similarly, the question of whether criminal behavior has a genetic basis is an empirical question, but the question of what actions ought to be considered illegal is not. It is especially important for researchers in psychology to be mindful of this distinction.

The third feature of science is that it creates **public knowledge**. After asking their empirical questions, making their systematic observations, and drawing their conclusions, scientists publish their work. This usually means writing an article for publication in a professional journal, in which they put their research question in the context of previous research, describe in detail the methods they used to answer their question, and clearly present their results and conclusions. Increasingly, scientists are opting to publish their work in open access journals, in which the articles are freely available to all – scientists and nonscientists alike. This important choice allows publicly-funded research to create knowledge that is truly public.

Publication is an essential feature of science for two reasons. One is that science is a social process—a large-scale collaboration among many researchers distributed across both time and space. Our current scientific knowledge of most topics is based on many different studies conducted by many different researchers who have shared their work publicly over many years. The second is that publication allows science to be self-correcting. Individual scientists understand that, despite their best efforts, their methods can be flawed and their conclusions incorrect. Publication allows others in the scientific community to detect and correct these errors so that, over time, scientific knowledge increasingly reflects the way the world actually is.

A good example of the self-correcting nature of science is the "Many Labs Replication Project" – a large and coordinated effort by prominent psychological scientists around the world to attempt to replicate findings from 13 classic and contemporary studies (Klein et al., 2013)[2]. One of the findings selected by these researchers for replication was the fascinating effect, first reported by Simone Schnall and her colleagues at the University of Plymouth, that washing one's hands leads people to view moral transgressions—ranging from keeping money inside a found wallet to using a kitten for sexual arousal—as less wrong (Schnall, Benton, & Harvey, 2008)[3]. If reliable, this effect might help explain why so many religious traditions associate physical cleanliness with moral purity. However, despite using the same materials and nearly identical procedures with a much larger sample, the "Many Labs" researchers were unable to replicate the original finding (Johnson, Cheung, & Donnellan, 2013)[4], suggesting that the original finding may have stemmed from the relatively small sample size (which can lead to unreliable results) used in the original study. To be clear, at this stage we are still unable to definitively conclude that the handwashing effect does not exist; however, the effort that has gone into testing its reliability certainly demonstrates the collaborative and cautious nature of scientific progress.

For more on the replication crisis in psychology see: http://nobaproject.com/modules/the-replication-crisis-in-psychology

# Science Versus Pseudoscience

**Pseudoscience** refers to activities and beliefs that are claimed to be scientific by their proponents—and may appear to be scientific at first glance—but are not. Consider the theory of biorhythms (not to be confused with sleep cycles or circadian rhythms that do have a scientific basis). The idea is that people's physical, intellectual, and emotional abilities run in cycles that begin when they are born and continue until they die. Allegedly, the physical cycle has a period of 23 days, the intellectual cycle a period of 33 days, and the emotional cycle a period of 28 days. So, for example, if you had the option of when to schedule an exam, you would want to schedule it for a time when your intellectual cycle will be at a high point. The theory of biorhythms has been around for more than 100 years, and you can find numerous popular books and websites about biorhythms, often containing impressive and scientific-sounding terms like *sinusoidal wave* and *bioelectricity*. The problem with biorhythms, however, is that scientific evidence indicates they do not exist (Hines, 1998)[5].

A set of beliefs or activities can be said to be pseudoscientific if (a) its adherents claim or imply that it is scientific but (b) it lacks one or more of the three features of science. For instance, it might lack systematic empiricism. Either there is no relevant scientific research or, as in the case of biorhythms, there is relevant scientific research but it is ignored. It might also lack public knowledge. People who promote the beliefs or activities might claim to have conducted scientific research but never publish that research in a way that allows others to evaluate it.

A set of beliefs and activities might also be pseudoscientific because it does not address empirical questions. The philosopher Karl Popper was especially concerned with this idea (Popper, 2002)[6]. He argued more specifically that any scientific claim must be expressed in such a way that there are observations that would—if they were made—count as evidence against the claim. In other words, scientific claims must be **falsifiable**. The claim that women talk more than men is falsifiable because systematic observations could reveal either that they do talk more than men or that they do not. As an example of an unfalsifiable claim, consider that many people who believe in extrasensory perception (ESP) and other psychic powers claim that such powers can disappear when they are observed too closely. This makes it so that no possible observation would count as evidence against ESP. If a careful test of a self-proclaimed psychic showed that she predicted the future at better-than-chance levels, this would be consistent with the claim that she had psychic powers. But if she failed to predict the future at better-than-chance levels, this would also be consistent with the claim because her powers can supposedly disappear when they are observed too closely.

Why should we concern ourselves with pseudoscience? There are at least three reasons. One is that learning about pseudoscience helps bring the fundamental features of science—and their importance—into sharper focus. A second is that biorhythms, psychic powers, astrology, and many other pseudoscientific beliefs are widely held and are promoted on the Internet, on television, and in books and magazines. Far from being harmless, the promotion of these beliefs often results in great personal toll as, for example, believers in pseudoscience opt for "treatments" such as homeopathy for serious medical conditions instead of empirically-supported treatments. Learning what makes them pseudoscientific can help us to identify and evaluate such beliefs and practices when we encounter them. A third reason is that many pseudosciences purport to explain some aspect of human behavior and mental processes, including biorhythms, astrology, graphology (handwriting analysis), and magnet therapy for pain control. It is important for students of psychology to distinguish their own field clearly from this "pseudo psychology."

### The Skeptic's Dictionary

An excellent source for information on pseudoscience is *The Skeptic's Dictionary* (http://www.skepdic.com). Among the pseudoscientific beliefs and practices you can learn about are the following:

- **Cryptozoology.** The study of "hidden" creatures like Bigfoot, the Loch Ness monster, and the chupacabra.
- **Pseudoscientific psychotherapies.** Past-life regression, rebirthing therapy, and bioscream therapy, among others.
- **Homeopathy.** The treatment of medical conditions using natural substances that have been diluted sometimes to the point of no longer being present.
- **Pyramidology.** Odd theories about the origin and function of the Egyptian pyramids (e.g., that they were built by extraterrestrials) and the idea that pyramids, in general, have healing and other special powers.

Another excellent online resource is *Neurobonkers* (http://neurobonkers.com), which regularly posts articles that investigate claims that pertain specifically to psychological science.

# Notes

1. Stanovich, K. E. (2010). *How to think straight about psychology* (9th ed.). Boston, MA: Allyn & Bacon.
2. Klein, R. A., Ratliff, K. A., Vianello, M., Adams, R. B., Bahník, S., Bernstein, M. J., . . . Nosek, B. A. (2013). Investigating variation in replicability: A "many labs" replication project. *Social Psychology, 45*(3), 142-152. doi: 10.1027/1864-9335/a000178
3. Schnall, S., Benton, J., & Harvey, S. (2008). With a clean conscience: Cleanliness reduces the severity of moral judgments. *Psychological Science, 19*(12), 1219-1222. doi: 10.1111/j.1467-9280.2008.02227.x
4. Johnson, D. J., Cheung, F., & Donnellan, M. B. (2013). Does cleanliness influence moral judgments? A direct replication of Schnall, Benton, and Harvey (2008). *Social Psychology, 45*(3), 209-215. doi: 10.1027/1864-9335/a000186
5. Hines, T. M. (1998). Comprehensive review of biorhythm theory. *Psychological Reports, 83*, 19–64.
6. Popper, K. R. (2002). *Conjectures and refutations: The growth of scientific knowledge.* New York, NY: Routledge.

# 3. Goals of Science

## The Broader Purposes of Scientific Research in Psychology

People have always been curious about the natural world, including themselves and their behavior (in fact, this is probably why you are studying psychology in the first place). Science grew out of this natural curiosity and has become the best way to achieve detailed and accurate knowledge. Keep in mind that most of the phenomena and theories that fill psychology textbooks are the products of scientific research. In a typical introductory psychology textbook, for example, one can learn about specific cortical areas for language and perception, principles of classical and operant conditioning, biases in reasoning and judgment, and people's surprising tendency to obey those in positions of authority. And scientific research continues because what we know right now only scratches the surface of what we *can* know.

## The Three Goals of Science

The first and most basic goal of science is **to describe**. This goal is achieved by making careful observations. As an example, perhaps I am interested in better understanding the medical conditions that medical marijuana patients use marijuana to treat. In this case, I could try to access records at several large medical marijuana licensing centers to see which conditions people are getting licensed to use medical marijuana. Or I could survey a large sample of medical marijuana patients and ask them to report which medical conditions they use marijuana to treat or manage. Indeed, research involving surveys of medical marijuana patients has been conducted and has found that the primary symptom medical marijuana patients use marijuana to treat is pain, followed by anxiety and depression (Sexton, Cuttler, Finnell, & Mischley, 2016).[1].

The second goal of science is **to predict**. Once we have observed with some regularity that two behaviors or events are systematically related to one another we can use that information to predict whether an event or behavior will occur in a certain situation. Once I know that most medical marijuana patients use marijuana to treat pain I can use that information to predict that an individual who uses medical marijuana likely experiences pain. Of course, my predictions will not be 100% accurate but if the relationship between medical marijuana use and pain is strong then my predictions will have greater than chance accuracy.

The third and ultimate goal of science is **to explain**. This goal involves determining the causes of behavior. For example, researchers might try to understand the mechanisms through which marijuana reduces pain. Does marijuana reduce inflammation which in turn reduces pain? Or does marijuana simply reduce the distress associated with pain rather than reducing pain itself? As you can see these questions tap at the underlying mechanisms and causal relationships.

## Basic versus Applied Research

Scientific research is often classified as being either basic or applied. **Basic research** in psychology is conducted primarily for the sake of achieving a more detailed and accurate understanding of human behavior, without necessarily trying to address any particular practical problem. The research of Mehl and his colleagues falls into this category. **Applied research** is conducted primarily to address some practical problem. Research on the effects of cell phone use on driving, for example, was prompted by safety concerns and has led to the enactment of laws to limit this practice. Although the distinction between basic and applied research is convenient, it is not always clear-cut. For example, basic research on sex differences in talkativeness could eventually have an effect on how marriage therapy is practiced, and applied research on the effect of cell phone use on driving could produce new insights into basic processes of perception, attention, and action.

## Notes

1. Sexton, M., Cuttler, C., Finnell, J., & Mischley, L (2016). A cross-sectional survey of medical cannabis users: Patterns of use and perceived efficacy. *Cannabis and Cannabinoid Research, 1*, 131-138. doi: 10.1089/can.2016.0007.

# 4. Science and Common Sense

*Learning Objectives*

1. Explain the limitations of common sense when it comes to achieving a detailed and accurate understanding of human behavior.
2. Give several examples of common sense or folk psychology that are incorrect.
3. Define skepticism and its role in scientific psychology.

## Can We Rely on Common Sense?

Some people wonder whether the scientific approach to psychology is necessary. Can we not reach the same conclusions based on common sense or intuition? Certainly we all have intuitive beliefs about people's behavior, thoughts, and feelings—and these beliefs are collectively referred to as **folk psychology**. Although much of our folk psychology is probably reasonably accurate, it is clear that much of it is not. For example, most people believe that anger can be relieved by "letting it out"—perhaps by punching something or screaming loudly. Scientific research, however, has shown that this approach tends to leave people feeling more angry, not less (Bushman, 2002)[1]. Likewise, most people believe that no one would confess to a crime that they had not committed unless perhaps that person was being physically tortured. But again, extensive empirical research has shown that false confessions are surprisingly common and occur for a variety of reasons (Kassin & Gudjonsson, 2004)[2].

### Some Great Myths

In 50 *Great Myths of Popular Psychology*, psychologist Scott Lilienfeld and colleagues discuss several widely held commonsense beliefs about human behavior that scientific research has shown to be incorrect (Lilienfeld, Lynn, Ruscio, & Beyerstein, 2010)[3]. Here is a short list:

- "People use only 10% of their brain power."
- "Most people experience a midlife crisis in their 40's or 50's."
- "Students learn best when teaching styles are matched to their learning styles."
- "Low self-esteem is a major cause of psychological problems."
- "Psychiatric admissions and crimes increase during full moons."

# How Could We Be So Wrong?

How can so many of our intuitive beliefs about human behavior be so wrong? Notice that this is an empirical question, and it just so happens that psychologists have conducted scientific research on it and identified many contributing factors (Gilovich, 1991)[4]. One is that forming detailed and accurate beliefs requires powers of observation, memory, and analysis to an extent that we do not naturally possess. It would be nearly impossible to count the number of words spoken by the women and men we happen to encounter, estimate the number of words they spoke per day, average these numbers for both groups, and compare them—all in our heads. This is why we tend to rely on mental shortcuts (what psychologists refer to as **heuristics**) in forming and maintaining our beliefs. For example, if a belief is widely shared—especially if it is endorsed by "experts"—and it makes intuitive sense, we tend to assume it is true. This is compounded by the fact that we then tend to focus on cases that confirm our intuitive beliefs and not on cases that dis-confirm them. This is called **confirmation bias**. For example, once we begin to believe that women are more talkative than men, we tend to notice and remember talkative women and silent men but ignore or forget silent women and talkative men. We also hold incorrect beliefs in part because it would be nice if they *were* true. For example, many people believe that calorie-reducing diets are an effective long-term treatment for obesity, yet a thorough review of the scientific evidence has shown that they are not (Mann et al., 2007)[5]. People may continue to believe in the effectiveness of dieting in part because it gives them hope for losing weight if they are obese or makes them feel good about their own "self-control" if they are not.

Scientists—especially psychologists—understand that they are just as susceptible as anyone else to intuitive but incorrect beliefs. This is why they cultivate an attitude of **skepticism**. Being skeptical does not mean being cynical or distrustful, nor does it mean questioning every belief or claim one comes across (which would be impossible anyway). Instead, it means pausing to consider alternatives and to search for evidence—especially systematically collected empirical evidence—when there is enough at stake to justify doing so. For example, imagine that you read a magazine article that claims that giving children a weekly allowance is a good way to help them develop financial responsibility. This is an interesting and potentially important claim (especially if you have children of your own). Taking an attitude of skepticism, however, would mean pausing to ask whether it might be instead that receiving an allowance merely teaches children to spend money—perhaps even to be more materialistic. Taking an attitude of skepticism would also mean asking what evidence supports the original claim. Is the author a scientific researcher? Is any scientific evidence cited? If the issue was important enough, it might also mean turning to the research literature to see if anyone else had studied it.

Because there is often not enough evidence to fully evaluate a belief or claim, scientists also cultivate a **tolerance for uncertainty**. They accept that there are many things that they simply do not know. For example, it turns out that there is no scientific evidence that receiving an allowance causes children to be more financially responsible, nor is there any scientific evidence that it causes them to be materialistic. Although this kind of uncertainty can be problematic from a practical perspective—for example, making it difficult to decide what to do when our children ask for an allowance—it is exciting from a scientific perspective. If we do not know the answer to an interesting and empirically testable question, science, and perhaps even you as a researcher, may be able to provide the answer.

# Notes

1. Bushman, B. J. (2002). Does venting anger feed or extinguish the flame? Catharsis, rumination, distraction, anger, and aggressive responding. *Personality and Social Psychology Bulletin, 28,* 724–731.

2. Kassin, S. M., & Gudjonsson, G. H. (2004). The psychology of confession evidence: A review of the literature and issues. *Psychological Science in the Public Interest, 5,* 33–67.

3. Lilienfeld, S. O., Lynn, S. J., Ruscio, J., & Beyerstein, B. L. (2010). *50 great myths of popular psychology.* Malden, MA: Wiley-Blackwell.

4. Gilovich, T. (1991). *How we know what isn't so: The fallibility of human reason in everyday life.* New York, NY: Free Press.

5. Mann, T., Tomiyama, A. J., Westling, E., Lew, A., Samuels, B., & Chatman, J. (2007). Medicare's search for effective obesity treatments: Diets are not the answer. *American Psychologist, 62,* 220–233.

# 5. Experimental and Clinical Psychologists

*Learning Objectives*

1. Define the clinical practice of psychology and distinguish it from experimental psychology.
2. Explain how science is relevant to clinical practice.
3. Define the concept of an empirically supported treatment and give some examples.

## Who Conducts Scientific Research in Psychology?

## Experimental Psychologists

Scientific research in psychology is generally conducted by people with doctoral degrees (usually the **doctor of philosophy [Ph.D.]**) and master's degrees in psychology and related fields, often supported by research assistants with bachelor's degrees or other relevant training. Some of them work for government agencies (e.g., doing research on the impact of public policies), national associations (e.g., the American Psychological Association), non-profit organizations (e.g., National Alliance on Mental Illness), or in the private sector (e.g., in product marketing and development; organizational behavior). However, the majority of them are college and university faculty, who often collaborate with their graduate and undergraduate students. Although some researchers are trained and licensed as clinicians for mental health work—especially those who conduct research in clinical psychology—the majority are not. Instead, they have expertise in one or more of the many other subfields of psychology: behavioral neuroscience, cognitive psychology, developmental psychology, personality psychology, social psychology, and so on. Doctoral-level researchers might be employed to conduct research full-time or, like many college and university faculty members, to conduct research in addition to teaching classes and serving their institution and community in other ways.

Of course, people also conduct research in psychology because they enjoy the intellectual and technical challenges involved and the satisfaction of contributing to scientific knowledge of human behavior. You might find that you enjoy the process too. If so, your college or university might offer opportunities to get involved in ongoing research as either a research assistant or a participant. Of course, you might find that you do not enjoy the process of conducting scientific research in psychology. But at least you will have a better understanding of where scientific knowledge in psychology comes from, an appreciation of its strengths and limitations, and an awareness of how it can be applied to solve practical problems in psychology and everyday life.

*Scientific Psychology Blogs*

A fun and easy way to follow current scientific research in psychology is to read any of the many excellent blogs devoted to summarizing and commenting on new findings. Among them are the following:

Research Digest, http://digest.bps.org.uk/
Talk Psych, http://www.talkpsych.com/
Brain Blogger, http://brainblogger.com/
Mind Hacks, http://mindhacks.com/
PsyBlog, http://www.spring.org.uk

You can also browse to http://www.researchblogging.org, select psychology as your topic, and read entries from a wide variety of blogs.

## Clinical Psychologists

Psychology is the scientific study of behavior and mental processes. But it is also the application of scientific research to "help people, organizations, and communities function better" (American Psychological Association, 2011)[1]. By far the most common and widely known application is the **clinical practice of psychology**–the diagnosis and treatment of psychological disorders and related problems. Let us use the term *clinical practice* broadly to refer to the activities of clinical and counseling psychologists, school psychologists, marriage and family therapists, licensed clinical social workers, and others who work with people individually or in small groups to identify and help address their psychological problems. It is important to consider the relationship between scientific research and clinical practice because many students are especially interested in clinical practice, perhaps even as a career.

The main point is that psychological disorders and other behavioral problems are part of the natural world. This means that questions about their nature, causes, and consequences are empirically testable and therefore subject to scientific study. As with other questions about human behavior, we cannot rely on our intuition or common sense for detailed and accurate answers. Consider, for example, that dozens of popular books and thousands of websites claim that adult children of alcoholics have a distinct personality profile, including low self-esteem, feelings of powerlessness, and difficulties with intimacy. Although this sounds plausible, scientific research has demonstrated that adult children of alcoholics are no more likely to have these problems than anybody else (Lilienfeld et al., 2010)[2]. Similarly, questions about whether a particular psychotherapy is effective are empirically testable questions that can be answered by scientific research. If a new psychotherapy is an effective treatment for depression, then systematic observation should reveal that depressed people who receive this psychotherapy improve more than a similar group of depressed people who do not receive this psychotherapy (or who receive some alternative treatment). Treatments that have been shown to work in this way are called **empirically supported treatments**.

## Empirically Supported Treatments

An empirically supported treatment is one that has been studied scientifically and shown to result in greater improvement than no treatment, a placebo, or some alternative treatment. These include many forms of psychotherapy, which can be as effective as standard drug therapies. Among the forms of psychotherapy with strong empirical support are the following:

- **Acceptance and committment therapy (ACT).** for depression, mixed anxiety disorders, psychosis, chronic pain, and obsessive-compulsive disorder.
- **Behavioral couples therapy.** For alcohol use disorders.
- **Cognitive behavioral therapy (CBT).** For many disorders including eating disorders, depression, anxiety disorders, etc.
- **Exposure therapy.** For post-traumatic stress disorder and phobias.
- **Exposure therapy with response prevention.** For obsessive-compulsive disorder.
- **Family-based treatment.** For eating disorders.

For a more complete list, see the following website, which is maintained by Division 12 of the American Psychological Association, the Society for Clinical Psychology: http://www.div12.org/psychological-treatments

Many in the clinical psychology community have argued that their field has not paid enough attention to scientific research—for example, by failing to use empirically supported treatments—and have suggested a variety of changes in the way clinicians are trained and treatments are evaluated and put into practice. Others believe that these claims are exaggerated and the suggested changes are unnecessary (Norcross, Beutler, & Levant, 2005)[3]. On both sides of the debate, however, there is agreement that a scientific approach to clinical psychology is essential if the goal is to diagnose and treat psychological problems based on detailed and accurate knowledge about those problems and the most effective treatments for them. So not only is it important for scientific research in clinical psychology to continue, but it is also important for clinicians who never conduct a scientific study themselves to be scientifically literate so that they can read and evaluate new research and make treatment decisions based on the best available evidence.

# Notes

1. American Psychological Association. (2011). *About APA.* Retrieved from http://www.apa.org/about
2. Lilienfeld, S. O., Lynn, S. J., Ruscio, J., & Beyerstein, B. L. (2010). *50 great myths of popular psychology.* Malden, MA: Wiley-Blackwell.
3. Norcross, J. C., Beutler, L. E., & Levant, R. F. (Eds.). (2005). *Evidence-based practices in mental health: Debate and dialogue on the fundamental questions.* Washington, DC: American Psychological Association.

# 6. Key Takeaways and Exercises

- Knowledge is acquired in many ways including intuition, authority, rationalism, empiricism, and the scientific method
- Science is a general way of understanding the natural world. Its three fundamental features are systematic empiricism, empirical questions, and public knowledge.
- Psychology is a science because it takes the scientific approach to understanding human behavior.
- Pseudoscience refers to beliefs and activities that are claimed to be scientific but lack one or more of the three features of science. It is important to distinguish the scientific approach to understanding human behavior from the many pseudoscientific approaches.
- Psychologists conduct research in order to describe basic phenomenon, to make predictions about future behaviors, and to explain the causes of behavior.
- Basic research is conducted to learn about human behavior for its own sake, and applied research is conducted to solve some practical problem. Both are valuable, and the distinction between the two is not always clear-cut.
- People's intuitions about human behavior, also known as folk psychology, often turn out to be wrong. This is one primary reason that psychology relies on science rather than common sense.
- Researchers in psychology cultivate certain critical-thinking attitudes. One is skepticism. They search for evidence and consider alternatives before accepting a claim about human behavior as true. Another is tolerance for uncertainty. They withhold judgment about whether a claim is true or not when there is insufficient evidence to decide.
- Scientific research in psychology is conducted mainly by people with doctoral degrees in psychology and related fields, most of whom are college and university faculty members. They do so for professional and for personal reasons, as well as to contribute to scientific knowledge about human behavior. Most psychologists are experimental psychologists and they conduct research.
- The clinical practice of psychology—the diagnosis and treatment of psychological problems—is one important application of the scientific discipline of psychology.
- Scientific research is relevant to clinical practice because it provides detailed and accurate knowledge about psychological problems and establishes whether treatments are effective.

## Exercises

- Practice: Consider three things you know and determine how you acquired that knowledge (authority, intuition, rationalism, empiricism, the scientific method).
- Practice: Try to generate different research questions to describe, predict, and explain a phenomenon that interests you.

- Practice: Based on your own experience or on things you have already learned about psychology, list three basic research questions and three applied research questions of interest to you.
- Practice: List three empirical questions about human behavior. List three nonempirical questions about human behavior.
- Practice: For each of the following intuitive beliefs about human behavior, list three reasons that it might be true and three reasons that it might not be true:

  ◦ You cannot truly love another person unless you love yourself.
  ◦ People who receive "crisis counseling" immediately after experiencing a traumatic event are better able to cope with that trauma in the long term.
  ◦ Studying is most effective when it is always done in the same location.

- Watch the following video, in which psychologist Scott Lilienfeld talks about confirmation bias, tunnel vision, and using evidence to evaluate the world around us:

*A YouTube element has been excluded from this version of the text. You can view it online here:*
*https://kpu.pressbooks.pub/psychmethods4e/?p=250*

  ◦ Reading in print? Go to https://youtu.be/Eut8jMfSA_k or scan this QR code with your phone:

- Discussion: Consider the following psychological claim. "People's choice of spouse is strongly influenced by their perception of their own parents. Some choose a spouse who is similar in some way to one of their parents. Others choose a spouse who is different from one of their parents." Is this claim falsifiable? Why or why not?
- Discussion: People sometimes suggest that psychology cannot be a science because either (a) human behavior cannot be predicted with perfect accuracy or (b) much of its subject matter (e.g., thoughts and feelings) cannot be observed directly. Do you agree or disagree with each of these ideas? Why?
- Watch the following video by PHD Comics for an overview of open access publishing and why it matters:

*A YouTube element has been excluded from this version of the text. You can view it online here:*
*https://kpu.pressbooks.pub/psychmethods4e/?p=250*

○ Reading in print? Go to https://youtu.be/L5rVH1KGBCY or scan this QR code with your phone:

- Discussion: Some clinicians argue that what they do is an "art form" based on intuition and personal experience and therefore cannot be evaluated scientifically. Write a paragraph about how satisfied you would be with such a clinician and why from each of three perspectives:

  - a potential client of the clinician
  - a judge who must decide whether to allow the clinician to testify as an expert witness in a child abuse case
  - an insurance company representative who must decide whether to reimburse the clinician for their services

- Practice: Create a short list of questions that a client could ask a clinician to determine whether they pay sufficient attention to scientific research.

# CHAPTER II
# OVERVIEW OF THE SCIENTIFIC METHOD

Here is the abstract of a 2014 article in the journal *Psychological Science*.

Taking notes on laptops rather than in longhand is increasingly common. Many researchers have suggested that laptop note taking is less effective than longhand note taking for learning. Prior studies have primarily focused on students' capacity for multitasking and distraction when using laptops. The present research suggests that even when laptops are used solely to take notes, they may still be impairing learning because their use results in shallower processing. In three studies, we found that students who took notes on laptops performed worse on conceptual questions than students who took notes longhand. We show that whereas taking more notes can be beneficial, laptop note takers' tendency to transcribe lectures verbatim rather than processing information and reframing it in their own words is detrimental to learning. (Mueler & Oppenheimer, 2014, p. 1159)[1]

In this abstract, the researcher has identified a research question—about the effect of taking notes on a laptop on learning—and identified why it is worthy of investigation—because the practice is ubiquitous and may be harmful to learning. In this chapter, we give you a broad overview of the various stages of the research process. These include finding a topic of investigation, reviewing the literature, refining your research question and generating a hypothesis, designing and conducting a study, analyzing the data, coming to conclusions, and reporting the results.

# 7. A Model of Scientific Research in Psychology

Figure 2.1 presents a simple model of scientific research in psychology. The researchers formulate a research question, conduct an empirical study designed to answer the question, analyze the resulting data, draw conclusions about the answer to the question, and publishes the results so that they become part of the research literature (i.e., all the published research in that field). Because the research literature is one of the primary sources of new research questions, this process can be thought of as a cycle. New research leads to new questions, which lead to new research, and so on. Figure 2.1 also indicates that research questions can originate outside of this cycle either with informal observations or with practical problems that need to be solved. But even in these cases, the researcher would start by checking the research literature to see if the question had already been answered and to refine it based on what previous research had already found.

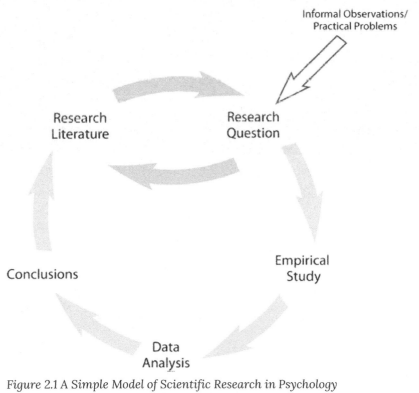

*Figure 2.1 A Simple Model of Scientific Research in Psychology*

The research by Mehl and his colleagues is described nicely by this model. Their research question—whether women are more talkative than men—was suggested to them both by people's stereotypes and by claims published in the research literature about the relative talkativeness of women and men. When they checked the research literature, however, they found that this question had not been adequately addressed in scientific studies. They then conducted a careful empirical study, analyzed the results (finding very little difference between women and men), formed their conclusions, and published their work so that it became part of the research literature. The publication of their article is not the end of the story, however, because their work suggests many new questions (about the reliability of the result, about potential cultural differences, etc.) that will likely be taken up by them and by other researchers inspired by their work.

*A YouTube element has been excluded from this version of the text. You can view it online here: https://kpu.pressbooks.pub/psychmethods4e/?p=32*

As another example, consider that as cell phones became more widespread during the 1990s, people began to wonder whether, and to what extent, cell phone use had a negative effect on driving. Many psychologists decided to tackle this question scientifically (e.g., Collet, Guillot, & Petit, 2010)[1]. It was clear from previously published research that engaging in a simple verbal task impairs performance on a perceptual or motor task carried out at the same time, but no one had studied the effect specifically of cell phone use on driving. Under carefully controlled conditions, these researchers compared people's driving performance while using a cell phone with their performance while not using a cell phone, both in the lab and on the road. They found that people's ability to detect road hazards, reaction time, and maintain control of the vehicle were all impaired by cell phone use. Each new study was published and became part of the growing research literature on this topic. For instance, other research teams subsequently demonstrated that cell phone conversations carry a greater risk than conversations with a passenger who is aware of driving conditions, which often become a point of conversation (e.g., Drews, Pasupathi, & Strayer, 2004)[2].

*Reading in print? Scan this QR code to view the video on your mobile device. Or go to youtu.be/ XToWVxS_9lA*

## Notes

1. Collet, C., Guillot, A., & Petit, C. (2010). Phoning while driving I: A review of epidemiological, psychological, behavioral and physiological studies. *Ergonomics, 53*, 589–601.
2. Drews, F. A., Pasupathi, M., & Strayer, D. L. (2004). Passenger and cell-phone conversations in simulated driving. *Proceedings of the Human Factors and Ergonomics Society Annual Meeting, 48*, 2210–2212.

# 8. Finding a Research Topic

*Learning Objectives*

1. Learn some common sources of research ideas.
2. Define the research literature in psychology and give examples of sources that are part of the research literature and sources that are not.
3. Describe and use several methods for finding previous research on a particular research idea or question.

Good research must begin with a good research question. Yet coming up with good research questions is something that novice researchers often find difficult and stressful. One reason is that this is a creative process that can appear mysterious—even magical—with experienced researchers seeming to pull interesting research questions out of thin air. However, psychological research on creativity has shown that it is neither as mysterious nor as magical as it appears. It is largely the product of ordinary thinking strategies and persistence (Weisberg, 1993)[1]. This section covers some fairly simple strategies for finding general research ideas, turning those ideas into empirically testable research questions, and finally evaluating those questions in terms of how interesting they are and how feasible they would be to answer.

## Finding Inspiration

Research questions often begin as more general research ideas—usually focusing on some behavior or psychological characteristic: talkativeness, learning, depression, bungee jumping, and so on. Before looking at how to turn such ideas into empirically testable research questions, it is worth looking at where such ideas come from in the first place. Three of the most common sources of inspiration are informal observations, practical problems, and previous research.

Informal observations include direct observations of our own and others' behavior as well as secondhand observations from non-scientific sources such as newspapers, books, blogs, and so on. For example, you might notice that you always seem to be in the slowest moving line at the grocery store. Could it be that most people think the same thing? Or you might read in a local newspaper about people donating money and food to a local family whose house has burned down and begin to wonder about who makes such donations and why. Some of the most famous research in psychology has been inspired by informal observations. Stanley Milgram's famous research on obedience to authority, for example, was inspired in part by journalistic reports of the trials of accused Nazi war criminals—many of whom claimed that they were only obeying orders. This led him to wonder about the extent to which ordinary people will commit immoral acts simply because they are ordered to do so by an authority figure (Milgram, 1963)[2].

Practical problems can also inspire research ideas, leading directly to applied research in such domains as law, health, education, and sports. Does taking lecture notes by hand improve students' exam performance? How effective is psychotherapy for depression compared to drug therapy? To what extent do cell phones impair people's driving ability? How can we teach children to read more efficiently? What is the best mental preparation for running a marathon?

Probably the most common inspiration for new research ideas, however, is previous research. Recall that science is a kind of large-scale collaboration in which many different researchers read and evaluate each other's work and conduct new studies to build on it. Of course, experienced researchers are familiar with previous research in their area of expertise and probably have a long list of ideas. This suggests that novice researchers can find inspiration by consulting with a more experienced researcher (e.g., students can consult a faculty member). But they can also find inspiration by picking up a copy of almost any professional journal and reading the titles and abstracts. In one typical issue of *Psychological Science*, for example, you can find articles on the perception of shapes, anti-Semitism, police lineups, the meaning of death, second-language learning, people who seek negative emotional experiences, and many other topics. If you can narrow your interests down to a particular topic (e.g., memory) or domain (e.g., health care), you can also look through more specific journals, such as *Memory & Cognition* or *Health Psychology*.

*A YouTube element has been excluded from this version of the text. You can view it online here: https://kpu.pressbooks.pub/psychmethods4e/?p=34*

# Reviewing the Research Literature

Once again, one of the most common sources of inspiration is previous research. Therefore, it is important to review the literature early in the research process. The **research literature** in any field is all the published research in that field. Reviewing the research literature means finding, reading, and summarizing the published research relevant to your topic of interest. In addition to helping you discover new research questions, reviewing the literature early in the research process can help you in several other ways.

*Reading in print? Scan this QR code to view the video on your mobile device. Or go to https://youtu.be/ nXNztCLYgxc*

- It can tell you if a research question has already been answered.
- It can help you evaluate the interestingness of a research question.
- It can give you ideas for how to conduct your own study.
- It can tell you how your study fits into the research literature.

The research literature in psychology is enormous—including millions of scholarly articles and books dating to the beginning of the field—and it continues to grow. Although its boundaries are somewhat fuzzy, the research literature definitely does not include self-help and other pop psychology books, dictionary and encyclopedia entries, websites, and similar sources that are intended mainly for the general public. These are considered unreliable because they are not reviewed by other researchers and are often based on little more than common sense or personal experience. Wikipedia contains much valuable information, but because its authors are anonymous and may not have any formal training or expertise in that subject area, and its content continually changes it is unsuitable as a basis of sound scientific research. For our purposes, it helps to define the research literature as consisting almost entirely of two types of sources: articles in professional journals, and scholarly books in psychology and related fields.

## Professional Journals

**Professional journals** are periodicals that publish original research articles. There are thousands of professional journals that publish research in psychology and related fields. They are usually published monthly or quarterly in individual issues, each of which contains several articles. The issues are organized into volumes, which usually consist of all the issues for a calendar year. Some journals are published in hard copy only, others in both hard copy and electronic form, and still others in electronic form only.

Most articles in professional journals are one of two basic types: empirical research reports and review articles. **Empirical research reports** describe one or more new empirical studies conducted by the authors. They introduce a research question, explain why it is interesting, review previous research, describe their method and results, and draw their conclusions. **Review articles** summarize previously published research on a topic and usually present new ways to organize or explain the results. When a review article is devoted primarily to presenting a new theory, it is often referred to as a **theoretical article**. When a review article provides a statistical summary of all of the previous results it is referred to as a **meta-analysis**.

*Figure 2.2 Small Sample of the Thousands of Professional Journals That Publish Research in Psychology and Related Fields*

Most professional journals in psychology undergo a process of **double-blind peer review**. Researchers who want to publish their work in the journal submit a manuscript to the editor—who is generally an established researcher too—who in turn sends it to two or three experts on the topic. Each reviewer reads the manuscript, writes a critical but constructive review, and sends the review back to the editor along with recommendations about whether the manuscript should be published or not. The editor then decides whether to accept the article for publication, ask the authors to make changes and resubmit it for further consideration, or reject it outright. In any case, the editor forwards the reviewers' written comments to the researchers so that they can revise their manuscript accordingly. This entire process is double-blind, as the reviewers do not know the identity of the researcher(s) and vice versa. Double-blind peer review is helpful because it ensures that the work meets basic standards of the field before it can enter the research literature. However, in order to increase transparency and accountability, some newer open access journals (e.g., Frontiers in Psychology) utilize an open peer review process wherein the identities of the reviewers (which remain concealed during the peer review process) are published alongside the journal article.

## Scholarly Books

**Scholarly books** are books written by researchers and practitioners mainly for use by other researchers and practitioners. A **monograph** is written by a single author or a small group of authors and usually, gives a coherent presentation of a topic much like an extended review article. **Edited volumes** have an editor or a small group of editors who recruit many authors to write separate chapters on different aspects of the same topic. Although edited volumes can also give a coherent presentation of the topic, it is not unusual for each chapter to take a different perspective or even for the authors of different chapters to openly disagree with each other. In general, scholarly books undergo a peer review process similar to that used by professional journals.

# Literature Search Strategies

## Using PsycINFO and Other Databases

The primary method used to search the research literature involves using one or more electronic databases. These include Academic Search Premier, JSTOR, and ProQuest for all academic disciplines, ERIC for education, and PubMed for medicine and related fields. The most important for our purposes, however, is PsycINFO, which is produced by the American Psychological Association (APA). **PsycINFO** is so comprehensive—covering thousands of professional journals and scholarly books going back more than 100 years—that for most purposes its content is synonymous with the research literature in psychology. Like most such databases, PsycINFO is usually available through your university library.

PsycINFO consists of individual records for each article, book chapter, or book in the database. Each record includes basic publication information, an abstract or summary of the work (like the one presented at the start of this chapter), and a list of other works cited by that work. A computer interface allows entering one or more search terms and returns any records that contain those search terms. (These interfaces are provided by different vendors and therefore can look somewhat different depending on the library you use.) Each record also contains lists of keywords that describe the content of the work and also a list of index terms. The index terms are especially helpful because they are standardized. Research on differences between females and males, for example, is always indexed under "Human Sex Differences." Research on note-taking is always indexed under the term "Learning Strategies." If you do not know the appropriate index terms, PsycINFO includes a thesaurus that can help you find them.

Given that there are nearly four million records in PsycINFO, you may have to try a variety of search terms in different combinations and at different levels of specificity before you find what you are looking for. Imagine, for example, that you are interested in the question of whether males and females differ in terms of their ability to recall experiences from when they were very young. If you were to enter the search term "memory," it would return far too many records to look through individually. This is where the thesaurus helps. Entering "memory" into the thesaurus provides several more specific index terms—one of which is "early memories." While searching for "early memories" among the index terms still returns too many to look through individually—combining it with "human sex differences" as a second search term returns fewer articles, many of which are highly relevant to the topic.

Depending on the vendor that provides the interface to PsycINFO, you may be able to save, print, or e-mail the relevant PsycINFO records. The records might even contain links to full-text copies of the works themselves. (PsycARTICLES is a database that provides full-text access to articles in all journals published by the APA.) If not, and you want a copy of the work, you will have to find out if your library carries the journal or has the book and the hard copy on the library shelves. Be sure to ask a librarian if you need help.

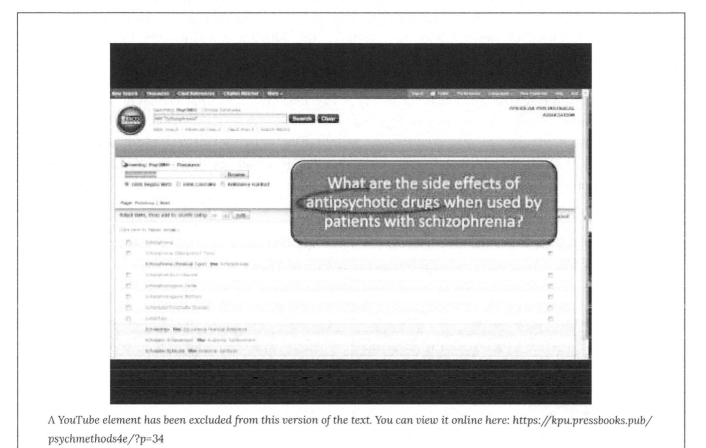

A YouTube element has been excluded from this version of the text. You can view it online here: https://kpu.pressbooks.pub/psychmethods4e/?p=34

## Using Other Search Techniques

In addition to entering search terms into PsycINFO and other databases, there are several other techniques you can use to search the research literature. First, if you have one good article or book chapter on your topic—a recent review article is best—you can look through the reference list of that article for other relevant articles, books, and book chapters. In fact, you should do this with any relevant article or book chapter you find. You can also start with a classic article or book

*Reading in print? Scan this QR code to view the video on your mobile device. Or go to https://youtu.be/fhhctbaVXvk*

chapter on your topic, find its record in PsycINFO (by entering the author's name or article's title as a search term), and link from there to a list of other works in PsycINFO that cite that classic article. This works because other researchers working on your topic are likely to be aware of the classic article and cite it in their own work. You can also do a general Internet search using search terms related to your topic or the name of a researcher who conducts research on your topic. This might lead you directly to works that are part of the research literature (e.g., articles in open-access journals or posted on researchers' own websites). The search engine Google Scholar is especially useful for this purpose. A general Internet search might also lead you to websites that are not part of the research literature but might provide references to works that are. Finally, you can talk to people (e.g., your instructor or other faculty members in psychology) who know something about your topic and can suggest relevant articles and book chapters.

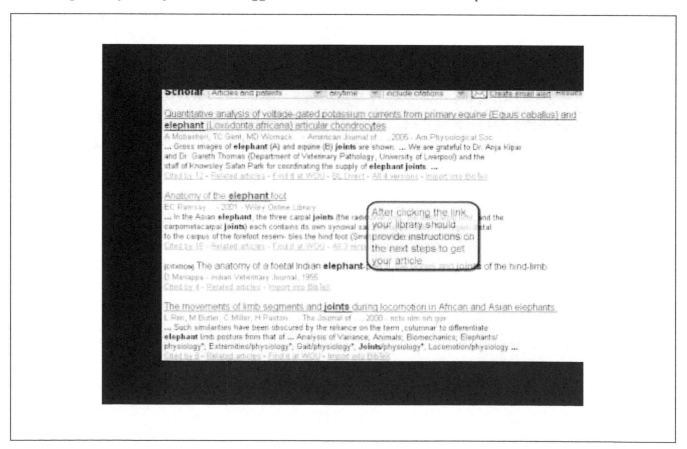

## What to Search For

When you do a literature review, you need to be selective. Not every article, book chapter, and book that relates to your research idea or question will be worth obtaining, reading, and integrating into your review. Instead, you want to focus on sources that help you do four basic things: (a) refine your research question, (b) identify appropriate research methods, (c) place your research in the context of previous research, and (d) write an effective research report. Several basic principles can help you find the most useful sources.

*Reading in print? Scan this QR code to view the video on your mobile device. Or go to https://youtu.be/ t1ZwgDeX2eQ*

First, it is best to focus on recent research, keeping in mind that what counts as recent depends on the topic. For newer topics that are actively being studied, "recent" might mean published in the past year or two. For older topics that are receiving less attention right now, "recent" might mean within the past 10 years. You will get a feel for what counts as recent for your topic when you start your literature search. A good general rule, however, is to start with sources published in the past five years. The main exception to this rule would be classic articles that turn up in the reference list of nearly every other source. If other researchers think that this work is important, even though it is old, then, by all means, you should include it in your review.

Second, you should look for review articles on your topic because they will provide a useful overview of it—often discussing important definitions, results, theories, trends, and controversies—giving you a good sense of where your own research fits into the literature. You should also look for empirical research reports addressing your question or similar questions, which can give you ideas about how to measure your variables and collect your data. As a general rule, it is good to use methods that others have already used successfully unless you have good reasons not to. Finally, you should look for sources that provide information that can help you argue for the interestingness of your research question. For a study on the effects of cell phone use on driving ability, for example, you might look for information about how widespread cell phone use is, how frequent and costly motor vehicle crashes are, and so on.

How many sources are enough for your literature review? This is a difficult question because it depends on how extensively your topic has been studied and also on your own goals. One study found that across a variety of professional journals in psychology, the average number of sources cited per article was about 50 (Adair & Vohra, 2003)[3]. This gives a rough idea of what professional researchers consider to be adequate. As a student, you might be assigned a much lower minimum number of references to include, but the principles for selecting the most useful ones remain the same.

# Notes

1. Weisberg, R. W. (1993). *Creativity: Beyond the myth of genius*. New York, NY: Freeman.
2. Milgram, S. (1963). Behavioral study of obedience. *Journal of Abnormal and Social Psychology, 67*, 371–378.
3. Adair, J. G., & Vohra, N. (2003). The explosion of knowledge, references, and citations: Psychology's unique response to a crisis. *American Psychologist, 58*, 15–23.

# 9. Generating Good Research Questions

## Generating Empirically Testable Research Questions

Once you have a research idea, you need to use it to generate one or more empirically testable research questions, that is, questions expressed in terms of a single variable or relationship between variables. One way to do this is to look closely at the discussion section in a recent research article on the topic. This is the last major section of the article, in which the researchers summarize their results, interpret them in the context of past research, and suggest directions for future research. These suggestions often take the form of specific research questions, which you can then try to answer with additional research. This can be a good strategy because it is likely that the suggested questions have already been identified as interesting and important by experienced researchers.

But you may also want to generate your own research questions. How can you do this? First, if you have a particular behavior or psychological characteristic in mind, you can simply conceptualize it as a variable and ask how frequent or intense it is. How many words on average do people speak per day? How accurate are our memories of traumatic events? What percentage of people have sought professional help for depression? If the question has never been studied scientifically—which is something that you will learn when you conduct your literature review—then it might be interesting and worth pursuing.

If scientific research has already answered the question of how frequent or intense the behavior or characteristic is, then you should consider turning it into a question about a relationship between that behavior or characteristic and some other variable. One way to do this is to ask yourself the following series of more general questions and write down all the answers you can think of.

- What are some possible causes of the behavior or characteristic?
- What are some possible effects of the behavior or characteristic?
- What types of people might exhibit more or less of the behavior or characteristic?
- What types of situations might elicit more or less of the behavior or characteristic?

In general, each answer you write down can be conceptualized as a second variable, suggesting a question about a relationship. If you were interested in talkativeness, for example, it might occur to you that a possible cause of this psychological characteristic is family size. Is there a relationship between family size and talkativeness? Or it might occur to you that people seem to be more talkative in same-sex groups than mixed-sex groups. Is there a difference in the average level of talkativeness of people in same-sex groups and people in mixed-sex groups? This approach should allow you to generate many different empirically testable questions about almost any behavior or psychological characteristic.

If through this process you generate a question that has never been studied scientifically–which again is something that you will learn in your literature review–then it might be interesting and worth pursuing. But what if you find that it has been studied scientifically? Although novice researchers often want to give up and move on to a new question at this point, this is not necessarily a good strategy. For one thing, the fact that the question has been studied scientifically and the research published suggests that it is of interest to the scientific community. For another, the question can almost certainly be refined so that its answer will still contribute something new to the research literature. Again, asking yourself a series of more general questions about the relationship is a good strategy.

- Are there other ways to define and measure the variables?
- Are there types of people for whom the relationship might be stronger or weaker?
- Are there situations in which the relationship might be stronger or weaker–including situations with practical importance?

For example, research has shown that women and men speak about the same number of words per day–but this was when talkativeness was measured in terms of the number of words spoken per day among university students in the United States and Mexico. We can still ask whether other ways of measuring talkativeness–perhaps the number of different people spoken to each day–produce the same result. Or we can ask whether studying elderly people or people from other cultures produces the same result. Again, this approach should help you generate many different research questions about almost any relationship.

## Evaluating Research Questions

Researchers usually generate many more research questions than they ever attempt to answer. This means they must have some way of evaluating the research questions they generate so that they can choose which ones to pursue. In this section, we consider two criteria for evaluating research questions: the interestingness of the question and the feasibility of answering it.

## Interestingness

How often do people tie their shoes? Do people feel pain when you punch them in the jaw? Are women more likely to wear makeup than men? Do people prefer vanilla or chocolate ice cream? Although it would be a fairly simple matter to design a study and collect data to answer these questions, you probably would not want to because they are not interesting. We are not talking here about whether a research question is interesting to us personally but whether it is interesting to people more generally and, especially, to the scientific community. But what makes a research question interesting in this sense? Here we look at three factors that affect the **interestingness** of a research question: the answer is in doubt, the answer fills a gap in the research literature, and the answer has important practical implications.

First, a research question is interesting to the extent that its answer is in doubt. Obviously, questions that have been answered by scientific research are no longer interesting as the subject of new empirical research. But the fact that a question has not been answered by scientific research does not necessarily make it interesting. There has to be some reasonable chance that the answer to the question will be something that we did not already know. But how can you assess this before actually collecting data? One approach is to try to think of reasons to expect different answers to the question—especially ones that seem to conflict with common sense. If you can think of reasons to expect at least two different answers, then the question might be interesting. If you can think of reasons to expect only one answer, then it probably is not. The question of whether women are more talkative than men is interesting because there are reasons to expect both answers. The existence of the stereotype itself suggests the answer could be yes, but the fact that women's and men's verbal abilities are fairly similar suggests the answer could be no. The question of whether people feel pain when you punch them in the jaw is not interesting because there is absolutely no reason to think that the answer could be anything other than a resounding yes.

A second important factor to consider when deciding if a research question is interesting is whether answering it will fill a gap in the research literature. Again, this means in part that the question has not already been answered by scientific research. But it also means that the question is in some sense a natural one for people who are familiar with the research literature. For example, the question of whether taking lecture notes by hand can help improve students' exam performance would be likely to occur to anyone who was familiar with research on note taking and the ineffectiveness of shallow processing on learning.

A final factor to consider when deciding whether a research question is interesting is whether its answer has important practical implications. Again, the question of whether taking notes by hand improves learning has important implications for education, including classroom policies concerning technology use. The question of whether cell phone use impairs driving is interesting because it is relevant to the personal safety of everyone who travels by car and to the debate over whether cell phone use should be restricted by law.

## Feasibility

A second important criterion for evaluating research questions is the **feasibility** of successfully answering them. There are many factors that affect feasibility, including time, money, equipment and materials, technical knowledge and skill, and access to research participants. Clearly, researchers need to take these factors into account so that they do not waste time and effort pursuing research that they cannot complete successfully.

Looking through a sample of professional journals in psychology will reveal many studies that are complicated and difficult to carry out. These include longitudinal designs in which participants are tracked over many years, neuroimaging studies in which participants' brain activity is measured while they carry out various mental tasks, and complex non-experimental studies involving several variables and complicated statistical analyses. Keep in mind, though, that such research tends to be carried out by teams of highly trained researchers whose work is often supported in part by government and private grants. Also, keep in mind that research does not have to be complicated or difficult to produce interesting and important results. Looking through a sample of professional journals will also reveal studies that are relatively simple and easy to carry out—perhaps involving a convenience sample of university students and a paper-and-pencil task.

A final point here is that it is generally good practice to use methods that have already been used successfully by other researchers. For example, if you want to manipulate people's moods to make some of them happy, it would be a good idea to use one of the many approaches that have been used successfully by other researchers (e.g., paying them a compliment). This is good not only for the sake of feasibility—the approach is "tried and true"—but also because it provides greater continuity with previous research. This makes it easier to compare your results with those of other researchers and to understand the implications of their research for yours, and vice versa.

# 10. Developing a Hypothesis

## Theories and Hypotheses

Before describing how to develop a hypothesis, it is important to distinguish between a theory and a hypothesis. A **theory** is a coherent explanation or interpretation of one or more phenomena. Although theories can take a variety of forms, one thing they have in common is that they go beyond the phenomena they explain by including variables, structures, processes, functions, or organizing principles that have not been observed directly. Consider, for example, Zajonc's theory of social facilitation and social inhibition (1965)[1]. He proposed that being watched by others while performing a task creates a general state of physiological arousal, which increases the likelihood of the dominant (most likely) response. So for highly practiced tasks, being watched increases the tendency to make correct responses, but for relatively unpracticed tasks, being watched increases the tendency to make incorrect responses. Notice that this theory—which has come to be called drive theory—provides an explanation of both social facilitation and social inhibition that goes beyond the phenomena themselves by including concepts such as "arousal" and "dominant response," along with processes such as the effect of arousal on the dominant response.

Outside of science, referring to an idea as a theory often implies that it is untested—perhaps no more than a wild guess. In science, however, the term theory has no such implication. A theory is simply an explanation or interpretation of a set of phenomena. It can be untested, but it can also be extensively tested, well supported, and accepted as an accurate description of the world by the scientific community. The theory of evolution by natural selection, for example, is a theory because it is an explanation of the diversity of life on earth—not because it is untested or unsupported by scientific research. On the contrary, the evidence for this theory is overwhelmingly positive and nearly all scientists accept its basic assumptions as accurate. Similarly, the "germ theory" of disease is a theory because it is an explanation of the origin of various diseases, not because there is any doubt that many diseases are caused by microorganisms that infect the body.

A **hypothesis**, on the other hand, is a specific prediction about a new phenomenon that should be observed if a particular theory is accurate. It is an explanation that relies on just a few key concepts. Hypotheses are often specific predictions about what will happen in a particular study. They are developed by considering existing evidence and using reasoning to infer what will happen in the specific context of interest. Hypotheses are often but not always derived from theories. So a hypothesis is often a prediction based on a theory but some hypotheses are a-theoretical and only after a set of observations have been made, is a theory developed. This is because theories are broad in nature and they explain larger bodies of data. So if our research question is really original then we may need to collect some data and make some observations before we can develop a broader theory.

Theories and hypotheses always have this *if-then* relationship. "*If* drive theory is correct, *then* cockroaches should run through a straight runway faster, and a branching runway more slowly, when other cockroaches are present." Although hypotheses are usually expressed as statements, they can always be rephrased as questions. "Do cockroaches run through a straight runway faster when other cockroaches are present?" Thus deriving hypotheses from theories is an excellent way of generating interesting research questions.

But how do researchers derive hypotheses from theories? One way is to generate a research question using the techniques discussed in this chapter and then ask whether any theory implies an answer to that question. For example, you might wonder whether expressive writing about positive experiences improves health as much as expressive writing about traumatic experiences. Although this question is an interesting one on its own, you might then ask whether the habituation theory—the idea that expressive writing causes people to habituate to negative thoughts and feelings—implies an answer. In this case, it seems clear that if the habituation theory is correct, then expressive writing about positive experiences should not be effective because it would not cause people to habituate to negative thoughts and feelings. A second way to derive hypotheses from theories is to focus on some component of the theory that has not yet been directly observed. For example, a researcher could focus on the process of habituation—perhaps hypothesizing that people should show fewer signs of emotional distress with each new writing session.

Among the very best hypotheses are those that distinguish between competing theories. For example, Norbert Schwarz and his colleagues considered two theories of how people make judgments about themselves, such as how assertive they are (Schwarz et al., 1991)[2]. Both theories held that such judgments are based on relevant examples that people bring to mind. However, one theory was that people base their judgments on the *number* of examples they bring to mind and the other was that people base their judgments on how *easily* they bring those examples to mind. To test these theories, the researchers asked people to recall either six times when they were assertive (which is easy for most people) or 12 times (which is difficult for most people). Then they asked them to judge their own assertiveness. Note that the number-of-examples theory implies that people who recalled 12 examples should judge themselves to be more assertive because they recalled more examples, but the ease-of-examples theory implies that participants who recalled six examples should judge themselves as more assertive because recalling the examples was easier. Thus the two theories made opposite predictions so that only one of the predictions could be confirmed. The surprising result was that participants who recalled fewer examples judged themselves to be more assertive—providing particularly convincing evidence in favor of the ease-of-retrieval theory over the number-of-examples theory.

# Theory Testing

The primary way that scientific researchers use theories is sometimes called the **hypothetico-deductive method** (although this term is much more likely to be used by philosophers of science than by scientists themselves). Researchers begin with a set of phenomena and either construct a theory to explain or interpret them or choose an existing theory to work with. They then make a prediction about some new phenomenon that should be observed if the theory is correct. Again, this prediction is called a hypothesis. The researchers then conduct an empirical study to test the hypothesis. Finally, they reevaluate the theory in light of the new results and revise it if necessary. This process is usually conceptualized as a cycle because the researchers can then derive a new hypothesis from the revised theory, conduct a new empirical study to test the hypothesis, and so on. As Figure 2.2 shows, this approach meshes nicely with the model of scientific research in psychology presented earlier in the textbook—creating a more detailed model of "theoretically motivated" or "theory-driven" research.

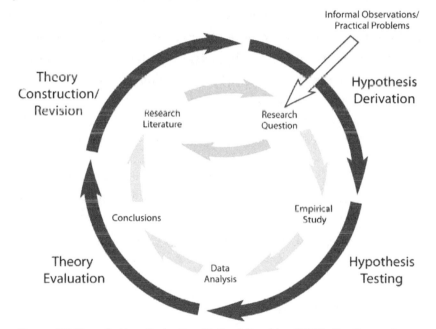

Figure 2.2 Hypothetico-Deductive Method Combined With the General Model of Scientific Research in Psychology Together they form a model of theoretically motivated research.

As an example, let us consider Zajonc's research on social facilitation and inhibition. He started with a somewhat contradictory pattern of results from the research literature. He then constructed his drive theory, according to which being watched by others while performing a task causes physiological arousal, which increases an organism's tendency to make the dominant response. This theory predicts social facilitation for well-learned tasks and social inhibition for poorly learned tasks. He now had a theory that organized previous results in a meaningful way—but he still needed to test it. He hypothesized that if his theory was correct, he should observe that the presence of others improves performance in a simple laboratory task but inhibits performance in a difficult version of the very same laboratory task. To test this hypothesis, one of the studies he conducted used cockroaches as subjects (Zajonc, Heingartner, &

Herman, 1969)[3]. The cockroaches ran either down a straight runway (an easy task for a cockroach) or through a cross-shaped maze (a difficult task for a cockroach) to escape into a dark chamber when a light was shined on them. They did this either while alone or in the presence of other cockroaches in clear plastic "audience boxes." Zajonc found that cockroaches in the straight runway reached their goal more quickly in the presence of other cockroaches, but cockroaches in the cross-shaped maze reached their goal more slowly when they were in the presence of other cockroaches. Thus he confirmed his hypothesis and provided support for his drive theory. (Zajonc also showed that drive theory existed in humans [Zajonc & Sales, 1966][4] in many other studies afterward).

## Incorporating Theory into Your Research

When you write your research report or plan your presentation, be aware that there are two basic ways that researchers usually include theory. The first is to raise a research question, answer that question by conducting a new study, and then offer one or more theories (usually more) to explain or interpret the results. This format works well for applied research questions and for research questions that existing theories do not address. The second way is to describe one or more existing theories, derive a hypothesis from one of those theories, test the hypothesis in a new study, and finally reevaluate the theory. This format works well when there is an existing theory that addresses the research question—especially if the resulting hypothesis is surprising or conflicts with a hypothesis derived from a different theory.

To use theories in your research will not only give you guidance in coming up with experiment ideas and possible projects, but it lends legitimacy to your work. Psychologists have been interested in a variety of human behaviors and have developed many theories along the way. Using established theories will help you break new ground as a researcher, not limit you from developing your own ideas.

## Characteristics of a Good Hypothesis

There are three general characteristics of a good hypothesis. First, a good hypothesis must be **testable and falsifiable**. We must be able to test the hypothesis using the methods of science and if you'll recall Popper's falsifiability criterion, it must be possible to gather evidence that will disconfirm the hypothesis if it is indeed false. Second, a good hypothesis must be **logical.** As described above, hypotheses are more than just a random guess. Hypotheses should be informed by previous theories or observations and logical reasoning. Typically, we begin with a broad and general theory and use *deductive reasoning* to generate a more specific hypothesis to test based on that theory. Occasionally, however, when there is no theory to inform our hypothesis, we use *inductive reasoning* which involves using specific observations or research findings to form a more general hypothesis. Finally, the hypothesis should be **positive.** That is, the hypothesis should make a positive statement about the existence of a relationship or effect, rather than a statement that a relationship or effect does not exist. As scientists, we don't set out to show that relationships do not exist or that effects do not occur so our hypotheses should not be worded in a way to suggest that an effect or relationship does not exist. The nature of science is to assume that something does not exist and then seek to find evidence to prove this wrong, to show that it really does exist. That may seem backward to you but that is the nature of the scientific method. The underlying reason for this is beyond the scope of this chapter but it has to do with statistical theory.

## Notes

1. Zajonc, R. B. (1965). Social facilitation. *Science*, 149, 269–274

2. Schwarz, N., Bless, H., Strack, F., Klumpp, G., Rittenauer-Schatka, H., & Simons, A. (1991). Ease of retrieval as information: Another look at the availability heuristic. *Journal of Personality and Social Psychology*, 61, 195–202.

3. Zajonc, R. B., Heingartner, A., & Herman, E. M. (1969). Social enhancement and impairment of performance in the cockroach. *Journal of Personality and Social Psychology*, 13, 83–92.

4. Zajonc, R.B. & Sales, S.M. (1966). Social facilitation of dominant and subordinate responses. *Journal of Experimental Social Psychology*, 2, 160-168.

# 11. Designing a Research Study

*Learning Objectives*

1. Define the concept of a variable, distinguish quantitative from categorical variables, and give examples of variables that might be of interest to psychologists.
2. Explain the difference between a population and a sample.
3. Distinguish between experimental and non-experimental research.
4. Distinguish between lab studies, field studies, and field experiments.

## Identifying and Defining the Variables and Population

## Variables and Operational Definitions

Part of generating a hypothesis involves identifying the variables that you want to study and operationally defining those variables so that they can be measured. Research questions in psychology are about variables. A **variable** is a quantity or quality that varies across people or situations. For example, the height of the students enrolled in a university course is a variable because it varies from student to student. The chosen major of the students is also a variable as long as not everyone in the class has declared the same major. Almost everything in our world varies and as such thinking of examples of constants (things that don't vary) is far more difficult. A rare example of a constant is the speed of light. Variables can be either quantitative or categorical. A **quantitative variable** is a quantity, such as height, that is typically measured by assigning a number to each individual. Other examples of quantitative variables include people's level of talkativeness, how depressed they are, and the number of siblings they have. A **categorical variable** is a quality, such as chosen major, and is typically measured by assigning a category label to each individual (e.g., Psychology, English, Nursing, etc.). Other examples include people's nationality, their occupation, and whether they are receiving psychotherapy.

After the researcher generates their hypothesis and selects the variables they want to manipulate and measure, the researcher needs to find ways to actually measure the variables of interest. This requires an **operational definition**—a definition of the variable in terms of precisely how it is to be measured. Most variables that researchers are interested in studying cannot be directly observed or measured and this poses a problem because empiricism (observation) is at the heart of the scientific method. Operationally defining a variable involves taking an abstract construct like depression that cannot be directly observed and transforming it into something that can be directly observed and measured. Most variables can be operationally defined in many different ways. For example, depression can be operationally defined as people's scores on a paper-and-pencil depression scale such as the Beck Depression Inventory, the number of depressive symptoms they are experiencing, or whether they have been diagnosed with major depressive disorder. Researchers are wise to choose an operational definition that has been used extensively in the research literature.

## Sampling and Measurement

In addition to identifying which variables to manipulate and measure, and operationally defining those variables, researchers need to identify the population of interest. Researchers in psychology are usually interested in drawing conclusions about some very large group of people. This is called the **population**. It could be all American teenagers, children with autism, professional athletes, or even just human beings—depending on the interests and goals of the researcher. But they usually study only a small subset or **sample** of the population. For example, a researcher might measure the talkativeness of a few hundred university students with the intention of drawing conclusions about the talkativeness of men and women in general. It is important, therefore, for researchers to use a representative sample—one that is similar to the population in important respects.

One method of obtaining a sample is **simple random sampling**, in which every member of the population has an equal chance of being selected for the sample. For example, a pollster could start with a list of all the registered voters in a city (the population), randomly select 100 of them from the list (the sample), and ask those 100 whom they intend to vote for. Unfortunately, random sampling is difficult or impossible in most psychological research because the populations are less clearly defined than the registered voters in a city. How could a researcher give all American teenagers or all children with autism an equal chance of being selected for a sample? The most common alternative to random sampling is **convenience sampling**, in which the sample consists of individuals who happen to be nearby and willing to participate (such as introductory psychology students). Of course, the obvious problem with convenience sampling is that the sample might not be representative of the population and therefore it may be less appropriate to generalize the results from the sample to that population.

## Experimental vs. Non-Experimental Research

The next step a researcher must take is to decide which type of approach they will use to collect the data. As you will learn in your research methods course there are many different approaches to research that can be divided in many different ways. One of the most fundamental distinctions is between experimental and non-experimental research.

# Experimental Research

Researchers who want to test hypotheses about causal relationships between variables (i.e., their goal is to explain) need to use an experimental method. This is because the experimental method is the only method that allows us to determine causal relationships. Using the experimental approach, researchers first manipulate one or more variables while attempting to control extraneous variables, and then they measure how the manipulated variables affect participants' responses.

The terms independent variable and dependent variable are used in the context of experimental research. The **independent variable** is the variable the experimenter manipulates (it is the presumed cause) and the **dependent variable** is the variable the experimenter measures (it is the presumed effect).

**Extraneous variables** are any variable other than the dependent variable. **Confounds** are a specific type of extraneous variable that systematically varies along with the variables under investigation and therefore provides an alternative explanation for the results. When researchers design an experiment they need to ensure that they control for confounds; they need to ensure that extraneous variables don't become confounding variables because in order to make a causal conclusion they need to make sure alternative explanations for the results have been ruled out.

As an example, if we manipulate the lighting in the room and examine the effects of that manipulation on workers' productivity, then the lighting conditions (bright lights vs. dim lights) would be considered the independent variable and the workers' productivity would be considered the dependent variable. If the bright lights are noisy then that noise would be a confound since the noise would be present whenever the lights are bright and the noise would be absent when the lights are dim. If noise is varying systematically with light then we wouldn't know if a difference in worker productivity across the two lighting conditions is due to noise or light. So confounds are bad, they disrupt our ability to make causal conclusions about the nature of the relationship between variables. However, if there is noise in the room both when the lights are on and when the lights are off then noise is merely an extraneous variable (it is a variable other than the independent or dependent variable) and we don't worry much about extraneous variables. This is because unless a variable varies systematically with the manipulated independent variable it cannot be a competing explanation for the results.

# Non-Experimental Research

Researchers who are simply interested in describing characteristics of people, describing relationships between variables, and using those relationships to make predictions can use non-experimental research. Using the non-experimental approach, the researcher simply measures variables as they naturally occur, but they do not manipulate them. For instance, if I just measured the number of traffic fatalities in America last year that involved the use of a cell phone but I did not actually manipulate cell phone use then this would be categorized as non-experimental research. Alternatively, if I stood at a busy intersection and recorded drivers' genders and whether or not they were using a cell phone when they passed through the intersection to see whether men or women are more likely to use a cell phone when driving, then this would be non-experimental research. It is important to point out that non-experimental does not mean nonscientific. Non-experimental research is scientific in nature. It can be used to fulfill two of the three goals of science (to describe and to predict). However, unlike with experimental research, we cannot make causal conclusions using this method; we cannot say that one variable causes another variable using this method.

## Laboratory vs. Field Research

The next major distinction between research methods is between laboratory and field studies. A **laboratory study** is a study that is conducted in the laboratory environment. In contrast, a **field study** is a study that is conducted in the real-world, in a natural environment.

Laboratory experiments typically have high **internal validity**. Internal validity refers to the degree to which we can confidently infer a causal relationship between variables. When we conduct an experimental study in a laboratory environment we have very high internal validity because we manipulate one variable while controlling all other outside extraneous variables. When we manipulate an independent variable and observe an effect on a dependent variable and we control for everything else so that the only difference between our experimental groups or conditions is the one manipulated variable then we can be quite confident that it is the independent variable that is causing the change in the dependent variable. In contrast, because field studies are conducted in the real-world, the experimenter typically has less control over the environment and potential extraneous variables, and this decreases internal validity, making it less appropriate to arrive at causal conclusions.

But there is typically a trade-off between internal and external validity. **External validity** simply refers to the degree to which we can generalize the findings to other circumstances or settings, like the real-world environment. When internal validity is high, external validity tends to be low; and when internal validity is low, external validity tends to be high. So laboratory studies are typically low in external validity, while field studies are typically high in external validity. Since field studies are conducted in the real-world environment it is far more appropriate to generalize the findings to that real-world environment than when the research is conducted in the more artificial sterile laboratory.

Finally, there are field studies which are non-experimental in nature because nothing is manipulated. But there are also **field experiments** where an independent variable is manipulated in a natural setting and extraneous variables are controlled. Depending on their overall quality and the level of control of extraneous variables, such field experiments can have high external and high internal validity.

# 12. Analyzing the Data

Once the study is complete and the observations have been made and recorded the researchers need to analyze the data and draw their conclusions. Typically, data are analyzed using both descriptive and inferential statistics. Descriptive statistics are used to summarize the data and inferential statistics are used to generalize the results from the sample to the population. In turn, inferential statistics are used to make conclusions about whether or not a theory has been supported, refuted, or requires modification.

## Descriptive Statistics

Descriptive statistics are used to organize or summarize a set of data. Examples include percentages, measures of central tendency (mean, median, mode), measures of dispersion (range, standard deviation, variance), and correlation coefficients.

Measures of central tendency are used to describe the typical, average and center of a distribution of scores. The **mode** is the most frequently occurring score in a distribution. The **median** is the midpoint of a distribution of scores. The **mean** is the average of a distribution of scores.

Measures of dispersion are also considered descriptive statistics. They are used to describe the degree of spread in a set of scores. So are all of the scores similar and clustered around the mean or is there a lot of variability in the scores? The **range** is a measure of dispersion that measures the distance between the highest and lowest scores in a distribution. The **standard deviation** is a more sophisticated measure of dispersion that measures the average distance of scores from the mean. The **variance** is just the standard deviation squared. So it also measures the distance of scores from the mean but in a different unit of measure.

Typically means and standard deviations are computed for experimental research studies in which an independent variable was manipulated to produce two or more groups and a dependent variable was measured quantitatively. The means from each experimental group or condition are calculated separately and are compared to see if they differ.

For non-experimental research, simple percentages may be computed to describe the percentage of people who engaged in some behavior or held some belief. But more commonly non-experimental research involves computing the correlation between two variables. A **correlation coefficient** describes the strength and direction of the relationship between two variables. The values of a correlation coefficient can range from –1.00 (the strongest possible negative relationship) to +1.00 (the strongest possible positive relationship). A value of 0 means there is no relationship between the two variables. Positive correlation coefficients indicate that as the values of one variable increase, so do the values of the other variable. A good example of a positive correlation is the correlation between height and weight, because as height increases weight also tends to increase. Negative correlation coefficients indicate that as the value of one variable increase, the values of the other variable decrease. An example of a negative correlation is the correlation between stressful life events and happiness; because as stress increases, happiness is likely to decrease.

# Inferential Statistics

As you learned in the section of this chapter on sampling, typically researchers sample from a population but ultimately they want to be able to generalize their results from the sample to a broader population. Researchers typically want to infer what the population is like based on the sample they studied. Inferential statistics are used for that purpose. **Inferential statistics** allow researchers to draw conclusions about a population based on data from a sample. Inferential statistics are crucial because the effects (i.e., the differences in the means or the correlation coefficient) that researchers find in a study may be due simply to random chance variability or they may be due to a real effect (i.e., they may reflect a real relationship between variables or a real effect of an independent variable on a dependent variable).

Researchers use inferential statistics to determine whether their effects are statistically significant. A **statistically significant** effect is one that is unlikely due to random chance and therefore likely represents a real effect in the population. More specifically results that have less than a 5% chance of being due to random error are typically considered statistically significant. When an effect is statistically significant it is appropriate to generalize the results from the sample to the population. In contrast, if inferential statistics reveal that there is more than a 5% chance that an effect could be due to chance error alone then the researcher must conclude that their result is not statistically significant.

It is important to keep in mind that statistics are probabilistic in nature. They allow researchers to determine whether the chances are low that their results are due to random error, but they don't provide any absolute certainty. Hopefully, when we conclude that an effect is statistically significant it is a real effect that we would find if we tested the entire population. And hopefully when we conclude that an effect is not statistically significant there really is no effect and if we tested the entire population we would find no effect. And that 5% threshold is set at 5% to ensure that there is a high probability that we make a correct decision and that our determination of statistical significance is an accurate reflection of reality.

But mistakes can always be made. Specifically, two kinds of mistakes can be made. First, researchers can make a **Type I error**, which is a false positive. It is when a researcher concludes that their results are statistically significant (so they say there is an effect in the population) when in reality there is no real effect in the population and the results are just due to chance (they are a fluke). When the threshold is set to 5%, which is the convention, then the researcher has a 5% chance or less of making a Type I error. You might wonder why researchers don't set it even lower to reduce the chances of making a Type I error. The reason is when the chances of making a Type I error are reduced, the chances of making a Type II error are increased. A **Type II error** is a missed opportunity. It is when a researcher concludes that their results are not statistically significant when in reality there is a real effect in the population and they just missed detecting it. Once again, these Type II errors are more likely to occur when the threshold is set too low (e.g., set at 1% instead of 5%) and/or when the sample was too small.

# 13. Drawing Conclusions and Reporting the Results

## Drawing Conclusions

Since statistics are probabilistic in nature and findings can reflect type I or type II errors, we cannot use the results of a single study to conclude with certainty that a theory is true. Rather theories are supported, refuted, or modified based on the results of research.

If the results are statistically significant and consistent with the hypothesis and the theory that was used to generate the hypothesis, then researchers can conclude that the theory is supported. Not only did the theory make an accurate prediction, but there is now a new phenomenon that the theory accounts for. If a hypothesis is disconfirmed in a systematic empirical study, then the theory has been weakened. It made an inaccurate prediction, and there is now a new phenomenon that it does not account for.

Although this seems straightforward, there are some complications. First, confirming a hypothesis can strengthen a theory but it can never prove a theory. In fact, scientists tend to avoid the word "prove" when talking and writing about theories. One reason for this avoidance is that the result may reflect a type I error. Another reason for this avoidance is that there may be other plausible theories that imply the same hypothesis, which means that confirming the hypothesis strengthens all those theories equally. A third reason is that it is always possible that another test of the hypothesis or a test of a new hypothesis derived from the theory will be disconfirmed. This difficulty is a version of the famous philosophical "problem of induction." One cannot definitively prove a general principle (e.g., "All swans are white.") just by observing confirming cases (e.g., white swans)—no matter how many. It is always possible that a disconfirming case (e.g., a black swan) will eventually come along. For these reasons, scientists tend to think of theories—even highly successful ones—as subject to revision based on new and unexpected observations.

A second complication has to do with what it means when a hypothesis is disconfirmed. According to the strictest version of the hypothetico-deductive method, disconfirming a hypothesis disproves the theory it was derived from. In formal logic, the premises "if A then B" and "not B" necessarily lead to the conclusion "not A." If A is the theory and B is the hypothesis ("if A then B"), then disconfirming the hypothesis ("not B") must mean that the theory is incorrect ("not A"). In practice, however, scientists do not give up on their theories so easily. One reason is that one disconfirmed hypothesis could be a missed opportunity (the result of a type II error) or it could be the result of a faulty research design. Perhaps the researcher did not successfully manipulate the independent variable or measure the dependent variable.

A disconfirmed hypothesis could also mean that some unstated but relatively minor assumption of the theory was not met. For example, if Zajonc had failed to find social facilitation in cockroaches, he could have concluded that drive theory is still correct but it applies only to animals with sufficiently complex nervous systems. That is, the evidence from a study can be used to modify a theory. This practice does not mean that researchers are free to ignore disconfirmations of their theories. If they cannot improve their research designs or modify their theories to account for repeated disconfirmations, then they eventually must abandon their theories and replace them with ones that are more successful.

The bottom line here is that because statistics are probabilistic in nature and because all research studies have flaws there is no such thing as scientific proof, there is only scientific evidence.

## Reporting the Results

The final step in the research process involves reporting the results. As described in the section on Reviewing the Research Literature in this chapter, results are typically reported in peer-reviewed journal articles and at conferences.

The most prestigious way to report one's findings is by writing a manuscript and having it published in a peer-reviewed scientific journal. Manuscripts published in psychology journals typically must adhere to the writing style of the American Psychological Association (APA style). You will likely be learning the major elements of this writing style in this course.

Another way to report findings is by writing a book chapter that is published in an edited book. Preferably the editor of the book puts the chapter through peer review but this is not always the case and some scientists are invited by editors to write book chapters.

A fun way to disseminate findings is to give a presentation at a conference. This can either be done as an oral presentation or a poster presentation. Oral presentations involve getting up in front of an audience of fellow scientists and giving a talk that might last anywhere from 10 minutes to 1 hour (depending on the conference) and then fielding questions from the audience. Alternatively, poster presentations involve summarizing the study on a large poster that provides a brief overview of the purpose, methods, results, and discussion. The presenter stands by their poster for an hour or two and discusses it with people who pass by. Presenting one's work at a conference is a great way to get feedback from one's peers before attempting to undergo the more rigorous peer-review process involved in publishing a journal article.

# 14. Key Takeaways and Exercise

- Research in psychology can be described by a simple cyclical model. A research question based on the research literature leads to an empirical study, the results of which are published and become part of the research literature.
- The research literature in psychology is all the published research in psychology, consisting primarily of articles in professional journals and scholarly books.
- Early in the research process, it is important to conduct a review of the research literature on your topic to refine your research question, identify appropriate research methods, place your question in the context of other research, and prepare to write an effective research report.
- There are several strategies for finding previous research on your topic. Among the best is using PsycINFO, a computer database that catalogs millions of articles, books, and book chapters in psychology and related fields.
- Research questions expressed in terms of variables and relationships between variables can be suggested by other researchers or generated by asking a series of more general questions about the behavior or psychological characteristic of interest.
- It is important to evaluate how interesting a research question is before designing a study and collecting data to answer it. Factors that affect interestingness are the extent to which the answer is in doubt, whether it fills a gap in the research literature, and whether it has important practical implications.
- It is also important to evaluate how feasible a research question will be to answer. Factors that affect feasibility include time, money, technical knowledge and skill, and access to special equipment and research participants.
- A theory is broad in nature and explains larger bodies of data. A hypothesis is more specific and makes a prediction about the outcome of a particular study.
- Working with theories is not "icing on the cake." It is a basic ingredient of psychological research.
- Like other scientists, psychologists use the hypothetico-deductive method. They construct theories to explain or interpret phenomena (or work with existing theories), derive hypotheses from their theories, test the hypotheses, and then reevaluate the theories in light of the new results.
- Variables vary across people or situations and may be quantitative (e.g., age) or categorical (e.g., course subject).
- A sample is a small subset of a larger population that is selected to participate in the research study. There are many different ways of sampling participants including convenience sampling and simple random sampling.
- Experimental research involves manipulating an independent variable to observe the effects on a measured dependent variable while non-experimental research involves measuring variables as they naturally occur (i.e., without manipulating anything).
- Research can be conducted in the field or the lab. Laboratory experiments tend to have high internal validity (allowing us to make strong causal conclusions), while field studies often have more external validity (allowing us to generalize to the real world).
- The mean, median, and mode are measures of central tendency used to describe the typical, average, or

center scores in a distribution. The range, standard deviation, and variance are measures of how dispersed or spread apart the scores are. Measures of central tendency and dispersion are important descriptive statistics.

- Inferential statistics allow researchers to determine whether their findings are statistically significant, that is, whether they are unlikely to be due to chance alone and therefore are likely to represent a real effect in the population.
- Since statistics are probabilistic in nature we never know if our conclusions are correct. We can make type I errors (concluding an effect is real when it is not) or type II errors (concluding there is no effect when there actually is a real effect in the population).
- Theories can be supported by not proved. Similarly, disconfirming a hypothesis does not necessarily mean that theory has been disproved.
- The final step of the research process involves reporting results at scientific conferences, in journal articles, and/or in books.

## Exercises

- Practice: Find a description of an empirical study in a professional journal or in one of the scientific psychology blogs. Then write a brief description of the research in terms of the cyclical model presented here. One or two sentences for each part of the cycle should suffice.
- Watch the following TED Ed video, in which David H. Schwartz provides an introduction to two types of empirical studies along with some methods that scientists use to increase the reliability of their results:

A YouTube element has been excluded from this version of the text. You can view it online here:
https://kpu.pressbooks.pub/psychmethods4e/?p=271

Reading in print? Go to https://youtu.be/GUpd2HJHUt8 or scan this QR code with your phone:

- Practice: Use the techniques discussed in this section to find 10 journal articles and book chapters on one of the following research ideas: memory for smells, aggressive driving, the causes of narcissistic personality disorder, the functions of the intraparietal sulcus, or prejudice against the physically handicapped.
- Watch the following video clip produced by UBCiSchool about how to read an academic paper (without losing your mind):

*A YouTube element has been excluded from this version of the text. You can view it online here:*
*https://kpu.pressbooks.pub/psychmethods4e/?p=271*

◦ Reading in print? Go to https://youtu.be/SKxm2HF_-k0 or scan this QR code with your phone:

- Practice: Generate three research ideas based on each of the following: informal observations, practical problems, and topics discussed in recent issues of professional journals.
- Practice: Generate an empirical research question about each of the following behaviors or psychological characteristics: long-distance running, getting tattooed, social anxiety, bullying, and memory for early childhood events.
- Practice: Evaluate each of the research questions you generated in Exercise 2 in terms of its interestingness based on the criteria discussed in this section.
- Practice: Find an issue of a journal that publishes short empirical research reports (e.g., *Psychological Science, Psychonomic Bulletin and Review, Personality and Social Psychology Bulletin*). Pick three studies, and rate each one in terms of how feasible it would be for you to replicate it with the resources available to you right now. Use the following rating scale: (1) You could replicate it essentially as reported. (2) You

could replicate it with some simplifications. (3) You could not replicate it. Explain each rating.
- Practice: Find a recent empirical research report in a professional journal. Read the introduction and highlight in different colors descriptions of theories and hypotheses.
- Practice: Using the research article you found in a professional journal identify whether the study was experimental or non-experimental. If it was experimental identify the independent and dependent variables.
- Practice: Using the research article you found in a professional journal identify which descriptive statistics were reported.
- Practice: Describe why theories can be supported but not proved.

# CHAPTER III
# RESEARCH ETHICS

In 1998 a medical journal called *The Lancet* published an article of interest to many psychologists. The researchers claimed to have shown a statistical relationship between receiving the combined measles, mumps, and rubella (MMR) vaccine and the development of autism—suggesting furthermore that the vaccine might even cause autism. One result of this report was that many parents decided not to have their children vaccinated, which of course put them at higher risk for measles, mumps, and rubella. However, follow-up studies by other researchers consistently failed to find a statistical relationship between the MMR vaccine and autism—and it is widely accepted now in the scientific community that there is no relationship. In addition, several more serious problems with the original research were uncovered. Among them were that the lead researcher stood to gain financially from his conclusions because he had patented a competing measles vaccine. He had also used biased methods to select and test his research participants and had used unapproved and medically unnecessary procedures on them. In 2010 *The Lancet* retracted the article, and the lead researcher's right to practice medicine was revoked (Burns, 2010).[1] [1]

In this chapter we explore the ethics of scientific research in psychology. We begin with a general framework for thinking about the ethics of scientific research in psychology. Then we look at some specific ethical codes for biomedical and behavioral researchers —focusing on the Ethics Code of the American Psychological Association. Finally, we consider some practical tips for conducting ethical research in psychology.

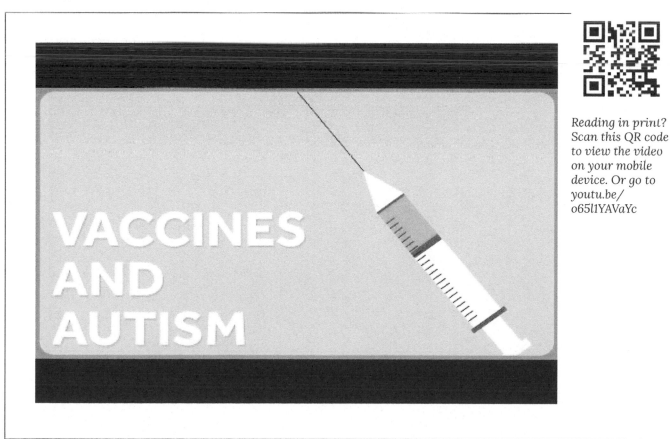

Reading in print? Scan this QR code to view the video on your mobile device. Or go to youtu.be/ o65l1YAVaYc

*A YouTube element has been excluded from this version of the text. You can view it online here: https://kpu.pressbooks.pub/psychmethods4e/?p=46*

# 15. Moral Foundations of Ethical Research

*Learning Objectives*

1. Describe a simple framework for thinking about ethical issues in psychological research.
2. Give examples of several ethical issues that arise in psychological research—including ones that affect research participants, the scientific community, and society more generally.

**Ethics** is the branch of philosophy that is concerned with morality—what it means to behave morally and how people can achieve that goal. It can also refer to a set of principles and practices that provide moral guidance in a particular field. There is an ethics of business, medicine, teaching, and of course, scientific research. As the opening example illustrates, many kinds of ethical issues can arise in scientific research, especially when it involves human participants. For this reason, it is useful to begin with a general framework for thinking through these issues.

## A Framework for Thinking About Research Ethics

Table 3.1 presents a framework for thinking through the ethical issues involved in psychological research. The rows of Table 3.1 represent four general moral principles that apply to scientific research: weighing risks against benefits, acting responsibly and with integrity, seeking justice, and respecting people's rights and dignity. (These principles are adapted from those in the American Psychological Association [APA] Ethics Code.) The columns of Table 3.1 represent three groups of people that are affected by scientific research: the research participants, the scientific community, and society more generally. The idea is that a thorough consideration of the ethics of any research project must take into account how each of the four moral principles applies to each of the three groups of people.

Table 3.1 A Framework for Thinking About Ethical Issues in Scientific Research

| | Who is affected? | | |
|---|---|---|---|
| Moral principle | Research participants | Scientific community | Society |
| Weighing risks against benefits | | | |
| Acting responsibly and with integrity | | | |
| Seeking justice | | | |
| Respecting people's rights and dignity | | | |

# Moral Principles

Let us look more closely at each of the moral principles and how they can be applied to each of the three groups.

## Weighing Risks Against Benefits

Scientific research in psychology can be ethical only if its risks are outweighed by its benefits. Among the risks to research participants are that a treatment might fail to help or even be harmful, a procedure might result in physical or psychological harm, and their right to privacy might be violated. Among the potential benefits are receiving a helpful treatment, learning about psychology, experiencing the satisfaction of contributing to scientific knowledge, and receiving money or course credit for participating. Scientific research can have risks and benefits to the scientific community and to society too (Rosenthal, 1994).[1] A risk to science is that if a research question is uninteresting or a study is poorly designed, then the time, money, and effort spent on that research could have been spent on more productive research. A risk to society is that research results could be misunderstood or misapplied with harmful consequences. The research that mistakenly linked the measles, mumps, and rubella (MMR) vaccine to autism resulted in both of these kinds of harm. Of course, the benefits of scientific research to science and society are that it advances scientific knowledge and can contribute to the welfare of society.

It is not necessarily easy to weigh the risks of research against its benefits because the risks and benefits may not be directly comparable. For example, it is common for the risks of a study to be primarily to the research participants but the benefits primarily for science or society. Consider, for example, Stanley Milgram's original study on obedience to authority (Milgram, 1963).[2] The participants were told that they were taking part in a study on the effects of punishment on learning and were instructed to give electric shocks to another participant each time that participant responded incorrectly on a learning task. With each incorrect response, the shock became stronger—eventually causing the other participant (who was in the next room) to protest, complain about his heart, scream in pain, and finally fall silent and stop responding. If the first participant hesitated or expressed concern, the researcher said that he must continue. In reality, the other participant was a **confederate** of the researcher—a helper who pretended to be a real participant—and the protests, complaints, and screams that the real participant heard were an audio recording that was activated when he flipped the switch to administer the "shocks." The surprising result of this study was that most of the real participants continued to administer the shocks right through the confederate's protests, complaints, and screams. Although this is considered one of the most important results in psychology—with implications for understanding events like the Holocaust or the mistreatment of prisoners by US soldiers at Abu Ghraib—it came at the cost of producing severe psychological stress in the research participants.

---

### Was It Worth It?

Much of the debate over the ethics of Milgram's obedience study concerns the question of whether the resulting scientific knowledge was worth the harm caused to the research participants. To get a better sense of the harm, consider Milgram's (1963) own description of it.

> In a large number of cases, the degree of tension reached extremes that are rarely seen in sociopsychological laboratory studies. Subjects were observed to sweat, tremble, stutter, bite their lips, groan, and dig their fingernails into their flesh....Fourteen of the 40 subjects showed definite signs of nervous laughter and smiling. The laughter seemed entirely out of place, even bizarre. Full-blown uncontrollable seizures [of laughter] were observed for three subjects. On one occasion we observed a seizure so violently convulsive that it was necessary to call a halt to the experiment (p. 375).

Milgram also noted that another observer reported that within 20 minutes one participant "was reduced to a twitching, stuttering wreck, who was rapidly approaching the point of nervous collapse" (p. 377)

To Milgram's credit, he went to great lengths to debrief his participants—including returning their mental states to normal—and to show that most of them thought the research was valuable and they were glad to have participated.

---

## Acting Responsibly and With Integrity

Researchers must act responsibly and with integrity. This means carrying out their research in a thorough and competent manner, meeting their professional obligations, and being truthful. Acting with integrity is important because it promotes trust, which is an essential element of all effective human relationships. Participants must be able to trust that researchers are being honest with them (e.g., about what the study involves), will keep their promises (e.g., to maintain confidentiality), and will carry out their research in ways that maximize benefits and minimize risk. An important issue here is the use of deception. Some research questions (such as Milgram's) are difficult or impossible to answer without deceiving research participants. Thus acting with integrity can conflict with doing research that advances scientific knowledge and benefits society. We will consider how psychologists generally deal with this conflict shortly.

The scientific community and society must also be able to trust that researchers have conducted their research thoroughly and competently and that they have reported on it honestly. Again, the example at the beginning of the chapter illustrates what can happen when this trust is violated. In this case, other researchers wasted resources on unnecessary follow-up research and people avoided the MMR vaccine, putting their children at increased risk of measles, mumps, and rubella. Indeed, many people, including children have died as a result of parents' misinformed decisions not to vaccinate their children.

## Seeking Justice

Researchers must conduct their research in a just manner. They should treat their participants fairly, for example, by giving them adequate compensation for their participation and making sure that benefits and risks are distributed across all participants. For example, in a study of a new and potentially beneficial psychotherapy, some participants might receive the psychotherapy while others serve as a control group that receives no treatment. If the psychotherapy turns out to be effective, it would be fair to offer it to participants in the control group when the study ends.

At a broader societal level, members of some groups have historically faced more than their fair share of the risks of scientific research, including people who are institutionalized, are disabled, or belong to racial or ethnic minorities. A particularly tragic example is the Tuskegee syphilis study conducted by the US Public Health Service from 1932 to 1972 (Reverby, 2009).[3] The participants in this study were poor African American men in the vicinity of Tuskegee, Alabama, who were told that they were being treated for "bad blood." Although they were given some free medical care, they were not treated for their syphilis. Instead, they were observed to see how the disease developed in untreated patients. Even after the use of penicillin became the standard treatment for syphilis in the 1940s, these men continued to be denied treatment without being given an opportunity to leave the study. The study was eventually discontinued only after details were made known to the general public by journalists and activists. It is now widely recognized that researchers need to consider issues of justice and fairness at the societal level.

---

### *"They Were Betrayed"*

In 1997—65 years after the Tuskegee Syphilis Study began and 25 years after it ended—President Bill Clinton formally apologized on behalf of the US government to those who were affected. Here is an excerpt from the apology:

So today America does remember the hundreds of men used in research without their knowledge and consent. We remember them and their family members. Men who were poor and African American, without resources and with few alternatives, they believed they had found hope when they were offered free medical care by the United States Public Health Service. They were betrayed.

---

Read the full text of the apology at http://www.cdc.gov/tuskegee/clintonp.htm.

## Respecting People's Rights and Dignity

Researchers must respect people's rights and dignity as human beings. One element of this is respecting their **autonomy**—their right to make their own choices and take their own actions free from coercion. Of fundamental importance here is the concept of **informed consent**. This means that researchers obtain and document people's agreement to participate in a study after having informed them of everything that might reasonably be expected to affect their decision. Consider the participants in the Tuskegee study. Although they agreed to participate in the study, they were not told that they had syphilis but would be denied treatment for it. Had they been told this basic fact about the study, it seems likely that they would not have agreed to participate. Likewise, had participants in Milgram's study been told that they might be "reduced to a twitching, stuttering wreck," it seems likely that many of them would not have agreed to participate. In neither of these studies did participants give true informed consent.

Another element of respecting people's rights and dignity is respecting their **privacy**—their right to decide what information about them is shared with others. This means that researchers must maintain **confidentiality**, which is essentially an agreement not to disclose participants' personal information without their consent or some appropriate legal authorization. Even more ideally participants can maintain **anonymity**, which is when their name and other personally identifiable information is not collected at all.

## Unavoidable Ethical Conflict

It may already be clear that ethical conflict in psychological research is unavoidable. Because there is little, if any, psychological research that is completely risk-free, there will almost always be a conflict between risks and benefits. Research that is beneficial to one group (e.g., the scientific community) can be harmful to another (e.g., the research participants), creating especially difficult tradeoffs. We have also seen that being completely truthful with research participants can make it difficult or impossible to conduct scientifically valid studies on important questions.

Of course, many ethical conflicts are fairly easy to resolve. Nearly everyone would agree that deceiving research participants and then subjecting them to physical harm would not be justified by filling a small gap in the research literature. But many ethical conflicts are not easy to resolve, and competent and well-meaning researchers can disagree about how to resolve them. Consider, for example, an actual study on "personal space" conducted in a public men's room (Middlemist, Knowles, & Matter, 1976).[4] The researchers secretly observed their participants to see whether it took them longer to begin urinating when there was another man (a confederate of the researchers) at a nearby urinal. While some critics found this to be an unjustified assault on human dignity (Koocher, 1977),[5] the researchers had carefully considered the ethical conflicts, resolved them as best they could, and concluded that the benefits of the research outweighed the risks (Middlemist, Knowles, & Matter, 1977).[6] For example, they had interviewed some preliminary participants and found that none of them was bothered by the fact that they had been observed.

The point here is that although it may not be possible to eliminate ethical conflict completely, it is possible to deal with it in responsible and constructive ways. In general, this means thoroughly and carefully thinking through the ethical issues that are raised, minimizing the risks, and weighing the risks against the benefits. It also means being able to explain one's ethical decisions to others, seeking feedback on them, and ultimately taking responsibility for them.

# Notes

1.  Rosenthal, R. M. (1994). Science and ethics in conducting, analyzing, and reporting psychological research. *Psychological Science, 5*, 127–133.
2.  Milgram, S. (1963). Behavioral study of obedience. *Journal of Abnormal and Social Psychology, 67*, 371–378.
3.  Reverby, S. M. (2009). *Examining Tuskegee: The infamous syphilis study and its legacy.* Chapel Hill, NC: University of North Carolina Press.
4.  Middlemist, R. D., Knowles, E. S., & Matter, C. F. (1976). Personal space invasions in the lavatory: Suggestive evidence for arousal. *Journal of Personality and Social Psychology, 33*, 541–546.
5.  Koocher, G. P. (1977). Bathroom behavior and human dignity. *Journal of Personality and Social Psychology, 35*, 120–121.
6.  Middlemist, R. D., Knowles, E. S., & Matter, C. F. (1977). What to do and what to report: A reply to Koocher. *Journal of Personality and Social Psychology, 35*, 122–125.

# 16. From Moral Principles to Ethics Codes

*Learning Objectives*

1. Describe the history of ethics codes for scientific research with human participants.
2. Summarize the American Psychological Association Ethics Code–especially as it relates to informed consent, deception, debriefing, research with nonhuman animals, and scholarly integrity.

The general moral principles of weighing risks against benefits, acting with integrity, seeking justice, and respecting people's rights and dignity provide a useful starting point for thinking about the ethics of psychological research because essentially everyone agrees on them. As we have seen, however, even people who agree on these general principles can disagree about specific ethical issues that arise in the course of conducting research. This is why there also exist more detailed and enforceable ethics codes that provide guidance on important issues that arise frequently. In this section, we begin with a brief historical overview of such ethics codes and then look closely at the one that is most relevant to psychological research–that of the American Psychological Association (APA).

## Historical Overview

One of the earliest ethics codes was the **Nuremberg Code**–a set of 10 principles written in 1947 in conjunction with the trials of Nazi physicians accused of shockingly cruel research on concentration camp prisoners during World War II. It provided a standard against which to compare the behavior of the men on trial–many of whom were eventually convicted and either imprisoned or sentenced to death. The Nuremberg Code was particularly clear about the importance of carefully weighing risks against benefits and the need for informed consent. The **Declaration of Helsinki** is a similar ethics code that was created by the World Medical Council in 1964. Among the standards that it added to the Nuremberg Code was that research with human participants should be based on a written **protocol**–a detailed description of the research–that is reviewed by an independent committee. The Declaration of Helsinki has been revised several times, most recently in 2004.

In the United States, concerns about the Tuskegee study and others led to the publication in 1978 of a set of federal guidelines called the **Belmont Report**. The Belmont Report explicitly recognized the principle of seeking **justice**, including the importance of conducting research in a way that distributes risks and benefits fairly across different groups at the societal level. It also recognized the importance of **respect for persons,** which acknowledges individuals' autonomy and protection for those with diminished autonomy (e.g., prisoners, children), and translates to the need for informed consent. Finally, it recognized the principle of **beneficence,** which underscores the importance of maximizing the benefits of research while minimizing harms to participants and society. The Belmont Report became the basis of a set of laws—the **Federal Policy for the Protection of Human Subjects**—that apply to research conducted, supported, or regulated by the federal government. An extremely important part of these regulations is that universities, hospitals, and other institutions that receive support from the federal government must establish an **institutional review board (IRB)**—a committee that is responsible for reviewing research protocols for potential ethical problems. An IRB must consist of at least five people with varying backgrounds, including members of different professions, scientists and nonscientists, men and women, and at least one person not otherwise affiliated with the institution. The IRB helps to make sure that the risks of the proposed research are minimized, the benefits outweigh the risks, the research is carried out in a fair manner, and the informed consent procedure is adequate.

The federal regulations also distinguish research that poses three levels of risk. **Exempt research** is the lowest level or risk and includes research on the effectiveness of normal educational activities, the use of standard psychological measures and surveys of a nonsensitive nature that are administered in a way that maintains confidentiality, and research using existing data from public sources. It is called exempt because once approved, it is exempt from regular, continuous review. **Expedited research** poses a somewhat higher risk than exempt, but still exposes participants to risks that are no greater than minimal risk (those encountered by healthy people in daily life or during routine physical or psychological examinations). Expedited review is done by by one member of the IRB or by a separate committee under the authority of the IRB that can only approve minimal risk research (many departments of psychology have such separate committees). Finally, research that does not qualify for exempt or expedited review is **greater than minimal risk research** must be reviewed by the full board of IRB members.

## Ethics Codes

The link that follows the list—from the Office of Human Subjects Research at the National Institutes of Health—allows you to read the ethics codes discussed in this section in their entirety. They are all highly recommended and, with the exception of the Federal Policy, short and easy to read.

- The Nuremberg Code
- The Declaration of Helsinki
- The Belmont Report
- Federal Policy for the Protection of Human Subjects

https://www.hhs.gov/ohrp/international/ethical-codes-and-research-standards/index.html

## APA Ethics Code

The APA's *Ethical Principles of Psychologists and Code of Conduct* (also known as the **APA Ethics Code**) was first published in 1953 and has been revised several times since then, most recently in 2010. It includes about 150 specific ethical standards that psychologists and their students are expected to follow. Much of the APA Ethics Code concerns the clinical practice of psychology—advertising one's services, setting and collecting fees, having personal relationships with clients, and so on. For our purposes, the most relevant part is *Standard 8: Research and Publication*. Although *Standard 8* is reproduced here in its entirety, we will consider some of its most important aspects—informed consent, deception, debriefing, the use of nonhuman animal subjects, and scholarly integrity—in more detail.

---

*APA Ethics Code Standard 8: Research and Publication*

8.01 Institutional Approval

When institutional approval is required, psychologists provide accurate information about their research proposals and obtain approval prior to conducting the research. They conduct the research in accordance with the approved research protocol.

8.02 Informed Consent to Research

3. When obtaining informed consent as required in Standard 3.10, Informed Consent, psychologists inform participants about (1) the purpose of the research, expected duration, and procedures; (2) their right to decline to participate and to withdraw from the research once participation has begun; (3) the foreseeable consequences of declining or withdrawing; (4) reasonably foreseeable factors that may be expected to influence their willingness to participate such as potential risks, discomfort, or adverse effects; (5) any prospective research benefits; (6) limits of confidentiality; (7) incentives for participation; and (8) whom to contact for questions about the research and research participants' rights. They provide opportunity for the prospective participants to ask questions and receive answers. (See also Standards 8.03, Informed Consent for Recording Voices and Images in Research; 8.05, Dispensing With Informed Consent for Research; and 8.07, Deception in Research.)

4. Psychologists conducting intervention research involving the use of experimental treatments clarify to participants at the outset of the research (1) the experimental nature of the treatment; (2) the services that will or will not be available to the control group(s) if appropriate; (3) the means by which assignment to treatment and control groups will be made; (4) available treatment alternatives if an individual does not wish to participate in the research or wishes to withdraw once a study has begun; and (5) compensation for or monetary costs of participating including, if appropriate, whether reimbursement from the participant or a third-party payor will be sought. (See also Standard 8.02a, Informed Consent to Research.)

8.03 Informed Consent for Recording Voices and Images in Research

Psychologists obtain informed consent from research participants prior to recording their voices or images for data collection unless (1) the research consists solely of naturalistic observations in public places, and it is not anticipated that the recording will be used in a manner that could cause personal identification or harm, or (2) the research design includes deception, and consent for the use of the recording is obtained during debriefing. (See also Standard 8.07, Deception in Research.)

8.04 Client/Patient, Student, and Subordinate Research Participants

1. When psychologists conduct research with clients/patients, students, or subordinates as participants, psychologists take steps to protect the prospective participants from adverse consequences of declining or withdrawing from participation.
2. When research participation is a course requirement or an opportunity for extra credit, the prospective participant is given the choice of equitable alternative activities.

8.05 Dispensing With Informed Consent for Research

Psychologists may dispense with informed consent only (1) where research would not reasonably be assumed to create distress or harm and involves (a) the study of normal educational practices, curricula, or classroom management methods conducted in educational settings; (b) only anonymous questionnaires, naturalistic observations, or archival research for which disclosure of responses would not place participants at risk of criminal or civil liability or damage their financial standing, employability, or reputation, and confidentiality is protected; or (c) the study of factors related to job or organization effectiveness conducted in organizational settings for which there is no risk to participants' employability, and confidentiality is protected or (2) where otherwise permitted by law or federal or institutional regulations.

8.06 Offering Inducements for Research Participation

1. Psychologists make reasonable efforts to avoid offering excessive or inappropriate financial or other inducements for research participation when such inducements are likely to coerce participation.
2. When offering professional services as an inducement for research participation, psychologists clarify the nature of the services, as well as the risks, obligations, and limitations. (See also Standard 6.05, Barter With Clients/Patients.)

8.07 Deception in Research

1. Psychologists do not conduct a study involving deception unless they have determined that the use of deceptive techniques is justified by the study's significant prospective scientific, educational, or applied value and that effective nondeceptive alternative procedures are not feasible.
2. Psychologists do not deceive prospective participants about research that is reasonably expected to cause physical pain or severe emotional distress.
3. Psychologists explain any deception that is an integral feature of the design and conduct of an experiment to participants as early as is feasible, preferably at the conclusion of their participation, but no later than at the conclusion of the data collection, and permit participants to withdraw their data. (See also Standard 8.08, Debriefing.)

8.08 Debriefing

1. Psychologists provide a prompt opportunity for participants to obtain appropriate information about the nature, results, and conclusions of the research, and they take reasonable steps to correct any misconceptions that participants may have of which the psychologists are aware.
2. If scientific or humane values justify delaying or withholding this information, psychologists take reasonable measures to reduce the risk of harm.
3. When psychologists become aware that research procedures have harmed a participant, they take reasonable steps to minimize the harm.

8.09 Humane Care and Use of Animals in Research

1. Psychologists acquire, care for, use, and dispose of animals in compliance with current federal, state, and local laws and regulations, and with professional standards.
2. Psychologists trained in research methods and experienced in the care of laboratory animals supervise all procedures involving animals and are responsible for ensuring appropriate consideration of their comfort, health, and humane treatment.
3. Psychologists ensure that all individuals under their supervision who are using animals have received instruction in research methods and in the care, maintenance, and handling of the species being used, to the extent appropriate to their role. (See also Standard 2.05, Delegation of Work to Others.)
4. Psychologists make reasonable efforts to minimize the discomfort, infection, illness, and pain of animal subjects.
5. Psychologists use a procedure subjecting animals to pain, stress, or privation only when an alternative procedure is unavailable and the goal is justified by its prospective scientific, educational, or applied value.
6. Psychologists perform surgical procedures under appropriate anesthesia and follow techniques to avoid infection and minimize pain during and after surgery.
7. When it is appropriate that an animal's life be terminated, psychologists proceed rapidly, with an effort to minimize pain and in accordance with accepted procedures.

8.10 Reporting Research Results

5. Psychologists do not fabricate data. (See also Standard 5.01a, Avoidance of False or Deceptive Statements.)
6. If psychologists discover significant errors in their published data, they take reasonable steps to correct such errors in a correction, retraction, erratum, or other appropriate publication means.

8.11 Plagiarism

Psychologists do not present portions of another's work or data as their own, even if the other work or data source is cited occasionally.

8.12 Publication Credit

8. Psychologists take responsibility and credit, including authorship credit, only for work they have actually performed or to which they have substantially contributed. (See also Standard 8.12b, Publication Credit.)
9. Principal authorship and other publication credits accurately reflect the relative scientific or professional contributions of the individuals involved, regardless of their relative status. Mere possession of an institutional position, such as department chair, does not justify authorship credit. Minor contributions to the research or to the writing for publications are acknowledged appropriately, such as in footnotes or in an introductory statement.
10. Except under exceptional circumstances, a student is listed as principal author on any multiple-authored article that is substantially based on the student's doctoral dissertation. Faculty advisors discuss publication credit with students as early as feasible and throughout the research and publication process as appropriate. (See also Standard 8.12b, Publication Credit.)

8.13 Duplicate Publication of Data

Psychologists do not publish, as original data, data that have been previously published. This does not preclude republishing data when they are accompanied by proper acknowledgment.

8.14 Sharing Research Data for Verification

1. After research results are published, psychologists do not withhold the data on which their conclusions are based from other competent professionals who seek to verify the substantive claims through reanalysis and who intend to use such data only for that purpose, provided that the confidentiality of the participants can be protected and unless legal rights concerning proprietary data preclude their release. This does not preclude psychologists from requiring that such individuals or groups be responsible for costs associated with the provision of such information.
2. Psychologists who request data from other psychologists to verify the substantive claims through reanalysis may use shared data only for the declared purpose. Requesting psychologists obtain prior written agreement for all other uses of the data.

8.15 Reviewers

Psychologists who review material submitted for presentation, publication, grant, or research proposal review respect the confidentiality of and the proprietary rights in such information of those who submitted it.

Source: You can read the full APA Ethics Code at http://www.apa.org/ethics/code/index.aspx.

# Informed Consent

Standards 8.02 to 8.05 are about informed consent. Again, informed consent means obtaining and documenting people's agreement to participate in a study, having informed them of everything that might reasonably be expected to affect their decision. This includes details of the procedure, the risks and benefits of the research, the fact that they have the right to decline to participate or to withdraw from the study, the consequences of doing so, and any legal limits to confidentiality. For example, some states require researchers who learn of child abuse or other crimes to report this information to authorities.

Although the process of obtaining informed consent often involves having participants read and sign a **consent form**, it is important to understand that this is not all it is. Although having participants read and sign a consent form might be enough when they are competent adults with the necessary ability and motivation, many participants do not actually read consent forms or read them but do not understand them. For example, participants often mistake consent forms for legal documents and mistakenly believe that by signing them they give up their right to sue the researcher (Mann, 1994).[1] Even with competent adults, therefore, it is good practice to tell participants about the risks and benefits, demonstrate the procedure, ask them if they have questions, and remind them of their right to withdraw at any time—in addition to having them read and sign a consent form.

Note also that there are situations in which informed consent is not necessary. These include situations in which the research is not expected to cause any harm and the procedure is straightforward or the study is conducted in the context of people's ordinary activities. For example, if you wanted to sit outside a public building and observe whether people hold the door open for people behind them, you would not need to obtain their informed consent. Similarly, if a college instructor wanted to compare two legitimate teaching methods across two sections of his research methods course, he would not need to obtain informed consent from his students.

## Deception

**Deception** of participants in psychological research can take a variety of forms: misinforming participants about the purpose of a study, using confederates, using phony equipment like Milgram's shock generator, and presenting participants with false feedback about their performance (e.g., telling them they did poorly on a test when they actually did well). Deception also includes not informing participants of the full design or true purpose of the research even if they are not actively misinformed (Sieber, Iannuzzo, & Rodriguez, 1995).[2] For example, a study on incidental learning—learning without conscious effort—might involve having participants read through a list of words in preparation for a "memory test" later. Although participants are likely to assume that the memory test will require them to recall the words, it might instead require them to recall the contents of the room or the appearance of the research assistant.

Some researchers have argued that deception of research participants is rarely if ever ethically justified. Among their arguments are that it prevents participants from giving truly informed consent, fails to respect their dignity as human beings, has the potential to upset them, makes them distrustful and therefore less honest in their responding, and damages the reputation of researchers in the field (Baumrind, 1985).[3]

Note, however, that the APA Ethics Code takes a more moderate approach—allowing deception when the benefits of the study outweigh the risks, participants cannot reasonably be expected to be harmed, the research question cannot be answered without the use of deception, and participants are informed about the deception as soon as possible. This approach acknowledges that not all forms of deception are equally bad. Compare, for example, Milgram's study in which he deceived his participants in several significant ways that resulted in their experiencing severe psychological stress with an incidental learning study in which a "memory test" turns out to be slightly different from what participants were expecting. It also acknowledges that some scientifically and socially important research questions can be difficult or impossible to answer without deceiving participants. Knowing that a study concerns the extent to which they obey authority, act aggressively toward a peer, or help a stranger is likely to change the way people behave so that the results no longer generalize to the real world.

## Debriefing

Standard 8.08 is about **debriefing**. This is the process of informing research participants as soon as possible of the purpose of the study, revealing any deception, and correcting any other misconceptions they might have as a result of participating. Debriefing also involves minimizing harm that might have occurred. For example, an experiment on the effects of being in a sad mood on memory might involve inducing a sad mood in participants by having them think sad thoughts, watch a sad video, and/or listen to sad music. Debriefing would be the time to return participants' moods to normal by having them think happy thoughts, watch a happy video, or listen to happy music.

## Nonhuman Animal Subjects

Standard 8.09 is about the humane treatment and care of nonhuman animal subjects. Although most contemporary research in psychology does not involve nonhuman animal subjects, a significant minority of it does—especially in the study of learning and conditioning, behavioral neuroscience, and the development of drug and surgical therapies for psychological disorders.

The use of nonhuman animal subjects in psychological research is similar to the use of deception in that there are those who argue that it is rarely, if ever, ethically acceptable (Bowd & Shapiro, 1993).[4] Clearly, nonhuman animals are incapable of giving informed consent. Yet they can be subjected to numerous procedures that are likely to cause them suffering. They can be confined, deprived of food and water, subjected to pain, operated on, and ultimately euthanized. (Of course, they can also be observed benignly in natural or zoo-like settings.) Others point out that psychological research on nonhuman animals has resulted in many important benefits to humans, including the development of behavioral therapies for many disorders, more effective pain control methods, and antipsychotic drugs (Miller, 1985).[5] It has also resulted in benefits to nonhuman animals, including alternatives to shooting and poisoning as means of controlling them.

As with deception, the APA acknowledges that the benefits of research on nonhuman animals can outweigh the costs, in which case it is ethically acceptable. However, researchers must use alternative methods when they can. When they cannot, they must acquire and care for their subjects humanely and minimize the harm to them. For more information on the APA's position on nonhuman animal subjects, see the website of the APA's Committee on Animal Research and Ethics (http://www.apa.org/science/leadership/care/index.aspx).

## Scholarly Integrity

Standards 8.10 to 8.15 are about scholarly integrity. These include the obvious points that researchers must not fabricate data or plagiarize. Plagiarism means using others' words or ideas without proper acknowledgment. Proper acknowledgment generally means indicating direct quotations with quotation marks *and* providing a citation to the source of any quotation or idea used. Self-plagiarism is also considered unethical and refers to publishing the same material more than once. In other words, researchers should not borrow prior phrasing from their other published works, just as students should not submit the same work to more than one class.

The remaining standards make some less obvious but equally important points. Researchers should not publish the same data a second time as though it were new, they should share their data with other researchers, and as peer reviewers, they should keep the unpublished research they review confidential. Note that the authors' names on published research—and the order in which those names appear—should reflect the importance of each person's contribution to the research. It would be unethical, for example, to include as an author someone who had made only minor contributions to the research (e.g., analyzing some of the data) or for a faculty member to make himself or herself the first author on research that was largely conducted by a student.

# Notes

1. Mann, T. (1994). Informed consent for psychological research: Do subjects comprehend consent forms and understand their legal rights? *Psychological Science, 5,* 140–143.
2. Sieber, J. E., Iannuzzo, R., & Rodriguez, B. (1995). Deception methods in psychology: Have they changed in 23 years? *Ethics & Behavior, 5,* 67–85.
3. Baumrind, D. (1985). Research using intentional deception: Ethical issues revisited. *American Psychologist, 40,* 165–174.
4. Bowd, A. D., & Shapiro, K. J. (1993). The case against animal laboratory research in psychology. *Journal of Social Issues, 49,* 133–142.
5. Miller, N. E. (1985). The value of behavioral research on animals. *American Psychologist, 40,* 423–440.

# 17. Putting Ethics Into Practice

*Learning Objectives*

1.  Describe several strategies for identifying and minimizing risks and deception in psychological research.
2.  Create thorough informed consent and debriefing procedures, including a consent form.

In this section, we look at some practical advice for conducting ethical research in psychology. Again, it is important to remember that ethical issues arise well before you begin to collect data and continue to arise through publication and beyond.

## Know and Accept Your Ethical Responsibilities

As the American Psychological Association (APA) Ethics Code notes in its introduction, "Lack of awareness or misunderstanding of an ethical standard is not itself a defense to a charge of unethical conduct." This is why the very first thing that you must do as a new researcher is to know and accept your ethical responsibilities. At a minimum, this means reading and understanding the relevant sections of the APA Ethics Code, distinguishing minimal risk from at-risk research, and knowing the specific policies and procedures of your institution—including how to prepare and submit a research protocol for institutional review board (IRB) review. If you are conducting research as a course requirement, there may be specific course standards, policies, and procedures. If any standard, policy, or procedure is unclear—or you are unsure what to do about an ethical issue that arises—you must seek clarification. You can do this by reviewing the relevant ethics codes, reading about how similar issues have been resolved by others, or consulting with more experienced researchers, your IRB, or your course instructor. Ultimately, you as the researcher must take responsibility for the ethics of the research you conduct.

## Identify and Minimize Risks

As you design your study, you must identify and minimize risks to participants. Start by listing all the risks, including risks of physical and psychological harm and violations of confidentiality. Remember that it is easy for researchers to see risks as less serious than participants do or even to overlook them completely. For example, one student researcher wanted to test people's sensitivity to violent images by showing them gruesome photographs of crime and accident scenes. Because she was an emergency medical technician, however, she greatly underestimated how disturbing these images were to most people. Remember too that some risks might apply only to some participants. For example, while most people would have no problem completing a survey about their fear of various crimes, those who have been a victim of one of those crimes might become upset. This is why you should seek input from a variety of people, including your research collaborators, more experienced researchers, and even from nonresearchers who might be better able to take the perspective of a participant.

Once you have identified the risks, you can often reduce or eliminate many of them. One way is to modify the research design. For example, you might be able to shorten or simplify the procedure to prevent boredom and frustration. You might be able to replace upsetting or offensive stimulus materials (e.g., graphic accident scene photos) with less upsetting or offensive ones (e.g., milder photos of the sort people are likely to see in the newspaper). A good example of modifying a research design is a 2009 replication of Milgram's study conducted by Jerry Burger. Instead of allowing his participants to continue administering shocks up to the 450-V maximum, the researcher always stopped the procedure when they were about to administer the 150-V shock (Burger, 2009).[1] This made sense because in Milgram's study (a) participants' severe negative reactions occurred after this point and (b) most participants who administered the 150-V shock continued all the way to the 450-V maximum. Thus the researcher was able to compare his results directly with Milgram's at every point up to the 150-V shock and also was able to estimate how many of his participants would have continued to the maximum—but without subjecting them to the severe stress that Milgram did. (The results, by the way, were that these contemporary participants were just as obedient as Milgram's were.)

A second way to minimize risks is to use a **pre-screening** procedure to identify and eliminate participants who are at high risk. You can do this in part through the informed consent process. For example, you can warn participants that a survey includes questions about their fear of crime and remind them that they are free to withdraw if they think this might upset them. Prescreening can also involve collecting data to identify and eliminate participants. For example, Burger used an extensive pre-screening procedure involving multiple questionnaires and an interview with a clinical psychologist to identify and eliminate participants with physical or psychological problems that put them at high risk.

A third way to minimize risks is to take active steps to maintain confidentiality. You should keep signed consent forms separately from any data that you collect and in such a way that no individual's name can be linked to their data. In addition, beyond people's sex and age, you should only collect personal information that you actually need to answer your research question. If people's sexual orientation or ethnicity is not clearly relevant to your research question, for example, then do not ask them about it. Be aware also that certain data collection procedures can lead to unintentional violations of confidentiality. When participants respond to an oral survey in a shopping mall or complete a questionnaire in a classroom setting, it is possible that their responses will be overheard or seen by others. If the responses are personal, it is better to administer the survey or questionnaire individually in private or to use other techniques to prevent the unintentional sharing of personal information.

## Identify and Minimize Deception

Remember that deception can take a variety of forms, not all of which involve actively misleading participants. It is also deceptive to allow participants to make incorrect assumptions (e.g., about what will be on a "memory test") or simply withhold information about the full design or purpose of the study. It is best to identify and minimize *all* forms of deception.

Remember that according to the APA Ethics Code, deception is ethically acceptable only if there is no way to answer your research question without it. Therefore, if your research design includes any form of active deception, you should consider whether it is truly necessary. Imagine, for example, that you want to know whether the age of college professors affects students' expectations about their teaching ability. You could do this by telling participants that you will show them photos of college professors and ask them to rate each one's teaching ability. But if the photos are not really of college professors but of your own family members and friends, then this would be deception. This deception could easily be eliminated, however, by telling participants instead to *imagine* that the photos are of college professors and to rate them *as if* they were.

In general, it is considered acceptable to wait until debriefing before you reveal your research question as long as you describe the procedure, risks, and benefits during the informed consent process. For example, you would not have to tell participants that you wanted to know whether the age of college professors affects people's expectations about them until the study was over. Not only is this information unlikely to affect people's decision about whether or not to participate in the study, but it has the potential to invalidate the results. Participants who know that age is the independent variable might rate the older and younger "professors" differently because they think you want them to. Alternatively, they might be careful to rate them the same so that they do not appear prejudiced. But even this extremely mild form of deception can be minimized by informing participants—orally, in writing, or both—that although you have accurately described the procedure, risks, and benefits, you will wait to reveal the research question until afterward. In essence, participants give their consent to be deceived or to have information withheld from them until later.

## Weigh the Risks Against the Benefits

Once the risks of the research have been identified and minimized, you need to weigh them against the benefits. This requires identifying all the benefits. Remember to consider benefits to the research participants, to science, and to society. If you are a student researcher, remember that one of the benefits is the knowledge you will gain about how to conduct scientific research in psychology—knowledge you can then use to complete your studies and succeed in graduate school or in your career.

If the research poses minimal risk—no more than in people's daily lives or routine physical or psychological examinations—then even a small benefit to participants, science, or society is generally considered enough to justify it. If it poses more than minimal risk, then there should be more benefits. If the research has the potential to upset some participants, for example, then it becomes more important that the study is well designed and can answer a scientifically interesting research question or have clear practical implications.

It would be unethical to subject people to pain, fear, or embarrassment for no better reason than to satisfy one's personal curiosity. In general, psychological research that has the potential to cause harm that is more than minor or lasts for more than a short time is rarely considered justified by its benefits.

## Create Informed Consent and Debriefing Procedures

Once you have settled on a research design, you need to create your informed consent and debriefing procedures. Start by deciding whether informed consent is necessary according to APA Standard 8.05. If informed consent is necessary, there are several things you should do. First, when you recruit participants—whether it is through word of mouth, posted advertisements, or a participant pool—provide them with as much information about the study as you can. This will allow those who might find the study objectionable to avoid it. Second, prepare a script or set of "talking points" to help you explain the study to your participants in simple everyday language. This should include a description of the procedure, the risks and benefits, and their right to withdraw at any time. Third, create an informed consent form that covers all the points in Standard 8.02a that participants can read and sign after you have described the study to them. Your university, department, or course instructor may have a sample consent form that you can adapt for your own study. If not, an Internet search will turn up several samples. Remember that if appropriate, both the oral and written parts of the informed consent process should include the fact that you are keeping some information about the design or purpose of the study from them but that you will reveal it during debriefing.

Debriefing is similar to informed consent in that you cannot necessarily expect participants to read and understand written debriefing forms. So again it is best to write a script or set of talking points with the goal of being able to explain the study in simple, everyday language. During the debriefing, you should reveal the research question and full design of the study. For example, if participants are tested under only one condition, then you should explain what happened in the other conditions. If you deceived your participants, you should reveal this as soon as possible, apologize for the deception, explain why it was necessary, and correct any misconceptions that participants might have as a result. Debriefing is also a good time to provide additional benefits to research participants by giving them relevant practical information or referrals to other sources of help. For example, in a study of attitudes toward domestic abuse, you could provide pamphlets about domestic abuse and referral information to the university counseling center for those who might want it.

Remember to schedule plenty of time for the informed consent and debriefing processes. They cannot be effective if you have to rush through them.

## Get Approval

The next step is to get institutional approval for your research based on the specific policies and procedures at your institution or for your course. This will generally require writing a protocol that describes the purpose of the study, the research design and procedure, the risks and benefits, the steps taken to minimize risks, and the informed consent and debriefing procedures. Do not think of the institutional approval process as merely an obstacle to overcome but as an opportunity to think through the ethics of your research and to consult with others who are likely to have more experience or different perspectives than you. If the IRB has questions or concerns about your research, address them promptly and in good faith. This might even mean making further modifications to your research design and procedure before resubmitting your protocol.

## Follow Through

Your concern with ethics should not end when your study receives institutional approval. It now becomes important to stick to the protocol you submitted or to seek additional approval for anything other than a minor change. During the research, you should monitor your participants for unanticipated reactions and seek feedback from them during debriefing. One criticism of Milgram's study is that although he did not know ahead of time that his participants would have such severe negative reactions, he certainly knew after he had tested the first several participants and should have made adjustments at that point (Baumrind, 1985).[2] Be alert also for potential violations of confidentiality. Keep the consent forms and the data safe and separate from each other and make sure that no one, intentionally or unintentionally, has access to any participant's personal information.

Finally, you must maintain your integrity through the publication process and beyond. Address publication credit—who will be authors on the research and the order of authors—with your collaborators early and avoid plagiarism in your writing. Remember that your scientific goal is to learn about the way the world actually is and that your scientific duty is to report on your results honestly and accurately. So do not be tempted to fabricate data or alter your results in any way. Besides, unexpected results are often as interesting, or more so, than expected ones.

## Notes

1.  Burger, J. M. (2009). Replicating Milgram: Would people still obey today? *American Psychologist, 64*, 1–11.
2.  Baumrind, D. (1985). Research using intentional deception: Ethical issues revisited. *American Psychologist, 40*, 165–174.

# 18. Key Takeaways and Exercises

- A wide variety of ethical issues arise in psychological research. Thinking them through requires considering how each of four moral principles (weighing risks against benefits, acting responsibly and with integrity, seeking justice, and respecting people's rights and dignity) applies to each of three groups of people (research participants, science, and society).
- Ethical conflict in psychological research is unavoidable. Researchers must think through the ethical issues raised by their research, minimize the risks, weigh the risks against the benefits, be able to explain their ethical decisions, seek feedback about these decisions from others, and ultimately take responsibility for them.
- There are several written ethics codes for research with human participants that provide specific guidance on the ethical issues that arise most frequently. These codes include the Nuremberg Code, the Declaration of Helsinki, the Belmont Report, and the Federal Policy for the Protection of Human Subjects.
- The APA Ethics Code is the most important ethics code for researchers in psychology. It includes many standards that are relevant mainly to clinical practice, but *Standard 8* concerns informed consent, deception, debriefing, the use of nonhuman animal subjects, and scholarly integrity in research.
- Research conducted at universities, hospitals, and other institutions that receive support from the federal government must be reviewed by an institutional review board (IRB)—a committee at the institution that reviews research protocols to make sure they conform to ethical standards.
- Informed consent is the process of obtaining and documenting people's agreement to participate in a study, having informed them of everything that might reasonably be expected to affect their decision. Although it often involves having them read and sign a consent form, it is not equivalent to reading and signing a consent form.
- Although some researchers argue that deception of research participants is never ethically justified, the APA Ethics Code allows for its use when the benefits of using it outweigh the risks, participants cannot reasonably be expected to be harmed, there is no way to conduct the study without deception, and participants are informed of the deception as soon as possible.
- It is your responsibility as a researcher to know and accept your ethical responsibilities.
- You can take several concrete steps to minimize risks and deception in your research. These include making changes to your research design, prescreening to identify and eliminate high-risk participants, and providing participants with as much information as possible during informed consent and debriefing.
- Your ethical responsibilities continue beyond IRB approval. You need to monitor participants' reactions, be alert for potential violations of confidentiality, and maintain scholarly integrity through the publication process.

- Practice: Imagine a study testing the effectiveness of a new drug for treating obsessive-compulsive disorder. Give a hypothetical example of an ethical issue from each cell of Table 3.1 "A Framework for Thinking About Ethical Issues in Scientific Research" that could arise in this research.
- Discussion: It has been argued that researchers are not ethically responsible for the misinterpretation or misuse of their research by others. Do you agree? Why or why not?
- Practice: Read the Nuremberg Code, the Belmont Report, and *Standard* 8 of the APA Ethics Code. List five specific similarities and five specific differences among them.
- Discussion: In a study on the effects of disgust on moral judgment, participants were asked to judge the morality of disgusting acts, including people eating a dead pet and passionate kissing between a brother and sister (Haidt, Koller, & Dias, 1993).[1] If you were on the IRB that reviewed this protocol, what concerns would you have with it? Refer to the appropriate sections of the APA Ethics Code.
- Discussion: How could you conduct a study on the extent to which people obey authority in a way that minimizes risks and deception as much as possible? (Note: Such a study would not have to look at all like Milgram's.)
- Practice: Find a study in a professional journal and create a consent form for that study. Be sure to include all the information in Standard 8.02.

# Notes

1.  Haidt, J., Koller, S. and Dias, M. (1993) Affect, culture, and morality, or is it wrong to eat your dog? Journal of Personality and Social Psychology, 65, 613-628. http://dx.doi.org/10.1037/0022-3514.65.4.613

# CHAPTER IV
# PSYCHOLOGICAL MEASUREMENT

Researchers Tara MacDonald and Alanna Martineau were interested in the effect of female university students' moods on their intentions to have unprotected sexual intercourse (MacDonald & Martineau, 2002)[1]. In a carefully designed empirical study, they found that being in a negative mood increased intentions to have unprotected sex—but only for students who were low in self-esteem. Although there are many challenges involved in conducting a study like this, one of the primary ones is the measurement of the relevant variables. In this study, the researchers needed to know whether each of their participants had high or low self-esteem, which of course required measuring their self-esteem. They also needed to be sure that their attempt to put people into a negative mood (by having them think negative thoughts) was successful, which required measuring their moods. Finally, they needed to see whether self-esteem and mood were related to participants' intentions to have unprotected sexual intercourse, which required measuring these intentions.

To students who are just getting started in psychological research, the challenge of measuring such variables might seem insurmountable. Is it really possible to measure things as intangible as self-esteem, mood, or an intention to do something? The answer is a resounding yes, and in this chapter we look closely at the nature of the variables that psychologists study and how they can be measured. We also look at some practical issues in psychological measurement.

## Do You Feel You Are a Person of Worth?

The Rosenberg Self-Esteem Scale (Rosenberg, 1989)[2] is one of the most common measures of self-esteem and the one that MacDonald and Martineau used in their study. Participants respond to each of the 10 items that follow with a rating on a 4-point scale: *Strongly Agree, Agree, Disagree, Strongly Disagree*. Score Items 1, 2, 4, 6, and 7 by assigning 3 points for each *Strongly Agree* response, 2 for each *Agree*, 1 for each *Disagree*, and 0 for each *Strongly Disagree*. Reverse the scoring for Items 3, 5, 8, 9, and 10 by assigning 0 points for each *Strongly Agree*, 1 point for each *Agree*, and so on. The overall score is the total number of points.

1. I feel that I'm a person of worth, at least on an equal plane with others.
2. I feel that I have a number of good qualities.
3. All in all, I am inclined to feel that I am a failure.
4. I am able to do things as well as most other people.
5. I feel I do not have much to be proud of.
6. I take a positive attitude toward myself.
7. On the whole, I am satisfied with myself.
8. I wish I could have more respect for myself.
9. I certainly feel useless at times.
10. At times I think I am no good at all.

# 19. Understanding Psychological Measurement

## What Is Measurement?

**Measurement** is the assignment of scores to individuals so that the scores represent some characteristic of the individuals. This very general definition is consistent with the kinds of measurement that everyone is familiar with—for example, weighing oneself by stepping onto a bathroom scale, or checking the internal temperature of a roasting turkey using a meat thermometer. It is also consistent with measurement in the other sciences. In physics, for example, one might measure the potential energy of an object in Earth's gravitational field by finding its mass and height (which of course requires measuring those variables) and then multiplying them together along with the gravitational acceleration of Earth (9.8 m/s2). The result of this procedure is a score that represents the object's potential energy.

This general definition of measurement is consistent with measurement in psychology too. (Psychological measurement is often referred to as **psychometrics**.) Imagine, for example, that a cognitive psychologist wants to measure a person's working memory capacity—their ability to hold in mind and think about several pieces of information all at the same time. To do this, she might use a backward digit span task, in which she reads a list of two digits to the person and asks them to repeat them in reverse order. She then repeats this several times, increasing the length of the list by one digit each time, until the person makes an error. The length of the longest list for which the person responds correctly is the score and represents their working memory capacity. Or imagine a clinical psychologist who is interested in how depressed a person is. He administers the Beck Depression Inventory, which is a 21-item self-report questionnaire in which the person rates the extent to which they have felt sad, lost energy, and experienced other symptoms of depression over the past 2 weeks. The sum of these 21 ratings is the score and represents the person's current level of depression.

The important point here is that measurement does not require any particular instruments or procedures.

What it *does* require is *some* systematic procedure for assigning scores to individuals or objects so that those scores represent the characteristic of interest.

## Psychological Constructs

Many variables studied by psychologists are straightforward and simple to measure. These include age, height, weight, and birth order. You can ask people how old they are and be reasonably sure that they know and will tell you. Although people might not know or want to tell you how much they weigh, you can have them step onto a bathroom scale. Other variables studied by psychologists—perhaps the majority—are not so straightforward or simple to measure. We cannot accurately assess people's level of intelligence by looking at them, and we certainly cannot put their self-esteem on a bathroom scale. These kinds of variables are called **constructs** (pronounced CON-*structs*) and include personality traits (e.g., extraversion), emotional states (e.g., fear), attitudes (e.g., toward taxes), and abilities (e.g., athleticism).

Psychological constructs cannot be observed directly. One reason is that they often represent *tendencies to* think, feel, or act in certain ways. For example, to say that a particular university student is highly extraverted does not necessarily mean that she is behaving in an extraverted way right now. In fact, she might be sitting quietly by herself, reading a book. Instead, it means that she has a general tendency to behave in extraverted ways (e.g., being outgoing, enjoying social interactions) across a variety of situations. Another reason psychological constructs cannot be observed directly is that they often involve internal processes. Fear, for example, involves the activation of certain central and peripheral nervous system structures, along with certain kinds of thoughts, feelings, and behaviors—none of which is necessarily obvious to an outside observer. Notice also that neither extraversion nor fear "reduces to" any particular thought, feeling, act, or physiological structure or process. Instead, each is a kind of summary of a complex set of behaviors and internal processes.

### The Big Five

The Big Five is a set of five broad dimensions that capture much of the variation in human personality. Each of the Big Five can even be defined in terms of six more specific constructs called "facets" (Costa & McCrae, 1992)[1].

| Big Five Dimenson | Facets | | | | | |
|---|---|---|---|---|---|---|
| Openness to Experience | Fantasy | Aesthetics | Feelings | Actions | Ideas | Values |
| Conscientiousness | Competence | Order | Dutifulness | Achievement Striving | Self-Discipline | Deliberation |
| Extraversion | Warmth | Gregariousness | Assertiveness | Activity | Excitement Seeking | Positive Emotions |
| Agreeableness | Trust | Straight-forwardness | Altruism | Compliance | Modesty | Tender-Mindedness |
| Neuroticism | Worry | Anger | Discourage-ment | Self-Consciousness | Impulsivity | Vulnerability |

Figure 4.1 The Big Five Personality Dimensions

The conceptual definition of a psychological construct describes the behaviors and internal processes that make up that construct, along with how it relates to other variables. For example, a conceptual definition of neuroticism (another one of the Big Five) would be that it is people's tendency to experience negative emotions such as anxiety, anger, and sadness across a variety of situations. This definition might also include that it has a strong genetic component, remains fairly stable over time, and is positively correlated with the tendency to experience pain and other physical symptoms.

Students sometimes wonder why, when researchers want to understand a construct like self-esteem or neuroticism, they do not simply look it up in the dictionary. One reason is that many scientific constructs do not have counterparts in everyday language (e.g., working memory capacity). More important, researchers are in the business of developing definitions that are more detailed and precise—and that more accurately describe the way the world is—than the informal definitions in the dictionary. As we will see, they do this by proposing conceptual definitions, testing them empirically, and revising them as necessary. Sometimes they throw them out altogether. This is why the research literature often includes different conceptual definitions of the same construct. In some cases, an older conceptual definition has been replaced by a newer one that fits and works better. In others, researchers are still in the process of deciding which of various conceptual definitions is the best.

## Operational Definitions

An **operational definition** is a definition of a variable in terms of precisely how it is to be measured. These measures generally fall into one of three broad categories. **Self-report measures** are those in which participants report on their own thoughts, feelings, and actions, as with the Rosenberg Self-Esteem Scale (Rosenberg, 1965)[2]. **Behavioral measures** are those in which some other aspect of participants' behavior is observed and recorded. This is an extremely broad category that includes the observation of people's behavior both in highly structured laboratory tasks and in more natural settings. A good example of the former would be measuring working memory capacity using the backward digit span task. A good example of the latter is a famous operational definition of physical aggression from researcher Albert Bandura and his colleagues (Bandura, Ross, & Ross, 1961)[3]. They let each of several children play for 20 minutes in a room that contained a clown-shaped punching bag called a Bobo doll. They filmed each child and counted the number of acts of physical aggression the child committed. These included hitting the doll with a mallet, punching it, and kicking it. Their operational definition, then, was the number of these specifically defined acts that the child committed during the 20-minute period. Finally, **physiological measures** are those that involve recording any of a wide variety of physiological processes, including heart rate and blood pressure, galvanic skin response, hormone levels, and electrical activity and blood flow in the brain.

For any given variable or construct, there will be multiple operational definitions. Stress is a good example. A rough conceptual definition is that stress is an adaptive response to a perceived danger or threat that involves physiological, cognitive, affective, and behavioral components. But researchers have operationally defined it in several ways. The Social Readjustment Rating Scale (Holmes & Rahe, 1967)[4] is a self-report questionnaire on which people identify stressful events that they have experienced in the past year and assigns points for each one depending on its severity. For example, a man who has been divorced (73 points), changed jobs (36 points), and had a change in sleeping habits (16 points) in the past year would have a total score of 125. The Hassles and Uplifts Scale (Delongis, Coyne, Dakof, Folkman & Lazarus, 1982)[5] is similar but focuses on everyday stressors like misplacing things and being concerned about one's weight. The Perceived Stress Scale (Cohen, Kamarck, & Mermelstein, 1983)[6] is another self-report measure that focuses on people's feelings of stress (e.g., "How often have you felt nervous and stressed?"). Researchers have also operationally defined stress in terms of several physiological variables including blood pressure and levels of the stress hormone cortisol.

When psychologists use multiple operational definitions of the same construct—either within a study or across studies—they are using **converging operations**. The idea is that the various operational definitions are "converging" or coming together on the same construct. When scores based on several different operational definitions are closely related to each other and produce similar patterns of results, this constitutes good evidence that the construct is being measured effectively and that it is useful. The various measures of stress, for example, are all correlated with each other and have all been shown to be correlated with other variables such as immune system functioning (also measured in a variety of ways) (Segerstrom & Miller, 2004)[7]. This is what allows researchers eventually to draw useful general conclusions, such as "stress is negatively correlated with immune system functioning," as opposed to more specific and less useful ones, such as "people's scores on the Perceived Stress Scale are negatively correlated with their white blood counts."

# Levels of Measurement

The psychologist S. S. Stevens suggested that scores can be assigned to individuals in a way that communicates more or less quantitative information about the variable of interest (Stevens, 1946)[8]. For example, the officials at a 100-m race could simply rank order the runners as they crossed the finish line (first, second, etc.), or they could time each runner to the nearest tenth of a second using a stopwatch (11.5 s, 12.1 s, etc.). In either case, they would be measuring the runners' times by systematically assigning scores to represent those times. But while the rank ordering procedure communicates the fact that the second-place runner took longer to finish than the first-place finisher, the stopwatch procedure also communicates *how much* longer the second-place finisher took. Stevens actually suggested four different **levels of measurement** (which he called "scales of measurement") that correspond to four types of information that can be communicated by a set of scores, and the statistical procedures that can be used with the information.

The **nominal level** of measurement is used for categorical variables and involves assigning scores that are category labels. Category labels communicate whether any two individuals are the same or different in terms of the variable being measured. For example, if you ask your participants about their marital status, you are engaged in nominal-level measurement. Or if you ask your participants to indicate which of several ethnicities they identify themselves with, you are again engaged in nominal-level measurement. The essential point about nominal scales is that they do not imply any ordering among the responses. For example, when classifying people according to their favorite color, there is no sense in which green is placed "ahead of" blue. Responses are merely categorized. Nominal scales thus embody the lowest level of measurement[9].

The remaining three levels of measurement are used for quantitative variables. The **ordinal level** of measurement involves assigning scores so that they represent the rank order of the individuals. Ranks communicate not only whether any two individuals are the same or different in terms of the variable being measured but also whether one individual is higher or lower on that variable. For example, a researcher wishing to measure consumers' satisfaction with their microwave ovens might ask them to specify their feelings as either "very dissatisfied," "somewhat dissatisfied," "somewhat satisfied," or "very satisfied." The items in this scale are ordered, ranging from least to most satisfied. This is what distinguishes ordinal from nominal scales. Unlike nominal scales, ordinal scales allow comparisons of the degree to which two individuals rate the variable. For example, our satisfaction ordering makes it meaningful to assert that one person is more satisfied than another with their microwave ovens. Such an assertion reflects the first person's use of a verbal label that comes later in the list than the label chosen by the second person.

On the other hand, ordinal scales fail to capture important information that will be present in the other levels of measurement we examine. In particular, the difference between two levels of an ordinal scale cannot be assumed to be the same as the difference between two other levels (just like you cannot assume that the gap between the runners in first and second place is equal to the gap between the runners in second and third place). In our satisfaction scale, for example, the difference between the responses "very dissatisfied" and "somewhat dissatisfied" is probably not equivalent to the difference between "somewhat dissatisfied" and "somewhat satisfied." Nothing in our measurement procedure allows us to determine whether the two differences reflect the same difference in psychological satisfaction. Statisticians express this point by saying that the differences between adjacent scale values do not necessarily represent equal intervals on the underlying scale giving rise to the measurements. (In our case, the underlying scale is the true feeling of satisfaction, which we are trying to measure.)

The **interval level** of measurement involves assigning scores using numerical scales in which intervals have the same interpretation throughout. As an example, consider either the Fahrenheit or Celsius temperature scales. The difference between 30 degrees and 40 degrees represents the same temperature difference as the difference between 80 degrees and 90 degrees. This is because each 10-degree interval has the same physical meaning (in terms of the kinetic energy of molecules).

Interval scales are not perfect, however. In particular, they do not have a true zero point even if one of the scaled values happens to carry the name "zero." The Fahrenheit scale illustrates the issue. Zero degrees Fahrenheit does not represent the complete absence of temperature (the absence of any molecular kinetic energy). In reality, the label "zero" is applied to its temperature for quite accidental reasons connected to the history of temperature measurement. Since an interval scale has no true zero point, it does not make sense to compute ratios of temperatures. For example, there is no sense in which the ratio of 40 to 20 degrees Fahrenheit is the same as the ratio of 100 to 50 degrees; no interesting physical property is preserved across the two ratios. After all, if the "zero" label were applied at the temperature that Fahrenheit happens to label as 10 degrees, the two ratios would instead be 30 to 10 and 90 to 40, no longer the same! For this reason, it does not make sense to say that 80 degrees is "twice as hot" as 40 degrees. Such a claim would depend on an arbitrary decision about where to "start" the temperature scale, namely, what temperature to call zero (whereas the claim is intended to make a more fundamental assertion about the underlying physical reality).

In psychology, the intelligence quotient (IQ) is often considered to be measured at the interval level. While it is technically possible to receive a score of 0 on an IQ test, such a score would not indicate the complete absence of IQ. Moreover, a person with an IQ score of 140 does not have twice the IQ of a person with a score of 70. However, the difference between IQ scores of 80 and 100 is the same as the difference between IQ scores of 120 and 140.

Finally, the **ratio level** of measurement involves assigning scores in such a way that there is a true zero point that represents the complete absence of the quantity. Height measured in meters and weight measured in kilograms are good examples. So are counts of discrete objects or events such as the number of siblings one has or the number of questions a student answers correctly on an exam. You can think of a ratio scale as the three earlier scales rolled up in one. Like a nominal scale, it provides a name or category for each object (the numbers serve as labels). Like an ordinal scale, the objects are ordered (in terms of the ordering of the numbers). Like an interval scale, the same difference at two places on the scale has the same meaning. However, in addition, the same ratio at two places on the scale also carries the same meaning (see Table 4.1).

The Fahrenheit scale for temperature has an arbitrary zero point and is therefore not a ratio scale. However, zero on the Kelvin scale is absolute zero. This makes the Kelvin scale a ratio scale. For example, if one temperature is twice as high as another as measured on the Kelvin scale, then it has twice the kinetic energy of the other temperature.

Another example of a ratio scale is the amount of money you have in your pocket right now (25 cents, 50 cents, etc.). Money is measured on a ratio scale because, in addition to having the properties of an interval scale, it has a true zero point: if you have zero money, this actually implies the absence of money. Since money has a true zero point, it makes sense to say that someone with 50 cents has twice as much money as someone with 25 cents.

Stevens's levels of measurement are important for at least two reasons. First, they emphasize the generality of the concept of measurement. Although people do not normally think of categorizing or ranking individuals as measurement, in fact, they are as long as they are done so that they represent some characteristic of the individuals. Second, the levels of measurement can serve as a rough guide to the statistical procedures that can be used with the data and the conclusions that can be drawn from them. With nominal-level measurement, for example, the only available measure of central tendency is the mode. With ordinal-level measurement, the median or mode can be used as indicators of central tendency. Interval and ratio-level measurement are typically considered the most desirable because they permit for any indicators of central tendency to be computed (i.e., mean, median, or mode). Also, ratio-level measurement is the only level that allows meaningful statements about ratios of scores. Once again, one cannot say that someone with an IQ of 140 is twice as intelligent as someone with an IQ of 70 because IQ is measured at the interval level, but one can say that someone with six siblings has twice as many as someone with three because number of siblings is measured at the ratio level.

Table 4.1 Summary of Levels of Measurements

| Level of Measurement | Category labels | Rank order | Equal intervals | True zero |
|---|---|---|---|---|
| NOMINAL | X | | | |
| ORDINAL | X | X | | |
| INTERVAL | X | X | X | |
| RATIO | X | X | X | X |

# Notes

1. Costa, P. T., Jr., & McCrae, R. R. (1992). Normal personality assessment in clinical practice: The NEO Personality Inventory. *Psychological Assessment*, 4, 5–13.
2. Rosenberg, M. (1965). *Society and the adolescent self-image*. Princeton, NJ: Princeton University Press
3. Bandura, A., Ross, D., & Ross, S. A. (1961). Transmission of aggression through imitation of aggressive models. *Journal of Abnormal and Social Psychology*, 63, 575–582.
4. Holmes, T. H., & Rahe, R. H. (1967). The Social Readjustment Rating Scale. *Journal of Psychosomatic Research*, 11(2), 213–218.
5. Delongis, A., Coyne, J. C., Dakof, G., Folkman, S., & Lazarus, R. S. (1982). Relationships of daily hassles, uplifts, and major life events to health status. *Health Psychology*, 1(2), 119–136.
6. Cohen, S., Kamarck, T., & Mermelstein, R. (1983). A global measure of perceived stress. *Journal of Health and Social Behavior*, 24, 386–396.
7. Segerstrom, S. E., & Miller, G. E. (2004). Psychological stress and the human immune system: A meta-analytic study of 30 years of inquiry. *Psychological Bulletin*, 130, 601–630.
8. Stevens, S. S. (1946). On the theory of scales of measurement. *Science*, 103, 677–680.
9. Levels of Measurement. Retrieved from http://wikieducator.org/

# 20. Reliability and Validity of Measurement

> ## Learning Objectives
>
> 1. Define reliability, including the different types and how they are assessed.
> 2. Define validity, including the different types and how they are assessed.
> 3. Describe the kinds of evidence that would be relevant to assessing the reliability and validity of a particular measure.

Again, measurement involves assigning scores to individuals so that they represent some characteristic of the individuals. But how do researchers know that the scores actually represent the characteristic, especially when it is a construct like intelligence, self-esteem, depression, or working memory capacity? The answer is that they conduct research using the measure to confirm that the scores make sense based on their understanding of the construct being measured. This is an extremely important point. Psychologists do not simply *assume* that their measures work. Instead, they collect data to *demonstrate* that they work. If their research does not demonstrate that a measure works, they stop using it.

As an informal example, imagine that you have been dieting for a month. Your clothes seem to be fitting more loosely, and several friends have asked if you have lost weight. If at this point your bathroom scale indicated that you had lost 10 pounds, this would make sense and you would continue to use the scale. But if it indicated that you had gained 10 pounds, you would rightly conclude that it was broken and either fix it or get rid of it. In evaluating a measurement method, psychologists consider two general dimensions: reliability and validity.

## Reliability

Reliability refers to the consistency of a measure. Psychologists consider three types of consistency: over time (test-retest reliability), across items (internal consistency), and across different researchers (inter-rater reliability).

## Test-Retest Reliability

When researchers measure a construct that they assume to be consistent across time, then the scores they obtain should also be consistent across time. Test-retest reliability is the extent to which this is actually the case. For example, intelligence is generally thought to be consistent across time. A person who is highly intelligent today will be highly intelligent next week. This means that any good measure of intelligence should produce roughly the same scores for this individual next week as it does today. Clearly, a measure that produces highly inconsistent scores over time cannot be a very good measure of a construct that is supposed to be consistent.

Assessing test-retest reliability requires using the measure on a group of people at one time, using it again on the *same* group of people at a later time, and then looking at the test-retest correlation between the two sets of scores. This is typically done by graphing the data in a scatterplot and computing the correlation coefficient. Figure 4.2 shows the correlation between two sets of scores of several university students on the Rosenberg Self-Esteem Scale, administered two times, a week apart. The correlation coefficient for these data is +.95. In general, a test-retest correlation of +.80 or greater is considered to indicate good reliability.

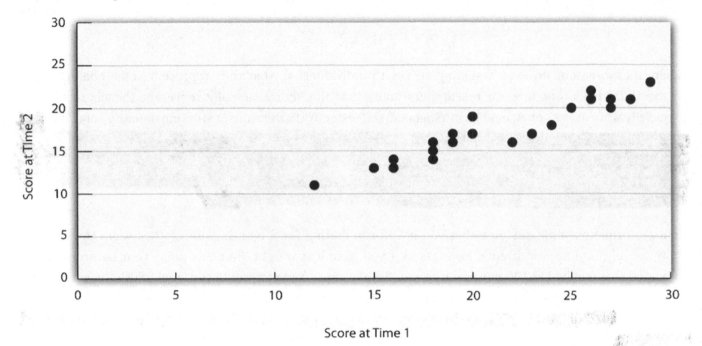

Figure 4.2 Test-Retest Correlation Between Two Sets of Scores of Several College Students on the Rosenberg Self-Esteem Scale, Given Two Times a Week Apart

Again, high test-retest correlations make sense when the construct being measured is assumed to be consistent over time, which is the case for intelligence, self-esteem, and the Big Five personality dimensions. But other constructs are not assumed to be stable over time. The very nature of mood, for example, is that it changes. So a measure of mood that produced a low test-retest correlation over a period of a month would not be a cause for concern.

## Internal Consistency

Another kind of reliability is **internal consistency**, which is the consistency of people's responses across the items on a multiple-item measure. In general, all the items on such measures are supposed to reflect the same underlying construct, so people's scores on those items should be correlated with each other. On the Rosenberg Self-Esteem Scale, people who agree that they are a person of worth should tend to agree that they have a number of good qualities. If people's responses to the different items are not correlated with each other, then it would no longer make sense to claim that they are all measuring the same underlying construct. This is as true for behavioral and physiological measures as for self-report measures. For example, people might make a series of bets in a simulated game of roulette as a measure of their level of risk seeking. This measure would be internally consistent to the extent that individual participants' bets were consistently high or low across trials.

Like test-retest reliability, internal consistency can only be assessed by collecting and analyzing data. One approach is to look at a **split-half correlation**. This involves splitting the items into two sets, such as the first and second halves of the items or the even- and odd-numbered items. Then a score is computed for each set of items, and the relationship between the two sets of scores is examined. For example, Figure 4.3 shows the split-half correlation between several university students' scores on the even-numbered items and their scores on the odd-numbered items of the Rosenberg Self-Esteem Scale. The correlation coefficient for these data is +.88. A split-half correlation of +.80 or greater is generally considered good internal consistency.

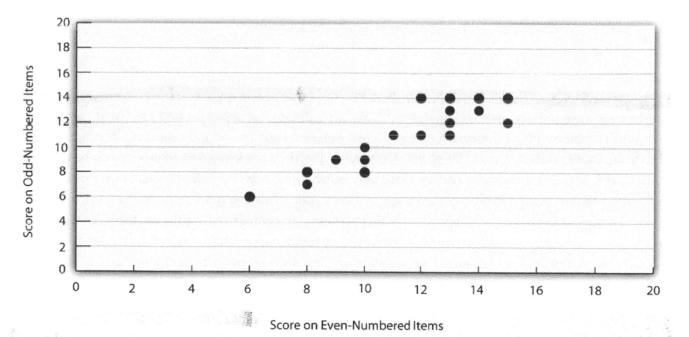

Figure 4.3 Split-Half Correlation Between Several College Students' Scores on the Even-Numbered Items and Their Scores on the Odd-Numbered Items of the Rosenberg Self-Esteem Scale

Perhaps the most common measure of internal consistency used by researchers in psychology is a statistic called **Cronbach's α** (the Greek letter alpha). Conceptually, α is the mean of all possible split-half correlations for a set of items. For example, there are 252 ways to split a set of 10 items into two sets of five. Cronbach's α would be the mean of the 252 split-half correlations. Note that this is not how α is actually computed, but it is a correct way of interpreting the meaning of this statistic. Again, a value of +.80 or greater is generally taken to indicate good internal consistency.

## Interrater Reliability

Many behavioral measures involve significant judgment on the part of an observer or a rater. **Interrater reliability** is the extent to which different observers are consistent in their judgments. For example, if you were interested in measuring university students' social skills, you could make video recordings of them as they interacted with another student whom they are meeting for the first time. Then you could have two or more observers watch the videos and rate each student's level of social skills. To the extent that each participant does, in fact, have some level of social skills that can be detected by an attentive observer, different observers' ratings should be highly correlated with each other. Inter-rater reliability would also have been measured in Bandura's Bobo doll study. In this case, the observers' ratings of how many acts of aggression a particular child committed while playing with the Bobo doll should have been highly positively correlated. Interrater reliability is often assessed using Cronbach's α when the judgments are quantitative or an analogous statistic called Cohen's κ (the Greek letter kappa) when they are categorical.

## Validity

**Validity** is the extent to which the scores from a measure represent the variable they are intended to. But how do researchers make this judgment? We have already considered one factor that they take into account—reliability. When a measure has good test-retest reliability and internal consistency, researchers should be more confident that the scores represent what they are supposed to. There has to be more to it, however, because a measure can be extremely reliable but have no validity whatsoever. As an absurd example, imagine someone who believes that people's index finger length reflects their self-esteem and therefore tries to measure self-esteem by holding a ruler up to people's index fingers. Although this measure would have extremely good test-retest reliability, it would have absolutely no validity. The fact that one person's index finger is a centimeter longer than another's would indicate nothing about which one had higher self-esteem.

Discussions of validity usually divide it into several distinct "types." But a good way to interpret these types is that they are other kinds of evidence—in addition to reliability—that should be taken into account when judging the validity of a measure. Here we consider three basic kinds: face validity, content validity, and criterion validity.

## Face Validity

**Face validity** is the extent to which a measurement method appears "on its face" to measure the construct of interest. Most people would expect a self-esteem questionnaire to include items about whether they see themselves as a person of worth and whether they think they have good qualities. So a questionnaire that included these kinds of items would have good face validity. The finger-length method of measuring self-esteem, on the other hand, seems to have nothing to do with self-esteem and therefore has poor face validity. Although face validity can be assessed quantitatively—for example, by having a large sample of people rate a measure in terms of whether it appears to measure what it is intended to—it is usually assessed informally.

Face validity is at best a very weak kind of evidence that a measurement method is measuring what it is supposed to. One reason is that it is based on people's intuitions about human behavior, which are frequently wrong. It is also the case that many established measures in psychology work quite well despite lacking face validity. The Minnesota Multiphasic Personality Inventory-2 (MMPI-2) measures many personality characteristics and disorders by having people decide whether each of over 567 different statements applies to them—where many of the statements do not have any obvious relationship to the construct that they measure. For example, the items "I enjoy detective or mystery stories" and "The sight of blood doesn't frighten me or make me sick" both measure the suppression of aggression. In this case, it is not the participants' literal answers to these questions that are of interest, but rather whether the pattern of the participants' responses to a series of questions matches those of individuals who tend to suppress their aggression.

## Content Validity

Content validity is the extent to which a measure "covers" the construct of interest. For example, if a researcher conceptually defines test anxiety as involving both sympathetic nervous system activation (leading to nervous feelings) and negative thoughts, then his measure of test anxiety should include items about both nervous feelings and negative thoughts. Or consider that attitudes are usually defined as involving thoughts, feelings, and actions toward something. By this conceptual definition, a person has a positive attitude toward exercise to the extent that they think positive thoughts about exercising, feels good about exercising, and actually exercises. So to have good content validity, a measure of people's attitudes toward exercise would have to reflect all three of these aspects. Like face validity, content validity is not usually assessed quantitatively. Instead, it is assessed by carefully checking the measurement method against the conceptual definition of the construct.

## Criterion Validity

Criterion validity is the extent to which people's scores on a measure are correlated with other variables (known as criteria) that one would expect them to be correlated with. For example, people's scores on a new measure of test anxiety should be negatively correlated with their performance on an important school exam. If it were found that people's scores were in fact negatively correlated with their exam performance, then this would be a piece of evidence that these scores really represent people's test anxiety. But if it were found that people scored equally well on the exam regardless of their test anxiety scores, then this would cast doubt on the validity of the measure.

A **criterion** can be any variable that one has reason to think should be correlated with the construct being measured, and there will usually be many of them. For example, one would expect test anxiety scores to be negatively correlated with exam performance and course grades and positively correlated with general anxiety and with blood pressure during an exam. Or imagine that a researcher develops a new measure of physical risk taking. People's scores on this measure should be correlated with their participation in "extreme" activities such as snowboarding and rock climbing, the number of speeding tickets they have received, and even the number of broken bones they have had over the years. When the criterion is measured at the same time as the construct, criterion validity is referred to as **concurrent validity**; however, when the criterion is measured at some point in the future (after the construct has been measured), it is referred to as **predictive validity** (because scores on the measure have "predicted" a future outcome).

Criteria can also include other measures of the same construct. For example, one would expect new measures of test anxiety or physical risk taking to be positively correlated with existing established measures of the same constructs. This is known as **convergent validity**.

Assessing convergent validity requires collecting data using the measure. Researchers John Cacioppo and Richard Petty did this when they created their self-report Need for Cognition Scale to measure how much people value and engage in thinking (Cacioppo & Petty, 1982)[1]. In a series of studies, they showed that people's scores were positively correlated with their scores on a standardized academic achievement test, and that their scores were negatively correlated with their scores on a measure of dogmatism (which represents a tendency toward obedience). In the years since it was created, the Need for Cognition Scale has been used in literally hundreds of studies and has been shown to be correlated with a wide variety of other variables, including the effectiveness of an advertisement, interest in politics, and juror decisions (Petty, Briñol, Loersch, & McCaslin, 2009)[2].

## Discriminant Validity

**Discriminant validity**, on the other hand, is the extent to which scores on a measure are *not* correlated with measures of variables that are conceptually distinct. For example, self-esteem is a general attitude toward the self that is fairly stable over time. It is not the same as mood, which is how good or bad one happens to be feeling right now. So people's scores on a new measure of self-esteem should not be very highly correlated with their moods. If the new measure of self-esteem were highly correlated with a measure of mood, it could be argued that the new measure is not really measuring self-esteem; it is measuring mood instead.

When they created the Need for Cognition Scale, Cacioppo and Petty also provided evidence of discriminant validity by showing that people's scores were not correlated with certain other variables. For example, they found only a weak correlation between people's need for cognition and a measure of their cognitive style—the extent to which they tend to think analytically by breaking ideas into smaller parts or holistically in terms of "the big picture." They also found no correlation between people's need for cognition and measures of their test anxiety and their tendency to respond in socially desirable ways. All these low correlations provide evidence that the measure is reflecting a conceptually distinct construct.

## Notes

1.  Cacioppo, J. T., & Petty, R. E. (1982). The need for cognition. *Journal of Personality and Social Psychology, 42*, 116–131.
2.  Petty, R. E, Briñol, P., Loersch, C., & McCaslin, M. J. (2009). The need for cognition. In M. R. Leary & R. H. Hoyle (Eds.), *Handbook of individual differences in social behavior* (pp. 318–329). New York, NY: Guilford Press.

# 21. Practical Strategies for Psychological Measurement

So far in this chapter, we have considered several basic ideas about the nature of psychological constructs and their measurement. But now imagine that you are in the position of actually having to measure a psychological construct for a research project. How should you proceed? Broadly speaking, there are four steps in the measurement process: (a) conceptually defining the construct, (b) operationally defining the construct, (c) implementing the measure, and (d) evaluating the measure. In this section, we will look at each of these steps in turn.

## Conceptually Defining the Construct

Having a clear and complete conceptual definition of a construct is a prerequisite for good measurement. For one thing, it allows you to make sound decisions about exactly how to measure the construct. If you had only a vague idea that you wanted to measure people's "memory," for example, you would have no way to choose whether you should have them remember a list of vocabulary words, a set of photographs, a newly learned skill, an experience from long ago, or have them remember to perform a task at a later time. Because psychologists now conceptualize memory as a set of semi-independent systems, you would have to be more precise about what you mean by "memory." If you are interested in long-term episodic memory (memory for previous experiences), then having participants remember a list of words that they learned last week would make sense, but having them try to remember to execute a task in the future would not. In general, there is no substitute for reading the research literature on a construct and paying close attention to how others have defined it.

# Operationally Defining the Construct

Once you have a conceptual definition of the construct you are interested in studying it is time to operationally define the construct. Recall an operational definition is a definition of the variable in terms of precisely how it is to be measured. Since most variables are relatively abstract concepts that cannot be directly observed (e.g., stress), and observation is at the heart of the scientific method, conceptual definitions must be transformed into something that can be directly observed and measured. Most variables can be operationally defined in many different ways. For example, stress can be operationally defined as people's scores on a stress scale such as the Perceived Stress Scale (Cohen, Kamarck, & Mermelstein, 1983) [1], cortisol concentrations in their saliva, or the number of stressful life events they have recently experienced. As described below, operationally defining your variable(s) of interest may involve using an existing measure or creating your own measure.

## Using an Existing Measure

It is usually a good idea to use an existing measure that has been used successfully in previous research. Among the advantages are that (a) you save the time and trouble of creating your own, (b) there is already some evidence that the measure is valid (if it has been used successfully), and (c) your results can more easily be compared with and combined with previous results. In fact, if there already exists a reliable and valid measure of a construct, other researchers might expect you to use it unless you have a good and clearly stated reason for not doing so.

If you choose to use an existing measure, you may still have to choose among several alternatives. You might choose the most common one, the one with the best evidence of reliability and validity, the one that best measures a particular aspect of a construct that you are interested in (e.g., a physiological measure of stress if you are most interested in its underlying physiology), or even the one that would be easiest to use. For example, the Ten-Item Personality Inventory (TIPI) is a self-report questionnaire that measures all the Big Five personality dimensions with just 10 items (Gosling, Rentfrow, & Swann, 2003) [2]. It is not as reliable or valid as longer and more comprehensive measures, but a researcher might choose to use it when testing time is severely limited.

When an existing measure was created primarily for use in scientific research, it is usually described in detail in a published research article and is free to use in your own research—with a proper citation. You might find that later researchers who use the same measure describe it only briefly but provide a reference to the original article, in which case you would have to get the details from the original article. The American Psychological Association also publishes the *Directory of Unpublished Experimental Measures* and PsycTESTS, which are extensive catalogs/collections of measures that have been used in previous research. Many existing measures—especially those that have applications in clinical psychology—are proprietary. This means that a publisher owns the rights to them and that you would have to purchase them. These include many standard intelligence tests, the Beck Depression Inventory, and the Minnesota Multiphasic Personality Inventory (MMPI). Details about many of these measures and how to obtain them can be found in other reference books, including *Tests in Print* and the *Mental Measurements Yearbook*. There is a good chance you can find these reference books in your university library.

## Creating Your Own Measure

Instead of using an existing measure, you might want to create your own. Perhaps there is no existing measure of the construct you are interested in or existing ones are too difficult or time-consuming to use. Or perhaps you want to use a new measure specifically to see whether it works in the same way as existing measures—that is, to evaluate convergent validity. In this section, we consider some general issues in creating new measures that apply equally to self-report, behavioral, and physiological measures. More detailed guidelines for creating self-report measures are presented in Chapter 7.

First, be aware that most new measures in psychology are really variations of existing measures, so you should still look to the research literature for ideas. Perhaps you can modify an existing questionnaire, create a paper-and-pencil version of a measure that is normally computerized (or vice versa), or adapt a measure that has traditionally been used for another purpose. For example, the famous Stroop task (Stroop, 1935)[3]—in which people quickly name the colors that various color words are printed in—has been adapted for the study of social anxiety. People high in social anxiety are slower at color naming when the words have negative social connotations such as "stupid" (Amir, Freshman, & Foa, 2002)[4].

When you create a new measure, you should strive for simplicity. Remember that your participants are not as interested in your research as you are and that they will vary widely in their ability to understand and carry out whatever task you give them. You should create a set of clear instructions using simple language that you can present in writing or read aloud (or both). It is also a good idea to include one or more practice items so that participants can become familiar with the task, and to build in an opportunity for them to ask questions before continuing. It is also best to keep the measure brief to avoid boring or frustrating your participants to the point that their responses start to become less reliable and valid.

The need for brevity, however, needs to be weighed against the fact that it is nearly always better for a measure to include multiple items rather than a single item. There are two reasons for this. One is a matter of content validity. Multiple items are often required to cover a construct adequately. The other is a matter of reliability. People's responses to single items can be influenced by all sorts of irrelevant factors—misunderstanding the particular item, a momentary distraction, or a simple error such as checking the wrong response option. But when several responses are summed or averaged, the effects of these irrelevant factors tend to cancel each other out to produce more reliable scores. Remember, however, that multiple items must be structured in a way that allows them to be combined into a single overall score by summing or averaging. To measure "financial responsibility," a student might ask people about their annual income, obtain their credit score, and have them rate how "thrifty" they are—but there is no obvious way to combine these responses into an overall score. To create a true multiple-item measure, the student might instead ask people to rate the degree to which 10 statements about financial responsibility describe them on the same five-point scale.

Finally, the very best way to assure yourself that your measure has clear instructions, includes sufficient practice, and is an appropriate length is to test several people. Observe them as they complete the task, time them, and ask them afterward to comment on how easy or difficult it was, whether the instructions were clear, and anything else you might be wondering about. Obviously, it is better to discover problems with a measure before beginning any large-scale data collection.

## Implementing the Measure

You will want to implement any measure in a way that maximizes its reliability and validity. In most cases, it is best to test everyone under similar conditions that, ideally, are quiet and free of distractions. Participants are often tested in groups because it is efficient, but be aware that it can create distractions that reduce the reliability and validity of the measure. As always, it is good to use previous research as a guide. If others have successfully tested people in groups using a particular measure, then you should consider doing it too.

Be aware also that people can react in a variety of ways to being measured that reduce the reliability and validity of the scores. Although some disagreeable participants might intentionally respond in ways meant to disrupt a study, participant reactivity is more likely to take the opposite form. Agreeable participants might respond in ways they believe they are expected to. Some participants might engage in **socially desirable responding**, doing or saying things because they think it is the socially appropriate thing. For example, people with low self-esteem agree that they feel they are a person of worth not because they really feel this way but because they believe this is the socially appropriate response and do not want to look bad in the eyes of the researcher. Additionally, research studies can have built-in **demand characteristics**: subtle cues that reveal how the researcher expects participants to behave. For example, a participant whose attitude toward exercise is measured immediately after she is asked to read a passage about the dangers of heart disease might reasonably conclude that the passage was meant to improve her attitude. As a result, she might respond more favorably because she believes she is expected to by the researcher. Finally, your own expectations can bias participants' behaviors in unintended ways.

There are several precautions you can take to minimize these kinds of reactivity. One is to make the procedure as clear and brief as possible so that participants are not tempted to vent their frustrations on your results. Another is to guarantee participants' anonymity and make clear to them that you are doing so. If you are testing them in groups, be sure that they are seated far enough apart that they cannot see each other's responses. Give them all the same type of writing implement so that they cannot be identified by, for example, the pink glitter pen that they used. You can even allow them to seal completed questionnaires into individual envelopes or put them into a drop box where they immediately become mixed with others' questionnaires. Although informed consent requires telling participants what they will be doing, it does not require revealing your hypothesis or other information that might suggest to participants how you expect them to respond. A questionnaire designed to measure financial responsibility need not be titled "Are You Financially Responsible?" It could be titled "Money Questionnaire" or have no title at all. Finally, the effects of your expectations can be minimized by arranging to have the measure administered by a helper who is "blind" or unaware of its intent or of any hypothesis being tested. Regardless of whether this is possible, you should standardize all interactions between researchers and participants—for example, by always reading the same set of instructions word for word.

# Evaluating the Measure

Once you have used your measure on a sample of people and have a set of scores, you are in a position to evaluate it more thoroughly in terms of reliability and validity. Even if the measure has been used extensively by other researchers and has already shown evidence of reliability and validity, you should not assume that it worked as expected for your particular sample and under your particular testing conditions. Regardless, you now have additional evidence bearing on the reliability and validity of the measure, and it would make sense to add that evidence to the research literature.

In most research designs, it is not possible to assess test-retest reliability because participants are tested at only one time. For a new measure, you might design a study specifically to assess its test-retest reliability by testing the same set of participants at two separate times. In other cases, a study designed to answer a different question still allows for the assessment of test-retest reliability. For example, a psychology instructor might measure his students' attitude toward critical thinking using the same measure at the beginning and end of the semester to see if there is any change. Even if there is no change, he could still look at the correlation between students' scores at the two times to assess the measure's test-retest reliability. It is also customary to assess internal consistency for any multiple-item measure—usually by looking at a split-half correlation or Cronbach's α.

Criterion validity can be assessed in various ways. For example, if your study included more than one measure of the same construct or measures of conceptually distinct constructs, then you should look at the correlations among these measures to be sure that they fit your expectations. Note also that a successful experimental manipulation also provides evidence of criterion validity. Recall that MacDonald and Martineau manipulated participant's moods by having them think either positive or negative thoughts, and after the manipulation, their mood measure showed a distinct difference between the two groups. This simultaneously provided evidence that their mood manipulation worked *and* that their mood measure was valid.

But what if your newly collected data cast doubt on the reliability or validity of your measure? The short answer is that you have to ask why. It could be that there is something wrong with your measure or how you administered it. It could be that there is something wrong with your conceptual definition. It could be that your experimental manipulation failed. For example, if a mood measure showed no difference between people whom you instructed to think positive versus negative thoughts, maybe it is because the participants did not actually think the thoughts they were supposed to or that the thoughts did not actually affect their moods. In short, it is "back to the drawing board" to revise the measure, revise the conceptual definition, or try a new manipulation.

# Notes

1. Cohen, S., Kamarck, T., & Mermelstein, R. (1983). A global measure of perceived stress. *Journal of Health and Social Behavior, 24,* 386-396.
2. Gosling, S. D., Rentfrow, P. J., & Swann, W. B., Jr. (2003). A very brief measure of the Big Five personality domains.

*Journal of Research in Personality, 37,* 504–528.

3. Stroop, J. R. (1935). Studies of interference in serial verbal reactions. *Journal of Experimental Psychology, 18,* 643–662.

4. Amir, N., Freshman, M., & Foa, E. (2002). Enhanced Stroop interference for threat in social phobia. *Journal of Anxiety Disorders, 16,* 1–9.

# 22. Key Takeaways and Exercises

- Practice: Complete the Rosenberg Self-Esteem Scale and compute your overall score.
- Practice: Think of three operational definitions for sexual jealousy, decisiveness, and social anxiety. Consider the possibility of self-report, behavioral, and physiological measures. Be as precise as you can.
- Practice: For each of the following variables, decide which level of measurement is being used.

  - A university instructor measures the time it takes her students to finish an exam by looking through the stack of exams at the end. She assigns the one on the bottom a score of 1, the one on top of that a 2, and so on.
  - A researcher accesses her participants' medical records and counts the number of times they have seen a doctor in the past year.
  - Participants in a research study are asked whether they are right-handed or left-handed.

- Practice: Ask several friends to complete the Rosenberg Self-Esteem Scale. Then assess its internal consistency by making a scatterplot to show the split-half correlation (even- vs. odd-numbered items). Compute the correlation coefficient too if you know how.
- Discussion: Think back to the last college exam you took and think of the exam as a psychological measure. What construct do you think it was intended to measure? Comment on its face and content validity. What data could you collect to assess its reliability and criterion validity?
- Practice: Write your own conceptual definition of self-confidence, irritability, and athleticism.
- Practice: Choose a construct (sexual jealousy, self-confidence, etc.) and find two measures of that construct in the research literature. If you were conducting your own study, which one (if either) would you use and why?

# CHAPTER V
# EXPERIMENTAL RESEARCH

In the late 1960s social psychologists John Darley and Bibb Latané proposed a counter-intuitive hypothesis. The more witnesses there are to an accident or a crime, the less likely any of them is to help the victim (Darley & Latané, 1968)[1].

They also suggested the theory that this phenomenon occurs because each witness feels less responsible for helping—a process referred to as the "diffusion of responsibility." Darley and Latané noted that their ideas were consistent with many real-world cases. For example, a New York woman named Catherine "Kitty" Genovese was assaulted and murdered while several witnesses evidently failed to help. But Darley and Latané also understood that such isolated cases did not provide convincing evidence for their hypothesized "bystander effect." There was no way to know, for example, whether any of the witnesses to Kitty Genovese's murder would have helped had there been fewer of them.

So to test their hypothesis, Darley and Latané created a simulated emergency situation in a laboratory. Each of their university student participants was isolated in a small room and told that they would be having a discussion about university life with other students via an intercom system. Early in the discussion, however, one of the students began having what seemed to be an epileptic seizure. Over the intercom came the following: "I could really-er-use some help so if somebody would-er-give me a little h-help-uh-er-er-er-er-er c-could somebody-er-er-help-er-uh-uh-uh (choking sounds)...I'm gonna die-er-er-I'm...gonna die-er-help-er-er-seizure-er- [chokes, then quiet]" (Darley & Latané, 1968, p. 379).

In actuality, there were no other students. These comments had been prerecorded and were played back to create the appearance of a real emergency. The key to the study was that some participants were told that the discussion involved only one other student (the victim), others were told that it involved two other students, and still others were told that it included five other students. Because this was the only difference between these three groups of participants, any difference in their tendency to help the victim would have to have been caused by it. And sure enough, the likelihood that the participant left the room to seek help for the "victim" decreased from 85% to 62% to 31% as the number of "witnesses" increased.

### The Parable of the 38 Witnesses

The story of Kitty Genovese has been told and retold in numerous psychology textbooks. The standard version is that there were 38 witnesses to the crime, that all of them watched (or listened) for an extended period of time, and that none of them did anything to help. However, recent scholarship suggests that the standard story is inaccurate in many ways (Manning, Levine, & Collins, 2007)[2]. For example, only six eyewitnesses testified at the trial, none of them was aware that they were witnessing a lethal assault, and there have been several reports of witnesses calling the police or even coming to the aid of Kitty Genovese. Although the standard story inspired a long line of research on the bystander effect and the diffusion of responsibility, it may also have directed researchers' and students' attention away from other equally interesting and important issues in the psychology of helping—including the conditions in which people do in fact respond collectively to emergency situations.

The research that Darley and Latané conducted was a particular kind of study called an experiment. Experiments are used to determine not only whether there is a meaningful relationship between two variables but also whether the relationship is a causal one that is supported by statistical analysis. For this reason, experiments are one of the most common and useful tools in the psychological researcher's toolbox. In this chapter, we look at experiments in detail. We will first consider what sets experiments apart from other kinds of studies and why they support causal conclusions while other kinds of studies do not. We then look at two basic ways of designing an experiment—between-subjects designs and within-subjects designs—and discuss their pros and cons. Finally, we consider several important practical issues that arise when conducting experiments.

# 23. Experiment Basics

## Learning Objectives

1. Explain what an experiment is and recognize examples of studies that are experiments and studies that are not experiments.
2. Distinguish between the manipulation of the independent variable and control of extraneous variables and explain the importance of each.
3. Recognize examples of confounding variables and explain how they affect the internal validity of a study.
4. Define what a control condition is, explain its purpose in research on treatment effectiveness, and describe some alternative types of control conditions.

## What Is an Experiment?

As we saw earlier in the book, an **experiment** is a type of study designed specifically to answer the question of whether there is a causal relationship between two variables. In other words, whether changes in one variable (referred to as an **independent variable**) cause a change in another variable (referred to as a **dependent variable**). Experiments have two fundamental features. The first is that the researchers manipulate, or systematically vary, the level of the independent variable. The different levels of the independent variable are called **conditions**. For example, in Darley and Latané's experiment, the independent variable was the number of witnesses that participants believed to be present. The researchers manipulated this independent variable by telling participants that there were either one, two, or five other students involved in the discussion, thereby creating three conditions. For a new researcher, it is easy to confuse these terms by believing there are three independent variables in this situation: one, two, or five students involved in the discussion, but there is actually only one independent variable (number of witnesses) with three different levels or conditions (one, two or five students). The second fundamental feature of an experiment is that the researcher exerts **control** over, or minimizes the variability in, variables other than the independent and dependent variable. These other variables are called **extraneous variables**. Darley and Latané tested all their participants in the same room, exposed them to the same emergency situation, and so on. They also randomly assigned their participants to conditions so that the three groups would be similar to each other to begin with. Notice that although the words manipulation and control have similar meanings in everyday language, researchers make a clear distinction between them. They manipulate the independent variable by systematically changing its levels and control other variables by holding them constant.

# Manipulation of the Independent Variable

Again, to **manipulate** an independent variable means to change its level systematically so that different groups of participants are exposed to different levels of that variable, or the same group of participants is exposed to different levels at different times. For example, to see whether expressive writing affects people's health, a researcher might instruct some participants to write about traumatic experiences and others to write about neutral experiences. The different levels of the independent variable are referred to as conditions, and researchers often give the conditions short descriptive names to make it easy to talk and write about them. In this case, the conditions might be called the "traumatic condition" and the "neutral condition."

Notice that the manipulation of an independent variable must involve the active intervention of the researcher. Comparing groups of people who differ on the independent variable before the study begins is not the same as manipulating that variable. For example, a researcher who compares the health of people who already keep a journal with the health of people who do not keep a journal has not manipulated this variable and therefore has not conducted an experiment. This distinction is important because groups that already differ in one way at the beginning of a study are likely to differ in other ways too. For example, people who choose to keep journals might also be more conscientious, more introverted, or less stressed than people who do not. Therefore, any observed difference between the two groups in terms of their health might have been caused by whether or not they keep a journal, or it might have been caused by any of the other differences between people who do and do not keep journals. Thus the active manipulation of the independent variable is crucial for eliminating potential alternative explanations for the results.

Of course, there are many situations in which the independent variable cannot be manipulated for practical or ethical reasons and therefore an experiment is not possible. For example, whether or not people have a significant early illness experience cannot be manipulated, making it impossible to conduct an experiment on the effect of early illness experiences on the development of hypochondriasis. This caveat does not mean it is impossible to study the relationship between early illness experiences and hypochondriasis—only that it must be done using nonexperimental approaches. We will discuss this type of methodology in detail later in the book.

Independent variables can be manipulated to create two conditions and experiments involving a single independent variable with two conditions are often referred to as a **single factor two-level design**. However, sometimes greater insights can be gained by adding more conditions to an experiment. When an experiment has one independent variable that is manipulated to produce more than two conditions it is referred to as a **single factor multi level design**. So rather than comparing a condition in which there was one witness to a condition in which there were five witnesses (which would represent a single-factor two-level design), Darley and Latané's experiment used a single factor multi-level design, by manipulating the independent variable to produce three conditions (a one witness, a two witnesses, and a five witnesses condition).

# Control of Extraneous Variables

As we have seen previously in the chapter, an extraneous variable is anything that varies in the context of a study other than the independent and dependent variables. In an experiment on the effect of expressive writing on health, for example, extraneous variables would include participant variables (individual differences) such as their writing ability, their diet, and their gender. They would also include situational or task variables such as the time of day when participants write, whether they write by hand or on a computer, and the weather. Extraneous variables pose a problem because many of them are likely to have some effect on the dependent variable. For example, participants' health will be affected by many things other than whether or not they engage in expressive writing. This influencing factor can make it difficult to separate the effect of the independent variable from the effects of the extraneous variables, which is why it is important to control extraneous variables by holding them constant.

## Extraneous Variables as "Noise"

Extraneous variables make it difficult to detect the effect of the independent variable in two ways. One is by adding variability or "noise" to the data. Imagine a simple experiment on the effect of mood (happy vs. sad) on the number of happy childhood events people are able to recall. Participants are put into a negative or positive mood (by showing them a happy or sad video clip) and then asked to recall as many happy childhood events as they can. The two leftmost columns of Table 5.1 show what the data might look like if there were no extraneous variables and the number of happy childhood events participants recalled was affected only by their moods. Every participant in the happy mood condition recalled exactly four happy childhood events, and every participant in the sad mood condition recalled exactly three. The effect of mood here is quite obvious. In reality, however, the data would probably look more like those in the two rightmost columns of Table 5.1. Even in the happy mood condition, some participants would recall fewer happy memories because they have fewer to draw on, use less effective recall strategies, or are less motivated. And even in the sad mood condition, some participants would recall more happy childhood memories because they have more happy memories to draw on, they use more effective recall strategies, or they are more motivated. Although the mean difference between the two groups is the same as in the idealized data, this difference is much less obvious in the context of the greater variability in the data. Thus one reason researchers try to control extraneous variables is so their data look more like the idealized data in Table 5.1, which makes the effect of the independent variable easier to detect (although real data never look quite *that* good).

**Table 5.1 Hypothetical Noiseless Data and Realistic Noisy Data**

| Idealized "noiseless" data | | Realistic "noisy" data | |
|---|---|---|---|
| Happy mood | Sad mood | Happy mood | Sad mood |
| 4 | 3 | 3 | 1 |
| 4 | 3 | 6 | 3 |
| 4 | 3 | 2 | 4 |
| 4 | 3 | 4 | 0 |
| 4 | 3 | 5 | 5 |
| 4 | 3 | 2 | 7 |
| 4 | 3 | 3 | 2 |
| 4 | 3 | 1 | 5 |
| 4 | 3 | 6 | 1 |
| 4 | 3 | 8 | 2 |
| M = 4 | M = 3 | M = 4 | M = 3 |

One way to control extraneous variables is to hold them constant. This technique can mean holding situation or task variables constant by testing all participants in the same location, giving them identical instructions, treating them in the same way, and so on. It can also mean holding participant variables constant. For example, many studies of language limit participants to right-handed people, who generally have their language areas isolated in their left cerebral hemispheres[1]. Left-handed people are more likely to have their language areas isolated in their right cerebral hemispheres or distributed across both hemispheres, which can change the way they process language and thereby add noise to the data.

In principle, researchers can control extraneous variables by limiting participants to one very specific category of person, such as 20-year-old, heterosexual, female, right-handed psychology majors. The obvious downside to this approach is that it would lower the external validity of the study—in particular, the extent to which the results can be generalized beyond the people actually studied. For example, it might be unclear whether results obtained with a sample of younger lesbian women would apply to older gay men. In many situations, the advantages of a diverse sample (increased external validity) outweigh the reduction in noise achieved by a homogeneous one.

## Extraneous Variables as Confounding Variables

The second way that extraneous variables can make it difficult to detect the effect of the independent variable is by becoming confounding variables. A **confounding variable** is an extraneous variable that differs on average *across* levels of the independent variable (i.e., it is an extraneous variable that varies systematically with the independent variable). For example, in almost all experiments, participants' intelligence quotients (IQs) will be an extraneous variable. But as long as there are participants with lower and higher IQs in each condition so that the average IQ is roughly equal across the conditions, then this variation is probably acceptable (and may even be desirable). What would be bad, however, would be for participants in one condition to have substantially lower IQs on average and participants in another condition to have substantially higher IQs on average. In this case, IQ would be a confounding variable.

To confound means to confuse, and this effect is exactly why confounding variables are undesirable. Because they differ systematically across conditions—just like the independent variable—they provide an alternative explanation for any observed difference in the dependent variable. Figure 5.1 shows the results of a hypothetical study, in which participants in a positive mood condition scored higher on a memory task than participants in a negative mood condition. But if IQ is a confounding variable—with participants in the positive mood condition having higher IQs on average than participants in the negative mood condition—then it is unclear whether it was the positive moods or the higher IQs that caused participants in the first condition to score higher. One way to avoid confounding variables is by holding extraneous variables constant. For example, one could prevent IQ from becoming a confounding variable by limiting participants only to those with IQs of exactly 100. But this approach is not always desirable for reasons we have already discussed. A second and much more general approach—random assignment to conditions—will be discussed in detail shortly.

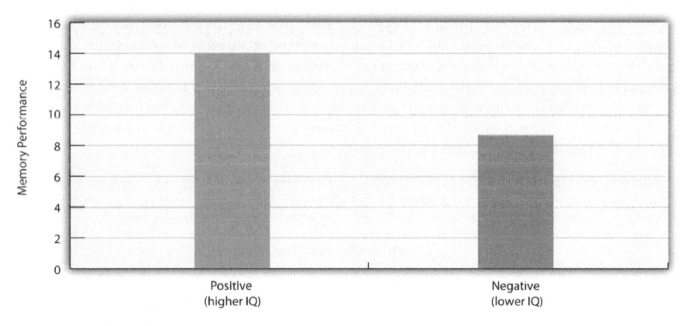

Figure 5.1 *Hypothetical Results From a Study on the Effect of Mood on Memory. Because IQ also differs across conditions, it is a confounding variable.*

## Treatment and Control Conditions

In psychological research, a **treatment** is any intervention meant to change people's behavior for the better. This intervention includes psychotherapies and medical treatments for psychological disorders but also interventions designed to improve learning, promote conservation, reduce prejudice, and so on. To determine whether a treatment works, participants are randomly assigned to either a **treatment condition**, in which they receive the treatment, or a **control condition**, in which they do not receive the treatment. If participants in the treatment condition end up better off than participants in the control condition—for example, they are less depressed, learn faster, conserve more, express less prejudice—then the researcher can conclude that the treatment works. In research on the effectiveness of psychotherapies and medical treatments, this type of experiment is often called a **randomized clinical trial**.

There are different types of control conditions. In a **no-treatment control condition**, participants receive no treatment whatsoever. One problem with this approach, however, is the existence of placebo effects. A **placebo** is a simulated treatment that lacks any active ingredient or element that should make it effective, and a **placebo effect** is a positive effect of such a treatment. Many folk remedies that seem to work—such as eating chicken soup for a cold or placing soap under the bed sheets to stop nighttime leg cramps—are probably nothing more than placebos. Although placebo effects are not well understood, they are probably driven primarily by people's expectations that they will improve. Having the expectation to improve can result in reduced stress, anxiety, and depression, which can alter perceptions and even improve immune system functioning (Price, Finniss, & Benedetti, 2008)[2].

Placebo effects are interesting in their own right (see Note "The Powerful Placebo"), but they also pose a serious problem for researchers who want to determine whether a treatment works. Figure 5.2 shows some hypothetical results in which participants in a treatment condition improved more on average than participants in a no-treatment control condition. If these conditions (the two leftmost bars in Figure 5.2) were the only conditions in this experiment, however, one could not conclude that the treatment worked. It could be instead that participants in the treatment group improved more because they expected to improve, while those in the no-treatment control condition did not.

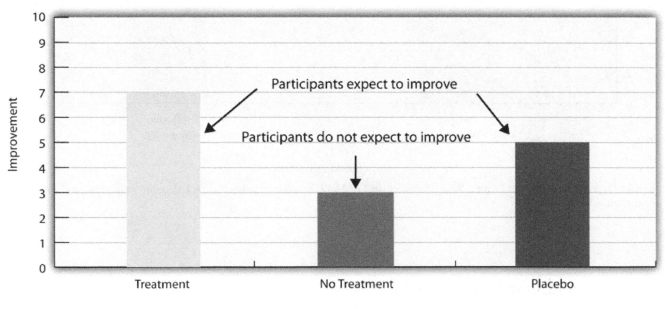

Figure 5.2 Hypothetical Results From a Study Including Treatment, No-Treatment, and Placebo Conditions

Fortunately, there are several solutions to this problem. One is to include a **placebo control condition**, in which participants receive a placebo that looks much like the treatment but lacks the active ingredient or element thought to be responsible for the treatment's effectiveness. When participants in a treatment condition take a pill, for example, then those in a placebo control condition would take an identical-looking pill that lacks the active ingredient in the treatment (a "sugar pill"). In research on psychotherapy effectiveness, the placebo might involve going to a psychotherapist and talking in an unstructured way about one's problems. The idea is that if participants in both the treatment and the placebo control groups expect to improve, then any improvement in the treatment group over and above that in the placebo control group must have been caused by the treatment and not by participants' expectations. This difference is what is shown by a comparison of the two outer bars in Figure 5.4.

Of course, the principle of informed consent requires that participants be told that they will be assigned to either a treatment or a placebo control condition—even though they cannot be told which until the experiment ends. In many cases the participants who had been in the control condition are then offered an opportunity to have the real treatment. An alternative approach is to use a **wait-list control condition**, in which participants are told that they will receive the treatment but must wait until the participants in the treatment condition have already received it. This disclosure allows researchers to compare participants who have received the treatment with participants who are not currently receiving it but who still expect to improve (eventually). A final solution to the problem of placebo effects is to leave out the control condition completely and compare any new treatment with the best available alternative treatment. For example, a new treatment for simple phobia could be compared with standard exposure therapy. Because participants in both conditions receive a treatment, their expectations about improvement should be similar. This approach also makes sense because once there is an effective treatment, the interesting question about a new treatment is not simply "Does it work?" but "Does it work better than what is already available?"

## The Powerful Placebo

Many people are not surprised that placebos can have a positive effect on disorders that seem fundamentally psychological, including depression, anxiety, and insomnia. However, placebos can also have a positive effect on disorders that most people think of as fundamentally physiological. These include asthma, ulcers, and warts (Shapiro & Shapiro, 1999)[3]. There is even evidence that placebo surgery—also called "sham surgery"—can be as effective as actual surgery.

Medical researcher J. Bruce Moseley and his colleagues conducted a study on the effectiveness of two arthroscopic surgery procedures for osteoarthritis of the knee (Moseley et al., 2002)[4]. The control participants in this study were prepped for surgery, received a tranquilizer, and even received three small incisions in their knees. But they did not receive the actual arthroscopic surgical procedure. Note that the IRB would have carefully considered the use of deception in this case and judged that the benefits of using it outweighed the risks and that there was no other way to answer the research question (about the effectiveness of a placebo procedure) without it. The surprising result was that all participants improved in terms of both knee pain and function, and the sham surgery group improved just as much as the treatment groups. According to the researchers, "This study provides strong evidence that arthroscopic lavage with or without débridement [the surgical procedures used] is not better than and appears to be equivalent to a placebo procedure in improving knee pain and self-reported function" (p. 85).

# Notes

1. Knecht, S., Dräger, B., Deppe, M., Bobe, L., Lohmann, H., Flöel, A., . . . Henningsen, H. (2000). Handedness and hemispheric language dominance in healthy humans. *Brain: A Journal of Neurology, 123*(12), 2512-2518. http://dx.doi.org/10.1093/brain/123.12.2512

2. Price, D. D., Finniss, D. G., & Benedetti, F. (2008). A comprehensive review of the placebo effect: Recent advances and current thought. *Annual Review of Psychology, 59,* 565–590.

3. Shapiro, A. K., & Shapiro, E. (1999). *The powerful placebo: From ancient priest to modern physician.* Baltimore, MD: Johns Hopkins University Press.

4. Moseley, J. B., O'Malley, K., Petersen, N. J., Menke, T. J., Brody, B. A., Kuykendall, D. H., ... Wray, N. P. (2002). A controlled trial of arthroscopic surgery for osteoarthritis of the knee. *The New England Journal of Medicine, 347,* 81–88.

# 24. Experimental Design

**Learning Objectives**

1.  Explain the difference between between-subjects and within-subjects experiments, list some of the pros and cons of each approach, and decide which approach to use to answer a particular research question.
2.  Define random assignment, distinguish it from random sampling, explain its purpose in experimental research, and use some simple strategies to implement it
3.  Define several types of carryover effect, give examples of each, and explain how counterbalancing helps to deal with them.

In this section, we look at some different ways to design an experiment. The primary distinction we will make is between approaches in which each participant experiences one level of the independent variable and approaches in which each participant experiences all levels of the independent variable. The former are called between-subjects experiments and the latter are called within-subjects experiments.

## Between-Subjects Experiments

In a **between-subjects experiment**, each participant is tested in only one condition. For example, a researcher with a sample of 100 university students might assign half of them to write about a traumatic event and the other half write about a neutral event. Or a researcher with a sample of 60 people with severe agoraphobia (fear of open spaces) might assign 20 of them to receive each of three different treatments for that disorder. It is essential in a between-subjects experiment that the researcher assigns participants to conditions so that the different groups are, on average, highly similar to each other. Those in a trauma condition and a neutral condition, for example, should include a similar proportion of men and women, and they should have similar average IQs, similar average levels of motivation, similar average numbers of health problems, and so on. This matching is a matter of controlling these extraneous participant variables across conditions so that they do not become confounding variables.

## Random Assignment

The primary way that researchers accomplish this kind of control of extraneous variables across conditions is called **random assignment**, which means using a random process to decide which participants are tested in which conditions. Do not confuse random assignment with random sampling. Random sampling is a method for selecting a sample from a population, and it is rarely used in psychological research. Random assignment is a method for assigning participants in a sample to the different conditions, and it is an important element of all experimental research in psychology and other fields too.

In its strictest sense, random assignment should meet two criteria. One is that each participant has an equal chance of being assigned to each condition (e.g., a 50% chance of being assigned to each of two conditions). The second is that each participant is assigned to a condition independently of other participants. Thus one way to assign participants to two conditions would be to flip a coin for each one. If the coin lands heads, the participant is assigned to Condition A, and if it lands tails, the participant is assigned to Condition B. For three conditions, one could use a computer to generate a random integer from 1 to 3 for each participant. If the integer is 1, the participant is assigned to Condition A; if it is 2, the participant is assigned to Condition B; and if it is 3, the participant is assigned to Condition C. In practice, a full sequence of conditions—one for each participant expected to be in the experiment—is usually created ahead of time, and each new participant is assigned to the next condition in the sequence as they are tested. When the procedure is computerized, the computer program often handles the random assignment.

One problem with coin flipping and other strict procedures for random assignment is that they are likely to result in unequal sample sizes in the different conditions. Unequal sample sizes are generally not a serious problem, and you should never throw away data you have already collected to achieve equal sample sizes. However, for a fixed number of participants, it is statistically most efficient to divide them into equal-sized groups. It is standard practice, therefore, to use a kind of modified random assignment that keeps the number of participants in each group as similar as possible. One approach is **block randomization**. In block randomization, all the conditions occur once in the sequence before any of them is repeated. Then they all occur again before any of them is repeated again. Within each of these "blocks," the conditions occur in a random order. Again, the sequence of conditions is usually generated before any participants are tested, and each new participant is assigned to the next condition in the sequence. Table 5.2 shows such a sequence for assigning nine participants to three conditions. The Research Randomizer website (http://www.randomizer.org) will generate block randomization sequences for any number of participants and conditions. Again, when the procedure is computerized, the computer program often handles the block randomization.

**Table 5.2 Block Randomization Sequence for Assigning Nine Participants to Three Conditions**

| Participant | Condition |
|---|---|
| 1 | A |
| 2 | C |
| 3 | B |
| 4 | B |
| 5 | C |
| 6 | A |
| 7 | C |
| 8 | B |
| 9 | A |

Random assignment is not guaranteed to control all extraneous variables across conditions. The process is random, so it is always possible that just by chance, the participants in one condition might turn out to be substantially older, less tired, more motivated, or less depressed on average than the participants in another condition. However, there are some reasons that this possibility is not a major concern. One is that random assignment works better than one might expect, especially for large samples. Another is that the inferential statistics that researchers use to decide whether a difference between groups reflects a difference in the population takes the "fallibility" of random assignment into account. Yet another reason is that even if random assignment does result in a confounding variable and therefore produces misleading results, this confound is likely to be detected when the experiment is replicated. The upshot is that random assignment to conditions—although not infallible in terms of controlling extraneous variables—is always considered a strength of a research design.

## Matched Groups

An alternative to simple random assignment of participants to conditions is the use of a **matched-groups design**. Using this design, participants in the various conditions are matched on the dependent variable or on some extraneous variable(s) prior the manipulation of the independent variable. This guarantees that these variables will not be confounded across the experimental conditions. For instance, if we want to determine whether expressive writing affects people's health then we could start by measuring various health-related variables in our prospective research participants. We could then use that information to rank-order participants according to how healthy or unhealthy they are. Next, the two healthiest participants would be randomly assigned to complete different conditions (one would be randomly assigned to the traumatic experiences writing condition and the other to the neutral writing condition). The next two healthiest participants would then be randomly assigned to complete different conditions, and so on until the two least healthy participants. This method would ensure that participants in the traumatic experiences writing condition are matched to participants in the neutral writing condition with respect to health at the beginning of the study. If at the end of the experiment, a difference in health was detected across the two conditions, then we would know that it is due to the writing manipulation and not to pre-existing differences in health.

# Within-Subjects Experiments

In a **within-subjects experiment**, each participant is tested under all conditions. Consider an experiment on the effect of a defendant's physical attractiveness on judgments of his guilt. Again, in a between-subjects experiment, one group of participants would be shown an attractive defendant and asked to judge his guilt, and another group of participants would be shown an unattractive defendant and asked to judge his guilt. In a within-subjects experiment, however, the same group of participants would judge the guilt of both an attractive and an unattractive defendant.

The primary advantage of this approach is that it provides maximum control of extraneous participant variables. Participants in all conditions have the same mean IQ, same socioeconomic status, same number of siblings, and so on—because they are the very same people. Within-subjects experiments also make it possible to use statistical procedures that remove the effect of these extraneous participant variables on the dependent variable and therefore make the data less "noisy" and the effect of the independent variable easier to detect. We will look more closely at this idea later in the book. However, not all experiments can use a within-subjects design nor would it be desirable to do so.

## Carryover Effects and Counterbalancing

The primary disadvantage of within-subjects designs is that they can result in order effects. An **order effect** occurs when participants' responses in the various conditions are affected by the order of conditions to which they were exposed. One type of order effect is a carryover effect. A **carryover effect** is an effect of being tested in one condition on participants' behavior in later conditions. One type of carryover effect is a **practice effect**, where participants perform a task better in later conditions because they have had a chance to practice it. Another type is a **fatigue effect**, where participants perform a task worse in later conditions because they become tired or bored. Being tested in one condition can also change how participants perceive stimuli or interpret their task in later conditions. This type of effect is called a **context effect (or contrast effect)**. For example, an average-looking defendant might be judged more harshly when participants have just judged an attractive defendant than when they have just judged an unattractive defendant. Within-subjects experiments also make it easier for participants to guess the hypothesis. For example, a participant who is asked to judge the guilt of an attractive defendant and then is asked to judge the guilt of an unattractive defendant is likely to guess that the hypothesis is that defendant attractiveness affects judgments of guilt. This knowledge could lead the participant to judge the unattractive defendant more harshly because he thinks this is what he is expected to do. Or it could make participants judge the two defendants similarly in an effort to be "fair."

Carryover effects can be interesting in their own right. (Does the attractiveness of one person depend on the attractiveness of other people that we have seen recently?) But when they are not the focus of the research, carryover effects can be problematic. Imagine, for example, that participants judge the guilt of an attractive defendant and then judge the guilt of an unattractive defendant. If they judge the unattractive defendant more harshly, this might be because of his unattractiveness. But it could be instead that they judge him more harshly because they are becoming bored or tired. In other words, the order of the conditions is a confounding variable. The attractive condition is always the first condition and the unattractive condition the second. Thus any difference between the conditions in terms of the dependent variable could be caused by the order of the conditions and not the independent variable itself.

There is a solution to the problem of order effects, however, that can be used in many situations. It is **counterbalancing**, which means testing different participants in different orders. The best method of counterbalancing is **complete counterbalancing** in which an equal number of participants complete each possible order of conditions. For example, half of the participants would be tested in the attractive defendant condition followed by the unattractive defendant condition, and others half would be tested in the unattractive condition followed by the attractive condition. With three conditions, there would be six different orders (ABC, ACB, BAC, BCA, CAB, and CBA), so some participants would be tested in each of the six orders. With four conditions, there would be 24 different orders; with five conditions there would be 120 possible orders. With counterbalancing, participants are assigned to orders randomly, using the techniques we have already discussed. Thus, random assignment plays an important role in within-subjects designs just as in between-subjects designs. Here, instead of randomly assigning to conditions, they are randomly assigned to different orders of conditions. In fact, it can safely be said that if a study does not involve random assignment in one form or another, it is not an experiment.

A more efficient way of counterbalancing is through a Latin square design which randomizes through having equal rows and columns. For example, if you have four treatments, you must have four versions. Like a Sudoku puzzle, no treatment can repeat in a row or column. For four versions of four treatments, the Latin square design would look like:

```
A  B  C  D
B  C  D  A
C  D  A  B
D  A  B  C
```

You can see in the diagram above that the square has been constructed to ensure that each condition appears at each ordinal position (A appears first once, second once, third once, and fourth once) and each condition precedes and follows each other condition one time. A Latin square for an experiment with 6 conditions would by 6 x 6 in dimension, one for an experiment with 8 conditions would be 8 x 8 in dimension, and so on. So while complete counterbalancing of 6 conditions would require 720 orders, a Latin square would only require 6 orders.

Finally, when the number of conditions is large experiments can use **random counterbalancing** in which the order of the conditions is randomly determined for each participant. Using this technique every possible order of conditions is determined and then one of these orders is randomly selected for each participant.

This is not as powerful a technique as complete counterbalancing or partial counterbalancing using a Latin squares design. Use of random counterbalancing will result in more random error, but if order effects are likely to be small and the number of conditions is large, this is an option available to researchers.

There are two ways to think about what counterbalancing accomplishes. One is that it controls the order of conditions so that it is no longer a confounding variable. Instead of the attractive condition always being first and the unattractive condition always being second, the attractive condition comes first for some participants and second for others. Likewise, the unattractive condition comes first for some participants and second for others. Thus any overall difference in the dependent variable between the two conditions cannot have been caused by the order of conditions. A second way to think about what counterbalancing accomplishes is that if there are carryover effects, it makes it possible to detect them. One can analyze the data separately for each order to see whether it had an effect.

### When 9 Is "Larger" Than 221

Researcher Michael Birnbaum has argued that the lack of context provided by between-subjects designs is often a bigger problem than the context effects created by within-subjects designs. To demonstrate this problem, he asked participants to rate two numbers on how large they were on a scale of 1-to-10 where 1 was "very very small" and 10 was "very very large". One group of participants were asked to rate the number 9 and another group was asked to rate the number 221 (Birnbaum, 1999)[1]. Participants in this between-subjects design gave the number 9 a mean rating of 5.13 and the number 221 a mean rating of 3.10. In other words, they rated 9 as larger than 221! According to Birnbaum, this difference is because participants spontaneously compared 9 with other one-digit numbers (in which case it is *relatively* large) and compared 221 with other three-digit numbers (in which case it is *relatively* small).

## Simultaneous Within-Subjects Designs

So far, we have discussed an approach to within-subjects designs in which participants are tested in one condition at a time. There is another approach, however, that is often used when participants make multiple responses in each condition. Imagine, for example, that participants judge the guilt of 10 attractive defendants and 10 unattractive defendants. Instead of having people make judgments about all 10 defendants of one type followed by all 10 defendants of the other type, the researcher could present all 20 defendants in a sequence that mixed the two types. The researcher could then compute each participant's mean rating for each type of defendant. Or imagine an experiment designed to see whether people with social anxiety disorder remember negative adjectives (e.g., "stupid," "incompetent") better than positive ones (e.g., "happy," "productive"). The researcher could have participants study a single list that includes both kinds of words and then have them try to recall as many words as possible. The researcher could then count the number of each type of word that was recalled.

# Between-Subjects or Within-Subjects?

Almost every experiment can be conducted using either a between-subjects design or a within-subjects design. This possibility means that researchers must choose between the two approaches based on their relative merits for the particular situation.

Between-subjects experiments have the advantage of being conceptually simpler and requiring less testing time per participant. They also avoid carryover effects without the need for counterbalancing. Within-subjects experiments have the advantage of controlling extraneous participant variables, which generally reduces noise in the data and makes it easier to detect any effect of the independent variable upon the dependent variable. Within-subjects experiments also require fewer participants than between-subjects experiments to detect an effect of the same size.

A good rule of thumb, then, is that if it is possible to conduct a within-subjects experiment (with proper counterbalancing) in the time that is available per participant—and you have no serious concerns about carryover effects—this design is probably the best option. If a within-subjects design would be difficult or impossible to carry out, then you should consider a between-subjects design instead. For example, if you were testing participants in a doctor's waiting room or shoppers in line at a grocery store, you might not have enough time to test each participant in all conditions and therefore would opt for a between-subjects design. Or imagine you were trying to reduce people's level of prejudice by having them interact with someone of another race. A within-subjects design with counterbalancing would require testing some participants in the treatment condition first and then in a control condition. But if the treatment works and reduces people's level of prejudice, then they would no longer be suitable for testing in the control condition. This difficulty is true for many designs that involve a treatment meant to produce long-term change in participants' behavior (e.g., studies testing the effectiveness of psychotherapy). Clearly, a between-subjects design would be necessary here.

Remember also that using one type of design does not preclude using the other type in a different study. There is no reason that a researcher could not use both a between-subjects design and a within-subjects design to answer the same research question. In fact, professional researchers often take exactly this type of mixed methods approach.

# Notes

1. Birnbaum, M.H. (1999). How to show that 9>221: Collect judgments in a between-subjects design. *Psychological Methods*, 4(3), 243-249.

# 25. Experimentation and Validity

## Four Big Validities

When we read about psychology experiments with a critical view, one question to ask is "is this study valid (accurate)?" However, that question is not as straightforward as it seems because, in psychology, there are many different kinds of validities. Researchers have focused on four validities to help assess whether an experiment is sound (Judd & Kenny, 1981; Morling, 2014)[12]: internal validity, external validity, construct validity, and statistical validity. We will explore each validity in depth.

## Internal Validity

Two variables being statistically related does not necessarily mean that one causes the other. In your psychology education, you have probably heard the term, "Correlation does not imply causation." For example, if it were the case that people who exercise regularly are happier than people who do not exercise regularly, this implication would not necessarily mean that exercising increases people's happiness. It could mean instead that greater happiness causes people to exercise or that something like better physical health causes people to exercise *and* be happier.

The purpose of an experiment, however, is to show that two variables are statistically related and to do so in a way that supports the conclusion that the independent variable caused any observed differences in the dependent variable. The logic is based on this assumption: If the researcher creates two or more highly similar conditions and then manipulates the independent variable to produce just one difference between them, then any later difference between the conditions must have been caused by the independent variable. For example, because the only difference between Darley and Latané's conditions was the number of students that participants believed to be involved in the discussion, this difference in belief must have been responsible for differences in helping between the conditions.

An empirical study is said to be high in **internal validity** if the way it was conducted supports the conclusion that the independent variable caused any observed differences in the dependent variable. Thus experiments are high in internal validity because the way they are conducted–with the manipulation of the independent variable and the control of extraneous variables (such as through the use of random assignment to minimize confounds)–provides strong support for causal conclusions. In contrast, non-experimental research designs (e.g., correlational designs), in which variables are measured but are not manipulated by an experimenter, are low in internal validity.

## External Validity

At the same time, the way that experiments are conducted sometimes leads to a different kind of criticism. Specifically, the need to manipulate the independent variable and control extraneous variables means that experiments are often conducted under conditions that seem artificial (Bauman, McGraw, Bartels, & Warren, 2014)[3]. In many psychology experiments, the participants are all undergraduate students and come to a classroom or laboratory to fill out a series of paper-and-pencil questionnaires or to perform a carefully designed computerized task. Consider, for example, an experiment in which researcher Barbara Fredrickson and her colleagues had undergraduate students come to a laboratory on campus and complete a math test while wearing a swimsuit (Fredrickson, Roberts, Noll, Quinn, & Twenge, 1998)[4]. At first, this manipulation might seem silly. When will undergraduate students ever have to complete math tests in their swimsuits outside of this experiment?

The issue we are confronting is that of **external validity**. An empirical study is high in external validity if the way it was conducted supports generalizing the results to people and situations beyond those actually studied. As a general rule, studies are higher in external validity when the participants and the situation studied are similar to those that the researchers want to generalize to and participants encounter every day, often described as **mundane realism**. Imagine, for example, that a group of researchers is interested in how shoppers in large grocery stores are affected by whether breakfast cereal is packaged in yellow or purple boxes. Their study would be high in external validity and have high mundane realism if they studied the decisions of ordinary people doing their weekly shopping in a real grocery store. If the shoppers bought much more cereal in purple boxes, the researchers would be fairly confident that this increase would be true for other shoppers in other stores. Their study would be relatively low in external validity, however, if they studied a sample of undergraduate students in a laboratory at a selective university who merely judged the appeal of various colors presented on a computer screen; however, this study would have high **psychological realism** where the same mental process is used in both the laboratory and in the real world. If the students judged purple to be more appealing than yellow, the researchers would not be very confident that this preference is relevant to grocery shoppers' cereal-buying decisions because of low external validity but they could be confident that the visual processing of colors has high psychological realism.

We should be careful, however, not to draw the blanket conclusion that experiments are low in external validity. One reason is that experiments need not seem artificial. Consider that Darley and Latané's experiment provided a reasonably good simulation of a real emergency situation. Or consider field experiments that are conducted entirely outside the laboratory. In one such experiment, Robert Cialdini and his colleagues studied whether hotel guests choose to reuse their towels for a second day as opposed to having them washed as a way of conserving water and energy (Cialdini, 2005)[5]. These researchers manipulated the message on a card left in a large sample of hotel rooms. One version of the message emphasized showing respect for the environment, another emphasized that the hotel would donate a portion of their savings to an environmental cause, and a third emphasized that most hotel guests choose to reuse their towels. The result was that guests who received the message that most hotel guests choose to reuse their towels, reused their own towels substantially more often than guests receiving either of the other two messages. Given the way they conducted their study, it seems very likely that their result would hold true for other guests in other hotels.

A second reason not to draw the blanket conclusion that experiments are low in external validity is that they are often conducted to learn about psychological processes that are likely to operate in a variety of people and situations. Let us return to the experiment by Fredrickson and colleagues. They found that the women in their study, but not the men, performed worse on the math test when they were wearing swimsuits. They argued that this gender difference was due to women's greater tendency to objectify themselves—to think about themselves from the perspective of an outside observer—which diverts their attention away from other tasks. They argued, furthermore, that this process of self-objectification and its effect on attention is likely to operate in a variety of women and situations—even if none of them ever finds herself taking a math test in her swimsuit.

## Construct Validity

In addition to the generalizability of the results of an experiment, another element to scrutinize in a study is the quality of the experiment's manipulations or the **construct validity**. The research question that Darley and Latané started with is "does helping behavior become diffused?" They hypothesized that participants in a lab would be less likely to help when they believed there were more potential helpers besides themselves. This conversion from research question to experiment design is called **operationalization** (see Chapter 4 for more information about the operational definition). Darley and Latané operationalized the independent variable of diffusion of responsibility by increasing the number of potential helpers. In evaluating this design, we would say that the construct validity was very high because the experiment's manipulations very clearly speak to the research question; there was a crisis, a way for the participant to help, and increasing the number of other students involved in the discussion, they provided a way to test diffusion.

What if the number of conditions in Darley and Latané's study changed? Consider if there were only two conditions: one student involved in the discussion or two. Even though we may see a decrease in helping by adding another person, it may not be a clear demonstration of diffusion of responsibility, just merely the presence of others. We might think it was a form of Bandura's concept of social inhibition. The construct validity would be lower. However, had there been five conditions, perhaps we would see the decrease continue with more people in the discussion or perhaps it would plateau after a certain number of people. In that situation, we may develop a more nuanced understanding of the phenomenon. But by adding still more conditions, the construct validity may not get higher. When designing your own experiment, consider how well the research question is operationalized your study.

## Statistical Validity

**Statistical validity** concerns the proper statistical treatment of data and the soundness of the researchers' statistical conclusions. There are many different types of inferential statistics tests (e.g., t-tests, ANOVA, regression, correlation) and statistical validity concerns the use of the proper type of test to analyze the data. When considering the proper type of test, researchers must consider the scale of measure their dependent variable was measured on and the design of their study. Further, many inferential statistics tests carry certain assumptions (e.g., the data are normally distributed) and statistical validity is threatened when these assumptions are not met but the statistics are used nonetheless.

One common critique of experiments is that a study did not have enough participants. The main reason for this criticism is that it is difficult to generalize about a population from a small sample. At the outset, it seems as though this critique is about external validity but there are studies where small sample sizes are not a problem (subsequent chapters will discuss how small samples, even of only one person, are still very illuminating for psychological research). Therefore, small sample sizes are actually a critique of statistical validity. The statistical validity speaks to whether the statistics conducted in the study are sound and support the conclusions that are made.

The proper statistical analysis should be conducted on the data to determine whether the difference or relationship that was predicted was indeed found. Interestingly, the likelihood of detecting an effect of the independent variable on the dependent variable depends on not just whether a relationship really exists between these variables, but also the number of conditions and the size of the sample. This is why it is important to conduct a power analysis when designing a study, which is a calculation that informs you of the number of participants you need to recruit to detect an effect of a specific size.

## Prioritizing Validities

These four big validities–internal, external, construct, and statistical–are useful to keep in mind when both reading about other experiments and designing your own. However, researchers must prioritize and often it is not possible to have high validity in all four areas. In Cialdini's study on towel usage in hotels, the external validity was high but the statistical validity was more modest. This discrepancy does not invalidate the study but it shows where there may be room for improvement for future follow-up studies (Goldstein, Cialdini, & Griskevicius, 2008)[6]. Morling (2014) points out that many psychology studies have high internal and construct validity but sometimes sacrifice external validity.

## Notes

1. Judd, C.M. & Kenny, D.A. (1981). *Estimating the effects of social interventions*. Cambridge, MA: Cambridge University Press.

2. Morling, B. (2014, April). Teach your students to be better consumers. *APS Observer*. Retrieved from http://www.psychologicalscience.org/index.php/publications/observer/2014/april-14/teach-your-students-to-be-better-consumers.html

3. Bauman, C.W., McGraw, A.P., Bartels, D.M., & Warren, C. (2014). Revisiting external validity: Concerns about trolley problems and other sacrificial dilemmas in moral psychology. *Social and Personality Psychology Compass, 8/9*, 536-554.

4. Fredrickson, B. L., Roberts, T.-A., Noll, S. M., Quinn, D. M., & Twenge, J. M. (1998). The swimsuit becomes you: Sex differences in self-objectification, restrained eating, and math performance. *Journal of Personality and Social Psychology, 75*, 269–284.

5. Cialdini, R. (2005, April). Don't throw in the towel: Use social influence research. *APS Observer*. Retrieved from http://www.psychologicalscience.org/index.php/publications/observer/2005/april-05/dont-throw-in-the-towel-use-social-influence-research.html

6. Goldstein, N. J., Cialdini, R. B., & Griskevicius, V. (2008). A room with a viewpoint: Using social norms to motivate environmental conservation in hotels. *Journal of Consumer Research, 35*, 472–482.

# 26. Practical Considerations

The information presented so far in this chapter is enough to design a basic experiment. When it comes time to conduct that experiment, however, several additional practical issues arise. In this section, we consider some of these issues and how to deal with them. Much of this information applies to non-experimental studies as well as experimental ones.

## Recruiting Participants

Of course, at the start of any research project, you should be thinking about how you will obtain your participants. Unless you have access to people with schizophrenia or incarcerated juvenile offenders, for example, then there is no point designing a study that focuses on these populations. But even if you plan to use a convenience sample, you will have to recruit participants for your study.

There are several approaches to recruiting participants. One is to use participants from a formal **subject pool**—an established group of people who have agreed to be contacted about participating in research studies. For example, at many colleges and universities, there is a subject pool consisting of students enrolled in introductory psychology courses who must participate in a certain number of studies to meet a course requirement. Researchers post descriptions of their studies and students sign up to participate, usually via an online system. Participants who are not in subject pools can also be recruited by posting or publishing advertisements or making personal appeals to groups that represent the population of interest. For example, a researcher interested in studying older adults could arrange to speak at a meeting of the residents at a retirement community to explain the study and ask for volunteers.

## The Volunteer Subject

Even if the participants in a study receive compensation in the form of course credit, a small amount of money, or a chance at being treated for a psychological problem, they are still essentially volunteers. This is worth considering because people who volunteer to participate in psychological research have been shown to differ in predictable ways from those who do not volunteer. Specifically, there is good evidence that on average, volunteers have the following characteristics compared with non-volunteers (Rosenthal & Rosnow, 1976)[1]:

- They are more interested in the topic of the research.
- They are more educated.
- They have a greater need for approval.
- They have higher IQ.
- They are more sociable.
- They are higher in social class.

This difference can be an issue of external validity if there is a reason to believe that participants with these characteristics are likely to behave differently than the general population. For example, in testing different methods of persuading people, a rational argument might work better on volunteers than it does on the general population because of their generally higher educational level and IQ.

In many field experiments, the task is not recruiting participants but selecting them. For example, researchers Nicolas Guéguen and Marie-Agnès de Gail conducted a field experiment on the effect of being smiled at on helping, in which the participants were shoppers at a supermarket. A confederate walking down a stairway gazed directly at a shopper walking up the stairway and either smiled or did not smile. Shortly afterward, the shopper encountered another confederate, who dropped some computer diskettes on the ground. The dependent variable was whether or not the shopper stopped to help pick up the diskettes (Guéguen & de Gail, 2003)[2]. There are two aspects of this study that are worth addressing here. First, notice that these participants were not "recruited," which means that the IRB would have taken care to ensure that dispensing with informed consent in this case was acceptable (e.g., the situation would not have been expected to cause any harm and the study was conducted in the context of people's ordinary activities). Second, even though informed consent was not necessary, the researchers still had to select participants from among all the shoppers taking the stairs that day. It is extremely important that this kind of selection be done according to a well-defined set of rules that are established before the data collection begins and can be explained clearly afterward. In this case, with each trip down the stairs, the confederate was instructed to gaze at the first person he encountered who appeared to be between the ages of 20 and 50. Only if the person gazed back did they become a participant in the study. The point of having a well-defined selection rule is to avoid bias in the selection of participants. For example, if the confederate was free to choose which shoppers he would gaze at, he might choose friendly-looking shoppers when he was set to smile and unfriendly-looking ones when he was not set to smile. As we will see shortly, such biases can be entirely unintentional.

## Standardizing the Procedure

It is surprisingly easy to introduce extraneous variables during the procedure. For example, the same experimenter might give clear instructions to one participant but vague instructions to another. Or one experimenter might greet participants warmly while another barely makes eye contact with them. To the extent that such variables affect participants' behavior, they add noise to the data and make the effect of the independent variable more difficult to detect. If they vary systematically across conditions, they become confounding variables and provide alternative explanations for the results. For example, if participants in a treatment group are tested by a warm and friendly experimenter and participants in a control group are tested by a cold and unfriendly one, then what appears to be an effect of the treatment might actually be an effect of experimenter demeanor. When there are multiple experimenters, the possibility of introducing extraneous variables is even greater, but is often necessary for practical reasons.

*Experimenter's Sex as an Extraneous Variable*

It is well known that whether research participants are male or female can affect the results of a study. But what about whether the experimenter is male or female? There is plenty of evidence that this matters too. Male and female experimenters have slightly different ways of interacting with their participants, and of course, participants also respond differently to male and female experimenters (Rosenthal, 1976)[3].

For example, in a recent study on pain perception, participants immersed their hands in icy water for as long as they could (Ibolya, Brake, & Voss, 2004)[4]. Male participants tolerated the pain longer when the experimenter was a woman, and female participants tolerated it longer when the experimenter was a man.

Researcher Robert Rosenthal has spent much of his career showing that this kind of unintended variation in the procedure does, in fact, affect participants' behavior. Furthermore, one important source of such variation is the experimenter's expectations about how participants "should" behave in the experiment. This outcome is referred to as an **experimenter expectancy effect** (Rosenthal, 1976)[5]. For example, if an experimenter expects participants in a treatment group to perform better on a task than participants in a control group, then they might unintentionally give the treatment group participants clearer instructions or more encouragement or allow them more time to complete the task. In a striking example, Rosenthal and Kermit Fode had several students in a laboratory course in psychology train rats to run through a maze. Although the rats were genetically similar, some of the students were told that they were working with "maze-bright" rats that had been bred to be good learners, and other students were told that they were working with "maze-dull" rats that had been bred to be poor learners. Sure enough, over five days of training, the "maze-bright" rats made more correct responses, made the correct response more quickly, and improved more steadily than the "maze-dull" rats (Rosenthal & Fode, 1963)[6]. Clearly, it had to have been the students' expectations about how the rats would perform that made the difference. But how? Some clues come from data gathered at the end of the study, which showed that students who expected their rats to learn quickly felt more positively about their animals and reported behaving toward them in a more friendly manner (e.g., handling them more).

The way to minimize unintended variation in the procedure is to standardize it as much as possible so that it is carried out in the same way for all participants regardless of the condition they are in. Here are several ways to do this:

- Create a written protocol that specifies everything that the experimenters are to do and say from the time they greet participants to the time they dismiss them.
- Create standard instructions that participants read themselves or that are read to them word for word by the experimenter.
- Automate the rest of the procedure as much as possible by using software packages for this purpose or even simple computer slide shows.
- Anticipate participants' questions and either raise and answer them in the instructions or develop standard answers for them.

- Train multiple experimenters on the protocol together and have them practice on each other.
- Be sure that each experimenter tests participants in all conditions.

Another good practice is to arrange for the experimenters to be "blind" to the research question or to the condition in which each participant is tested. The idea is to minimize experimenter expectancy effects by minimizing the experimenters' expectations. For example, in a drug study in which each participant receives the drug or a placebo, it is often the case that neither the participants nor the experimenter who interacts with the participants knows which condition they have been assigned to complete. Because both the participants and the experimenters are blind to the condition, this technique is referred to as a **double-blind study**. (A single-blind study is one in which only the participant is blind to the condition.) Of course, there are many times this blinding is not possible. For example, if you are both the investigator and the only experimenter, it is not possible for you to remain blind to the research question. Also, in many studies, the experimenter must know the condition because they must carry out the procedure in a different way in the different conditions.

"Placebo Blocker" retrieved from http://imgs.xkcd.com/comics/placebo_blocker.png (CC-BY-NC 2.5)

# Record Keeping

It is essential to keep good records when you conduct an experiment. As discussed earlier, it is typical for experimenters to generate a written sequence of conditions before the study begins and then to test each new participant in the next condition in the sequence. As you test them, it is a good idea to add to this list basic demographic information; the date, time, and place of testing; and the name of the experimenter who did the testing. It is also a good idea to have a place for the experimenter to write down comments about unusual occurrences (e.g., a confused or uncooperative participant) or questions that come up. This kind of information can be useful later if you decide to analyze sex differences or effects of different experimenters, or if a question arises about a particular participant or testing session.

Since participants' identities should be kept as confidential (or anonymous) as possible, their names and other identifying information should not be included with their data. In order to identify individual participants, it can, therefore, be useful to assign an identification number to each participant as you test them. Simply numbering them consecutively beginning with 1 is usually sufficient. This number can then also be written on any response sheets or questionnaires that participants generate, making it easier to keep them together.

## Manipulation Check

In many experiments, the independent variable is a construct that can only be manipulated indirectly. For example, a researcher might try to manipulate participants' stress levels indirectly by telling some of them that they have five minutes to prepare a short speech that they will then have to give to an audience of other participants. In such situations, researchers often include a **manipulation check** in their procedure. A manipulation check is a separate measure of the construct the researcher is trying to manipulate. The purpose of a manipulation check is to confirm that the independent variable was, in fact, successfully manipulated. For example, researchers trying to manipulate participants' stress levels might give them a paper-and-pencil stress questionnaire or take their blood pressure—perhaps right after the manipulation or at the end of the procedure—to verify that they successfully manipulated this variable.

Manipulation checks are particularly important when the results of an experiment turn out null. In cases where the results show no significant effect of the manipulation of the independent variable on the dependent variable, a manipulation check can help the experimenter determine whether the null result is due to a real absence of an effect of the independent variable on the dependent variable or if it is due to a problem with the manipulation of the independent variable. Imagine, for example, that you exposed participants to happy or sad movie music—intending to put them in happy or sad moods—but you found that this had no effect on the number of happy or sad childhood events they recalled. This could be because being in a happy or sad mood has no effect on memories for childhood events. But it could also be that the music was ineffective at putting participants in happy or sad moods. A manipulation check—in this case, a measure of participants' moods—would help resolve this uncertainty. If it showed that you had successfully manipulated participants' moods, then it would appear that there is indeed no effect of mood on memory for childhood events. But if it showed that you did not successfully manipulate participants' moods, then it would appear that you need a more effective manipulation to answer your research question.

Manipulation checks are usually done at the end of the procedure to be sure that the effect of the manipulation lasted throughout the entire procedure and to avoid calling unnecessary attention to the manipulation (to avoid a demand characteristic). However, researchers are wise to include a manipulation check in a pilot test of their experiment so that they avoid spending a lot of time and resources on an experiment that is doomed to fail and instead spend that time and energy finding a better manipulation of the independent variable.

# Pilot Testing

It is always a good idea to conduct a **pilot test** of your experiment. A pilot test is a small-scale study conducted to make sure that a new procedure works as planned. In a pilot test, you can recruit participants formally (e.g., from an established participant pool) or you can recruit them informally from among family, friends, classmates, and so on. The number of participants can be small, but it should be enough to give you confidence that your procedure works as planned. There are several important questions that you can answer by conducting a pilot test:

- Do participants understand the instructions?
- What kind of misunderstandings do participants have, what kind of mistakes do they make, and what kind of questions do they ask?
- Do participants become bored or frustrated?
- Is an indirect manipulation effective? (You will need to include a manipulation check.)
- Can participants guess the research question or hypothesis (are there demand characteristics)?
- How long does the procedure take?
- Are computer programs or other automated procedures working properly?
- Are data being recorded correctly?

Of course, to answer some of these questions you will need to observe participants carefully during the procedure and talk with them about it afterward. Participants are often hesitant to criticize a study in front of the researcher, so be sure they understand that their participation is part of a pilot test and you are genuinely interested in feedback that will help you improve the procedure. If the procedure works as planned, then you can proceed with the actual study. If there are problems to be solved, you can solve them, pilot test the new procedure, and continue with this process until you are ready to proceed.

# Notes

1. Rosenthal, R., & Rosnow, R. L. (1976). *The volunteer subject*. New York, NY: Wiley.
2. Guéguen, N., & de Gail, Marie-Agnès. (2003). The effect of smiling on helping behavior: Smiling and good Samaritan behavior. *Communication Reports, 16*, 133–140.
3. Rosenthal, R. (1976). *Experimenter effects in behavioral research* (enlarged ed.). New York, NY: Wiley.
4. Ibolya, K., Brake, A., & Voss, U. (2004). The effect of experimenter characteristics on pain reports in women and men. *Pain, 112*, 142–147.
5. Rosenthal, R. (1976). *Experimenter effects in behavioral research* (enlarged ed.). New York, NY: Wiley.
6. Rosenthal, R., & Fode, K. (1963). The effect of experimenter bias on performance of the albino rat. *Behavioral Science, 8*, 183-189.

# 27. Key Takeaways and Exercises

- An experiment is a type of empirical study that features the manipulation of an independent variable, the measurement of a dependent variable, and control of extraneous variables.
- An extraneous variable is any variable other than the independent and dependent variables. A confound is an extraneous variable that varies systematically with the independent variable.
- Experimental research on the effectiveness of a treatment requires both a treatment condition and a control condition, which can be a no-treatment control condition, a placebo control condition, or a wait-list control condition. Experimental treatments can also be compared with the best available alternative.
- Experiments can be conducted using either between-subjects or within-subjects designs. Deciding which to use in a particular situation requires careful consideration of the pros and cons of each approach.
- Random assignment to conditions in between-subjects experiments or counterbalancing of orders of conditions in within-subjects experiments is a fundamental element of experimental research. The purpose of these techniques is to control extraneous variables so that they do not become confounding variables.
- Studies are high in internal validity to the extent that the way they are conducted supports the conclusion that the independent variable caused any observed differences in the dependent variable. Experiments are generally high in internal validity because of the manipulation of the independent variable and control of extraneous variables.
- Studies are high in external validity to the extent that the result can be generalized to people and situations beyond those actually studied. Although experiments can seem "artificial"—and low in external validity—it is important to consider whether the psychological processes under study are likely to operate in other people and situations.
- There are several effective methods you can use to recruit research participants for your experiment, including through formal subject pools, advertisements, and personal appeals. Field experiments require well-defined participant selection procedures.
- It is important to standardize experimental procedures to minimize extraneous variables, including experimenter expectancy effects.
- It is important to conduct one or more small-scale pilot tests of an experiment to be sure that the procedure works as planned.

- Practice: List five variables that can be manipulated by the researcher in an experiment. List five variables that cannot be manipulated by the researcher in an experiment.
- Practice: For each of the following topics, decide whether that topic could be studied using an

experimental research design and explain why or why not.

- Effect of parietal lobe damage on people's ability to do basic arithmetic.
- Effect of being clinically depressed on the number of close friendships people have.
- Effect of group training on the social skills of teenagers with Asperger's syndrome.
- Effect of paying people to take an IQ test on their performance on that test.

- Discussion: Imagine that an experiment shows that participants who receive psychodynamic therapy for a dog phobia improve more than participants in a no-treatment control group. Explain a fundamental problem with this research design and at least two ways that it might be corrected.
- Discussion: For each of the following topics, list the pros and cons of a between-subjects and within-subjects design and decide which would be better.

  - You want to test the relative effectiveness of two training programs for running a marathon.
  - Using photographs of people as stimuli, you want to see if smiling people are perceived as more intelligent than people who are not smiling.
  - In a field experiment, you want to see if the way a panhandler is dressed (neatly vs. sloppily) affects whether or not passersby give him any money.
  - You want to see if concrete nouns (e.g., dog) are recalled better than abstract nouns (e.g., truth).

- Practice: List two ways that you might recruit participants from each of the following populations:

  - elderly adults
  - unemployed people
  - regular exercisers
  - math majors

- Discussion: Imagine a study in which you will visually present participants with a list of 20 words, one at a time, wait for a short time, and then ask them to recall as many of the words as they can. In the stressed condition, they are told that they might also be chosen to give a short speech in front of a small audience. In the unstressed condition, they are not told that they might have to give a speech. What are several specific things that you could do to standardize the procedure?

# CHAPTER VI
# NON-EXPERIMENTAL RESEARCH

What do the following classic studies have in common?

- Stanley Milgram found that about two thirds of his research participants were willing to administer dangerous shocks to another person just because they were told to by an authority figure (Milgram, 1963)[1].
- Elizabeth Loftus and Jacqueline Pickrell showed that it is relatively easy to "implant" false memories in people by repeatedly asking them about childhood events that did not actually happen to them (Loftus & Pickrell, 1995)[2].
- John Cacioppo and Richard Petty evaluated the validity of their Need for Cognition Scale—a measure of the extent to which people like and value thinking—by comparing the scores of university professors with those of factory workers (Cacioppo & Petty, 1982)[3].
- David Rosenhan found that confederates who went to psychiatric hospitals claiming to have heard voices saying things like "empty" and "thud" were labeled as schizophrenic by the hospital staff and kept there even though they behaved normally in all other ways (Rosenhan, 1973)[4].

The answer for purposes of this chapter is that they are not experiments. In this chapter, we look more closely at non-experimental research. We begin with a general definition of non-experimental research, along with a discussion of when and why non-experimental research is more appropriate than experimental research. We then look separately at two important types of non-experimental research: correlational research and observational research.

# 28. Overview of Non-Experimental Research

*Learning Objectives*

1. Define non-experimental research, distinguish it clearly from experimental research, and give several examples.
2. Explain when a researcher might choose to conduct non-experimental research as opposed to experimental research.

## What Is Non-Experimental Research?

**Non-experimental research** is research that lacks the manipulation of an independent variable. Rather than manipulating an independent variable, researchers conducting non-experimental research simply measure variables as they naturally occur (in the lab or real world).

Most researchers in psychology consider the distinction between experimental and non-experimental research to be an extremely important one. This is because although experimental research can provide strong evidence that changes in an independent variable cause differences in a dependent variable, non-experimental research generally cannot. As we will see, however, this inability to make causal conclusions does not mean that non-experimental research is less important than experimental research. It is simply used in cases where experimental research is not able to be carried out.

## When to Use Non-Experimental Research

As we saw in the last chapter, experimental research is appropriate when the researcher has a specific research question or hypothesis about a causal relationship between two variables—and it is possible, feasible, and ethical to manipulate the independent variable. It stands to reason, therefore, that non-experimental research is appropriate—even necessary—when these conditions are not met. There are many times in which non-experimental research is preferred, including when:

- the research question or hypothesis relates to a single variable rather than a statistical relationship between two variables (e.g., how accurate are people's first impressions?).
- the research question pertains to a non-causal statistical relationship between variables (e.g., is there a correlation between verbal intelligence and mathematical intelligence?).
- the research question is about a causal relationship, but the independent variable cannot be

manipulated or participants cannot be randomly assigned to conditions or orders of conditions for practical or ethical reasons (e.g., does damage to a person's hippocampus impair the formation of long-term memory traces?).
- the research question is broad and exploratory, or is about what it is like to have a particular experience (e.g., what is it like to be a working mother diagnosed with depression?).

Again, the choice between the experimental and non-experimental approaches is generally dictated by the nature of the research question. Recall the three goals of science are to describe, to predict, and to explain. If the goal is to explain and the research question pertains to causal relationships, then the experimental approach is typically preferred. If the goal is to describe or to predict, a non-experimental approach is appropriate. But the two approaches can also be used to address the same research question in complementary ways. For example, in Milgram's original (non-experimental) obedience study, he was primarily interested in one variable—the extent to which participants obeyed the researcher when he told them to shock the confederate—and he observed all participants performing the same task under the same conditions. However, Milgram subsequently conducted experiments to explore the factors that affect obedience. He manipulated several independent variables, such as the distance between the experimenter and the participant, the participant and the confederate, and the location of the study (Milgram, 1974)[1].

## Types of Non-Experimental Research

Non-experimental research falls into two broad categories: correlational research and observational research.

The most common type of non-experimental research conducted in psychology is correlational research. Correlational research is considered non-experimental because it focuses on the statistical relationship between two variables but does not include the manipulation of an independent variable. More specifically, in **correlational research**, the researcher measures two variables with little or no attempt to control extraneous variables and then assesses the relationship between them. As an example, a researcher interested in the relationship between self-esteem and school achievement could collect data on students' self-esteem and their GPAs to see if the two variables are statistically related.

**Observational research** is non-experimental because it focuses on making observations of behavior in a natural or laboratory setting without manipulating anything. Milgram's original obedience study was non-experimental in this way. He was primarily interested in the extent to which participants obeyed the researcher when he told them to shock the confederate and he observed all participants performing the same task under the same conditions. The study by Loftus and Pickrell described at the beginning of this chapter is also a good example of observational research. The variable was whether participants "remembered" having experienced mildly traumatic childhood events (e.g., getting lost in a shopping mall) that they had not actually experienced but that the researchers asked them about repeatedly. In this particular study, nearly a third of the participants "remembered" at least one event. (As with Milgram's original study, this study inspired several later experiments on the factors that affect false memories).

## Cross-Sectional, Longitudinal, and Cross-Sequential Studies

When psychologists wish to study change over time (for example, when developmental psychologists wish to study aging) they usually take one of three non-experimental approaches: cross-sectional, longitudinal, or cross-sequential. Cross-sectional studies involve comparing two or more pre-existing groups of people (e.g., children at different stages of development). What makes this approach non-experimental is that there is no manipulation of an independent variable and no random assignment of participants to groups. Using this design, developmental psychologists compare groups of people of different ages (e.g., young adults spanning from 18-25 years of age versus older adults spanning 60-75 years of age) on various dependent variables (e.g., memory, depression, life satisfaction). Of course, the primary limitation of using this design to study the effects of aging is that differences between the groups other than age may account for differences in the dependent variable. For instance, differences between the groups may reflect the generation that people come from (a cohort effect) rather than a direct effect of age. For this reason, longitudinal studies, in which one group of people is followed over time as they age, offer a superior means of studying the effects of aging. However, longitudinal studies are by definition more time consuming and so require a much greater investment on the part of the researcher and the participants. A third approach, known as cross-sequential studies, combines elements of both cross-sectional and longitudinal studies. Rather than measuring differences between people in different age groups or following the same people over a long period of time, researchers adopting this approach choose a smaller period of time during which they follow people in different age groups. For example, they might measure changes over a ten year period among participants who at the start of the study fall into the following age groups: 20 years old, 30 years old, 40 years old, 50 years old, and 60 years old. This design is advantageous because the researcher reaps the immediate benefits of being able to compare the age groups after the first assessment. Further, by following the different age groups over time they can subsequently determine whether the original differences they found across the age groups are due to true age effects or cohort effects.

The types of research we have discussed so far are all quantitative, referring to the fact that the data consist of numbers that are analyzed using statistical techniques. But as you will learn in this chapter, many observational research studies are more qualitative in nature. In qualitative research, the data are usually nonnumerical and therefore cannot be analyzed using statistical techniques. Rosenhan's observational study of the experience of people in psychiatric wards was primarily qualitative. The data were the notes taken by the "pseudopatients"–the people pretending to have heard voices–along with their hospital records. Rosenhan's analysis consists mainly of a written description of the experiences of the pseudopatients, supported by several concrete examples. To illustrate the hospital staff's tendency to "depersonalize" their patients, he noted, "Upon being admitted, I and other pseudopatients took the initial physical examinations in a semi-public room, where staff members went about their own business as if we were not there" (Rosenhan, 1973, p. 256)[2]. Qualitative data has a separate set of analysis tools depending on the research question. For example, thematic analysis would focus on themes that emerge in the data or conversation analysis would focus on the way the words were said in an interview or focus group.

# Internal Validity Revisited

Recall that internal validity is the extent to which the design of a study supports the conclusion that changes in the independent variable caused any observed differences in the dependent variable. Figure 6.1 shows how experimental, quasi-experimental, and non-experimental (correlational) research vary in terms of internal validity. Experimental research tends to be highest in internal validity because the use of manipulation (of the independent variable) and control (of extraneous variables) help to rule out alternative explanations for the observed relationships. If the average score on the dependent variable in an experiment differs across conditions, it is quite likely that the independent variable is responsible for that difference. Non-experimental (correlational) research is lowest in internal validity because these designs fail to use manipulation or control. Quasi-experimental research (which will be described in more detail in a subsequent chapter) falls in the middle because it contains some, but not all, of the features of a true experiment. For instance, it may fail to use random assignment to assign participants to groups or fail to use counterbalancing to control for potential order effects. Imagine, for example, that a researcher finds two similar schools, starts an anti-bullying program in one, and then finds fewer bullying incidents in that "treatment school" than in the "control school." While a comparison is being made with a control condition, the inability to randomly assign children to schools could still mean that students in the treatment school differed from students in the control school in some other way that could explain the difference in bullying (e.g., there may be a selection effect).

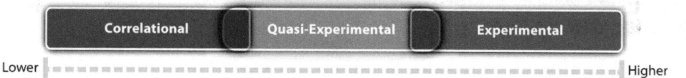

## Internal Validity

*Figure 6.1 Internal Validity of Correlation, Quasi-Experimental, and Experimental Studies. Experiments are generally high in internal validity, quasi-experiments lower, and correlation (non-experimental) studies lower still.*

Notice also in Figure 6.1 that there is some overlap in the internal validity of experiments, quasi-experiments, and correlational (non-experimental) studies. For example, a poorly designed experiment that includes many confounding variables can be lower in internal validity than a well-designed quasi-experiment with no obvious confounding variables. Internal validity is also only one of several validities that one might consider, as noted in Chapter 5.

## Notes

1. Milgram, S. (1974). *Obedience to authority: An experimental view.* New York, NY: Harper & Row.
2. Rosenhan, D. L. (1973). On being sane in insane places. *Science, 179,* 250–258.

# 29. Correlational Research

*Learning Objectives*

1. Define correlational research and give several examples.
2. Explain why a researcher might choose to conduct correlational research rather than experimental research or another type of non-experimental research.
3. Interpret the strength and direction of different correlation coefficients.
4. Explain why correlation does not imply causation.

## What Is Correlational Research?

Correlational research is a type of non-experimental research in which the researcher measures two variables (binary or continuous) and assesses the statistical relationship (i.e., the correlation) between them with little or no effort to control extraneous variables. There are many reasons that researchers interested in statistical relationships between variables would choose to conduct a correlational study rather than an experiment. The first is that they do not believe that the statistical relationship is a causal one or are not interested in causal relationships. Recall two goals of science are to describe and to predict and the correlational research strategy allows researchers to achieve both of these goals. Specifically, this strategy can be used to describe the strength and direction of the relationship between two variables and if there is a relationship between the variables then the researchers can use scores on one variable to predict scores on the other (using a statistical technique called regression, which is discussed further in the section on Complex Correlation in this chapter).

Another reason that researchers would choose to use a correlational study rather than an experiment is that the statistical relationship of interest is thought to be causal, but the researcher *cannot* manipulate the independent variable because it is impossible, impractical, or unethical. For example, while a researcher might be interested in the relationship between the frequency people use cannabis and their memory abilities they cannot ethically manipulate the frequency that people use cannabis. As such, they must rely on the correlational research strategy; they must simply measure the frequency that people use cannabis and measure their memory abilities using a standardized test of memory and then determine whether the frequency people use cannabis is statistically related to memory test performance.

Correlation is also used to establish the reliability and validity of measurements. For example, a researcher might evaluate the validity of a brief extraversion test by administering it to a large group of participants along with a longer extraversion test that has already been shown to be valid. This researcher might then check to see whether participants' scores on the brief test are strongly correlated with their scores on the longer one. Neither test score is thought to cause the other, so there is no independent variable to manipulate. In fact, the terms *independent variable* and *dependent variable* do not apply to this kind of research.

Another strength of correlational research is that it is often higher in external validity than experimental research. Recall there is typically a trade-off between internal validity and external validity. As greater controls are added to experiments, internal validity is increased but often at the expense of external validity as artificial conditions are introduced that do not exist in reality. In contrast, correlational studies typically have low internal validity because nothing is manipulated or controlled but they often have high external validity. Since nothing is manipulated or controlled by the experimenter the results are more likely to reflect relationships that exist in the real world.

Finally, extending upon this trade-off between internal and external validity, correlational research can help to provide converging evidence for a theory. If a theory is supported by a true experiment that is high in internal validity as well as by a correlational study that is high in external validity then the researchers can have more confidence in the validity of their theory. As a concrete example, correlational studies establishing that there is a relationship between watching violent television and aggressive behavior have been complemented by experimental studies confirming that the relationship is a causal one (Bushman & Huesmann, 2001)[1].

## Does Correlational Research Always Involve Quantitative Variables?

A common misconception among beginning researchers is that correlational research must involve two quantitative variables, such as scores on two extraversion tests or the number of daily hassles and number of symptoms people have experienced. However, the defining feature of correlational research is that the two variables are measured—neither one is manipulated—and this is true regardless of whether the variables are quantitative or categorical. Imagine, for example, that a researcher administers the Rosenberg Self-Esteem Scale to 50 American college students and 50 Japanese college students. Although this "feels" like a between-subjects experiment, it is a correlational study because the researcher did not manipulate the students' nationalities. The same is true of the study by Cacioppo and Petty comparing college faculty and factory workers in terms of their need for cognition. It is a correlational study because the researchers did not manipulate the participants' occupations.

Figure 6.2 shows data from a hypothetical study on the relationship between whether people make a daily list of things to do (a "to-do list") and stress. Notice that it is unclear whether this is an experiment or a correlational study because it is unclear whether the independent variable was manipulated. If the researcher randomly assigned some participants to make daily to-do lists and others not to, then it is an experiment. If the researcher simply asked participants whether they made daily to-do lists, then it is a correlational study. The distinction is important because if the study was an experiment, then it could be concluded that making the daily to-do lists reduced participants' stress. But if it was a correlational study, it could only be concluded that these variables are statistically related. Perhaps being stressed has a negative effect on people's ability to plan ahead (the directionality problem). Or perhaps people who are more conscientious are more likely to make to-do lists and less likely to be stressed (the third-variable problem). The crucial point is that what defines a study as experimental or correlational is not the variables being studied, nor whether the variables are quantitative or categorical, nor the type of graph or statistics used to analyze the data. What defines a study is *how* the study is conducted.

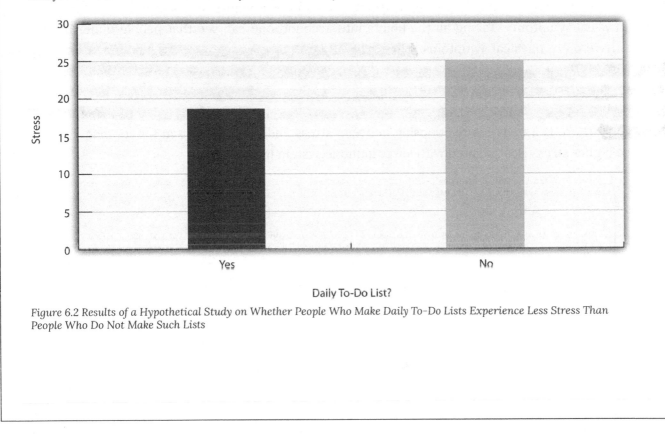

Figure 6.2 Results of a Hypothetical Study on Whether People Who Make Daily To-Do Lists Experience Less Stress Than People Who Do Not Make Such Lists

## Data Collection in Correlational Research

Again, the defining feature of correlational research is that neither variable is manipulated. It does not matter how or where the variables are measured. A researcher could have participants come to a laboratory to complete a computerized backward digit span task and a computerized risky decision-making task and then assess the relationship between participants' scores on the two tasks. Or a researcher could go to a shopping mall to ask people about their attitudes toward the environment and their shopping habits and then assess the relationship between these two variables. Both of these studies would be correlational because no independent variable is manipulated.

# Correlations Between Quantitative Variables

Correlations between quantitative variables are often presented using **scatterplots**. Figure 6.3 shows some hypothetical data on the relationship between the amount of stress people are under and the number of physical symptoms they have. Each point in the scatterplot represents one person's score on both variables. For example, the circled point in Figure 6.3 represents a person whose stress score was 10 and who had three physical symptoms. Taking all the points into account, one can see that people under more stress tend to have more physical symptoms. This is a good example of a **positive relationship**, in which higher scores on one variable tend to be associated with higher scores on the other. In other words, they move in the same direction, either both up or both down. A **negative relationship** is one in which higher scores on one variable tend to be associated with lower scores on the other. In other words, they move in opposite directions. There is a negative relationship between stress and immune system functioning, for example, because higher stress is associated with lower immune system functioning.

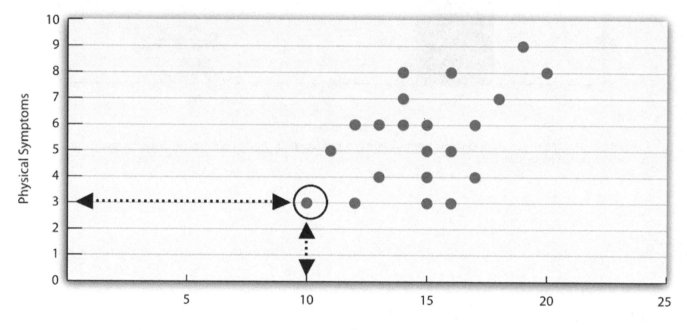

Figure 6.3 Scatterplot Showing a Hypothetical Positive Relationship Between Stress and Number of Physical Symptoms. The circled point represents a person whose stress score was 10 and who had three physical symptoms. Pearson's r for these data is +.51.

The strength of a correlation between quantitative variables is typically measured using a statistic called **Pearson's Correlation Coefficient (or Pearson's r)**. As Figure 6.4 shows, Pearson's r ranges from –1.00 (the strongest possible negative relationship) to +1.00 (the strongest possible positive relationship). A value of 0 means there is no relationship between the two variables. When Pearson's r is 0, the points on a scatterplot form a shapeless "cloud." As its value moves toward –1.00 or +1.00, the points come closer and closer to falling on a single straight line. Correlation coefficients near ±.10 are considered small, values near ± .30 are considered medium, and values near ±.50 are considered large. Notice that the sign of Pearson's r is unrelated to its strength. Pearson's *r* values of +.30 and –.30, for example, are equally strong; it is just that one represents a moderate positive relationship and the other a moderate negative relationship. With the exception of reliability coefficients, most correlations that we find in Psychology are small or moderate in size. The website http://rpsychologist.com/d3/correlation/, created by Kristoffer Magnusson, provides an excellent interactive visualization of correlations that permits you to adjust the strength and direction of a correlation while witnessing the corresponding changes to the scatterplot.

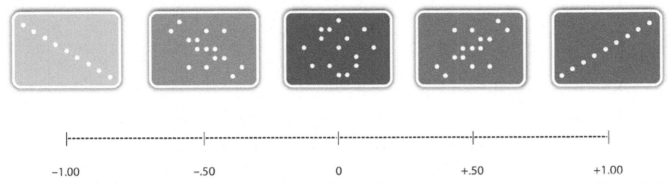

*Figure 6.4 Range of Pearson's r, From –1.00 (Strongest Possible Negative Relationship), Through 0 (No Relationship), to +1.00 (Strongest Possible Positive Relationship)*

There are two common situations in which the value of Pearson's *r* can be misleading. Pearson's *r* is a good measure only for linear relationships, in which the points are best approximated by a straight line. It is not a good measure for nonlinear relationships, in which the points are better approximated by a curved line. Figure 6.5, for example, shows a hypothetical relationship between the amount of sleep people get per night and their level of depression. In this example, the line that best approximates the points is a curve—a kind of upside-down "U"—because people who get about eight hours of sleep tend to be the least depressed. Those who get too little sleep and those who get too much sleep tend to be more depressed. Even though Figure 6.5 shows a fairly strong relationship between depression and sleep, Pearson's *r* would be close to zero because the points in the scatterplot are not well fit by a single straight line. This means that it is important to make a scatterplot and confirm that a relationship is approximately linear before using Pearson's *r*. Nonlinear relationships are fairly common in psychology, but measuring their strength is beyond the scope of this book.

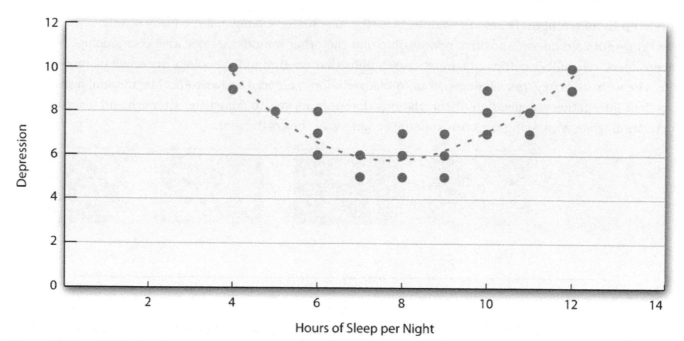

*Figure 6.5 Hypothetical Nonlinear Relationship Between Sleep and Depression*

The other common situations in which the value of Pearson's r can be misleading is when one or both of the variables have a limited range in the sample relative to the population. This problem is referred to as **restriction of range**. Assume, for example, that there is a strong negative correlation between people's age and their enjoyment of hip hop music as shown by the scatterplot in Figure 6.6. Pearson's r here is −.77. However, if we were to collect data only from 18- to 24-year-olds—represented by the shaded area of Figure 6.6—then the relationship would seem to be quite weak. In fact, Pearson's r for this restricted range of ages is 0. It is a good idea, therefore, to design studies to avoid restriction of range. For example, if age is one of your primary variables, then you can plan to collect data from people of a wide range of ages. Because restriction of range is not always anticipated or easily avoidable, however, it is good practice to examine your data for possible restriction of range and to interpret Pearson's r in light of it. (There are also statistical methods to correct Pearson's r for restriction of range, but they are beyond the scope of this book).

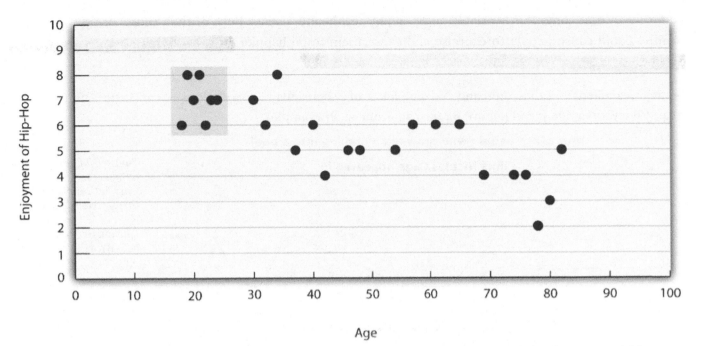

Figure 6.6 *Hypothetical Data Showing How a Strong Overall Correlation Can Appear to Be Weak When One Variable Has a Restricted Range. The overall correlation here is –.77, but the correlation for the 18- to 24-year-olds (in the blue box) is 0.*

## Correlation Does Not Imply Causation

You have probably heard repeatedly that "Correlation does not imply causation." An amusing example of this comes from a 2012 study that showed a positive correlation (Pearson's $r$ = 0.79) between the per capita chocolate consumption of a nation and the number of Nobel prizes awarded to citizens of that nation[2]. It seems clear, however, that this does not mean that eating chocolate causes people to win Nobel prizes, and it would not make sense to try to increase the number of Nobel prizes won by recommending that parents feed their children more chocolate.

There are two reasons that correlation does not imply causation. The first is called the **directionality problem**. Two variables, X and Y, can be statistically related because X causes Y or because Y causes X. Consider, for example, a study showing that whether or not people exercise is statistically related to how happy they are—such that people who exercise are happier on average than people who do not. This statistical relationship is consistent with the idea that exercising causes happiness, but it is also consistent with the idea that happiness causes exercise. Perhaps being happy gives people more energy or leads them to seek opportunities to socialize with others by going to the gym. The second reason that correlation does not imply causation is called the **third-variable problem**. Two variables, X and Y, can be statistically related not because X causes Y, or because Y causes X, but because some third variable, Z, causes both X and Y. For example, the fact that nations that have won more Nobel prizes tend to have higher chocolate consumption probably reflects geography in that European countries tend to have higher rates of per capita chocolate consumption *and* invest more in education and technology (once again, per capita) than many other countries in the world. Similarly, the statistical relationship between exercise and happiness could mean that some third variable, such as physical health, causes both of the others. Being physically healthy could cause people to exercise and cause them to be happier. Correlations that are a result of a third-variable are often referred to as **spurious correlations**.

Some excellent and amusing examples of spurious correlations can be found at http://www.tylervigen.com (Figure 6.7 provides one such example).

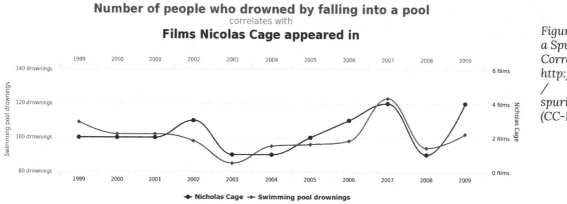

**Number of people who drowned by falling into a pool**
correlates with
**Films Nicolas Cage appeared in**

*Figure 6.7 Example of a Spurious Correlation. Source: http://tylervigen.com / spurious-correlations (CC-BY 4.0)*

*"Lots of Candy Could Lead to Violence"*

Although researchers in psychology know that correlation does not imply causation, many journalists do not. One website about correlation and causation, http://jonathan.mueller.faculty.noctrl.edu/100/correlation_or_causation.htm, links to dozens of media reports about real biomedical and psychological research. Many of the headlines suggest that a causal relationship has been demonstrated when a careful reading of the articles shows that it has not because of the directionality and third-variable problems.

One such article is about a study showing that children who ate candy every day were more likely than other children to be arrested for a violent offense later in life. But could candy really "lead to" violence, as the headline suggests? What alternative explanations can you think of for this statistical relationship? How could the headline be rewritten so that it is not misleading?

As you have learned by reading this book, there are various ways that researchers address the directionality and third-variable problems. The most effective is to conduct an experiment. For example, instead of simply measuring how much people exercise, a researcher could bring people into a laboratory and randomly assign half of them to run on a treadmill for 15 minutes and the rest to sit on a couch for 15 minutes. Although this seems like a minor change to the research design, it is extremely important. Now if the exercisers end up in more positive moods than those who did not exercise, it cannot be because their moods affected how much they exercised (because it was the *researcher* who used random assignment to determine how much they exercised). Likewise, it cannot be because some third variable (e.g., physical health) affected both how much they exercised and what mood they were in. Thus experiments eliminate the directionality and third-variable problems and allow researchers to draw firm conclusions about causal relationships.

# Notes

1. Bushman, B. J., & Huesmann, L. R. (2001). Effects of televised violence on aggression. In D. Singer & J. Singer (Eds.), *Handbook of children and the media* (pp. 223–254). Thousand Oaks, CA: Sage.

2. Messerli, F. H. (2012). Chocolate consumption, cognitive function, and Nobel laureates. *New England Journal of Medicine, 367*, 1562-1564.

# 30. Complex Correlation

### Learning Objectives

1. Explain some reasons that researchers use complex correlational designs.
2. Create and interpret a correlation matrix.
3. Describe how researchers can use partial correlation and multiple regression to statistically control for third variables.

As we have already seen, researchers conduct correlational studies rather than experiments when they are interested in noncausal relationships or when they are interested in causal relationships but the independent variable cannot be manipulated for practical or ethical reasons. In this section, we look at some approaches to complex correlational research that involve measuring several variables and assessing the relationships among them.

## Assessing Relationships Among Multiple Variables

Most complex correlational research involves measuring several variables—either binary or continuous—and then assessing the statistical relationships among them. For example, researchers Nathan Radcliffe and William Klein studied a sample of middle-aged adults to see how their level of optimism (measured by using a short questionnaire called the Life Orientation Test) relates to several other variables related to having a heart attack (Radcliffe & Klein, 2002)[1]. These included their health, their knowledge of heart attack risk factors, and their beliefs about their own risk of having a heart attack. They found that more optimistic participants were healthier (e.g., they exercised more and had lower blood pressure), knew about heart attack risk factors, and correctly believed their own risk to be lower than that of their peers.

In another example, Ernest Jouriles and his colleagues measured adolescents' experiences of physical and psychological relationship aggression and their psychological distress. Because measures of physical aggression (such as the Conflict in Adolescent Dating Relationships Inventory and the Relationship Violence Interview) often tend to result in highly skewed distributions, the researchers transformed their measures of physical aggression into a dichotomous (i.e., binary) measure (0 = did not occur, 1 = did occur). They did the same with their measures of psychological aggression and then measured the correlations among these variables, finding that adolescents who experienced physical aggression were moderately likely to also have experienced psychological aggression and that experiencing psychological aggression was related to symptoms of psychological distress. (Jouriles, Garrido, Rosenfield, & McDonald, 2009)[2]

This approach is often used to assess the validity of new psychological measures. For example, when John

Cacioppo and Richard Petty created their Need for Cognition Scale—a measure of the extent to which people like to think and value thinking—they used it to measure the need for cognition for a large sample of college students, along with three other variables: intelligence, socially desirable responding (the tendency to give what one thinks is the "appropriate" response), and dogmatism (Cacioppo & Petty, 1982)[3]. The results of this study are summarized in Table 6.1, which is a correlation matrix showing the correlation (Pearson's $r$) between every possible pair of variables in the study. For example, the correlation between the need for cognition and intelligence was +.39, the correlation between intelligence and socially desirable responding was +.02, and so on. (Only half the matrix is filled in because the other half would contain exactly the same information. Also, because the correlation between a variable and itself is always +1.00, these values are replaced with dashes throughout the matrix.) In this case, the overall pattern of correlations was consistent with the researchers' ideas about how scores on the need for cognition should be related to these other constructs.

Table 6.1 Correlation Matrix Showing Correlations Among the Need for Cognition and Three Other Variables Based on Research by Cacioppo and Petty (1982)

|  | Need for cognition | Intelligence | Social desirability | Dogmatism |
|---|---|---|---|---|
| Need for cognition | – | | | |
| Intelligence | +.39 | – | | |
| Social desirability | +.08 | +.02 | – | |
| Dogmatism | −.27 | −.23 | +.03 | – |

# Factor Analysis

When researchers study relationships among a large number of conceptually similar variables, they often use a complex statistical technique called **factor analysis**. In essence, factor analysis organizes the variables into a smaller number of clusters, such that they are strongly correlated within each cluster but weakly correlated between clusters. Each cluster is then interpreted as multiple measures of the same underlying construct. These underlying constructs are also called "factors." For example, when people perform a wide variety of mental tasks, factor analysis typically organizes them into two main factors—one that researchers interpret as mathematical intelligence (arithmetic, quantitative estimation, spatial reasoning, and so on) and another that they interpret as verbal intelligence (grammar, reading comprehension, vocabulary, and so on). The Big Five personality factors have been identified through factor analyses of people's scores on a large number of more specific traits. For example, measures of warmth, gregariousness, activity level, and positive emotions tend to be highly correlated with each other and are interpreted as representing the construct of extraversion. As a final example, researchers Peter Rentfrow and Samuel Gosling asked more than 1,700 university students to rate how much they liked 14 different popular genres of music (Rentfrow & Gosling, 2008)[4]. They then submitted these 14 variables to a factor analysis, which identified four distinct factors. The researchers called them *Reflective and Complex* (blues, jazz, classical, and folk), *Intense and Rebellious* (rock, alternative, and heavy metal), *Upbeat and Conventional* (country, soundtrack, religious, pop), and *Energetic and Rhythmic* (rap/hip-hop, soul/funk, and electronica); see Table 6.2.

*Table 6.2 Factor Loadings of the 14 Music Genres on Four Varimax-Rotated Principal Components. Based on Research by Rentfrow and Gosling (2003)*

| Genre | Music-preference dimension | | | |
|---|---|---|---|---|
| | Reflective and Complex | Intense and Rebellious | Upbeat and Conventional | Energetic and Rhythmic |
| Blues | **.85** | .01 | -.09 | .12 |
| Jazz | **.83** | .04 | .07 | .15 |
| Classical | **.66** | .14 | .02 | -.13 |
| Folk | **.64** | .09 | .15 | -.16 |
| Rock | .17 | **.85** | -.04 | -.07 |
| Alternative | .02 | **.80** | .13 | .04 |
| Heavy metal | .07 | **.75** | -.11 | .04 |
| Country | -.06 | .05 | **.72** | -.03 |
| Sound tracks | .01 | .04 | **.70** | .17 |
| Religious | .23 | -.21 | **.64** | -.01 |
| Pop | -.20 | .06 | **.59** | .45 |
| Rap/hip-hop | -.19 | -.12 | .17 | **.79** |
| Soul/funk | .39 | -.11 | .11 | **.69** |
| Electronica/dance | -.02 | .15 | -.01 | **.60** |

Note. N = 1,704. All factor loadings .40 or larger are in italics; the highest factor loadings for each dimension are listed in boldface type.

Two additional points about factor analysis are worth making here. One is that factors are not categories. Factor analysis does not tell us that people are *either* extraverted *or* conscientious or that they like *either* "reflective and complex" music *or* "intense and rebellious" music. Instead, factors are constructs that operate independently of each other. So people who are high in extraversion might be high or low in conscientiousness, and people who like reflective and complex music might or might not also like intense and rebellious music. The second point is that factor analysis reveals only the underlying structure of the variables. It is up to researchers to interpret and label the factors and to explain the origin of that particular factor structure. For example, one reason that extraversion and the other Big Five operate as separate factors is that they appear to be controlled by different genes (Plomin, DeFries, McClean, & McGuffin, 2008)[5].

## Exploring Causal Relationships

Another important use of complex correlational research is to explore possible causal relationships among variables. This might seem surprising given the oft-quoted saying that "correlation does not imply causation." It is true that correlational research cannot unambiguously establish that one variable causes another. Complex correlational research, however, can often be used to rule out other plausible interpretations. The primary way of doing this is through the **statistical control** of potential third variables. Instead of controlling these variables through random assignment or by holding them constant as in an experiment, the researcher instead measures them and includes them in the statistical analysis called **partial correlation**. Using this technique, researchers can examine the relationship between two variables, while statistically controlling for one or more potential third variables.

For example, assume a researcher was interested in the relationship between watching violent television shows and aggressive behavior but she was concerned that socioeconomic status (SES) might represent a third variable that is driving this relationship. In this case, she could conduct a study in which she measures the amount of violent television that participants watch in their everyday life, the number of acts of aggression that they have engaged in, and their SES. She could first examine the correlation between violent television viewing and aggression. Let's say she found a correlation of +.35, which would be considered a moderate sized positive correlation. Next, she could use partial correlation to reexamine this relationship after statistically controlling for SES. This technique would allow her to examine the relationship between the part of violent television viewing that is independent of SES and the part of aggressive behavior that is independent of SES. If she found that the partial correlation between violent television viewing and aggression while controlling for SES was +.34, that would suggest that the relationship between violent television viewing and aggression is largely independent of SES (i.e., SES is not a third variable driving this relationship). On the other hand, if she found that after statistically controlling for SES the correlation between violent television viewing and aggression dropped to +.03, then that would suggest that SES is indeed a third variable that is driving the relationship. If, however, she found that statistically controlling for SES reduced the magnitude of the correlation from +.35 to +.20, then this would suggest that SES accounts for some, but not all, of the relationship between television violence and aggression. It is important to note that while partial correlation provides an important tool for researchers to statistically control for third variables, researchers using this technique are still limited in their ability to arrive at causal conclusions because this technique does not take care of the directionality problem and there may be other third variables driving the relationship that the researcher did not consider and statistically control.

## Regression

Once a relationship between two variables has been established, researchers can use that information to make predictions about the value of one variable given the value of another variable. For, instance, once we have established that there is a correlation between IQ and GPA we can use people's IQ scores to predict their GPA. Thus, while correlation coefficients can be used to describe the strength and direction of relationships between variables, **regression** is a statistical technique that allows researchers to predict one variable given another. Regression can also be used to describe more complex relationships between more than two variables. Typically the variable that is used to make the prediction is referred to as the **predictor variable** and the variable that is being predicted is called the **outcome variable or criterion variable**. This regression equation has the following general form:

$$Y = b_1X_1$$

Y in this formula represents the person's predicted score on the outcome variable, $b_1$ represents the slope of the line depicting the relationship between two variables (or the regression weight), and $X_1$ represents the person's score on the predictor variable. You can see that to predict a person's score on the outcome variable (Y), one simply needs to multiply their score on the predictor variable (X) by the regression weight ($b_1$)

While **simple regression** involves using one variable to predict another, **multiple regression** involves measuring several variables (X1, X2, X3,...Xi), and using them to predict some outcome variable (Y). Multiple regression can also be used to simply describe the relationship between a single outcome variable (Y) and a set of predictor variables (X1, X2, X3,...Xi). The result of a multiple regression analysis is an equation that expresses the outcome variable as an additive combination of the predictor variables. This regression equation has the following general form:

$$Y = b_1X_1 + b_2X_2 + b_3X_3 + \dots + b_iX_i$$

The regression weights ($b_1$, $b_2$, and so on) indicate how large a contribution a predictor variable makes, on average, to the prediction of the outcome variable. Specifically, they indicate how much the outcome variable changes for each one-unit change in the predictor variable.

The advantage of multiple regression is that it can show whether a predictor variable makes a contribution to an outcome variable *over and above* the contributions made by other predictor variables (i.e., it can be used to show whether a predictor variable is related to an outcome variable after statistically controlling for other predictor variables). As a hypothetical example, imagine that a researcher wants to know how income and health relate to happiness. This is tricky because income and health are themselves related to each other. Thus if people with greater incomes tend to be happier, then perhaps this is only because they tend to be healthier. Likewise, if people who are healthier tend to be happier, perhaps this is only because they tend to make more money. But a multiple regression analysis including both income and health as predictor variables would show whether each one makes a contribution to the prediction of happiness when the other is taken into account (when it is statistically controlled). In other words, multiple regression would allow the researcher to examine whether that part of income that is unrelated to health predicts or relates to happiness as well as whether that part of health that is unrelated to income predicts or relates to happiness. Research like this, by the way, has shown both income and health make extremely small contributions to happiness except in the case of severe poverty or illness (Diener, 2000[6]).

The examples discussed in this section only scratch the surface of how researchers use complex correlational research to explore possible causal relationships among variables. It is important to keep in mind, however, that purely correlational approaches cannot unambiguously establish that one variable causes another. The best they can do is show patterns of relationships that are consistent with some causal interpretations and inconsistent with others.

## Notes

1. Radcliffe, N. M., & Klein, W. M. P. (2002). Dispositional, unrealistic, and comparative optimism: Differential relations

with knowledge and processing of risk information and beliefs about personal risk. *Personality and Social Psychology Bulletin, 28,* 836–846.

2. Jouriles, E. N., Garrido, E., Rosenfield, D., & McDonald, R. (2009). Experiences of psychological and physical aggression in adolescent romantic relationships: Links to psychological distress. *Child Abuse & Neglect, 33*(7), 451–460.

3. Cacioppo, J. T., & Petty, R. E. (1982). The need for cognition. *Journal of Personality and Social Psychology, 42,* 116–131.

4. Rentfrow, P. J., & Gosling, S. D. (2008). The do re mi's of everyday life: The structure and personality correlates of music preferences. *Journal of Personality and Social Psychology, 84,* 1236–1256.

5. Plomin, R., DeFries, J. C., McClearn, G. E., & McGuffin, P. (2008). *Behavioral genetics* (5th ed.). New York, NY: Worth.

6. Diener, E. (2000). Subjective well-being: The science of happiness, and a proposal for a national index. *American Psychologist, 55,* 34–43.

# 31. Qualitative Research

## What Is Qualitative Research?

This textbook is primarily about **quantitative research,** in part because most studies conducted in psychology are quantitative in nature. Quantitative researchers typically start with a focused research question or hypothesis, collect a small amount of numerical data from a large number of individuals, describe the resulting data using statistical techniques, and draw general conclusions about some large population. Although this method is by far the most common approach to conducting empirical research in psychology, there is an important alternative called **qualitative research**. Qualitative research originated in the disciplines of anthropology and sociology but is now used to study psychological topics as well. Qualitative researchers generally begin with a less focused research question, collect large amounts of relatively "unfiltered" data from a relatively small number of individuals, and describe their data using nonstatistical techniques, such as grounded theory, thematic analysis, critical discourse analysis, or interpretative phenomenological analysis. They are usually less concerned with drawing general conclusions about human behavior than with understanding in detail the *experience* of their research participants.

Consider, for example, a study by researcher Per Lindqvist and his colleagues, who wanted to learn how the families of teenage suicide victims cope with their loss (Lindqvist, Johansson, & Karlsson, 2008)[1]. They did not have a specific research question or hypothesis, such as, What percentage of family members join suicide support groups? Instead, they wanted to understand the variety of reactions that families had, with a focus on what it is like from *their* perspectives. To address this question, they interviewed the families of 10 teenage suicide victims in their homes in rural Sweden. The interviews were relatively unstructured, beginning with a general request for the families to talk about the victim and ending with an invitation to talk about anything else that they wanted to tell the interviewer. One of the most important themes that emerged from these interviews was that even as life returned to "normal," the families continued to struggle with the question of why their loved one committed suicide. This struggle appeared to be especially difficult for families in which the suicide was most unexpected.

# The Purpose of Qualitative Research

Again, this textbook is primarily about quantitative research in psychology. The strength of quantitative research is its ability to provide precise answers to specific research questions and to draw general conclusions about human behavior. This method is how we know that people have a strong tendency to obey authority figures, for example, and that female undergraduate students are not substantially more talkative than male undergraduate students. But while quantitative research is good at providing precise answers to specific research questions, it is not nearly as good at *generating* novel and interesting research questions. Likewise, while quantitative research is good at drawing general conclusions about human behavior, it is not nearly as good at providing detailed descriptions of the behavior of particular groups in particular situations. And quantitative research is not very good at communicating what it is actually like to be a member of a particular group in a particular situation.

But the relative weaknesses of quantitative research are the relative strengths of qualitative research. Qualitative research can help researchers to generate new and interesting research questions and hypotheses. The research of Lindqvist and colleagues, for example, suggests that there may be a general relationship between how unexpected a suicide is and how consumed the family is with trying to understand why the teen committed suicide. This relationship can now be explored using quantitative research. But it is unclear whether this question would have arisen at all without the researchers sitting down with the families and listening to what they themselves wanted to say about their experience. Qualitative research can also provide rich and detailed descriptions of human behavior in the real-world contexts in which it occurs. Among qualitative researchers, this depth is often referred to as "thick description" (Geertz, 1973)[2]. Similarly, qualitative research can convey a sense of what it is actually like to be a member of a particular group or in a particular situation–what qualitative researchers often refer to as the "lived experience" of the research participants. Lindqvist and colleagues, for example, describe how all the families spontaneously offered to show the interviewer the victim's bedroom or the place where the suicide occurred–revealing the importance of these physical locations to the families. It seems unlikely that a quantitative study would have discovered this detail.

Table 6.3 Some contrasts between qualitative and quantitative research

| Qualitative | Quantitative |
| --- | --- |
| 1. In-depth information about relatively few people | 1. Less depth information with larger samples |
| 2. Conclusions are based on interpretations drawn by the investigator | 2. Conclusions are based on statistical analyses |
| 3. Global and exploratory | 3. Specific and focused |

# Data Collection and Analysis in Qualitative Research

Data collection approaches in qualitative research are quite varied and can involve naturalistic observation, participant observation, archival data, artwork, and many other things. But one of the most common approaches, especially for psychological research, is to conduct **interviews**. Interviews in qualitative research can be unstructured—consisting of a small number of general questions or prompts that allow participants to talk about what is of interest to them—or structured, where there is a strict script that the interviewer does not deviate from. Most interviews are in between the two and are called semi-structured interviews, where the researcher has a few consistent questions and can follow up by asking more detailed questions about the topics that come up. Such interviews can be lengthy and detailed, but they are usually conducted with a relatively small sample. The unstructured interview was the approach used by Lindqvist and colleagues in their research on the families of suicide victims because the researchers were aware that how much was disclosed about such a sensitive topic should be led by the families, not by the researchers.

Another approach used in qualitative research involves small groups of people who participate together in interviews focused on a particular topic or issue, known as **focus groups**. The interaction among participants in a focus group can sometimes bring out more information than can be learned in a one-on-one interview. The use of focus groups has become a standard technique in business and industry among those who want to understand consumer tastes and preferences. The content of all focus group interviews is usually recorded and transcribed to facilitate later analyses. However, we know from social psychology that group dynamics are often at play in any group, including focus groups, and it is useful to be aware of those possibilities. For example, the desire to be liked by others can lead participants to provide inaccurate answers that they believe will be perceived favorably by the other participants. The same may be said for personality characteristics. For example, highly extraverted participants can sometimes dominate discussions within focus groups.

## Data Analysis in Qualitative Research

Although quantitative and qualitative research generally differ along several important dimensions (e.g., the specificity of the research question, the type of data collected), it is the method of data analysis that distinguishes them more clearly than anything else. To illustrate this idea, imagine a team of researchers that conducts a series of unstructured interviews with people recovering from alcohol use disorder to learn about the role of their religious faith in their recovery. Although this project sounds like qualitative research, imagine further that once they collect the data, they code the data in terms of how often each participant mentions God (or a "higher power"), and they then use descriptive and inferential statistics to find out whether those who mention God more often are more successful in abstaining from alcohol. Now it sounds like quantitative research. In other words, the quantitative-qualitative distinction depends more on what researchers do with the data they have collected than with why or how they collected the data.

But what does qualitative data analysis look like? Just as there are many ways to collect data in qualitative research, there are many ways to analyze data. Here we focus on one general approach called **grounded theory** (Glaser & Strauss, 1967)[3]. This approach was developed within the field of sociology in the 1960s and has gradually gained popularity in psychology. Remember that in quantitative research, it is typical for the researcher to start with a theory, derive a hypothesis from that theory, and then collect data to test that specific hypothesis. In qualitative research using grounded theory, researchers start with the data and develop a theory or an interpretation that is "grounded in" those data. They do this analysis in stages. First, they identify ideas that are repeated throughout the data. Then they organize these ideas into a smaller number of broader themes. Finally, they write a **theoretical narrative**–an interpretation of the data in terms of the themes that they have identified. This theoretical narrative focuses on the subjective experience of the participants and is usually supported by many direct quotations from the participants themselves.

As an example, consider a study by researchers Laura Abrams and Laura Curran, who used the grounded theory approach to study the experience of postpartum depression symptoms among low-income mothers (Abrams & Curran, 2009)[4]. Their data were the result of unstructured interviews with 19 participants. Table 6.4 shows the five broad themes the researchers identified and the more specific repeating ideas that made up each of those themes. In their research report, they provide numerous quotations from their participants, such as this one from "Destiny:"

> Well, just recently my apartment was broken into and the fact that his Medicaid for some reason was cancelled so a lot of things was happening within the last two weeks all at one time. So that in itself I don't want to say almost drove me mad but it put me in a funk....Like I really was depressed. (p. 357)

Their theoretical narrative focused on the participants' experience of their symptoms, not as an abstract "affective disorder" but as closely tied to the daily struggle of raising children alone, under often difficult circumstances.

*Table 6.4 Themes and Repeating Ideas in a Study of Postpartum Depression Among Low-Income Mothers. Based on Research by Abrams and Curran (2009).*

| Theme | Repeating ideas |
| --- | --- |
| Ambivalence | "I wasn't prepared for this baby," "I didn't want to have any more children." |
| Caregiving overload | "Please stop crying," "I need a break," "I can't do this anymore." |
| Juggling | "No time to breathe," "Everyone depends on me," "Navigating the maze." |
| Mothering alone | "I really don't have any help," "My baby has no father." |
| Real-life worry | "I don't have any money," "Will my baby be OK?" "It's not safe here." |

# The Quantitative-Qualitative "Debate"

Given their differences, it may come as no surprise that quantitative and qualitative research in psychology and related fields do not coexist in complete harmony. Some quantitative researchers criticize qualitative methods on the grounds that they lack objectivity, are difficult to evaluate in terms of reliability and validity, and do not allow generalization to people or situations other than those actually studied. At the same time, some qualitative researchers criticize quantitative methods on the grounds that they overlook the richness of human behavior and experience and instead answer simple questions about easily quantifiable variables.

In general, however, qualitative researchers are well aware of the issues of objectivity, reliability, validity, and generalizability. In fact, they have developed a number of frameworks for addressing these issues (which are beyond the scope of our discussion). And in general, quantitative researchers are well aware of the issue of oversimplification. They do not believe that all human behavior and experience can be adequately described in terms of a small number of variables and the statistical relationships among them. Instead, they use simplification as a strategy for uncovering general principles of human behavior.

Many researchers from both the quantitative and qualitative camps now agree that the two approaches can and should be combined into what has come to be called **mixed-methods research** (Todd, Nerlich, McKeown, & Clarke, 2004)[5]. (In fact, the studies by Lindqvist and colleagues and by Abrams and Curran both combined quantitative and qualitative approaches.) One approach to combining quantitative and qualitative research is to use qualitative research for hypothesis generation and quantitative research for hypothesis testing. Again, while a qualitative study might suggest that families who experience an unexpected suicide have more difficulty resolving the question of why, a well-designed quantitative study could test a hypothesis by measuring these specific variables in a large sample. A second approach to combining quantitative and qualitative research is referred to as **triangulation**. The idea is to use both quantitative and qualitative methods simultaneously to study the same general questions and to compare the results. If the results of the quantitative and qualitative methods converge on the same general conclusion, they reinforce and enrich each other. If the results diverge, then they suggest an interesting new question: Why do the results diverge and how can they be reconciled?

Using qualitative research can often help clarify quantitative results via triangulation. Trenor, Yu, Waight, Zerda, and Sha (2008)[6] investigated the experience of female engineering students at a university. In the first phase, female engineering students were asked to complete a survey, where they rated a number of their perceptions, including their sense of belonging. Their results were compared across the student ethnicities, and statistically, the various ethnic groups showed no differences in their ratings of their sense of belonging. One might look at that result and conclude that ethnicity does not have anything to do with one's sense of belonging. However, in the second phase, the authors also conducted interviews with the students, and in those interviews, many minority students reported how the diversity of cultures at the university enhanced their sense of belonging. Without the qualitative component, we might have drawn the wrong conclusion about the quantitative results.

This example shows how qualitative and quantitative research work together to help us understand human behavior. Some researchers have characterized qualitative research as best for identifying behaviors or the phenomenon whereas quantitative research is best for understanding meaning or identifying the mechanism. However, Bryman (2012)[7] argues for breaking down the divide between these arbitrarily different ways of investigating the same questions.

# Notes

1. Lindqvist, P., Johansson, L., & Karlsson, U. (2008). In the aftermath of teenage suicide: A qualitative study of the psychosocial consequences for the surviving family members. BMC Psychiatry, 8, 26. Retrieved from http://www.biomedcentral.com/1471-244X/8/26

2. Geertz, C. (1973). The interpretation of cultures. New York, NY: Basic Books.

3. Glaser, B. G., & Strauss, A. L. (1967). The discovery of grounded theory: Strategies for qualitative research. Chicago, IL: Aldine.

4. Abrams, L. S., & Curran, L. (2009). "And you're telling me not to stress?" A grounded theory study of postpartum depression symptoms among low-income mothers. *Psychology of Women Quarterly*, 33, 351–362.

5. Todd, Z., Nerlich, B., McKeown, S., & Clarke, D. D. (2004) *Mixing methods in psychology: The integration of qualitative and quantitative methods in theory and practice*. London, UK: Psychology Press.

6. Trenor, J.M., Yu, S.L., Waight, C.L., Zerda. K.S & Sha T.-L. (2008). The relations of ethnicity to female engineering students' educational experiences and college and career plans in an ethnically diverse learning environment. *Journal of Engineering Education*, 97(4), 449-465.

7. Bryman, A. (2012). *Social Research Methods*, 4th ed. Oxford: OUP.

# 32. Observational Research

*Learning Objectives*

1. List the various types of observational research methods and distinguish between each.
2. Describe the strengths and weakness of each observational research method.

## What Is Observational Research?

The term **observational research** is used to refer to several different types of non-experimental studies in which behavior is systematically observed and recorded. The goal of observational research is to describe a variable or set of variables. More generally, the goal is to obtain a snapshot of specific characteristics of an individual, group, or setting. As described previously, observational research is non-experimental because nothing is manipulated or controlled, and as such we cannot arrive at causal conclusions using this approach. The data that are collected in observational research studies are often qualitative in nature but they may also be quantitative or both (mixed-methods). There are several different types of observational methods that will be described below.

## Naturalistic Observation

**Naturalistic observation** is an observational method that involves observing people's behavior in the environment in which it typically occurs. Thus naturalistic observation is a type of field research (as opposed to a type of laboratory research). Jane Goodall's famous research on chimpanzees is a classic example of naturalistic observation. Dr. Goodall spent three decades observing chimpanzees in their natural environment in East Africa. She examined such things as chimpanzee's social structure, mating patterns, gender roles, family structure, and care of offspring by observing them in the wild. However, naturalistic observation could more simply involve observing shoppers in a grocery store, children on a school playground, or psychiatric inpatients in their wards. Researchers engaged in naturalistic observation usually make their observations as unobtrusively as possible so that participants are not aware that they are being studied. Such an approach is called **disguised naturalistic observation.** Ethically, this method is considered to be acceptable if the participants remain anonymous and the behavior occurs in a public setting where people would not normally have an expectation of privacy. Grocery shoppers putting items into their shopping carts, for example, are engaged in public behavior that is easily observable by store employees and other shoppers. For this reason, most researchers would consider it ethically acceptable to observe them for a study. On the other hand, one of the arguments against the ethicality of the naturalistic observation of "bathroom behavior" discussed earlier in the book is that people have a reasonable expectation of privacy even in a public restroom and that this expectation was violated.

In cases where it is not ethical or practical to conduct disguised naturalistic observation, researchers can conduct **undisguised naturalistic observation** where the participants are made aware of the researcher presence and monitoring of their behavior. However, one concern with undisguised naturalistic observation is reactivity. **Reactivity** refers to when a measure changes participants' behavior. In the case of undisguised naturalistic observation, the concern with reactivity is that when people know they are being observed and studied, they may act differently than they normally would. This type of reactivity is known as the **Hawthorne effect**. For instance, you may act much differently in a bar if you know that someone is observing you and recording your behaviors and this would invalidate the study. So disguised observation is less reactive and therefore can have higher validity because people are not aware that their behaviors are being observed and recorded. However, we now know that people often become used to being observed and with time they begin to behave naturally in the researcher's presence. In other words, over time people habituate to being observed. Think about reality shows like Big Brother or Survivor where people are constantly being observed and recorded. While they may be on their best behavior at first, in a fairly short amount of time they are flirting, having sex, wearing next to nothing, screaming at each other, and occasionally behaving in ways that are embarrassing.

## Participant Observation

Another approach to data collection in observational research is participant observation. In **participant observation**, researchers become active participants in the group or situation they are studying. Participant observation is very similar to naturalistic observation in that it involves observing people's behavior in the environment in which it typically occurs. As with naturalistic observation, the data that are collected can include interviews (usually unstructured), notes based on their observations and interactions, documents, photographs, and other artifacts. The only difference between naturalistic observation and participant observation is that researchers engaged in participant observation become active members of the group or situations they are studying. The basic rationale for participant observation is that there may be important information that is only accessible to, or can be interpreted only by, someone who is an active participant in the group or situation. Like naturalistic observation, participant observation can be either disguised or undisguised. In **disguised participant observation,** the researchers pretend to be members of the social group they are observing and conceal their true identity as researchers.

In a famous example of disguised participant observation, Leon Festinger and his colleagues infiltrated a doomsday cult known as the Seekers, whose members believed that the apocalypse would occur on December 21, 1954. Interested in studying how members of the group would cope psychologically when the prophecy inevitably failed, they carefully recorded the events and reactions of the cult members in the days before and after the supposed end of the world. Unsurprisingly, the cult members did not give up their belief but instead convinced themselves that it was their faith and efforts that saved the world from destruction.

Festinger and his colleagues later published a book about this experience, which they used to illustrate the theory of cognitive dissonance (Festinger, Riecken, & Schachter, 1956)[1].

In contrast with **undisguised participant observation,** the researchers become a part of the group they are studying and they disclose their true identity as researchers to the group under investigation. Once again there are important ethical issues to consider with disguised participant observation. First no informed consent can be obtained and second deception is being used. The researcher is deceiving the participants by intentionally withholding information about their motivations for being a part of the social group they are studying. But sometimes disguised participation is the only way to access a protective group (like a cult). Further, disguised participant observation is less prone to reactivity than undisguised participant observation.

Rosenhan's study (1973)[2] of the experience of people in a psychiatric ward would be considered disguised participant observation because Rosenhan and his pseudopatients were admitted into psychiatric hospitals on the pretense of being patients so that they could observe the way that psychiatric patients are treated by staff. The staff and other patients were unaware of their true identities as researchers.

Another example of participant observation comes from a study by sociologist Amy Wilkins on a university-based religious organization that emphasized how happy its members were (Wilkins, 2008)[3]. Wilkins spent 12 months attending and participating in the group's meetings and social events, and she interviewed several group members. In her study, Wilkins identified several ways in which the group "enforced" happiness—for example, by continually talking about happiness, discouraging the expression of negative emotions, and using happiness as a way to distinguish themselves from other groups.

One of the primary benefits of participant observation is that the researchers are in a much better position to understand the viewpoint and experiences of the people they are studying when they are a part of the social group. The primary limitation with this approach is that the mere presence of the observer could affect the behavior of the people being observed. While this is also a concern with naturalistic observation, additional concerns arise when researchers become active members of the social group they are studying because that they may change the social dynamics and/or influence the behavior of the people they are studying. Similarly, if the researcher acts as a participant observer there can be concerns with biases resulting from developing relationships with the participants. Concretely, the researcher may become less objective resulting in more experimenter bias.

## Structured Observation

Another observational method is **structured observation**. Here the investigator makes careful observations of one or more specific behaviors in a particular setting that is more structured than the settings used in naturalistic or participant observation. Often the setting in which the observations are made is not the natural setting. Instead, the researcher may observe people in the laboratory environment. Alternatively, the researcher may observe people in a natural setting (like a classroom setting) that they have structured some way, for instance by introducing some specific task participants are to engage in or by introducing a specific social situation or manipulation.

Structured observation is very similar to naturalistic observation and participant observation in that in all three cases researchers are observing naturally occurring behavior; however, the emphasis in structured observation is on gathering quantitative rather than qualitative data. Researchers using this approach are interested in a limited set of behaviors. This allows them to quantify the behaviors they are observing. In other words, structured observation is less global than naturalistic or participant observation because the researcher engaged in structured observations is interested in a small number of specific behaviors. Therefore, rather than recording everything that happens, the researcher only focuses on very specific behaviors of interest.

Researchers Robert Levine and Ara Norenzayan used structured observation to study differences in the "pace of life" across countries (Levine & Norenzayan, 1999)[4]. One of their measures involved observing pedestrians in a large city to see how long it took them to walk 60 feet. They found that people in some countries walked reliably faster than people in other countries. For example, people in Canada and Sweden covered 60 feet in just under 13 seconds on average, while people in Brazil and Romania took close to 17 seconds. When structured observation takes place in the complex and even chaotic "real world," the questions of when, where, and under what conditions the observations will be made, and who exactly will be observed are important to consider. Levine and Norenzayan described their sampling process as follows:

> "Male and female walking speed over a distance of 60 feet was measured in at least two locations in main downtown areas in each city. Measurements were taken during main business hours on clear summer days. All locations were flat, unobstructed, had broad sidewalks, and were sufficiently uncrowded to allow pedestrians to move at potentially maximum speeds. To control for the effects of socializing, only pedestrians walking alone were used. Children, individuals with obvious physical handicaps, and window-shoppers were not timed. Thirty-five men and 35 women were timed in most cities." (p. 186).

Precise specification of the sampling process in this way makes data collection manageable for the observers, and it also provides some control over important extraneous variables. For example, by making their observations on clear summer days in all countries, Levine and Norenzayan controlled for effects of the weather on people's walking speeds. In Levine and Norenzayan's study, measurement was relatively straightforward. They simply measured out a 60-foot distance along a city sidewalk and then used a stopwatch to time participants as they walked over that distance.

As another example, researchers Robert Kraut and Robert Johnston wanted to study bowlers' reactions to their shots, both when they were facing the pins and then when they turned toward their companions (Kraut & Johnston, 1979)[5]. But what "reactions" should they observe? Based on previous research and their own pilot testing, Kraut and Johnston created a list of reactions that included "closed smile," "open smile," "laugh," "neutral face," "look down," "look away," and "face cover" (covering one's face with one's hands). The observers committed this list to memory and then practiced by coding the reactions of bowlers who had been videotaped. During the actual study, the observers spoke into an audio recorder, describing the reactions they observed. Among the most interesting results of this study was that bowlers rarely smiled while they still faced the pins. They were much more likely to smile after they turned toward their companions, suggesting that smiling is not purely an expression of happiness but also a form of social communication.

In yet another example (this one in a laboratory environment), Dov Cohen and his colleagues had observers rate the emotional reactions of participants who had just been deliberately bumped and insulted by a confederate after they dropped off a completed questionnaire at the end of a hallway. The confederate was posing as someone who worked in the same building and who was frustrated by having to close a file drawer twice in order to permit the participants to walk past them (first to drop off the questionnaire at the end of the hallway and once again on their way back to the room where they believed the study they signed up for was taking place). The two observers were positioned at different ends of the hallway so that they could read the participants' body language and hear anything they might say. Interestingly, the researchers hypothesized that participants from the southern United States, which is one of several places in the world that has a "culture of honor," would react with more aggression than participants from the northern United States, a prediction that was in fact supported by the observational data (Cohen, Nisbett, Bowdle, & Schwarz, 1996)[6].

When the observations require a judgment on the part of the observers—as in the studies by Kraut and Johnston and Cohen and his colleagues—a process referred to as **coding** is typically required. Coding generally requires clearly defining a set of target behaviors. The observers then categorize participants individually in terms of which behavior they have engaged in and the number of times they engaged in each behavior. The observers might even record the duration of each behavior. The target behaviors must be defined in such a way that guides different observers to code them in the same way. This difficulty with coding illustrates the issue of interrater reliability, as mentioned in Chapter 4. Researchers are expected to demonstrate the interrater reliability of their coding procedure by having multiple raters code the same behaviors independently and then showing that the different observers are in close agreement. Kraut and Johnston, for example, video recorded a subset of their participants' reactions and had two observers independently code them. The two observers showed that they agreed on the reactions that were exhibited 97% of the time, indicating good interrater reliability.

One of the primary benefits of structured observation is that it is far more efficient than naturalistic and participant observation. Since the researchers are focused on specific behaviors this reduces time and expense. Also, often times the environment is structured to encourage the behaviors of interest which again means that researchers do not have to invest as much time in waiting for the behaviors of interest to naturally occur. Finally, researchers using this approach can clearly exert greater control over the environment. However, when researchers exert more control over the environment it may make the environment less natural which decreases external validity. It is less clear for instance whether structured observations made in a laboratory environment will generalize to a real world environment. Furthermore, since researchers engaged in structured observation are often not disguised there may be more concerns with reactivity.

## Case Studies

A **case study** is an in-depth examination of an individual. Sometimes case studies are also completed on social units (e.g., a cult) and events (e.g., a natural disaster). Most commonly in psychology, however, case studies provide a detailed description and analysis of an individual. Often the individual has a rare or unusual condition or disorder or has damage to a specific region of the brain.

Like many observational research methods, case studies tend to be more qualitative in nature. Case study methods involve an in-depth, and often a longitudinal examination of an individual. Depending on the focus of the case study, individuals may or may not be observed in their natural setting. If the natural setting is not what is of interest, then the individual may be brought into a therapist's office or a researcher's lab for study. Also, the bulk of the case study report will focus on in-depth descriptions of the person rather than on statistical analyses. With that said some quantitative data may also be included in the write-up of a case study. For instance, an individual's depression score may be compared to normative scores or their score before and after treatment may be compared. As with other qualitative methods, a variety of different methods and tools can be used to collect information on the case. For instance, interviews, naturalistic observation, structured observation, psychological testing (e.g., IQ test), and/or physiological measurements (e.g., brain scans) may be used to collect information on the individual.

HM is one of the most notorious case studies in psychology. HM suffered from intractable and very severe epilepsy. A surgeon localized HM's epilepsy to his medial temporal lobe and in 1953 he removed large sections of his hippocampus in an attempt to stop the seizures. The treatment was a success, in that it resolved his epilepsy and his IQ and personality were unaffected. However, the doctors soon realized that HM exhibited a strange form of amnesia, called anterograde amnesia. HM was able to carry out a conversation and he could remember short strings of letters, digits, and words. Basically, his short term memory was preserved. However, HM could not commit new events to memory. He lost the ability to transfer information from his short-term memory to his long term memory, something memory researchers call consolidation. So while he could carry on a conversation with someone, he would completely forget the conversation after it ended. This was an extremely important case study for memory researchers because it suggested that there's a dissociation between short-term memory and long-term memory, it suggested that these were two different abilities sub-served by different areas of the brain. It also suggested that the temporal lobes are particularly important for consolidating new information (i.e., for transferring information from short-term memory to long-term memory).

*Reading in print? Scan this QR code to view the video on your mobile device. Or go to youtu.be/ KkaXNvzE4pk*

*A YouTube element has been excluded from this version of the text. You can view it online here: https://kpu.pressbooks.pub/psychmethods4e/?p=78*

The history of psychology is filled with influential cases studies, such as Sigmund Freud's description of "Anna O." (see Note 6.1 "The Case of "Anna O."") and John Watson and Rosalie Rayner's description of Little Albert (Watson & Rayner, 1920)[7], who allegedly learned to fear a white rat—along with other furry objects—when the researchers repeatedly made a loud noise every time the rat approached him.

### The Case of "Anna O."

Sigmund Freud used the case of a young woman he called "Anna O." to illustrate many principles of his theory of psychoanalysis (Freud, 1961)[8]. (Her real name was Bertha Pappenheim, and she was an early feminist who went on to make important contributions to the field of social work.) Anna had come to Freud's colleague Josef Breuer around 1880 with a variety of odd physical and psychological symptoms. One of them was that for several weeks she was unable to drink any fluids. According to Freud,

> She would take up the glass of water that she longed for, but as soon as it touched her lips she would push it away like someone suffering from hydrophobia....She lived only on fruit, such as melons, etc., so as to lessen her tormenting thirst. (p. 9)

But according to Freud, a breakthrough came one day while Anna was under hypnosis.

[S]he grumbled about her English "lady-companion," whom she did not care for, and went on to describe, with every sign of disgust, how she had once gone into this lady's room and how her little dog—horrid creature!—had drunk out of a glass there. The patient had said nothing, as she had wanted to be polite. After giving further energetic expression to the anger she had held back, she asked for something to drink, drank a large quantity of water without any difficulty, and awoke from her hypnosis with the glass at her lips; and thereupon the disturbance vanished, never to return. (p.9)

Freud's interpretation was that Anna had repressed the memory of this incident along with the emotion that it triggered and that this was what had caused her inability to drink. Furthermore, he believed that her recollection of the incident, along with her expression of the emotion she had repressed, caused the symptom to go away.

As an illustration of Freud's theory, the case study of Anna O. is quite effective. As evidence for the theory, however, it is essentially worthless. The description provides no way of knowing whether Anna had really repressed the memory of the dog drinking from the glass, whether this repression had caused her inability to drink, or whether recalling this "trauma" relieved the symptom. It is also unclear from this case study how typical or atypical Anna's experience was.

*Figure 10.1 Anna O. "Anna O." was the subject of a famous case study used by Freud to illustrate the principles of psychoanalysis. Source: http://en.wikipedia.org/wiki/ File:Pappenheim_1882.jpg*

Case studies are useful because they provide a level of detailed analysis not found in many other research methods and greater insights may be gained from this more detailed analysis. As a result of the case study, the researcher may gain a sharpened understanding of what might become important to look at more extensively in future more controlled research. Case studies are also often the only way to study rare conditions because it may be impossible to find a large enough sample of individuals with the condition to use quantitative methods. Although at first glance a case study of a rare individual might seem to tell us little about ourselves, they often do provide insights into normal behavior. The case of HM provided important insights into the role of the hippocampus in memory consolidation.

However, it is important to note that while case studies can provide *insights* into certain areas and variables to study, and can be useful in helping develop theories, they should never be used as evidence for theories. In other words, case studies can be used as inspiration to formulate theories and hypotheses, but those hypotheses and theories then need to be formally tested using more rigorous quantitative methods. The reason case studies shouldn't be used to provide support for theories is that they suffer from problems with both internal and external validity. Case studies lack the proper controls that true experiments contain. As such, they suffer from problems with internal validity, so they cannot be used to determine causation. For instance, during HM's surgery, the surgeon may have accidentally lesioned another area of HM's brain (a possibility suggested by the dissection of HM's brain following his death) and that lesion may have contributed to his inability to consolidate new information. The fact is, with case studies we cannot rule out these sorts of alternative explanations. So, as with all observational methods, case studies do not permit determination of causation. In addition, because case studies are often of a single individual, and typically an abnormal individual, researchers cannot generalize their conclusions to other individuals. Recall that with most research designs there is a trade-off between internal and external validity. With case studies, however, there are problems with both internal validity and external validity. So there are limits both to the ability to determine causation and to generalize the results. A final limitation of case studies is that ample opportunity exists for the theoretical biases of the researcher to color or bias the case description. Indeed, there have been accusations that the woman who studied HM destroyed a lot of her data that were not published and she has been called into question for destroying contradictory data that didn't support her theory about how memories are consolidated. There is a fascinating New York Times article that describes some of the controversies that ensued after HM's death and analysis of his brain that can be found at: https://www.nytimes.com/2016/08/07/magazine/the-brain-that-couldnt-remember.html?_r=0

# Archival Research

Another approach that is often considered observational research involves analyzing archival data that have already been collected for some other purpose. An example is a study by Brett Pelham and his colleagues on "implicit egotism"–the tendency for people to prefer people, places, and things that are similar to themselves (Pelham, Carvallo, & Jones, 2005)[9]. In one study, they examined Social Security records to show that women with the names Virginia, Georgia, Louise, and Florence were especially likely to have moved to the states of Virginia, Georgia, Louisiana, and Florida, respectively.

As with naturalistic observation, measurement can be more or less straightforward when working with archival data. For example, counting the number of people named Virginia who live in various states based on Social Security records is relatively straightforward. But consider a study by Christopher Peterson and his colleagues on the relationship between optimism and health using data that had been collected many years before for a study on adult development (Peterson, Seligman, & Vaillant, 1988)[10]. In the 1940s, healthy male college students had completed an open-ended questionnaire about difficult wartime experiences.

In the late 1980s, Peterson and his colleagues reviewed the men's questionnaire responses to obtain a measure of explanatory style–their habitual ways of explaining bad events that happen to them. More pessimistic people tend to blame themselves and expect long-term negative consequences that affect many aspects of their lives, while more optimistic people tend to blame outside forces and expect limited negative consequences. To obtain a measure of explanatory style for each participant, the researchers used a procedure in which all negative events mentioned in the questionnaire responses, and any causal explanations for them were identified and written on index cards. These were given to a separate group of raters who rated each explanation in terms of three separate dimensions of optimism-pessimism. These ratings were then averaged to produce an explanatory style score for each participant. The researchers then assessed the statistical relationship between the men's explanatory style as undergraduate students and archival measures of their health at approximately 60 years of age. The primary result was that the more optimistic the men were as undergraduate students, the healthier they were as older men. Pearson's $r$ was +.25.

This method is an example of **content analysis**–a family of systematic approaches to measurement using complex archival data. Just as structured observation requires specifying the behaviors of interest and then noting them as they occur, content analysis requires specifying keywords, phrases, or ideas and then finding all occurrences of them in the data. These occurrences can then be counted, timed (e.g., the amount of time devoted to entertainment topics on the nightly news show), or analyzed in a variety of other ways.

# Notes

1. Festinger, L., Riecken, H., & Schachter, S. (1956). When prophecy fails: A social and psychological study of a modern group that predicted the destruction of the world. University of Minnesota Press.

2. Rosenhan, D. L. (1973). On being sane in insane places. *Science, 179*, 250–258.

3. Wilkins, A. (2008). "Happier than Non-Christians": Collective emotions and symbolic boundaries among evangelical Christians. *Social Psychology Quarterly, 71*, 281–301.

4. Levine, R. V., & Norenzayan, A. (1999). The pace of life in 31 countries. *Journal of Cross-Cultural Psychology, 30*, 178–205.

5. Kraut, R. E., & Johnston, R. E. (1979). Social and emotional messages of smiling: An ethological approach. *Journal of Personality and Social Psychology, 37*, 1539–1553.

6. Cohen, D., Nisbett, R. E., Bowdle, B. F., & Schwarz, N. (1996). Insult, aggression, and the southern culture of honor: An "experimental ethnography." *Journal of Personality and Social Psychology, 70*(5), 945-960.

7. Watson, J. B., & Rayner, R. (1920). Conditioned emotional reactions. *Journal of Experimental Psychology, 3*, 1–14.

8. Freud, S. (1961). *Five lectures on psycho-analysis.* New York, NY: Norton.

9. Pelham, B. W., Carvallo, M., & Jones, J. T. (2005). Implicit egotism. *Current Directions in Psychological Science, 14*, 106–110.

10. Peterson, C., Seligman, M. E. P., & Vaillant, G. E. (1988). Pessimistic explanatory style is a risk factor for physical illness: A thirty-five year longitudinal study. *Journal of Personality and Social Psychology, 55*, 23–27.

# 33. Key Takeaways and Exercises

- Non-experimental research is research that lacks the manipulation of an independent variable.
- There are two broad types of non-experimental research. Correlational research that focuses on statistical relationships between variables that are measured but not manipulated; and observational research in which participants are observed and their behavior is recorded without the researcher interfering or manipulating any variables.
- In general, experimental research is high in internal validity, correlational research is low in internal validity, and quasi-experimental research is in between.
- Correlational research involves measuring two variables and assessing the relationship between them, with no manipulation of an independent variable.
- Correlation does not imply causation. A statistical relationship between two variables, X and Y, does not necessarily mean that X causes Y. It is also possible that Y causes X, or that a third variable, Z, causes both X and Y.
- While correlational research cannot be used to establish causal relationships between variables, correlational research does allow researchers to achieve many other important objectives (establishing reliability and validity, providing converging evidence, describing relationships, and making predictions)
- Correlation coefficients can range from -1 to +1. The sign indicates the direction of the relationship between the variables and the numerical value indicates the strength of the relationship.
- Researchers often use complex correlational research to explore relationships among several variables in the same study.
- Complex correlational research can be used to explore possible causal relationships among variables using techniques such as partial correlation and multiple regression. Such designs can show patterns of relationships that are consistent with some causal interpretations and inconsistent with others, but they cannot unambiguously establish that one variable causes another.
- Qualitative research is an important alternative to quantitative research in psychology. It generally involves asking broader research questions, collecting more detailed data (e.g., interviews), and using non-statistical analyses.
- Many researchers conceptualize quantitative and qualitative research as complementary and advocate combining them. For example, qualitative research can be used to generate hypotheses and quantitative research to test them.
- There are several different approaches to observational research including naturalistic observation, participant observation, structured observation, case studies, and archival research.
- Naturalistic observation is used to observe people in their natural setting; participant observation involves becoming an active member of the group being observed; structured observation involves coding a small number of behaviors in a quantitative manner; case studies are typically used to collect in-depth information on a single individual; and archival research involves analyzing existing data.

- Discussion: For each of the following studies, decide which type of research design it is and explain why.

    - A researcher conducts detailed interviews with unmarried teenage fathers to learn about how they feel and what they think about their role as fathers and summarizes their feelings in a written narrative.
    - A researcher measures the impulsivity of a large sample of drivers and looks at the statistical relationship between this variable and the number of traffic tickets the drivers have received.
    - A researcher randomly assigns patients with low back pain either to a treatment involving hypnosis or to a treatment involving exercise. She then measures their level of low back pain after 3 months.

- Discussion: For each of the following, decide whether it is most likely that the study described is experimental or non-experimental and explain why.

    - A cognitive psychologist compares the ability of people to recall words that they were instructed to "read" with their ability to recall words that they were instructed to "imagine."
    - A manager studies the correlation between new employees' college grade point averages and their first-year performance reports.
    - An automotive engineer installs different stick shifts in a new car prototype, each time asking several people to rate how comfortable the stick shift feels.
    - A food scientist studies the relationship between the temperature inside people's refrigerators and the amount of bacteria on their food.
    - A social psychologist tells some research participants that they need to hurry over to the next building to complete a study. She tells others that they can take their time. Then she observes whether they stop to help a research assistant who is pretending to be hurt.

- Practice: For each of the following statistical relationships, decide whether the directionality problem is present and think of at least one plausible third variable.

    - People who eat more lobster tend to live longer.
    - People who exercise more tend to weigh less.
    - College students who drink more alcohol tend to have poorer grades.

- Practice: Construct a correlation matrix for a hypothetical study including the variables of depression, anxiety, self-esteem, and happiness. Include the Pearson's $r$ values that you would expect.
- Discussion: Imagine a correlational study that looks at intelligence, the need for cognition, and high school students' performance in a critical thinking course. A multiple regression analysis shows that intelligence is not related to performance in the class but that the need for cognition is. Explain what this study has shown in terms of what is related to good performance in the critical thinking course.
- Discussion: What are some ways in which a qualitative study of girls who play youth baseball would likely differ from a quantitative study on the same topic? How would the data differ by interviewing girls one-on-one rather than conducting focus groups or surveys?
- Practice: Find and read a published case study in psychology. (Use *case study* as a key term in a PsycINFO search.) Then do the following:

    - Describe one problem related to internal validity.

- Describe one problem related to external validity.
- Generate one hypothesis suggested by the case study that might be interesting to test in a subsequent study.

# CHAPTER VII
# SURVEY RESEARCH

Shortly after the terrorist attacks in New York City and Washington, DC, in September of 2001, researcher Jennifer Lerner and her colleagues conducted an Internet-based survey of nearly 2,000 American teens and adults ranging in age from 13 to 88 (Lerner, Gonzalez, Small, & Fischhoff, 2003)[1]. They asked participants about their reactions to the attacks and for their judgments of various terrorism-related and other risks. Among the results were that the participants tended to overestimate most risks, that females did so more than males, and that there were no differences between teens and adults. The most interesting result, however, had to do with the fact that some participants were "primed" to feel anger by asking them what made them angry about the attacks and by presenting them with a photograph and audio clip intended to evoke anger. Others were primed to feel fear by asking them what made them fearful about the attacks and by presenting them with a photograph and audio clip intended to evoke fear. As the researchers hypothesized, the participants who were primed to feel anger perceived less risk than the participants who had been primed to feel fear—showing how risk perceptions are strongly tied to specific emotions.

The study by Lerner and her colleagues is an example of survey research in psychology—the topic of this chapter. We begin with an overview of survey research, including its definition, some history, and a bit about who conducts it and why. We then look at survey responding as a psychological process and the implications of this for constructing good survey questionnaires. Finally, we consider some issues related to actually conducting survey research, including sampling the participants and collecting the data.

# 34. Overview of Survey Research

**Learning Objectives**

1. Define what survey research is, including its two important characteristics.
2. Describe several different ways that survey research can be used and give some examples.

## What Is Survey Research?

**Survey research** is a quantitative and qualitative method with two important characteristics. First, the variables of interest are measured using self-reports (using questionnaires or interviews). In essence, survey researchers ask their participants (who are often called **respondents** in survey research) to report directly on their own thoughts, feelings, and behaviors. Second, considerable attention is paid to the issue of sampling. In particular, survey researchers have a strong preference for large random samples because they provide the most accurate estimates of what is true in the population. In fact, survey research may be the only approach in psychology in which random sampling is routinely used. Beyond these two characteristics, almost anything goes in survey research. Surveys can be long or short. They can be conducted in person, by telephone, through the mail, or over the Internet. They can be about voting intentions, consumer preferences, social attitudes, health, or anything else that it is possible to ask people about and receive meaningful answers. Although survey data are often analyzed using statistics, there are many questions that lend themselves to more qualitative analysis.

Most survey research is non experimental. It is used to describe single variables (e.g., the percentage of voters who prefer one presidential candidate or another, the prevalence of schizophrenia in the general population, etc.) and also to assess statistical relationships between variables (e.g., the relationship between income and health). But surveys can also be used within experimental research. The study by Lerner and her colleagues is a good example. Their use of self-report measures and a large national sample identifies their work as survey research. But their manipulation of an independent variable (anger vs. fear) to assess its effect on a dependent variable (risk judgments) also identifies their work as experimental.

## History and Uses of Survey Research

Survey research may have its roots in English and American "social surveys" conducted around the turn of the 20th century by researchers and reformers who wanted to document the extent of social problems such as poverty (Converse, 1987)[1]. By the 1930s, the US government was conducting surveys to document economic and social conditions in the country. The need to draw conclusions about the entire population helped spur advances in sampling procedures. At about the same time, several researchers who had already made a name for themselves in market research, studying consumer preferences for American businesses, turned their attention to election polling. A watershed event was the presidential election of 1936 between Alf Landon and Franklin Roosevelt. A magazine called *Literary Digest* conducted a survey by sending ballots (which were also subscription requests) to millions of Americans. Based on this "straw poll," the editors predicted that Landon would win in a landslide. At the same time, the new pollsters were using scientific methods with much smaller samples to predict just the opposite—that Roosevelt would win in a landslide. In fact, one of them, George Gallup, publicly criticized the methods of *Literary Digest* before the election and all but guaranteed that his prediction would be correct. And of course, it was, demonstrating the effectiveness of careful survey methodology (We will consider the reasons that Gallup was right later in this chapter). Gallup's demonstration of the power of careful survey methods led later researchers to to local, and in 1948, the first national election survey by the Survey Research Center at the University of Michigan. This work eventually became the American National Election Studies (https://electionstudies.org/) as a collaboration of Stanford University and the University of Michigan, and these studies continue today.

From market research and election polling, survey research made its way into several academic fields, including political science, sociology, and public health—where it continues to be one of the primary approaches to collecting new data. Beginning in the 1930s, psychologists made important advances in questionnaire design, including techniques that are still used today, such as the Likert scale. (See "What Is a Likert Scale?" in Section 7.2 "Constructing Survey Questionnaires".) Survey research has a strong historical association with the social psychological study of attitudes, stereotypes, and prejudice. Early attitude researchers were also among the first psychologists to seek larger and more diverse samples than the convenience samples of university students that were routinely used in psychology (and still are).

Survey research continues to be important in psychology today. For example, survey data have been instrumental in estimating the prevalence of various mental disorders and identifying statistical relationships among those disorders and with various other factors. The National Comorbidity Survey is a large-scale mental health survey conducted in the United States (see http://www.hcp.med.harvard.edu/ ncs). In just one part of this survey, nearly 10,000 adults were given a structured mental health interview in their homes in 2002 and 2003. Table 7.1 presents results on the lifetime prevalence of some anxiety, mood, and substance use disorders. (Lifetime prevalence is the percentage of the population that develops the problem sometime in their lifetime.) Obviously, this kind of information can be of great use both to basic researchers seeking to understand the causes and correlates of mental disorders as well as to clinicians and policymakers who need to understand exactly how common these disorders are.

**Table 7.1 Some Lifetime Prevalence Results From the National Comorbidity Survey**

**Lifetime prevalence***

| Disorder | Total | Female | Male |
|---|---|---|---|
| Generalized anxiety disorder | 5.7 | 7.1 | 4.2 |
| Obsessive-compulsive disorder | 2.3 | 3.1 | 1.6 |
| Major depressive disorder | 16.9 | 20.2 | 13.2 |
| Bipolar disorder | 4.4 | 4.5 | 4.3 |
| Alcohol abuse | 13.2 | 7.5 | 19.6 |
| Drug abuse | 8.0 | 4.8 | 11.6 |

***The lifetime prevalence of a disorder is the percentage of people in the population that develop that disorder at any time in their lives.**

And as the opening example makes clear, survey research can even be used as a data collection method within experimental research to test specific hypotheses about causal relationships between variables. Such studies, when conducted on large and diverse samples, can be a useful supplement to laboratory studies conducted on university students. Survey research is thus a flexible approach that can be used to study a variety of basic and applied research questions.

# Notes

1. Converse, J. M. (1987). *Survey research in the United States: Roots and emergence, 1890–1960*. Berkeley, CA: University of California Press.

# 35. Constructing Surveys

**Learning Objectives**

1. Describe the cognitive processes involved in responding to a survey item.
2. Explain what a context effect is and give some examples.
3. Create a simple survey questionnaire based on principles of effective item writing and organization.

The heart of any survey research project is the survey itself. Although it is easy to think of interesting questions to ask people, constructing a good survey is not easy at all. The problem is that the answers people give can be influenced in unintended ways by the wording of the items, the order of the items, the response options provided, and many other factors. At best, these influences add noise to the data. At worst, they result in systematic biases and misleading results. In this section, therefore, we consider some principles for constructing surveys to minimize these unintended effects and thereby maximize the reliability and validity of respondents' answers.

## Survey Responding as a Psychological Process

Before looking at specific principles of survey construction, it will help to consider survey responding as a psychological process.

## A Cognitive Model

Figure 7.1 presents a model of the cognitive processes that people engage in when responding to a survey item (Sudman, Bradburn, & Schwarz, 1996)[1]. Respondents must interpret the question, retrieve relevant information from memory, form a tentative judgment, convert the tentative judgment into one of the response options provided (e.g., a rating on a 1-to-7 scale), and finally edit their response as necessary.

*Figure 7.1 Model of the Cognitive Processes Involved in Responding to a Survey Item*

Consider, for example, the following questionnaire item:

How many alcoholic drinks do you consume in a typical day?

- _____ a lot more than average
- _____ somewhat more than average
- _____ average
- _____ somewhat fewer than average
- _____ a lot fewer than average

Although this item at first seems straightforward, it poses several difficulties for respondents. First, they must interpret the question. For example, they must decide whether "alcoholic drinks" include beer and wine (as opposed to just hard liquor) and whether a "typical day" is a typical weekday, typical weekend day, or both. Even though Chang and Krosnick (2003)[2] found that asking about "typical" behavior has been shown to be more valid than asking about "past" behavior, their study compared "typical week" to "past week" and may be different when considering typical weekdays or weekend days). Once respondents have interpreted the question, they must retrieve relevant information from memory to answer it. But what information should they retrieve, and how should they go about retrieving it? They might think vaguely about some recent occasions on which they drank alcohol, they might carefully try to recall and count the number of alcoholic drinks they consumed last week, or they might retrieve some existing beliefs that they have about themselves (e.g., "I am not much of a drinker"). Then they must use this information to arrive at a tentative judgment about how many alcoholic drinks they consume in a typical day. For example, this mental calculation might mean dividing the number of alcoholic drinks they consumed last week by seven to come up with an average number per day. Then they must format this tentative answer in terms of the response options actually provided. In this case, the options pose additional problems of interpretation. For example, what does "average" mean, and what would count as "somewhat more" than average? Finally, they must decide whether they want to report the response they have come up with or whether they want to edit it in some way. For example, if they believe that they drink a lot more than average, they might not want to report that for fear of looking bad in the eyes of the researcher, so instead, they may opt to select the "somewhat more than average" response option.

From this perspective, what at first appears to be a simple matter of asking people how much they drink (and receiving a straightforward answer from them) turns out to be much more complex.

## Context Effects on Survey Responses

Again, this complexity can lead to unintended influences on respondents' answers. These are often referred to as **context effects** because they are not related to the content of the item but to the context in which the item appears (Schwarz & Strack, 1990)[3]. For example, there is an **item-order effect** when the order in which the items are presented affects people's responses. One item can change how participants interpret a later item or change the information that they retrieve to respond to later items. For example, researcher Fritz Strack and his colleagues asked college students about both their general life satisfaction and their dating frequency (Strack, Martin, & Schwarz, 1988)[4]. When the life satisfaction item came first, the correlation between the two was only –.12, suggesting that the two variables are only weakly related. But when the dating frequency item came first, the correlation between the two was +.66, suggesting that those who date more have a strong tendency to be more satisfied with their lives. Reporting the dating frequency first made that information more accessible in memory so that they were more likely to base their life satisfaction rating on it.

The response options provided can also have unintended effects on people's responses (Schwarz, 1999)[5]. For example, when people are asked how often they are "really irritated" and given response options ranging from "less than once a year" to "more than once a month," they tend to think of major irritations and report being irritated infrequently. But when they are given response options ranging from "less than once a day" to "several times a month," they tend to think of minor irritations and report being irritated frequently. People also tend to assume that middle response options represent what is normal or typical. So if they think of themselves as normal or typical, they tend to choose middle response options. For example, people are likely to report watching more television when the response options are centered on a middle option of 4 hours than when centered on a middle option of 2 hours. To mitigate against order effects, rotate questions and response items when there is no natural order. Counterbalancing or randomizing the order of presentation of the questions in online surveys are good practices for survey questions and can reduce response order effects that show that among undecided voters, the first candidate listed in a ballot receives a 2.5% boost simply by virtue of being listed first[6]!

## Writing Survey Items

## Types of Items

Questionnaire items can be either open-ended or closed-ended. **Open-ended items** simply ask a question and allow participants to answer in whatever way they choose. The following are examples of open-ended questionnaire items.

- "What is the most important thing to teach children to prepare them for life?"
- "Please describe a time when you were discriminated against because of your age."
- "Is there anything else you would like to tell us about?"

Open-ended items are useful when researchers do not know how participants might respond or when they want to avoid influencing their responses. Open-ended items are more qualitative in nature, so they tend to be used when researchers have more vaguely defined research questions—often in the early stages of a research project. Open-ended items are relatively easy to write because there are no response options to worry about. However, they take more time and effort on the part of participants, and they are more difficult for the researcher to analyze because the answers must be transcribed, coded, and submitted to some form of qualitative analysis, such as content analysis. Another disadvantage is that respondents are more likely to skip open-ended items because they take longer to answer. It is best to use open-ended questions when the answer is unsure or for quantities which can easily be converted to categories later in the analysis.

**Closed-ended items** ask a question and provide a set of response options for participants to choose from. The alcohol item just mentioned is an example, as are the following:

How old are you?

- _____ Under 18
- _____ 18 to 34
- _____ 35 to 49
- _____ 50 to 70
- _____ Over 70

On a scale of 0 (no pain at all) to 10 (worst pain ever experienced), how much pain are you in right now?

Have you ever in your adult life been depressed for a period of 2 weeks or more? Yes    No

Closed-ended items are used when researchers have a good idea of the different responses that participants might make. They are more quantitative in nature, so they are also used when researchers are interested in a well-defined variable or construct such as participants' level of agreement with some statement, perceptions of risk, or frequency of a particular behavior. Closed-ended items are more difficult to write because they must include an appropriate set of response options. However, they are relatively quick and easy for participants to complete. They are also much easier for researchers to analyze because the responses can be easily converted to numbers and entered into a spreadsheet. For these reasons, closed-ended items are much more common.

All closed-ended items include a set of response options from which a participant must choose. For categorical variables like sex, race, or political party preference, the categories are usually listed and participants choose the one (or ones) to which they belong. For quantitative variables, a rating scale is typically provided. A **rating scale** is an ordered set of responses that participants must choose from. Figure 7.2 shows several examples. The number of response options on a typical rating scale ranges from three to 11—although five and seven are probably most common. Five-point scales are best for unipolar scales where only one construct is tested, such as frequency (Never, Rarely, Sometimes, Often, Always). Seven-point scales are best for bipolar scales where there is a dichotomous spectrum, such as liking (Like very much, Like somewhat, Like slightly, Neither like nor dislike, Dislike slightly, Dislike somewhat, Dislike very much). For bipolar questions, it is useful to offer an earlier question that branches them into an area of the scale; if asking about liking ice cream, first ask "Do you generally like or dislike ice cream?" Once the respondent chooses like or dislike, refine it by offering them relevant choices from the seven-point scale. Branching improves both reliability and validity (Krosnick & Berent, 1993)[7]. Although you often see scales with numerical labels, it is best to only present verbal labels to the respondents but convert them to numerical values in the analyses. Avoid partial labels or length or overly specific labels. In some cases, the verbal labels can be supplemented with (or even replaced by) meaningful graphics. The last rating scale shown in Figure 7.3 is a visual-analog scale, on which participants make a mark somewhere along the horizontal line to indicate the magnitude of their response.

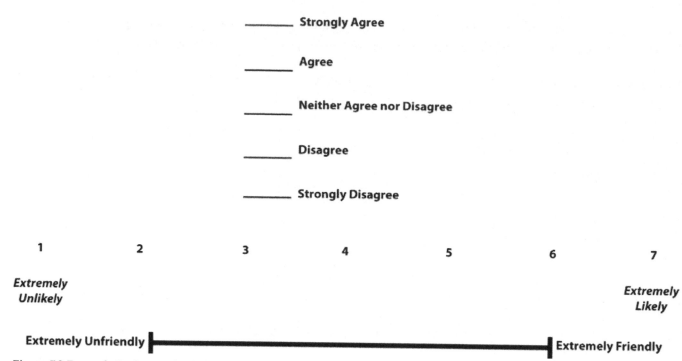

Figure 7.2 Example Rating Scales for Closed-Ended Questionnaire Items

## What Is a Likert Scale?

In reading about psychological research, you are likely to encounter the term *Likert scale*. Although this term is sometimes used to refer to almost any rating scale (e.g., a 0-to-10 life satisfaction scale), it has a much more precise meaning.

In the 1930s, researcher Rensis Likert (pronounced LICK-ert) created a new approach for measuring people's attitudes (Likert, 1932)[8]. It involves presenting people with several statements—including both favorable and unfavorable statements—about some person, group, or idea. Respondents then express their agreement or disagreement with each statement on a 5-point scale: *Strongly Agree, Agree, Neither Agree nor Disagree, Disagree, Strongly Disagree*. Numbers are assigned to each response and then summed across all items to produce a score representing the attitude toward the person, group, or idea. For items that are phrased in an opposite direction (e.g., negatively worded statements instead of positively worded statements), reverse coding is used so that the numerical scoring of statements also runs in the opposite direction. The entire set of items came to be called a Likert scale.

Thus unless you are measuring people's attitude toward something by assessing their level of agreement with several statements about it, it is best to avoid calling it a Likert scale. You are probably just using a "rating scale."

# Writing Effective Items

We can now consider some principles of writing questionnaire items that minimize unintended context effects and maximize the reliability and validity of participants' responses. A rough guideline for writing questionnaire items is provided by the BRUSO model (Peterson, 2000)[9]. An acronym, **BRUSO** stands for "brief," "relevant," "unambiguous," "specific," and "objective." Effective questionnaire items are *brief* and to the point. They avoid long, overly technical, or unnecessary words. This brevity makes them easier for respondents to understand and faster for them to complete. Effective questionnaire items are also *relevant* to the research question. If a respondent's sexual orientation, marital status, or income is not relevant, then items on them should probably not be included. Again, this makes the questionnaire faster to complete, but it also avoids annoying respondents with what they will rightly perceive as irrelevant or even "nosy" questions. Effective questionnaire items are also *unambiguous*; they can be interpreted in only one way. Part of the problem with the alcohol item presented earlier in this section is that different respondents might have different ideas about what constitutes "an alcoholic drink" or "a typical day." Effective questionnaire items are also *specific* so that it is clear to respondents what their response *should* be about and clear to researchers what it *is* about. A common problem here is closed-ended items that are "double barrelled." They ask about two conceptually separate issues but allow only one response. For example, "Please rate the extent to which you have been feeling anxious and depressed." This item should probably be split into two separate items—one about anxiety and one about depression. Finally, effective questionnaire items are *objective* in the sense that they do not reveal the researcher's own opinions or lead participants to answer in a particular way. Table 7.2 shows some examples of poor and effective questionnaire items based on the BRUSO criteria. The best way to know how people interpret the wording of the question is to conduct a pilot test and ask a few people to explain how they interpreted the question.

*Table 7.2 BRUSO Model of Writing Effective Questionnaire Items, Plus Examples*

| Criterion | Poor | Effective |
|---|---|---|
| B–Brief | "Are you now or have you ever been the possessor of a firearm?" | "Have you ever owned a gun?" |
| R–Relevant | "What is your sexual orientation?" | Do not include this item unless it is clearly relevant to the research. |
| U–Unambiguous | "Are you a gun person?" | "Do you currently own a gun?" |
| S–Specific | "How much have you read about the new gun control measure and sales tax?" | "How much have you read about the new sales tax?" |
| O–Objective | "How much do you support the new gun control measure?" | "What is your view of the new gun control measure?" |

For closed-ended items, it is also important to create an appropriate response scale. For categorical variables, the categories presented should generally be mutually exclusive and exhaustive. Mutually exclusive categories do not overlap. For a religion item, for example, the categories of *Christian* and *Catholic* are not mutually exclusive but *Protestant* and *Catholic* are mutually exclusive. Exhaustive categories cover all possible responses. Although *Protestant* and *Catholic* are mutually exclusive, they are not exhaustive because there are many other religious categories that a respondent might select: *Jewish*, *Hindu*, *Buddhist*, and so on. In many cases, it is not feasible to include every possible category, in which case an *Other* category, with a space for the respondent to fill in a more specific response, is a good solution. If respondents could belong to more than one category (e.g., race), they should be instructed to choose all categories that apply.

For rating scales, five or seven response options generally allow about as much precision as respondents are capable of. However, numerical scales with more options can sometimes be appropriate. For dimensions such as attractiveness, pain, and likelihood, a 0-to-10 scale will be familiar to many respondents and easy for them to use. Regardless of the number of response options, the most extreme ones should generally be "balanced" around a neutral or modal midpoint. An example of an unbalanced rating scale measuring perceived likelihood might look like this:

*Unlikely | Somewhat Likely | Likely | Very Likely | Extremely Likely*

A balanced version might look like this:

*Extremely Unlikely | Somewhat Unlikely | As Likely as Not | Somewhat Likely |Extremely Likely*

Note, however, that a middle or neutral response option does not have to be included. Researchers sometimes choose to leave it out because they want to encourage respondents to think more deeply about their response and not simply choose the middle option by default. However, including middle alternatives on bipolar dimensions can be used to allow people to choose an option that is neither.

*"Question" retrieved from*
*http://imgs.xkcd.com/comics/*
*question.png (CC-BY-NC 2.5)*

## Formatting the Survey

Writing effective items is only one part of constructing a survey. For one thing, every survey should have a written or spoken introduction that serves two basic functions (Peterson, 2000)[10]. One is to encourage respondents to participate in the survey. In many types of research, such encouragement is not necessary either because participants do not know they are in a study (as in naturalistic observation) or because they are part of a subject pool and have already shown their willingness to participate by signing up and showing up for the study. Survey research usually catches respondents by surprise when they answer their phone, go to their mailbox, or check their e-mail—and the researcher must make a good case for why they should agree to participate. Thus the introduction should briefly explain the purpose of the survey and its importance, provide information about the sponsor of the survey (university-based surveys tend to generate higher response rates), acknowledge the importance of the respondent's participation, and describe any incentives for participating.

The second function of the introduction is to establish informed consent. Remember that this involves describing to respondents everything that might affect their decision to participate. This includes the topics covered by the survey, the amount of time it is likely to take, the respondent's option to withdraw at any time, confidentiality issues, and so on. Written consent forms are not always used in survey research (when the research is of minimal risk and completion of the survey instrument is often accepted by the IRB as evidence of consent to participate), so it is important that this part of the introduction be well documented and presented clearly and in its entirety to every respondent.

The introduction should be followed by the substantive questionnaire items. But first, it is important to present clear instructions for completing the questionnaire, including examples of how to use any unusual response scales. Remember that the introduction is the point at which respondents are usually most interested and least fatigued, so it is good practice to start with the most important items for purposes of the research and proceed to less important items. Items should also be grouped by topic or by type. For example, items using the same rating scale (e.g., a 5-point agreement scale) should be grouped together if possible to make things faster and easier for respondents. Demographic items are often presented last because they are least interesting to participants but also easy to answer in the event respondents have become tired or bored. Of course, any survey should end with an expression of appreciation to the respondent.

# Notes

1. Sudman, S., Bradburn, N. M., & Schwarz, N. (1996). *Thinking about answers: The application of cognitive processes to survey methodology.* San Francisco, CA: Jossey-Bass.
2. Chang, L., & Krosnick, J.A. (2003). Measuring the frequency of regular behaviors: Comparing the 'typical week' to the 'past week'. *Sociological Methodology, 33,* 55-80.
3. Schwarz, N., & Strack, F. (1990). Context effects in attitude surveys: Applying cognitive theory to social research. In W. Stroebe & M. Hewstone (Eds.), *European review of social psychology* (Vol. 2, pp. 31–50). Chichester, UK: Wiley.
4. Strack, F., Martin, L. L., & Schwarz, N. (1988). Priming and communication: The social determinants of information use in judgments of life satisfaction. *European Journal of Social Psychology, 18,* 429–442.
5. Schwarz, N. (1999). Self-reports: How the questions shape the answers. *American Psychologist, 54,* 93–105.
6. Miller, J.M. & Krosnick, J.A. (1998). The impact of candidate name order on election outcomes. *Public Opinion Quarterly, 62*(3), 291-330.
7. Krosnick, J.A. & Berent, M.K. (1993). Comparisons of party identification and policy preferences: The impact of survey question format. *American Journal of Political Science, 27*(3), 941-964.
8. Likert, R. (1932). A technique for the measurement of attitudes. *Archives of Psychology,140,* 1–55.
9. Peterson, R. A. (2000). *Constructing effective questionnaires.* Thousand Oaks, CA: Sage.
10. Peterson, R. A. (2000). *Constructing effective questionnaires.* Thousand Oaks, CA: Sage.

# 36. Conducting Surveys

### Learning Objectives

1. Explain the difference between probability and non-probability sampling, and describe the major types of probability sampling.
2. Define sampling bias in general and non-response bias in particular. List some techniques that can be used to increase the response rate and reduce non-response bias.
3. List the four major ways to conduct a survey along with some pros and cons of each.

In this section, we consider how to go about conducting a survey. We first consider the issue of sampling, followed by some different methods of actually collecting survey data.

## Sampling

Essentially all psychological research involves sampling—selecting a sample to study from the population of interest. Sampling falls into two broad categories. The first category, **Probability sampling**, occurs when the researcher can specify the probability that each member of the population will be selected for the sample. The second is **Non-probability sampling**, which occurs when the researcher cannot specify these probabilities. Most psychological research involves non-probability sampling. For example, **Convenience sampling**—studying individuals who happen to be nearby and willing to participate—is a very common form of non-probability sampling used in psychological research. Other forms of non-probability sampling include **snowball sampling** (in which existing research participants help recruit additional participants for the study), **quota sampling** (in which subgroups in the sample are recruited to be proportional to those subgroups in the population), and **self-selection sampling** (in which individuals choose to take part in the research on their own accord, without being approached by the researcher directly).

Survey researchers, however, are much more likely to use some form of probability sampling. This tendency is because the goal of most survey research is to make accurate estimates about what is true in a particular population, and these estimates are most accurate when based on a probability sample. For example, it is important for survey researchers to base their estimates of election outcomes—which are often decided by only a few percentage points—on probability samples of likely registered voters.

Compared with non-probability sampling, probability sampling requires a very clear specification of the population, which of course depends on the research questions to be answered. The population might be all registered voters in Washington State, all American consumers who have purchased a car in the past year, women in the Seattle over 40 years old who have received a mammogram in the past decade, or all the alumni of a particular university. Once the population has been specified, probability sampling requires a **sampling frame**. This sampling frame is essentially a list of all the members of the population from which to select the respondents. Sampling frames can come from a variety of sources, including telephone directories, lists of registered voters, and hospital or insurance records. In some cases, a map can serve as a sampling frame, allowing for the selection of cities, streets, or households.

There are a variety of different probability sampling methods. **Simple random sampling** is done in such a way that each individual in the population has an equal probability of being selected for the sample. This type of sampling could involve putting the names of all individuals in the sampling frame into a hat, mixing them up, and then drawing out the number needed for the sample. Given that most sampling frames take the form of computer files, random sampling is more likely to involve computerized sorting or selection of respondents. A common approach in telephone surveys is random-digit dialing, in which a computer randomly generates phone numbers from among the possible phone numbers within a given geographic area.

A common alternative to simple random sampling is **stratified random sampling**, in which the population is divided into different subgroups or "strata" (usually based on demographic characteristics) and then a random sample is taken from each "stratum." **Proportionate stratified random sampling** can be used to select a sample in which the proportion of respondents in each of various subgroups matches the proportion in the population. For example, because about 12.6% of the American population is African American, stratified random sampling can be used to ensure that a survey of 1,000 American adults includes about 126 African-American respondents. **Disproportionate stratified random sampling** can also be used to sample extra respondents from particularly small subgroups—allowing valid conclusions to be drawn about those subgroups. For example, because Asian Americans make up a relatively small percentage of the American population (about 5.6%), a simple random sample of 1,000 American adults might include too few Asian Americans to draw any conclusions about them as distinct from any other subgroup. If representation is important to the research question, however, then disproportionate stratified random sampling could be used to ensure that enough Asian-American respondents are included in the sample to draw valid conclusions about Asian Americans a whole.

Yet another type of probability sampling is **cluster sampling**, in which larger clusters of individuals are randomly sampled and then individuals within each cluster are randomly sampled. This is the only probability sampling method that does not require a sampling frame. For example, to select a sample of small-town residents in Washington, a researcher might randomly select several small towns and then randomly select several individuals within each town. Cluster sampling is especially useful for surveys that involve face-to-face interviewing because it minimizes the amount of traveling that the interviewers must do. For example, instead of traveling to 200 small towns to interview 200 residents, a research team could travel to 10 small towns and interview 20 residents of each. The National Comorbidity Survey was done using a form of cluster sampling.

How large does a survey sample need to be? In general, this estimate depends on two factors. One is the level of confidence in the result that the researcher wants. The larger the sample, the closer any statistic based on that sample will tend to be to the corresponding value in the population. The other factor is a practical constraint in the form of the budget of the study. Larger samples provide greater confidence, but they take more time, effort, and money to obtain. Taking these two factors into account, most survey research uses sample sizes that range from about 100 to about 1,000. Conducting a power analysis prior to launching the survey helps to guide the researcher in making this trade-off.

*Sample Size and Population Size*

Why is a sample of about 1,000 considered to be adequate for most survey research—even when the population is much larger than that? Consider, for example, that a sample of only 1,000 American adults is generally considered a good sample of the roughly 252 million adults in the American population—even though it includes only about 0.000004% of the population! The answer is a bit surprising.

One part of the answer is that a statistic based on a larger sample will tend to be closer to the population value and that this can be characterized mathematically. Imagine, for example, that in a sample of registered voters, exactly 50% say they intend to vote for the incumbent. If there are 100 voters in this sample, then there is a 95% chance that the true percentage in the population is between 40 and 60. But if there are 1,000 voters in the sample, then there is a 95% chance that the true percentage in the population is between 47 and 53. Although this "95% confidence interval" continues to shrink as the sample size increases, it does so at a slower rate. For example, if there are 2,000 voters in the sample, then this reduction only reduces the 95% confidence interval to 48 to 52. In many situations, the small increase in confidence beyond a sample size of 1,000 is not considered to be worth the additional time, effort, and money.

Another part of the answer—and perhaps the more surprising part—is that confidence intervals depend only on the size of the sample and not on the size of the population. So a sample of 1,000 would produce a 95% confidence interval of 47 to 53 regardless of whether the population size was a hundred thousand, a million, or a hundred million.

# Sampling Bias

Probability sampling was developed in large part to address the issue of sampling bias. **Sampling bias** occurs when a sample is selected in such a way that it is not representative of the entire population and therefore produces inaccurate results. This bias was the reason that the *Literary Digest* straw poll was so far off in its prediction of the 1936 presidential election. The mailing lists used came largely from telephone directories and lists of registered automobile owners, which over-represented wealthier people, who were more likely to vote for Landon. Gallup was successful because he knew about this bias and found ways to sample less wealthy people as well.

There is one form of sampling bias that even careful random sampling is subject to. It is almost never the case that everyone selected for the sample actually responds to the survey. Some may have died or moved away, and others may decline to participate because they are too busy, are not interested in the survey topic, or do not participate in surveys on principle. If these survey non-responders differ from survey responders in systematic ways, then this difference can produce **non-response bias**. For example, in a mail survey on alcohol consumption, researcher Vivienne Lahaut and colleagues found that only about half the sample responded after the initial contact and two follow-up reminders (Lahaut, Jansen, van de Mheen, & Garretsen, 2002)[1]. The danger here is that the half who responded might have different patterns of alcohol consumption than the half who did not, which could lead to inaccurate conclusions on the part of the researchers. So to test for non-response bias, the researchers later made unannounced visits to the homes of a subset of the non-responders—coming back up to five times if they did not find them at home. They found that the original non-responders included an especially high proportion of abstainers (nondrinkers), which meant that their estimates of alcohol consumption based only on the original responders were too high.

Although there are methods for statistically correcting for non-response bias, they are based on assumptions about the non-responders—for example, that they are more similar to late responders than to early responders—which may not be correct. For this reason, the best approach to minimizing non-response bias is to minimize the number of non-responders—that is, to maximize the response rate. There is a large research literature on the factors that affect survey response rates (Groves et al., 2004)[2]. In general, in-person interviews have the highest response rates, followed by telephone surveys, and then mail and Internet surveys. Among the other factors that increase response rates are sending potential respondents a short pre-notification message informing them that they will be asked to participate in a survey in the near future and sending simple follow-up reminders to non-responders after a few weeks. The perceived length and complexity of the survey can also make a difference, which is why it is important to keep survey questionnaires as short, simple, and on topic as possible. Finally, offering an incentive—especially cash—is a reliable way to increase response rates. However, ethically, there are limits to offering incentives that may be so large as to be considered coercive.

## Conducting the Survey

The four main ways to conduct surveys are through in-person interviews, by telephone, through the mail, and over the internet. As with other aspects of survey design, the choice depends on both the researcher's goals and the budget. In-person interviews have the highest response rates and provide the closest personal contact with respondents. Personal contact can be important, for example, when the interviewer must see and make judgments about respondents, as is the case with some mental health interviews. But in-person interviewing is by far the most costly approach. Telephone surveys have lower response rates and still provide some personal contact with respondents. They can also be costly but are generally less so than in-person interviews. Traditionally, telephone directories have provided fairly comprehensive sampling frames. However, this trend is less true today as more people choose to only have cell phones and do not install land lines that would be included in telephone directories. Mail surveys are less costly still but generally have even lower response rates—making them most susceptible to non-response bias.

Not surprisingly, internet surveys are becoming more common. They are increasingly easy to construct and use (see "Online Survey Creation"). Although initial contact can be made by mail with a link provided to the survey, this approach does not necessarily produce higher response rates than an ordinary mail survey. A better approach is to make initial contact by email with a link directly to the survey. This approach can work well when the population consists of the members of an organization who have known email addresses and regularly use them (e.g., a university community). For other populations, it can be difficult or impossible to find a comprehensive list of email addresses to serve as a sampling frame. Alternatively, a request to participate in the survey with a link to it can be posted on websites known to be visited by members of the population. But again it is very difficult to get anything approaching a random sample this way because the members of the population who visit the websites are likely to be different from the population as a whole. However, internet survey methods are in rapid development. Because of their low cost, and because more people are online than ever before, internet surveys are likely to become the dominant approach to survey data collection in the near future.

Finally, it is important to note that some of the concerns that people have about collecting data online (e.g., that internet-based findings differ from those obtained with other methods) have been found to be myths. Table 7.3 (adapted from Gosling, Vazire, Srivastava, & John, 2004)[3] addresses three such preconceptions about data collected in web-based studies:

*Table 7.3 Some Preconceptions and Findings Pertaining to Web-based Studies*

| Preconception | Finding |
| --- | --- |
| Internet samples are not demographically diverse | Internet samples are more diverse than traditional samples in many domains, although they are not completely representative of the population |
| Internet samples are maladjusted, socially isolated, or depressed | Internet users do not differs from nonusers on markers of adjustment and depression |
| Internet-based findings differ from those obtained with other methods | Evidence so far suggests that internet-based findings are consistent with findings based on traditional methods (e.g., on self-esteem, personality), but more data are needed. |

*Online Survey Creation*

There are now several online tools for creating online questionnaires. After a questionnaire is created, a link to it can then be emailed to potential respondents or embedded in a web page. The following websites are among those that offer free accounts. Although the free accounts limit the number of questionnaire items and the number of respondents, they can be useful for doing small-scale surveys and for practicing the principles of good questionnaire construction. Here are some commonly used online survey tools:

- SurveyMonkey–https://surveymonkey.com
- PsyToolkit–https://www.psytoolkit.org/ (free, noncommercial, and does many experimental paradigms)
- Qualtrics–https://www.qualtrics.com/
- PsycData–https://www.psychdata.com/

A small note of caution: the data from US survey software are held on US servers, and are subject to be seized as granted through the Patriot Act. To avoid infringing on any rights, the following is a list of online survey sites that are hosted in Canada:

- Fluid Surveys–http://fluidsurveys.com/
- Simple Survey–http://www.simplesurvey.com/
- Lime Survey–https://www.limesurvey.org

There are also survey sites hosted in other countries outside of North America.

Another new tool for survey researchers is Mechanical Turk (MTurk) created by Amazon.com https://www.mturk.com Originally created for simple usability testing, MTurk has a database of over 500,000 workers from over 190 countries[4]. You can put simple tasks (for example, different question wording to test your survey items), set parameters as your sample frame dictates and deploy your experiment at a very low cost (for example, a few cents for less than 5 minutes). MTurk has been lauded as an inexpensive way to gather high-quality data (Buhrmester, Kwang, & Gosling, 2011)[5].

# Notes

1. Lahaut, V. M. H. C. J., Jansen, H. A. M., van de Mheen, D., & Garretsen, H. F. L. (2002). Non-response bias in a sample survey on alcohol consumption. *Alcohol and Alcoholism*, 37, 256–260.

2. Groves, R. M., Fowler, F. J., Couper, M. P., Lepkowski, J. M., Singer, E., & Tourangeau, R. (2004). *Survey methodology*. Hoboken, NJ: Wiley.

3. Gosling, S. D., Vazire, S., Srivastava, S., & John, O. P. (2004). Should we trust web-based studies? A comparative analysis of six preconceptions about internet questionnaires. *American Psychologist*, 59(2), 93-104.

4. Natala@aws. (2011, January 26). Re: MTurk CENSUS: About how many workers were on Mechanical Turk in 2010? Message posted to Amazon Web Services Discussion Forums. Retrieved from https://forums.aws.amazon.com/thread.jspa?threadID=58891

5. Buhrmester, M., Kwang, T., & Gosling, S.D. (2011). Amazon's Mechanical Turk: A new source of inexpensive, yet high quality, data? *Perspectives on Psychological Science*, 6(1), 3-5.

# 37. Key Takeaways and Exercises

- Survey research features the use of self-report measures on carefully selected samples. It is a flexible approach that can be used to study a wide variety of basic and applied research questions.
- Survey research has its roots in applied social research, market research, and election polling. It has since become an important approach in many academic disciplines, including political science, sociology, public health, and, of course, psychology.
- Survey research involves asking respondents to self-report on their own thoughts, feelings, and behaviors.
- Most survey research is non-experimental in nature (it is used to describe variables or measure statistical relationships between variables) but surveys can also be used to measure dependent variables in true experiments.
- Responding to a survey item is itself a complex cognitive process that involves interpreting the question, retrieving information, making a tentative judgment, putting that judgment into the required response format, and editing the response.
- Survey responses are subject to numerous context effects due to question wording, item order, response options, and other factors. Researchers should be sensitive to such effects when constructing surveys and interpreting survey results.
- Survey items are either open-ended or closed-ended. Open-ended items simply ask a question and allow respondents to answer in whatever way they want. Closed-ended items ask a question and provide several response options that respondents must choose from.
- Use verbal labels instead of numerical labels although the responses can be converted to numerical data in the analyses.
- According to the BRUSO model, questionnaire items should be brief, relevant, unambiguous, specific, and objective.
- Survey research usually involves probability sampling, in which each member of the population has a known probability of being selected for the sample. Types of probability sampling include simple random sampling, stratified random sampling, and cluster sampling.
- Sampling bias occurs when a sample is selected in such a way that it is not representative of the population and therefore produces inaccurate results. The most pervasive form of sampling bias is non-response bias, which occurs when people who do not respond to the survey differ in important ways from people who do respond. The best way to minimize non-response bias is to maximize the response rate by prenotifying respondents, sending them reminders, constructing questionnaires that are short and easy to complete, and offering incentives.
- Surveys can be conducted in person, by telephone, through the mail, and on the internet. In-person interviewing has the highest response rates but is the most expensive. Mail and internet surveys are less expensive but have much lower response rates. Internet surveys are likely to become the dominant approach because of their low cost.

- Discussion: Think of a question that each of the following professionals might try to answer using survey research.

  - a social psychologist
  - an educational researcher
  - a market researcher who works for a supermarket chain
  - the mayor of a large city
  - the head of a university police force

- Discussion: Write a survey item and then write a short description of how someone might respond to that item based on the cognitive model of survey responding (or choose any item on the Rosenberg Self-Esteem Scale at http://www.bsos.umd.edu/socy/research/rosenberg.htm).

- Practice: Write survey items for each of the following general questions. In some cases, a series of items, rather than a single item, might be necessary.

  - How much does the respondent use Facebook?
  - How much exercise does the respondent get?
  - How likely does the respondent think it is that the incumbent will be re-elected in the next presidential election?
  - To what extent does the respondent experience "road rage"?

- Discussion: If possible, identify an appropriate sampling frame for each of the following populations. If there is no appropriate sampling frame, explain why.

  - students at a particular university
  - adults living in the state of Washington
  - households in Pullman, Washington
  - people with low self-esteem

- Practice: Use one of the online survey creation tools to create a 10-item survey questionnaire on a topic of your choice.

# CHAPTER VIII
# QUASI-EXPERIMENTAL RESEARCH

The prefix *quasi* means "resembling." Thus quasi-experimental research is research that resembles experimental research but is not true experimental research. Recall with a true between-groups experiment, random assignment to conditions is used to ensure the groups are equivalent and with a true within-subjects design counterbalancing is used to guard against order effects. Quasi-experiments are missing one of these safeguards. Although an independent variable is manipulated, either a control group is missing or participants are not randomly assigned to conditions (Cook & Campbell, 1979)[1].

Because the independent variable is manipulated before the dependent variable is measured, quasi-experimental research eliminates the directionality problem associated with non-experimental research. But because either counterbalancing techniques are not used or participants are not randomly assigned to conditions—making it likely that there are other differences between conditions—quasi-experimental research does not eliminate the problem of confounding variables. In terms of internal validity, therefore, quasi-experiments are generally somewhere between non-experimental studies and true experiments.

Quasi-experiments are most likely to be conducted in field settings in which random assignment is difficult or impossible. They are often conducted to evaluate the effectiveness of a treatment—perhaps a type of psychotherapy or an educational intervention. There are many different kinds of quasi-experiments, but we will discuss just a few of the most common ones in this chapter.

# 38. One-Group Designs

## One-Group Posttest Only Design

In a **one-group posttest only design,** a treatment is implemented (or an independent variable is manipulated) and then a dependent variable is measured once after the treatment is implemented. Imagine, for example, a researcher who is interested in the effectiveness of an anti-drug education program on elementary school students' attitudes toward illegal drugs. The researcher could implement the anti-drug program, and then immediately after the program ends, the researcher could measure students' attitudes toward illegal drugs.

This is the weakest type of quasi-experimental design. A major limitation to this design is the lack of a control or comparison group. There is no way to determine what the attitudes of these students would have been if they hadn't completed the anti-drug program. Despite this major limitation, results from this design are frequently reported in the media and are often misinterpreted by the general population. For instance, advertisers might claim that 80% of women noticed their skin looked bright after using Brand X cleanser for a month. If there is no comparison group, then this statistic means little to nothing.

## One-Group Pretest-Posttest Design

In a **one-group pretest-posttest design**, the dependent variable is measured once before the treatment is implemented and once after it is implemented. Let's return to the example of a researcher who is interested in the effectiveness of an anti-drug education program on elementary school students' attitudes toward illegal drugs. The researcher could measure the attitudes of students at a particular elementary school during one week, implement the anti-drug program during the next week, and finally, measure their attitudes again the following week. The pretest-posttest design is much like a within-subjects experiment in which each participant is tested first under the control condition and then under the treatment condition. It is unlike a within-subjects experiment, however, in that the order of conditions is not counterbalanced because it typically is not possible for a participant to be tested in the treatment condition first and then in an "untreated" control condition.

If the average posttest score is better than the average pretest score (e.g., attitudes toward illegal drugs are more negative after the anti-drug educational program), then it makes sense to conclude that the treatment might be responsible for the improvement. Unfortunately, one often cannot conclude this with a high degree of certainty because there may be other explanations for why the posttest scores may have changed. These alternative explanations pose threats to internal validity.

One alternative explanation goes under the name of **history**. Other things might have happened between the pretest and the posttest that caused a change from pretest to posttest. Perhaps an anti-drug program aired on television and many of the students watched it, or perhaps a celebrity died of a drug overdose and many of the students heard about it.

Another alternative explanation goes under the name of **maturation**. Participants might have changed between the pretest and the posttest in ways that they were going to anyway because they are growing and learning. If it were a year long anti-drug program, participants might become less impulsive or better reasoners and this might be responsible for the change in their attitudes toward illegal drugs.

Another threat to the internal validity of one-group pretest-posttest designs is **testing**, which refers to when the act of measuring the dependent variable during the pretest affects participants' responses at posttest. For instance, completing the measure of attitudes towards illegal drugs may have had an effect on those attitudes. Simply completing this measure may have inspired further thinking and conversations about illegal drugs that then produced a change in posttest scores.

Similarly, **instrumentation** can be a threat to the internal validity of studies using this design. Instrumentation refers to when the basic characteristics of the measuring instrument change over time. When human observers are used to measure behavior, they may over time gain skill, become fatigued, or change the standards on which observations are based. So participants may have taken the measure of attitudes toward illegal drugs very seriously during the pretest when it was novel but then they may have become bored with the measure at posttest and been less careful in considering their responses.

Another alternative explanation for a change in the dependent variable in a pretest-posttest design is **regression to the mean**. This refers to the statistical fact that an individual who scores extremely high or extremely low on a variable on one occasion will tend to score less extremely on the next occasion. For example, a bowler with a long-term average of 150 who suddenly bowls a 220 will almost certainly score lower in the next game. Her score will "regress" toward her mean score of 150. Regression to the mean can be a problem when participants are selected for further study *because* of their extreme scores. Imagine, for example, that only students who scored especially high on the test of attitudes toward illegal drugs (those with extremely favorable attitudes toward drugs) were given the anti-drug program and then were retested. Regression to the mean all but guarantees that their scores will be lower at the posttest even if the training program has no effect.

A closely related concept—and an extremely important one in psychological research—is **spontaneous remission**. This is the tendency for many medical and psychological problems to improve over time without any form of treatment. The common cold is a good example. If one were to measure symptom severity in 100 common cold sufferers today, give them a bowl of chicken soup every day, and then measure their symptom severity again in a week, they would probably be much improved. This does not mean that the chicken soup was responsible for the improvement, however, because they would have been much improved without any treatment at all. The same is true of many psychological problems. A group of severely depressed people today is likely to be less depressed on average in 6 months. In reviewing the results of several studies of treatments for depression, researchers Michael Posternak and Ivan Miller found that participants in waitlist control conditions improved an average of 10 to 15% before they received any treatment at all (Posternak & Miller, 2001)[1]. Thus one must generally be very cautious about inferring causality from pretest-posttest designs.

A common approach to ruling out the threats to internal validity described above is by revisiting the research design to include a control group, one that does not receive the treatment effect. A control group would be subject to the same threats from history, maturation, testing, instrumentation, regression to the mean, and spontaneous remission and so would allow the researcher to measure the actual effect of the treatment (if any). Of course, including a control group would mean that this is no longer a one-group design.

*Does Psychotherapy Work?*

Early studies on the effectiveness of psychotherapy tended to use pretest-posttest designs. In a classic 1952 article, researcher Hans Eysenck summarized the results of 24 such studies showing that about two thirds of patients improved between the pretest and the posttest (Eysenck, 1952)[2]. But Eysenck also compared these results with archival data from state hospital and insurance company records showing that similar patients recovered at about the same rate *without* receiving psychotherapy. This parallel suggested to Eysenck that the improvement that patients showed in the pretest-posttest studies might be no more than spontaneous remission. Note that Eysenck did not conclude that psychotherapy was ineffective. He merely concluded that there was no evidence that it was, and he wrote of "the necessity of properly planned and executed experimental studies into this important field" (p. 323). You can read the entire article here:

http://psychclassics.yorku.ca/Eysenck/psychotherapy.htm

Fortunately, many other researchers took up Eysenck's challenge, and by 1980 hundreds of experiments had been conducted in which participants were randomly assigned to treatment and control conditions, and the results were summarized in a classic book by Mary Lee Smith, Gene Glass, and Thomas Miller (Smith, Glass, & Miller, 1980)[3]. They found that overall psychotherapy was quite effective, with about 80% of treatment participants improving more than the average control participant. Subsequent research has focused more on the conditions under which different types of psychotherapy are more or less effective.

# Interrupted Time Series Design

A variant of the pretest-posttest design is the **interrupted time-series design**. A time series is a set of measurements taken at intervals over a period of time. For example, a manufacturing company might measure its workers' productivity each week for a year. In an interrupted time series-design, a time series like this one is "interrupted" by a treatment. In one classic example, the treatment was the reduction of the work shifts in a factory from 10 hours to 8 hours (Cook & Campbell, 1979)[4]. Because productivity increased rather quickly after the shortening of the work shifts, and because it remained elevated for many months afterward, the researcher concluded that the shortening of the shifts caused the increase in productivity. Notice that the interrupted time-series design is like a pretest-posttest design in that it includes measurements of the dependent variable both before and after the treatment. It is unlike the pretest-posttest design, however, in that it includes multiple pretest and posttest measurements.

Figure 8.1 shows data from a hypothetical interrupted time-series study. The dependent variable is the number of student absences per week in a research methods course. The treatment is that the instructor begins publicly taking attendance each day so that students know that the instructor is aware of who is present and who is absent. The top panel of Figure 8.1 shows how the data might look if this treatment worked. There is a consistently high number of absences before the treatment, and there is an immediate and sustained drop in absences after the treatment. The bottom panel of Figure 8.1 shows how the data might look if this treatment did not work. On average, the number of absences after the treatment is about the same as the number before. This figure also illustrates an advantage of the interrupted time-series design over a simpler pretest-posttest design. If there had been only one measurement of absences before the treatment at Week 7 and one afterward at Week 8, then it would have looked as though the treatment were responsible for the reduction. The multiple measurements both before and after the treatment suggest that the reduction between Weeks 7 and 8 is nothing more than normal week-to-week variation.

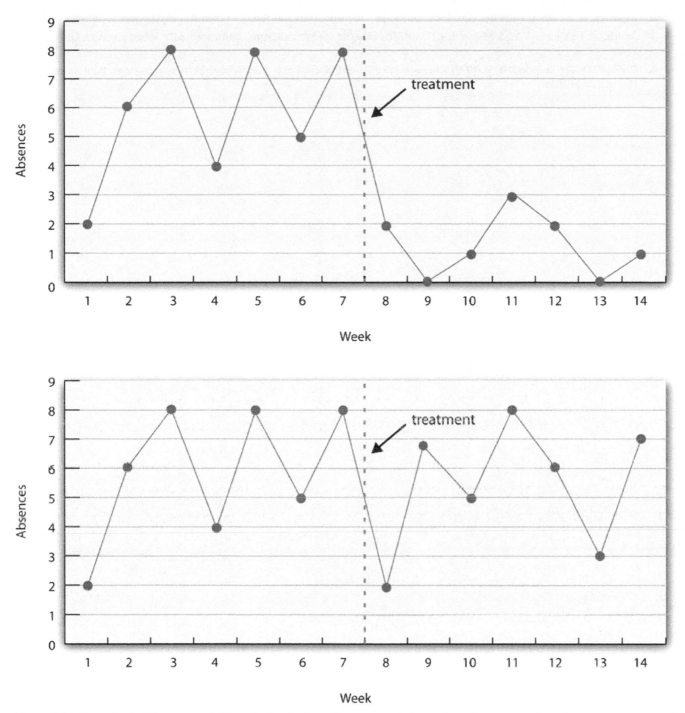

Figure 8.1 A Hypothetical Interrupted Time-Series Design. The top panel shows data that suggest that the treatment caused a reduction in absences. The bottom panel shows data that suggest that it did not.

## Notes

1. Posternak, M. A., & Miller, I. (2001). Untreated short-term course of major depression: A meta-analysis of studies using outcomes from studies using wait-list control groups. *Journal of Affective Disorders, 66*, 139–146.

2.  Eysenck, H. J. (1952). The effects of psychotherapy: An evaluation. *Journal of Consulting Psychology, 16*, 319–324.

3.  Smith, M. L., Glass, G. V., & Miller, T. I. (1980). *The benefits of psychotherapy*. Baltimore, MD: Johns Hopkins University Press.

4.  Cook, T. D., & Campbell, D. T. (1979). *Quasi-experimentation: Design & analysis issues in field settings*. Boston, MA: Houghton Mifflin.

# 39. Non-Equivalent Groups Designs

### Learning Objectives

1. Describe the different types of nonequivalent groups quasi-experimental designs.
2. Identify some of the threats to internal validity associated with each of these designs.

Recall that when participants in a between-subjects experiment are randomly assigned to conditions, the resulting groups are likely to be quite similar. In fact, researchers consider them to be equivalent. When participants are not randomly assigned to conditions, however, the resulting groups are likely to be dissimilar in some ways. For this reason, researchers consider them to be nonequivalent. A **nonequivalent groups design**, then, is a between-subjects design in which participants have not been randomly assigned to conditions. There are several types of nonequivalent groups designs we will consider.

## Posttest Only Nonequivalent Groups Design

The first nonequivalent groups design we will consider is the **posttest only nonequivalent groups design.** In this design, participants in one group are exposed to a treatment, a nonequivalent group is not exposed to the treatment, and then the two groups are compared. Imagine, for example, a researcher who wants to evaluate a new method of teaching fractions to third graders. One way would be to conduct a study with a treatment group consisting of one class of third-grade students and a control group consisting of another class of third-grade students. This design would be a nonequivalent groups design because the students are not randomly assigned to classes by the researcher, which means there could be important differences between them. For example, the parents of higher achieving or more motivated students might have been more likely to request that their children be assigned to Ms. Williams's class. Or the principal might have assigned the "troublemakers" to Mr. Jones's class because he is a stronger disciplinarian. Of course, the teachers' styles, and even the classroom environments might be very different and might cause different levels of achievement or motivation among the students. If at the end of the study there was a difference in the two classes' knowledge of fractions, it might have been caused by the difference between the teaching methods—but it might have been caused by any of these confounding variables.

Of course, researchers using a posttest only nonequivalent groups design can take steps to ensure that their groups are as similar as possible. In the present example, the researcher could try to select two classes at the same school, where the students in the two classes have similar scores on a standardized math test and the teachers are the same sex, are close in age, and have similar teaching styles. Taking such steps would increase the internal validity of the study because it would eliminate some of the most important confounding variables. But without true random assignment of the students to conditions, there remains the possibility of other important confounding variables that the researcher was not able to control.

## Pretest-Posttest Nonequivalent Groups Design

Another way to improve upon the posttest only nonequivalent groups design is to add a pretest. In the **pretest-posttest nonequivalent groups design** there is a treatment group that is given a pretest, receives a treatment, and then is given a posttest. But at the same time there is a nonequivalent control group that is given a pretest, does not receive the treatment, and then is given a posttest. The question, then, is not simply whether participants who receive the treatment improve, but whether they improve *more* than participants who do not receive the treatment.

Imagine, for example, that students in one school are given a pretest on their attitudes toward drugs, then are exposed to an anti-drug program, and finally, are given a posttest. Students in a similar school are given the pretest, not exposed to an anti-drug program, and finally, are given a posttest. Again, if students in the treatment condition become more negative toward drugs, this change in attitude could be an effect of the treatment, but it could also be a matter of history or maturation. If it really is an effect of the treatment, then students in the treatment condition should become more negative than students in the control condition. But if it is a matter of history (e.g., news of a celebrity drug overdose) or maturation (e.g., improved reasoning), then students in the two conditions would be likely to show similar amounts of change. This type of design does not completely eliminate the possibility of confounding variables, however. Something could occur at one of the schools but not the other (e.g., a student drug overdose), so students at the first school would be affected by it while students at the other school would not.

Returning to the example of evaluating a new measure of teaching third graders, this study could be improved by adding a pretest of students' knowledge of fractions. The changes in scores from pretest to posttest would then be evaluated and compared across conditions to determine whether one group demonstrated a bigger improvement in knowledge of fractions than another. Of course, the teachers' styles, and even the classroom environments might still be very different and might cause different levels of achievement or motivation among the students that are independent of the teaching intervention. Once again, differential history also represents a potential threat to internal validity. If asbestos is found in one of the schools causing it to be shut down for a month then this interruption in teaching could produce a difference across groups on posttest scores.

If participants in this kind of design are randomly assigned to conditions, it becomes a true between-groups experiment rather than a quasi-experiment. In fact, it is the kind of experiment that Eysenck called for–and that has now been conducted many times–to demonstrate the effectiveness of psychotherapy.

# Interrupted Time-Series Design with Nonequivalent Groups

One way to improve upon the interrupted time-series design is to add a control group. The **interrupted time-series design with nonequivalent groups** involves taking a set of measurements at intervals over a period of time both before and after an intervention of interest in two or more nonequivalent groups. Once again consider the manufacturing company that measures its workers' productivity each week for a year before and after reducing work shifts from 10 hours to 8 hours. This design could be improved by locating another manufacturing company who does not plan to change their shift length and using them as a nonequivalent control group. If productivity increased rather quickly after the shortening of the work shifts in the treatment group but productivity remained consistent in the control group, then this provides better evidence for the effectiveness of the treatment.

Similarly, in the example of examining the effects of taking attendance on student absences in a research methods course, the design could be improved by using students in another section of the research methods course as a control group. If a consistently higher number of absences was found in the treatment group before the intervention, followed by a sustained drop in absences after the treatment, while the nonequivalent control group showed consistently high absences across the semester then this would provide superior evidence for the effectiveness of the treatment in reducing absences.

# Pretest-Posttest Design With Switching Replication

Some of these nonequivalent control group designs can be further improved by adding a switching replication. Using a **pretest-posttest design with switching replication design,** nonequivalent groups are administered a pretest of the dependent variable, then one group receives a treatment while a nonequivalent control group does not receive a treatment, the dependent variable is assessed again, and then the treatment is added to the control group, and finally the dependent variable is assessed one last time.

As a concrete example, let's say we wanted to introduce an exercise intervention for the treatment of depression. We recruit one group of patients experiencing depression and a nonequivalent control group of students experiencing depression. We first measure depression levels in both groups, and then we introduce the exercise intervention to the patients experiencing depression, but we hold off on introducing the treatment to the students. We then measure depression levels in both groups. If the treatment is effective we should see a reduction in the depression levels of the patients (who received the treatment) but not in the students (who have not yet received the treatment). Finally, while the group of patients continues to engage in the treatment, we would introduce the treatment to the students with depression. Now and only now should we see the students' levels of depression decrease.

One of the strengths of this design is that it includes a built in replication. In the example given, we would get evidence for the efficacy of the treatment in two different samples (patients and students). Another strength of this design is that it provides more control over history effects. It becomes rather unlikely that some outside event would perfectly coincide with the introduction of the treatment in the first group and with the delayed introduction of the treatment in the second group. For instance, if a change in the weather occurred when we first introduced the treatment to the patients, and this explained their reductions in depression the second time that depression was measured, then we would see depression levels decrease in both the groups. Similarly, the switching replication helps to control for maturation and instrumentation. Both groups would be expected to show the same rates of spontaneous remission of depression and if the instrument for assessing depression happened to change at some point in the study the change would be consistent across both of the groups. Of course, demand characteristics, placebo effects, and experimenter expectancy effects can still be problems. But they can be controlled for using some of the methods described in Chapter 5.

## Switching Replication with Treatment Removal Design

In a basic pretest-posttest design with switching replication, the first group receives a treatment and the second group receives the same treatment a little bit later on (while the initial group continues to receive the treatment). In contrast, in a **switching replication with treatment removal design**, the treatment is removed from the first group when it is added to the second group. Once again, let's assume we first measure the depression levels of patients with depression and students with depression. Then we introduce the exercise intervention to only the patients. After they have been exposed to the exercise intervention for a week we assess depression levels again in both groups. If the intervention is effective then we should see depression levels decrease in the patient group but not the student group (because the students haven't received the treatment yet). Next, we would remove the treatment from the group of patients with depression. So we would tell them to stop exercising. At the same time, we would tell the student group to start exercising. After a week of the students exercising and the patients not exercising, we would reassess depression levels. Now if the intervention is effective we should see that the depression levels have decreased in the student group but that they have increased in the patient group (because they are no longer exercising).

Demonstrating a treatment effect in two groups staggered over time and demonstrating the reversal of the treatment effect after the treatment has been removed can provide strong evidence for the efficacy of the treatment. In addition to providing evidence for the replicability of the findings, this design can also provide evidence for whether the treatment continues to show effects after it has been withdrawn.

# 40. Key Takeaways and Exercises

## Key Takeaways

- Quasi-experimental research involves the manipulation of an independent variable without the random assignment of participants to conditions or counterbalancing of orders of conditions.
- There are three types of quasi-experimental designs that are within-subjects in nature. These are the one-group posttest only design, the one-group pretest-posttest design, and the interrupted time-series design.
- There are five types of quasi-experimental designs that are between-subjects in nature. These are the posttest only design with nonequivalent groups, the pretest-posttest design with nonequivalent groups, the interrupted time-series design with nonequivalent groups, the pretest-posttest design with switching replication, and the switching replication with treatment removal design.
- Quasi-experimental research eliminates the directionality problem because it involves the manipulation of the independent variable. However, it does not eliminate the problem of confounding variables, because it does not involve random assignment to conditions or counterbalancing. For these reasons, quasi-experimental research is generally higher in internal validity than non-experimental studies but lower than true experiments.
- Of all of the quasi-experimental designs, those that include a switching replication are highest in internal validity.

## Exercises

- Practice: Imagine that two professors decide to test the effect of giving daily quizzes on student performance in a statistics course. They decide that Professor A will give quizzes but Professor B will not. They will then compare the performance of students in their two sections on a common final exam. List five other variables that might differ between the two sections that could affect the results.
- Discussion: Imagine that a group of obese children is recruited for a study in which their weight is measured, then they participate for 3 months in a program that encourages them to be more active, and finally their weight is measured again. Explain how each of the following might affect the results:

    ◦ regression to the mean
    ◦ spontaneous remission
    ◦ history
    ◦ maturation

# CHAPTER IX
# FACTORIAL DESIGNS

In Chapter 1 we briefly described a study conducted by Simone Schnall and her colleagues, in which they found that washing one's hands leads people to view moral transgressions as less wrong (Schnall, Benton, & Harvey, 2008)[1]. In a different but related study, Schnall and her colleagues investigated whether feeling physically disgusted causes people to make harsher moral judgments (Schnall, Haidt, Clore, & Jordan, 2008)[2]. In this experiment, they manipulated participants' feelings of disgust by testing them in either a clean room or a messy room that contained dirty dishes, an overflowing wastebasket, and a chewed-up pen. They also used a self-report questionnaire to measure the amount of attention that people pay to their own bodily sensations. They called this "private body consciousness." They measured their primary dependent variable, the harshness of people's moral judgments, by describing different behaviors (e.g., eating one's dead dog, failing to return a found wallet) and having participants rate the moral acceptability of each one on a scale of 1 to 7. Finally, the researchers asked participants to rate their current level of disgust and other emotions. The primary results of this study were that participants in the messy room were, in fact, more disgusted and made harsher moral judgments than participants in the clean room—but only if they scored relatively high in private body consciousness.

The research designs we have considered so far have been simple—focusing on a question about one variable or about a relationship between two variables. But in many ways, the complex design of this experiment undertaken by Schnall and her colleagues is more typical of research in psychology. Fortunately, we have already covered the basic elements of such designs in previous chapters. In this chapter, we look closely at how and why researchers use **factorial designs,** which are experiments that include more than one independent variable.

# 41. Setting Up a Factorial Experiment

*Learning Objectives*

1. Explain why researchers often include multiple independent variables in their studies.
2. Define factorial design, and use a factorial design table to represent and interpret simple factorial designs.

Just as it is common for studies in psychology to include multiple levels of a single independent variable (placebo, new drug, old drug), it is also common for them to include multiple independent variables. Schnall and her colleagues studied the effect of both disgust and private body consciousness in the same study. Researchers' inclusion of multiple independent variables in one experiment is further illustrated by the following actual titles from various professional journals:

- The Effects of Temporal Delay and Orientation on Haptic Object Recognition
- Opening Closed Minds: The Combined Effects of Intergroup Contact and Need for Closure on Prejudice
- Effects of Expectancies and Coping on Pain-Induced Intentions to Smoke
- The Effect of Age and Divided Attention on Spontaneous Recognition
- The Effects of Reduced Food Size and Package Size on the Consumption Behavior of Restrained and Unrestrained Eaters

Just as including multiple levels of a single independent variable allows one to answer more sophisticated research questions, so too does including multiple independent variables in the same experiment. For example, instead of conducting one study on the effect of disgust on moral judgment and another on the effect of private body consciousness on moral judgment, Schnall and colleagues were able to conduct one study that addressed both questions. But including multiple independent variables also allows the researcher to answer questions about whether the effect of one independent variable depends on the level of another. This is referred to as an interaction between the independent variables. Schnall and her colleagues, for example, observed an interaction between disgust and private body consciousness because the effect of disgust depended on whether participants were high or low in private body consciousness. As we will see, interactions are often among the most interesting results in psychological research.

# Factorial Designs

## Overview

By far the most common approach to including multiple independent variables (which are often called factors) in an experiment is the factorial design. In a **factorial design**, each level of one independent variable is combined with each level of the others to produce all possible combinations. Each combination, then, becomes a condition in the experiment. Imagine, for example, an experiment on the effect of cell phone use (yes vs. no) and time of day (day vs. night) on driving ability. This is shown in the **factorial design table** in Figure 9.1. The columns of the table represent cell phone use, and the rows represent time of day. The four cells of the table represent the four possible combinations or conditions: using a cell phone during the day, not using a cell phone during the day, using a cell phone at night, and not using a cell phone at night. This particular design is referred to as a 2 × 2 (read "two-by-two") factorial design because it combines two variables, each of which has two levels.

If one of the independent variables had a third level (e.g., using a handheld cell phone, using a hands-free cell phone, and not using a cell phone), then it would be a 3 × 2 factorial design, and there would be six distinct conditions. Notice that the number of possible conditions is the product of the numbers of levels. A 2 × 2 factorial design has four conditions, a 3 × 2 factorial design has six conditions, a 4 × 5 factorial design would have 20 conditions, and so on. Also notice that each number in the notation represents one factor, one independent variable. So by looking at how many numbers are in the notation, you can determine how many independent variables there are in the experiment. 2 x 2, 3 x 3, and 2 x 3 designs all have two numbers in the notation and therefore all have two independent variables. The numerical value of each of the numbers represents the number of levels of each independent variable. A 2 means that the independent variable has two levels, a 3 means that the independent variable has three levels, a 4 means it has four levels, etc. To illustrate a 3 x 3 design has two independent variables, each with three levels, while a 2 x 2 x 2 design has three independent variables, each with two levels.

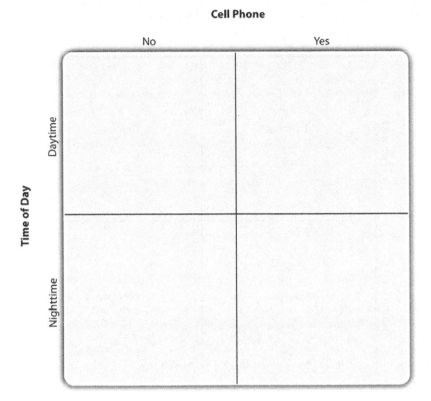

*Figure 9.1 Factorial Design Table Representing a 2 × 2 Factorial Design*

In principle, factorial designs can include any number of independent variables with any number of levels. For example, an experiment could include the type of psychotherapy (cognitive vs. behavioral), the length of the psychotherapy (2 weeks vs. 2 months), and the sex of the psychotherapist (female vs. male). This would be a 2 × 2 × 2 factorial design and would have eight conditions. Figure 9.2 shows one way to represent this design. In practice, it is unusual for there to be more than three independent variables with more than two or three levels each. This is for at least two reasons: For one, the number of conditions can quickly become unmanageable. For example, adding a fourth independent variable with three levels (e.g., therapist experience: low vs. medium vs. high) to the current example would make it a 2 × 2 × 2 × 3 factorial design with 24 distinct conditions. Second, the number of participants required to populate all of these conditions (while maintaining a reasonable ability to detect a real underlying effect) can render the design unfeasible (for more information, see the discussion about the importance of adequate statistical power in Chapter 13). As a result, in the remainder of this section, we will focus on designs with two independent variables. The general principles discussed here extend in a straightforward way to more complex factorial designs.

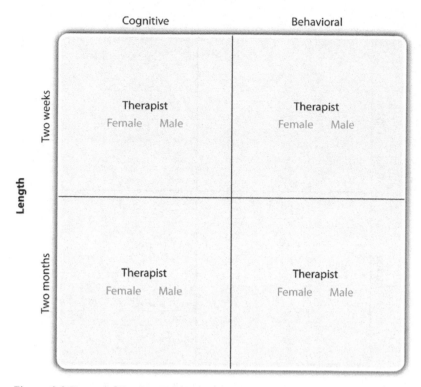

**Psychotherapy Type**

Figure 9.2 Factorial Design Table Representing a 2 × 2 × 2 Factorial Design

## Assigning Participants to Conditions

Recall that in a simple between-subjects design, each participant is tested in only one condition. In a simple within-subjects design, each participant is tested in all conditions. In a factorial experiment, the decision to take the between-subjects or within-subjects approach must be made separately for each independent variable. In a **between-subjects factorial design**, all of the independent variables are manipulated between subjects. For example, all participants could be tested either while using a cell phone *or* while not using a cell phone and either during the day *or* during the night. This would mean that each participant would be tested in one and only one condition. In a within-subjects factorial design, all of the independent variables are manipulated within subjects. All participants could be tested both while using a cell phone *and* while not using a cell phone and both during the day *and* during the night. This would mean that each participant would need to be tested in all four conditions. The advantages and disadvantages of these two approaches are the same as those discussed in Chapter 5. The between-subjects design is conceptually simpler, avoids order/carryover effects, and minimizes the time and effort of each participant. The within-subjects design is more efficient for the researcher and controls extraneous participant variables.

Since factorial designs have more than one independent variable, it is also possible to manipulate one independent variable between subjects and another within subjects. This is called a **mixed factorial design**. For example, a researcher might choose to treat cell phone use as a within-subjects factor by testing the same participants both while using a cell phone and while not using a cell phone (while counterbalancing the order of these two conditions). But they might choose to treat time of day as a between-subjects factor by testing each participant either during the day or during the night (perhaps because this only requires them to come in for testing once). Thus each participant in this mixed design would be tested in two of the four conditions.

Regardless of whether the design is between subjects, within subjects, or mixed, the actual assignment of participants to conditions or orders of conditions is typically done randomly.

## Non-Manipulated Independent Variables

In many factorial designs, one of the independent variables is a **non-manipulated independent variable**. The researcher measures it but does not manipulate it. The study by Schnall and colleagues is a good example. One independent variable was disgust, which the researchers manipulated by testing participants in a clean room or a messy room. The other was private body consciousness, a participant variable which the researchers simply measured. Another example is a study by Halle Brown and colleagues in which participants were exposed to several words that they were later asked to recall (Brown, Kosslyn, Delamater, Fama, & Barsky, 1999)[1]. The manipulated independent variable was the type of word. Some were negative health-related words (e.g., *tumor, coronary*), and others were not health related (e.g., *election, geometry*). The non-manipulated independent variable was whether participants were high or low in hypochondriasis (excessive concern with ordinary bodily symptoms). The result of this study was that the participants high in hypochondriasis were better than those low in hypochondriasis at recalling the health-related words, but they were no better at recalling the non-health-related words.

Such studies are extremely common, and there are several points worth making about them. First, non-manipulated independent variables are usually participant variables (private body consciousness, hypochondriasis, self-esteem, gender, and so on), and as such, they are by definition between-subjects factors. For example, people are either low in hypochondriasis or high in hypochondriasis; they cannot be tested in both of these conditions. Second, such studies are generally considered to be experiments as long as at least one independent variable is manipulated, regardless of how many non-manipulated independent variables are included. Third, it is important to remember that causal conclusions can only be drawn about the manipulated independent variable. For example, Schnall and her colleagues were justified in concluding that disgust affected the harshness of their participants' moral judgments because they manipulated that variable and randomly assigned participants to the clean or messy room. But they would not have been justified in concluding that participants' private body consciousness affected the harshness of their participants' moral judgments because they did not manipulate that variable. It could be, for example, that having a strict moral code and a heightened awareness of one's body are both caused by some third variable (e.g., neuroticism). Thus it is important to be aware of which variables in a study are manipulated and which are not.

# Non-Experimental Studies With Factorial Designs

Thus far we have seen that factorial experiments can include manipulated independent variables or a combination of manipulated and non-manipulated independent variables. But factorial designs can also include *only* non-manipulated independent variables, in which case they are no longer experiments but are instead non-experimental in nature. Consider a hypothetical study in which a researcher simply measures both the moods and the self-esteem of several participants—categorizing them as having either a positive or negative mood and as being either high or low in self-esteem—along with their willingness to have unprotected sexual intercourse. This can be conceptualized as a 2 × 2 factorial design with mood (positive vs. negative) and self-esteem (high vs. low) as non-manipulated between-subjects factors. Willingness to have unprotected sex is the dependent variable.

Again, because neither independent variable in this example was manipulated, it is a non-experimental study rather than an experiment. (The similar study by MacDonald and Martineau [2002][2] was an experiment because they manipulated their participants' moods.) This is important because, as always, one must be cautious about inferring causality from non-experimental studies because of the directionality and third-variable problems. For example, an effect of participants' moods on their willingness to have unprotected sex might be caused by any other variable that happens to be correlated with their moods.

# Notes

1.  Brown, H. D., Kosslyn, S. M., Delamater, B., Fama, A., & Barsky, A. J. (1999). Perceptual and memory biases for health-related information in hypochondriacal individuals. *Journal of Psychosomatic Research, 47,* 67–78.
2.  MacDonald, T. K., & Martineau, A. M. (2002). Self-esteem, mood, and intentions to use condoms: When does low self-esteem lead to risky health behaviors? *Journal of Experimental Social Psychology, 38,* 299–306.

# 42. Interpreting the Results of a Factorial Experiment

*Learning Objectives*

1. Distinguish between main effects and interactions, and recognize and give examples of each.
2. Sketch and interpret bar graphs and line graphs showing the results of studies with simple factorial designs.
3. Distinguish between main effects and simple effects, and recognize when an analysis of simple effects is required.

## Graphing the Results of Factorial Experiments

The results of factorial experiments with two independent variables can be graphed by representing one independent variable on the x-axis and representing the other by using different colored bars or lines. (The y-axis is always reserved for the dependent variable.) Figure 9.3 shows results for two hypothetical factorial experiments. The top panel shows the results of a 2 × 2 design. Time of day (day vs. night) is represented by different locations on the x-axis, and cell phone use (no vs. yes) is represented by different-colored bars. (It would also be possible to represent cell phone use on the x-axis and time of day as different-colored bars. The choice comes down to which way seems to communicate the results most clearly.) The bottom panel of Figure 9.3 shows the results of a 4 × 2 design in which one of the variables is quantitative. This variable, psychotherapy length, is represented along the x-axis, and the other variable (psychotherapy type) is represented by differently formatted lines. This is a line graph rather than a bar graph because the variable on the x-axis is quantitative with a small number of distinct levels. Line graphs are also appropriate when representing measurements made over a time interval (also referred to as time series information) on the x-axis.

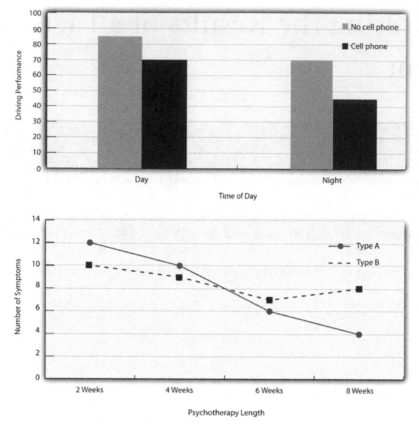

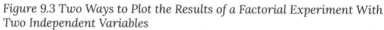

Figure 9.3 Two Ways to Plot the Results of a Factorial Experiment With Two Independent Variables

# Main Effects

In factorial designs, there are three kinds of results that are of interest: main effects, interaction effects, and simple effects. A **main effect** is the effect of one independent variable on the dependent variable—averaging across the levels of the other independent variable. Thus there is one main effect to consider for each independent variable in the study. The top panel of Figure 9.3 shows a main effect of cell phone use because driving performance was better, on average, when participants were not using cell phones than when they were. The blue bars are, on average, higher than the red bars. It also shows a main effect of time of day because driving performance was better during the day than during the night—both when participants were using cell phones and when they were not. Main effects are independent of each other in the sense that whether or not there is a main effect of one independent variable says nothing about whether or not there is a main effect of the other. The bottom panel of Figure 9.3, for example, shows a clear main effect of psychotherapy length. The longer the psychotherapy, the better it worked.

# Interactions

There is an **interaction** effect (or just "interaction") when the effect of one independent variable depends on the level of another. Although this might seem complicated, you already have an intuitive understanding of interactions. As an everyday example, assume your friend asks you to go to a movie with another friend. Your response to her is, "well it depends on which movie you are going to see and who else is coming." You really want to see the big blockbuster summer hit but have little interest in seeing the cheesy romantic comedy. In other words, there is a main effect of type of movie on your decision. If your decision to go to see either of these movies further depends on who she is bringing with her then there is an interaction. For instance, if you will go to see the cheesy romantic comedy if she brings her hot friend you want to get to know better, but you will not go to this movie if she brings anyone else, then there is an interaction. Drug interactions are another good illustration of everyday interactions. Many older men take Viagara to assist them in the bedroom, and many men take nitrates to treat angina or chest pain. So each of these drugs is beneficial on its own (there are main effects of each on older men's well-being). But the combination of these two drugs can be lethal. In other words, there is a very important interaction between Viagara and heart medication that older men need to be aware of to prevent their untimely demise.

Let's now consider some examples of interactions from research. It probably would not surprise you to hear that the effect of receiving psychotherapy is stronger among people who are highly motivated to change than among people who are not motivated to change. This is an interaction because the effect of one independent variable (whether or not one receives psychotherapy) depends on the level of another (motivation to change). Schnall and her colleagues also demonstrated an interaction because the effect of whether the room was clean or messy on participants' moral judgments depended on whether the participants were low or high in private body consciousness. If they were high in private body consciousness, then those in the messy room made harsher judgments. If they were low in private body consciousness, then whether the room was clean or messy did not matter.

In many studies, the primary research question is about an interaction. The study by Brown and her colleagues was inspired by the idea that people with hypochondriasis are especially attentive to any negative health-related information. This led to the hypothesis that people high in hypochondriasis would recall negative health-related words more accurately than people low in hypochondriasis but recall non-health-related words about the same as people low in hypochondriasis. And of course, this is exactly what happened in this study.

## Types of Interactions

The effect of one independent variable can depend on the level of the other in several different ways. First, there can be **spreading interactions**. Examples of spreading interactions are shown in the top two panels of Figure 9.4. In the top panel, independent variable "B" has an effect at level 1 of independent variable "A" (there is a difference in the height of the blue and red bars on the left side of the graph) but no effect at level 2 of independent variable "A." (there is no difference in the height of the blue and red bars on the right side of the graph). This is much like the study of Schnall and her colleagues where there was an effect of disgust for those high in private body consciousness but not for those low in private body consciousness. In the middle panel, independent variable "B" has a stronger effect at level 1 of independent variable "A" than at level 2 (there is a larger difference in the height of the blue and red bars on the left side of the graph and a smaller difference in the height of the blue and red bars on the right side of the graph). This is like the hypothetical driving example where there was a strong effect of using a cell phone at night and a weaker effect of using a cell phone during the day. So to summarize, for spreading interactions there is an effect of one independent variable at one level of the other independent variable and there is either a weak effect or no effect of that independent variable at the other level of the other independent variable.

The second type of interaction that can be found is a **cross-over interaction.** A cross-over interaction is depicted in the bottom panel of Figure 9.4, independent variable "B" again has an effect at both levels of independent variable "A," but the effects are in opposite directions. Another example of a crossover interaction comes from a study by Kathy Gilliland on the effect of caffeine on the verbal test scores of introverts and extraverts (Gilliland, 1980)[1]. Introverts perform better than extraverts when they have not ingested any caffeine. But extraverts perform better than introverts when they have ingested 4 mg of caffeine per kilogram of body weight.

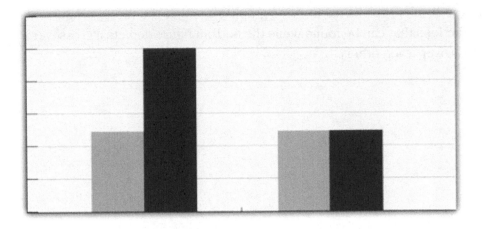

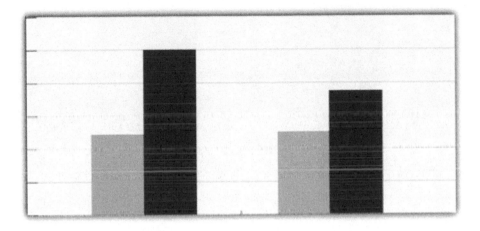

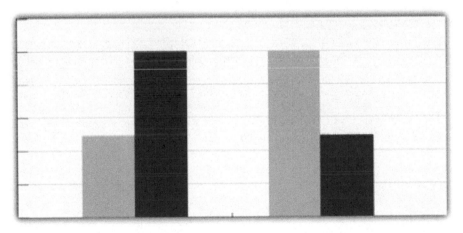

*Figure 9.4 Bar Graphs Showing Three Types of Interactions. In the top panel, one independent variable has an effect at one level of the second independent variable but not at the other. In the middle panel, one independent variable has a stronger effect at one level of the second independent variable than at the other. In the bottom panel, one independent variable has the opposite effect at one level of the second independent variable than at the other.*

Figure 9.5 shows examples of these same kinds of interactions when one of the independent variables is quantitative and the results are plotted in a line graph. Note that the top two figures depict the two kinds of spreading interactions that can be found while the bottom figure depicts a crossover interaction (the two lines literally "cross over" each other).

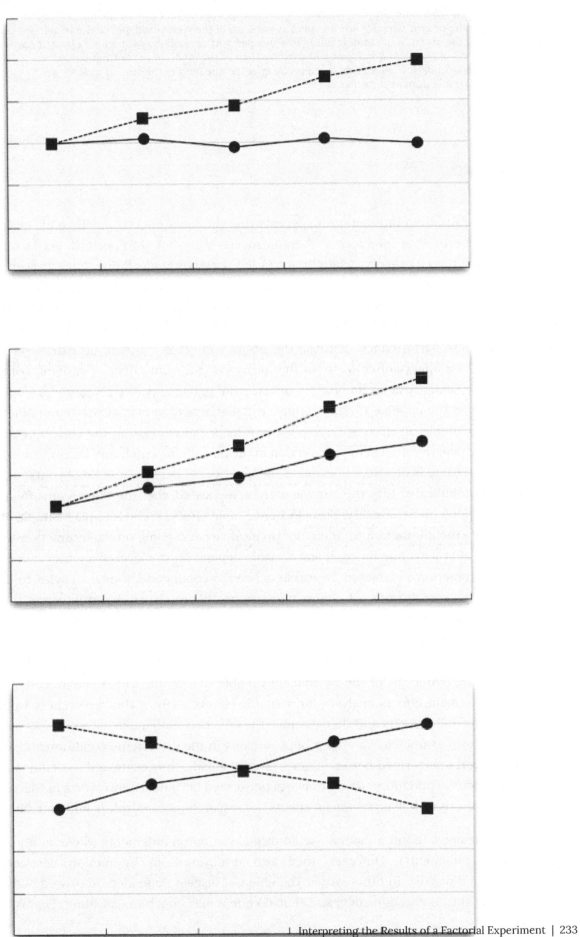

*Figure 9.5 Line Graphs Showing Different Types of Interactions. In the top panel, one independent variable has an effect at one level of the second independent variable but not at the other. In the middle panel, one independent variable has a stronger effect at one level of the second independent variable than at the other. In the bottom panel, one independent variable has the opposite effect at one level of the second independent variable than at the other.*

# Simple Effects

When researchers find an interaction it suggests that the main effects may be a bit misleading. Think of the example of a crossover interaction where introverts were found to perform better on a test of verbal test performance than extraverts when they had not ingested any caffeine, but extraverts were found to perform better than introverts when they had ingested 4 mg of caffeine per kilogram of body weight. To examine the main effect of caffeine consumption, the researchers would have averaged across introversion and extraversion and simply looked at whether overall those who ingested caffeine had better or worse verbal memory test performance. Because the positive effect of caffeine on extraverts would be wiped out by the negative effects of caffeine on the introverts, no main effect of caffeine consumption would have been found. Similarly, to examine the main effect of personality, the researchers would have averaged across the levels of the caffeine variable to look at the effects of personality (introversion vs. extraversion) independent of caffeine. In this case, the positive effects extraversion in the caffeine condition would be wiped out by the negative effects of extraversion in the no caffeine condition. Does the absence of any main effects mean that there is no effect of caffeine and no effect of personality? No of course not. The presence of the interaction indicates that the story is more complicated, that the effects of caffeine on verbal test performance depend on personality. This is where simple effects come into play. **Simple effects** are a way of breaking down the interaction to figure out precisely what is going on. An interaction simply informs us that the effects of at least one independent variable depend on the level of another independent variable. Whenever an interaction is detected, researchers need to conduct additional analyses to determine where that interaction is coming from. Of course one may be able to visualize and interpret the interaction on a graph but a simple effects analysis provides researchers with a more sophisticated means of breaking down the interaction. Specifically, a simple effects analysis allows researchers to determine the effects of each independent variable at each level of the other independent variable. So while the researchers would average across the two levels of the personality variable to examine the effects of caffeine on verbal test performance in a main effects analysis, for a simple effects analysis the researchers would examine the effects of caffeine in introverts and then examine the effects of caffeine in extraverts. As we saw previously, the researchers also examined the effects of personality in the no caffeine condition and found that in this condition introverts performed better than extraverts. Finally, they examined the effects of personality in the caffeine condition and found that extraverts performed better than introverts in this condition. For a 2 x 2 design like this, there will be two main effects the researchers can explore and four simple effects.

Schnall and colleagues found a main effect of disgust on moral judgments (those in a messy room made harsher moral judgments). However, they also discovered an interaction between private body consciousness and disgust. In other words, the effect of disgust depended on private body consciousness. The presence of this interaction suggests the main effect may be a bit misleading. That is, it is not entirely accurate to say that those in a messy room made harsher moral judgments because this was only true for half of the participants. Using simple effects analyses, they were able to further demonstrate that for people high in private body consciousness, there was an effect of disgust on moral judgments. Further, they found that for those low in private body consciousness there was no effect of disgust on moral judgments. By examining the effect of disgust at each level of body consciousness using simple effects analyses, Schnall and colleagues were able to better understand the nature of the interaction.

As described previously, Brown and colleagues found an interaction between type of words (health related or not health related) and hypochondriasis (high or low) on word recall. To break down this interaction using simple effects analyses they examined the effect of hypochondriasis at each level of word type. Specifically, they examined the effect of hypochondriasis on recall of health-related words and then they subsequently examined the effect of hypochondriasis on recall of non-health related words. They found that people high in hypochondriasis were able to recall more health-related words than people low in hypochondriasis. In contrast, there was no effect of hypochondriasis on the recall of non-health related words.

Once again examining simple effects provides a means of breaking down the interaction and therefore it is only necessary to conduct these analyses when an interaction is present. When there is no interaction then the main effects will tell the complete and accurate story. To summarize, rather than averaging across the levels of the other independent variable, as is done in a main effects analysis, simple effects analyses are used to examine the effects of each independent variable at each level of the other independent variable(s). So a researcher using a 2×2 design with four conditions would need to look at 2 main effects and 4 simple effects. A researcher using a 2×3 design with six conditions would need to look at 2 main effects and 5 simple effects, while a researcher using a 3×3 design with nine conditions would need to look at 2 main effects and 6 simple effects. As you can see, while the number of main effects depends simply on the number of independent variables included (one main effect can be explored for each independent variable), the number of simple effects analyses depends on the number of levels of the independent variables (because a separate analysis of each independent variable is conducted at each level of the other independent variable).

## Notes

1. Gilliland, K. (1980). The interactive effect of introversion-extraversion with caffeine induced arousal on verbal performance. *Journal of Research in Personality*, 14, 482–492.

# 43. Key Takeaways and Exercises

- Researchers often include multiple independent variables in their experiments. The most common approach is the factorial design, in which each level of one independent variable is combined with each level of the others to create all possible conditions.
- Each independent variable can be manipulated between-subjects or within-subjects.
- Non-manipulated independent variables (gender) can be included in factorial designs, however, they limit the causal conclusions that can be made about the effects of the non-manipulated variable on the dependent variable.
- In a factorial design, the main effect of an independent variable is its overall effect averaged across all other independent variables. There is one main effect for each independent variable.
- There is an interaction between two independent variables when the effect of one depends on the level of the other. Some of the most interesting research questions and results in psychology are specifically about interactions.
- A simple effects analysis provides a means for researchers to break down interactions by examining the effect of each independent variable at each level of the other independent variable.

*Exercises*

- Practice: Return to the five article titles presented at the beginning of this section. For each one, identify the independent variables and the dependent variable.
- Practice: Create a factorial design table for an experiment on the effects of room temperature and noise level on performance on the MCAT. Be sure to indicate whether each independent variable will be manipulated between-subjects or within-subjects and explain why.
- Practice: Sketch 8 different bar graphs to depict each of the following possible results in a 2 x 2 factorial experiment:

  - No main effect of A; no main effect of B; no interaction
  - Main effect of A; no main effect of B; no interaction
  - No main effect of A; main effect of B; no interaction
  - Main effect of A; main effect of B; no interaction
  - Main effect of A; main effect of B; interaction
  - Main effect of A; no main effect of B; interaction
  - No main effect of A; main effect of B; interaction
  - No main effect of A; no main effect of B; interaction

# CHAPTER X
# SINGLE-SUBJECT RESEARCH

Researcher Vance Hall and his colleagues were faced with the challenge of increasing the extent to which six disruptive elementary school students stayed focused on their schoolwork (Hall, Lund, & Jackson, 1968)[1]. For each of several days, the researchers carefully recorded whether or not each student was doing schoolwork every 10 seconds during a 30-minute period. Once they had established this baseline, they introduced a treatment. The treatment was that when the student was doing schoolwork, the teacher gave him or her positive attention in the form of a comment like "good work" or a pat on the shoulder. The result was that all of the students dramatically increased their time spent on schoolwork and decreased their disruptive behavior during this treatment phase. For example, a student named Robbie originally spent 25% of his time on schoolwork and the other 75% "snapping rubber bands, playing with toys from his pocket, and talking and laughing with peers" (p. 3). During the treatment phase, however, he spent 71% of his time on schoolwork and only 29% on other activities. Finally, when the researchers had the teacher stop giving positive attention, the students all decreased their studying and increased their disruptive behavior. This confirmed that it was, in fact, the positive attention that was responsible for the increase in studying. This was one of the first studies to show that attending to positive behavior—and ignoring negative behavior—could be a quick and effective way to deal with problem behavior in an applied setting.

Most of this textbook is about what can be called group research, which typically involves studying a large number of participants and combining their data to draw general conclusions about human behavior. The study by Hall and his colleagues, in contrast, is an example of single-subject research, which typically involves studying a small number of participants and focusing closely on each individual. In this chapter, we consider this alternative approach. We begin with an overview of single-subject research, including some assumptions on which it is based, who conducts it, and why they do. We then look at some basic single-subject research designs and how the data from those designs are analyzed. Finally, we consider some of the strengths and weaknesses of single-subject research as compared with group research and see how these two approaches can complement each other.

# 44. Overview of Single-Subject Research

*Learning Objectives*

1. Explain what single-subject research is, including how it differs from other types of psychological research.
2. Explain who uses single-subject research and why.

## What Is Single-Subject Research?

**Single-subject research** is a type of quantitative research that involves studying in detail the behavior of each of a small number of participants. Note that the term *single-subject* does not mean that only one participant is studied; it is more typical for there to be somewhere between two and 10 participants. (This is why single-subject research designs are sometimes called small-*n* designs, where *n* is the statistical symbol for the sample size.) Single-subject research can be contrasted with **group research**, which typically involves studying large numbers of participants and examining their behavior primarily in terms of group means, standard deviations, and so on. The majority of this textbook is devoted to understanding group research, which is the most common approach in psychology. But single-subject research is an important alternative, and it is the primary approach in some more applied areas of psychology.

Before continuing, it is important to distinguish single-subject research from case studies and other more qualitative approaches that involve studying in detail a small number of participants. As described in Chapter 6, case studies involve an in-depth analysis and description of an individual, which is typically primarily qualitative in nature. More broadly speaking, qualitative research focuses on understanding people's subjective experience by observing behavior and collecting relatively unstructured data (e.g., detailed interviews) and analyzing those data using narrative rather than quantitative techniques. Single-subject research, in contrast, focuses on understanding objective behavior through experimental manipulation and control, collecting highly structured data, and analyzing those data quantitatively.

## Assumptions of Single-Subject Research

Again, single-subject research involves studying a small number of participants and focusing intensively on the behavior of each one. But why take this approach instead of the group approach? There are several important assumptions underlying single-subject research, and it will help to consider them now.

First and foremost is the assumption that it is important to focus intensively on the behavior of individual participants. One reason for this is that group research can hide individual differences and generate results that do not represent the behavior of any individual. For example, a treatment that has a positive effect for half the people exposed to it but a negative effect for the other half would, on average, appear to have no effect at all. Single-subject research, however, would likely reveal these individual differences. A second reason to focus intensively on individuals is that sometimes it is the behavior of a particular individual that is primarily of interest. A school psychologist, for example, might be interested in changing the behavior of a particular disruptive student. Although previous published research (both single-subject and group research) is likely to provide some guidance on how to do this, conducting a study on this student would be more direct and probably more effective.

A second assumption of single-subject research is that it is important to discover causal relationships through the manipulation of an independent variable, the careful measurement of a dependent variable, and the control of extraneous variables. For this reason, single-subject research is often considered a type of experimental research with good internal validity. Recall, for example, that Hall and his colleagues measured their dependent variable (studying) many times—first under a no-treatment control condition, then under a treatment condition (positive teacher attention), and then again under the control condition. Because there was a clear increase in studying when the treatment was introduced, a decrease when it was removed, and an increase when it was reintroduced, there is little doubt that the treatment was the cause of the improvement.

A third assumption of single-subject research is that it is important to study strong and consistent effects that have biological or social importance. Applied researchers, in particular, are interested in treatments that have substantial effects on important behaviors and that can be implemented reliably in the real-world contexts in which they occur. This is sometimes referred to as **social validity** (Wolf, 1976)[1]. The study by Hall and his colleagues, for example, had good social validity because it showed strong and consistent effects of positive teacher attention on a behavior that is of obvious importance to teachers, parents, and students. Furthermore, the teachers found the treatment easy to implement, even in their often-chaotic elementary school classrooms.

## Who Uses Single-Subject Research?

Single-subject research has been around as long as the field of psychology itself. In the late 1800s, one of psychology's founders, Wilhelm Wundt, studied sensation and consciousness by focusing intensively on each of a small number of research participants. Herman Ebbinghaus's research on memory and Ivan Pavlov's research on classical conditioning are other early examples, both of which are still described in almost every introductory psychology textbook.

In the middle of the 20th century, B. F. Skinner clarified many of the assumptions underlying single-subject research and refined many of its techniques (Skinner, 1938)[2]. He and other researchers then used it to describe how rewards, punishments, and other external factors affect behavior over time. This work was carried out primarily using nonhuman subjects—mostly rats and pigeons. This approach, which Skinner called the **experimental analysis of behavior**—remains an important subfield of psychology and continues to rely almost exclusively on single-subject research. For excellent examples of this work, look at any issue of the *Journal of the Experimental Analysis of Behavior*. By the 1960s, many researchers were interested in using this approach to conduct applied research primarily with humans—a subfield now called **applied behavior analysis** (Baer, Wolf, & Risley, 1968)[3]. Applied behavior analysis plays an especially important role in contemporary research on developmental disabilities, education, organizational behavior, and health, among many other areas. Excellent examples of this work (including the study by Hall and his colleagues) can be found in the *Journal of Applied Behavior Analysis*.

Although most contemporary single-subject research is conducted from the behavioral perspective, it can in principle be used to address questions framed in terms of any theoretical perspective. For example, a studying technique based on cognitive principles of learning and memory could be evaluated by testing it on individual high school students using the single-subject approach. The single-subject approach can also be used by clinicians who take any theoretical perspective—behavioral, cognitive, psychodynamic, or humanistic—to study processes of therapeutic change with individual clients and to document their clients' improvement (Kazdin, 1982)[4].

# Notes

1. Wolf, M. (1976). Social validity: The case for subjective measurement or how applied behavior analysis is finding its heart. *Journal of Applied Behavior Analysis, 11,* 203–214.
2. Skinner, B. F. (1938). *The behavior of organisms: An experimental analysis.* New York, NY: Appleton-Century-Crofts.
3. Baer, D. M., Wolf, M. M., & Risley, T. R. (1968). Some current dimensions of applied behavior analysis. *Journal of Applied Behavior Analysis, 1,* 91–97.
4. Kazdin, A. E. (1982). *Single-case research designs: Methods for clinical and applied settings.* New York, NY: Oxford University Press.

# 45. Single-Subject Research Designs

## General Features of Single-Subject Designs

Before looking at any specific single-subject research designs, it will be helpful to consider some features that are common to most of them. Many of these features are illustrated in Figure 10.1, which shows the results of a generic single-subject study. First, the dependent variable (represented on the $y$-axis of the graph) is measured repeatedly over time (represented by the $x$-axis) at regular intervals. Second, the study is divided into distinct phases, and the participant is tested under one condition per phase. The conditions are often designated by capital letters: A, B, C, and so on. Thus Figure 10.1 represents a design in which the participant was tested first in one condition (A), then tested in another condition (B), and finally retested in the original condition (A). (This is called a reversal design and will be discussed in more detail shortly.)

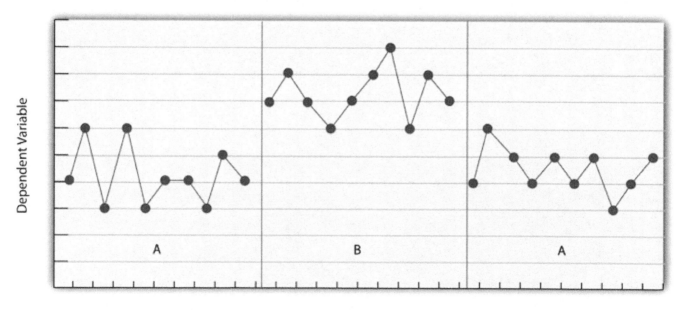

Figure 10.1 Results of a Generic Single-Subject Study Illustrating Several Principles of Single-Subject Research

Another important aspect of single-subject research is that the change from one condition to the next does not usually occur after a fixed amount of time or number of observations. Instead, it depends on the participant's behavior. Specifically, the researcher waits until the participant's behavior in one condition becomes fairly consistent from observation to observation before changing conditions. This is sometimes referred to as the **steady state strategy** (Sidman, 1960)[1]. The idea is that when the dependent variable has reached a steady state, then any change across conditions will be relatively easy to detect. Recall that we encountered this same principle when discussing experimental research more generally. The effect of an independent variable is easier to detect when the "noise" in the data is minimized.

## Reversal Designs

The most basic single-subject research design is the **reversal design**, also called the **ABA design**. During the first phase, A, a **baseline** is established for the dependent variable. This is the level of responding before any treatment is introduced, and therefore the baseline phase is a kind of control condition. When steady state responding is reached, phase B begins as the researcher introduces the treatment. There may be a period of adjustment to the treatment during which the behavior of interest becomes more variable and begins to increase or decrease. Again, the researcher waits until that dependent variable reaches a steady state so that it is clear whether and how much it has changed. Finally, the researcher removes the treatment and again waits until the dependent variable reaches a steady state. This basic reversal design can also be extended with the reintroduction of the treatment (ABAB), another return to baseline (ABABA), and so on.

The study by Hall and his colleagues employed an ABAB reversal design. Figure 10.2 approximates the data for Robbie. The percentage of time he spent studying (the dependent variable) was low during the first baseline phase, increased during the first treatment phase until it leveled off, decreased during the second baseline phase, and again increased during the second treatment phase.

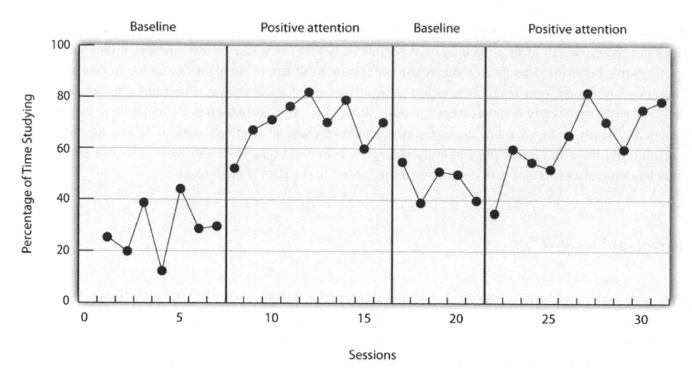

Figure 10.2 *An Approximation of the Results for Hall and Colleagues' Participant Robbie in Their ABAB Reversal Design*

Why is the reversal—the removal of the treatment—considered to be necessary in this type of design? Why use an ABA design, for example, rather than a simpler AB design? Notice that an AB design is essentially an interrupted time-series design applied to an individual participant. Recall that one problem with that design is that if the dependent variable changes after the treatment is introduced, it is not always clear that the treatment was responsible for the change. It is possible that something else changed at around the same time and that this extraneous variable is responsible for the change in the dependent variable. But if the dependent variable changes with the introduction of the treatment and then changes *back* with the removal of the treatment (assuming that the treatment does not create a permanent effect), it is much clearer that the treatment (and removal of the treatment) is the cause. In other words, the reversal greatly increases the internal validity of the study.

There are close relatives of the basic reversal design that allow for the evaluation of more than one treatment. In a **multiple-treatment reversal design**, a baseline phase is followed by separate phases in which different treatments are introduced. For example, a researcher might establish a baseline of studying behavior for a disruptive student (A), then introduce a treatment involving positive attention from the teacher (B), and then switch to a treatment involving mild punishment for not studying (C). The participant could then be returned to a baseline phase before reintroducing each treatment—perhaps in the reverse order as a way of controlling for carryover effects. This particular multiple-treatment reversal design could also be referred to as an ABCACB design.

In an **alternating treatments design**, two or more treatments are alternated relatively quickly on a regular schedule. For example, positive attention for studying could be used one day and mild punishment for not studying the next, and so on. Or one treatment could be implemented in the morning and another in the afternoon. The alternating treatments design can be a quick and effective way of comparing treatments, but only when the treatments are fast acting.

## Multiple-Baseline Designs

There are two potential problems with the reversal design—both of which have to do with the removal of the treatment. One is that if a treatment is working, it may be unethical to remove it. For example, if a treatment seemed to reduce the incidence of self-injury in a child with an intellectual delay, it would be unethical to remove that treatment just to show that the incidence of self-injury increases. The second problem is that the dependent variable may not return to baseline when the treatment is removed. For example, when positive attention for studying is removed, a student might continue to study at an increased rate. This could mean that the positive attention had a lasting effect on the student's studying, which of course would be good. But it could also mean that the positive attention was not really the cause of the increased studying in the first place. Perhaps something else happened at about the same time as the treatment—for example, the student's parents might have started rewarding him for good grades. One solution to these problems is to use a **multiple-baseline design**, which is represented in Figure 10.3. There are three different types of multiple-baseline designs which we will now consider.

## Multiple-Baseline Design Across Participants

In one version of the design, a baseline is established for each of several participants, and the treatment is then introduced for each one. In essence, each participant is tested in an AB design. The key to this design is that the treatment is introduced at a different *time* for each participant. The idea is that if the dependent variable changes when the treatment is introduced for one participant, it might be a coincidence. But if the dependent variable changes when the treatment is introduced for multiple participants—especially when the treatment is introduced at different times for the different participants—then it is unlikely to be a coincidence.

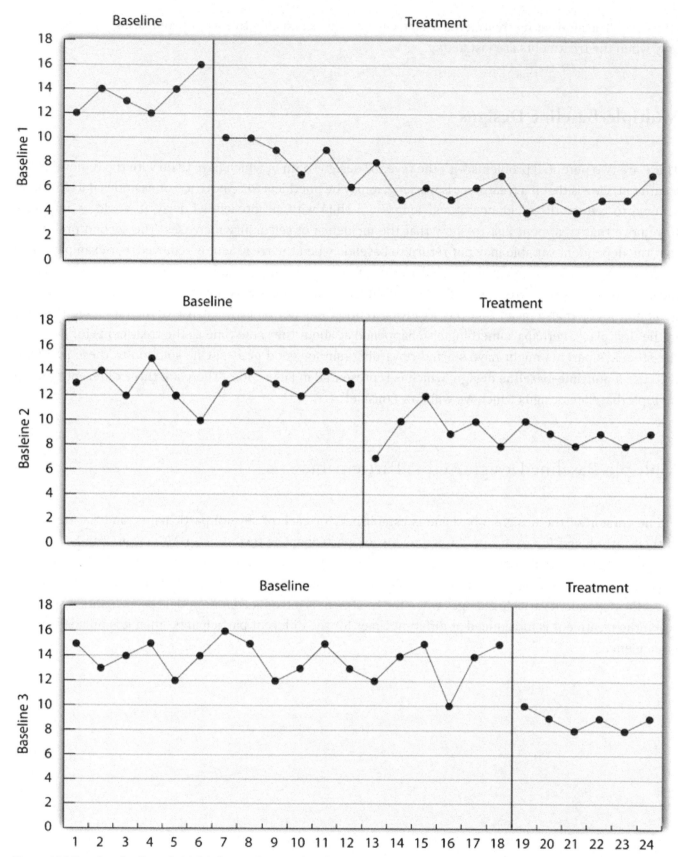

Figure 10.3 Results of a Generic Multiple-Baseline Study. The multiple baselines can be for different participants, dependent variables, or settings. The treatment is introduced at a different time on each baseline.

As an example, consider a study by Scott Ross and Robert Horner (Ross & Horner, 2009)[2]. They were interested in how a school-wide bullying prevention program affected the bullying behavior of particular problem students. At each of three different schools, the researchers studied two students who had regularly engaged in bullying. During the baseline phase, they observed the students for 10-minute periods each day during lunch recess and counted the number of aggressive behaviors they exhibited toward their peers. After 2 weeks, they implemented the program at one school. After 2 more weeks, they implemented it at the second school. And after 2 more weeks, they implemented it at the third school. They found that the number of aggressive behaviors exhibited by each student dropped shortly after the program was implemented at the student's school. Notice that if the researchers had only studied one school or if they had introduced the treatment at the same time at all three schools, then it would be unclear whether the reduction in aggressive behaviors was due to the bullying program or something else that happened at about the same time it was introduced (e.g., a holiday, a television program, a change in the weather). But with their multiple-baseline design, this kind of coincidence would have to happen three separate times—a very unlikely occurrence—to explain their results.

## Multiple-Baseline Design Across Behaviors

In another version of the multiple-baseline design, multiple baselines are established for the same participant but for different dependent variables, and the treatment is introduced at a different time for each dependent variable. Imagine, for example, a study on the effect of setting clear goals on the productivity of an office worker who has two primary tasks: making sales calls and writing reports. Baselines for both tasks could be established. For example, the researcher could measure the number of sales calls made and reports written by the worker each week for several weeks. Then the goal-setting treatment could be introduced for *one* of these tasks, and at a later time the same treatment could be introduced for the other task. The logic is the same as before. If productivity increases on one task after the treatment is introduced, it is unclear whether the treatment caused the increase. But if productivity increases on both tasks after the treatment is introduced—especially when the treatment is introduced at two different times—then it seems much clearer that the treatment was responsible.

## Multiple-Baseline Design Across Settings

In yet a third version of the multiple-baseline design, multiple baselines are established for the same participant but in different settings. For example, a baseline might be established for the amount of time a child spends reading during his free time at school and during his free time at home. Then a treatment such as positive attention might be introduced first at school and later at home. Again, if the dependent variable changes after the treatment is introduced in each setting, then this gives the researcher confidence that the treatment is, in fact, responsible for the change.

# Data Analysis in Single-Subject Research

In addition to its focus on individual participants, single-subject research differs from group research in the way the data are typically analyzed. As we have seen throughout the book, group research involves combining data across participants. Group data are described using statistics such as means, standard deviations, correlation coefficients, and so on to detect general patterns. Finally, inferential statistics are used to help decide whether the result for the sample is likely to generalize to the population. Single-subject research, by contrast, relies heavily on a very different approach called **visual inspection**. This means plotting individual participants' data as shown throughout this chapter, looking carefully at those data, and making judgments about whether and to what extent the independent variable had an effect on the dependent variable. Inferential statistics are typically not used.

In visually inspecting their data, single-subject researchers take several factors into account. One of them is changes in the **level** of the dependent variable from condition to condition. If the dependent variable is much higher or much lower in one condition than another, this suggests that the treatment had an effect. A second factor is **trend**, which refers to gradual increases or decreases in the dependent variable across observations. If the dependent variable begins increasing or decreasing with a change in conditions, then again this suggests that the treatment had an effect. It can be especially telling when a trend changes directions—for example, when an unwanted behavior is increasing during baseline but then begins to decrease with the introduction of the treatment. A third factor is **latency**, which is the time it takes for the dependent variable to begin changing after a change in conditions. In general, if a change in the dependent variable begins shortly after a change in conditions, this suggests that the treatment was responsible.

In the top panel of Figure 10.4, there are fairly obvious changes in the level and trend of the dependent variable from condition to condition. Furthermore, the latencies of these changes are short; the change happens immediately. This pattern of results strongly suggests that the treatment was responsible for the changes in the dependent variable. In the bottom panel of Figure 10.4, however, the changes in level are fairly small. And although there appears to be an increasing trend in the treatment condition, it looks as though it might be a continuation of a trend that had already begun during baseline. This pattern of results strongly suggests that the treatment was not responsible for any changes in the dependent variable—at least not to the extent that single-subject researchers typically hope to see.

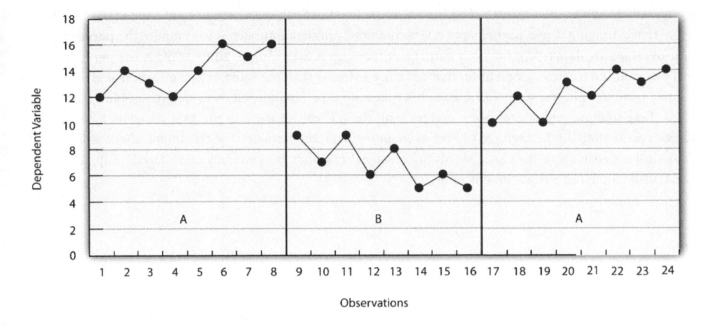

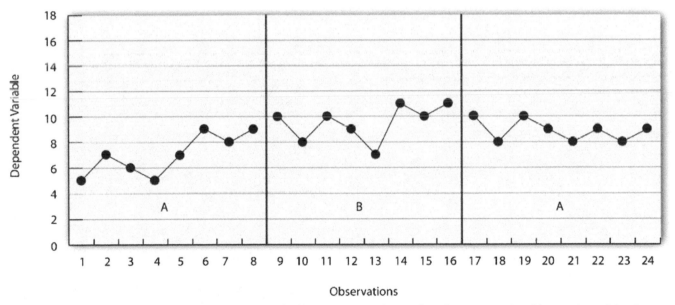

Figure 10.4 Results of a Generic Single-Subject Study Illustrating Level, Trend, and Latency. Visual inspection of the data suggests an effective treatment in the top panel but an ineffective treatment in the bottom panel.

The results of single-subject research can also be analyzed using statistical procedures—and this is becoming more common. There are many different approaches, and single-subject researchers continue to debate which are the most useful. One approach parallels what is typically done in group research. The mean and standard deviation of each participant's responses under each condition are computed and compared, and inferential statistical tests such as the *t* test or analysis of variance are applied (Fisch, 2001)[3]. (Note that averaging *across* participants is less common.) Another approach is to compute the **percentage of non-overlapping data** (PND) for each participant (Scruggs & Mastropieri, 2001)[4]. This is the percentage of responses in the treatment condition that are more extreme than the most extreme response in a relevant control condition. In the study of Hall and his colleagues, for example, all measures of Robbie's study time in the first treatment condition were greater than the highest measure in the first baseline, for a PND of 100%. The greater the percentage of non-overlapping data, the stronger the treatment effect. Still, formal statistical approaches to data analysis in single-subject research are generally considered a supplement to visual inspection, not a replacement for it.

# Notes

1.  Sidman, M. (1960). *Tactics of scientific research: Evaluating experimental data in psychology*. Boston, MA: Authors Cooperative.

2.  Ross, S. W., & Horner, R. H. (2009). Bully prevention in positive behavior support. *Journal of Applied Behavior Analysis, 42,* 747–759.

3.  Fisch, G. S. (2001). Evaluating data from behavioral analysis: Visual inspection or statistical models. *Behavioral Processes, 54,* 137–154.

4.  Scruggs, T. E., & Mastropieri, M. A. (2001). How to summarize single-participant research: Ideas and applications. *Exceptionality, 9,* 227–244.

# 46. The Single-Subject Versus Group "Debate"

*Learning Objectives*

1. Explain some of the points of disagreement between advocates of single-subject research and advocates of group research.
2. Identify several situations in which single-subject research would be appropriate and several others in which group research would be appropriate.

Single-subject research is similar to group research—especially experimental group research—in many ways. They are both quantitative approaches that try to establish causal relationships by manipulating an independent variable, measuring a dependent variable, and controlling extraneous variables. But there are important differences between these approaches too, and these differences sometimes lead to disagreements. It is worth addressing the most common points of disagreement between single-subject researchers and group researchers and how these disagreements can be resolved. As we will see, single-subject research and group research are probably best conceptualized as complementary approaches.

## Data Analysis

One set of disagreements revolves around the issue of data analysis. Some advocates of group research worry that visual inspection is inadequate for deciding whether and to what extent a treatment has affected a dependent variable. One specific concern is that visual inspection is not sensitive enough to detect weak effects. A second is that visual inspection can be unreliable, with different researchers reaching different conclusions about the same set of data (Danov & Symons, 2008)[1]. A third is that the results of visual inspection—an overall judgment of whether or not a treatment was effective—cannot be clearly and efficiently summarized or compared across studies (unlike the measures of relationship strength typically used in group research).

In general, single-subject researchers share these concerns. However, they also argue that their use of the steady state strategy, combined with their focus on strong and consistent effects, minimizes most of them. If the effect of a treatment is difficult to detect by visual inspection because the effect is weak or the data are noisy, then single-subject researchers look for ways to increase the strength of the effect or reduce the noise in the data by controlling extraneous variables (e.g., by administering the treatment more consistently). If the effect is still difficult to detect, then they are likely to consider it neither strong enough nor consistent enough to be of further interest. Many single-subject researchers also point out that statistical analysis is becoming increasingly common and that many of them are using this as a supplement to visual inspection—especially for the purpose of comparing results across studies (Scruggs & Mastropieri, 2001)[2].

Turning the tables, some advocates of single-subject research worry about the way that group researchers analyze their data. Specifically, they point out that focusing on group means can be highly misleading. Again, imagine that a treatment has a strong positive effect on half the people exposed to it and an equally strong negative effect on the other half. In a traditional between-subjects experiment, the positive effect on half the participants in the treatment condition would be statistically cancelled out by the negative effect on the other half. The mean for the treatment group would then be the same as the mean for the control group, making it seem as though the treatment had no effect when in fact it had a strong effect on every single participant!

But again, group researchers share this concern. Although they do focus on group statistics, they also emphasize the importance of examining distributions of individual scores. For example, if some participants were positively affected by a treatment and others negatively affected by it, this would produce a bimodal distribution of scores and could be detected by looking at a histogram of the data. The use of within-subjects designs is another strategy that allows group researchers to observe effects at the individual level and even to specify what percentage of individuals exhibit strong, medium, weak, and even negative effects. Finally, factorial designs can be used to examine whether the effects of an independent variable on a dependent variable differ in different groups of participants (introverts vs. extraverts).

## External Validity

The second issue about which single-subject and group researchers sometimes disagree has to do with external validity—the ability to generalize the results of a study beyond the people and specific situation actually studied. In particular, advocates of group research point out the difficulty in knowing whether results for just a few participants are likely to generalize to others in the population. Imagine, for example, that in a single-subject study, a treatment has been shown to reduce self-injury for each of two children with intellectual disabilities. Even if the effect is strong for these two children, how can one know whether this treatment is likely to work for other children with intellectual delays?

Again, single-subject researchers share this concern. In response, they note that the strong and consistent effects they are typically interested in—even when observed in small samples—are likely to generalize to others in the population. Single-subject researchers also note that they place a strong emphasis on replicating their research results. When they observe an effect with a small sample of participants, they typically try to replicate it with another small sample—perhaps with a slightly different type of participant or under slightly different conditions. Each time they observe similar results, they rightfully become more confident in the generality of those results. Single-subject researchers can also point to the fact that the principles of classical and operant conditioning—most of which were discovered using the single-subject approach—have been successfully generalized across an incredibly wide range of species and situations.

And, once again turning the tables, single-subject researchers have concerns of their own about the external validity of group research. One extremely important point they make is that studying large groups of participants does not entirely solve the problem of generalizing to other *individuals*. Imagine, for example, a treatment that has been shown to have a small positive effect on average in a large group study. It is likely that although many participants exhibited a small positive effect, others exhibited a large positive effect, and still others exhibited a small negative effect. When it comes to applying this treatment to another large *group*, we can be fairly sure that it will have a small effect on average. But when it comes to applying this treatment to another *individual*, we cannot be sure whether it will have a small, a large, or even a negative effect. Another point that single-subject researchers make is that group researchers also face a similar problem when they study a single situation and then generalize their results to other situations. For example, researchers who conduct a study on the effect of cell phone use on drivers on a closed oval track probably want to apply their results to drivers in many other real-world driving situations. But notice that this requires generalizing from a single situation to a population of situations. Thus the ability to generalize is based on much more than just the sheer number of participants one has studied. It requires a careful consideration of the similarity of the participants *and* situations studied to the population of participants and situations to which one wants to generalize (Shadish, Cook, & Campbell, 2002)[3].

## Single-Subject and Group Research as Complementary Methods

As with quantitative and qualitative research, it is probably best to conceptualize single-subject research and group research as complementary methods that have different strengths and weaknesses and that are appropriate for answering different kinds of research questions (Kazdin, 1982)[4]. Single-subject research is particularly good for testing the effectiveness of treatments on individuals when the focus is on strong, consistent, and biologically or socially important effects. It is also especially useful when the behavior of particular individuals is of interest. Clinicians who work with only one individual at a time may find that it is their only option for doing systematic quantitative research.

Group research, on the other hand, is ideal for testing the effectiveness of treatments at the group level. Among the advantages of this approach is that it allows researchers to detect weak effects, which can be of interest for many reasons. For example, finding a weak treatment effect might lead to refinements of the treatment that eventually produce a larger and more meaningful effect. Group research is also good for studying interactions between treatments and participant characteristics. For example, if a treatment is effective for those who are high in motivation to change and ineffective for those who are low in motivation to change, then a group design can detect this much more efficiently than a single-subject design. Group research is also necessary to answer questions that cannot be addressed using the single-subject approach, including questions about independent variables that cannot be manipulated (e.g., number of siblings, extraversion, culture).

Finally, it is important to understand that the single-subject and group approaches represent different research traditions. This factor is probably the most important one affecting which approach a researcher uses. Researchers in the experimental analysis of behavior and applied behavior analysis learn to conceptualize their research questions in ways that are amenable to the single-subject approach. Researchers in most other areas of psychology learn to conceptualize their research questions in ways that are amenable to the group approach. At the same time, there are many topics in psychology in which research from the two traditions have informed each other and been successfully integrated. One example is research suggesting that both animals and humans have an innate "number sense"–an awareness of how many objects or events of a particular type have they have experienced without actually having to count them (Dehaene, 2011)[5]. Single-subject research with rats and birds and group research with human infants have shown strikingly similar abilities in those populations to discriminate small numbers of objects and events. This number sense–which probably evolved long before humans did–may even be the foundation of humans' advanced mathematical abilities.

## The Principle of Converging Evidence

Now that you have been introduced to many of the most commonly used research methods in psychology it should be readily apparent that no design is perfect. Every research design has strengths and weakness. True experiments typically have high internal validity but may have problems with external validity, while non-experimental research (e.g., correlational research) often has good external validity but poor internal validity. Each study brings us closer to the truth but no single study can ever be considered definitive. This is one reason why, in science, we say there is no such thing as scientific proof, there is only scientific evidence.

While the media will often try to reach strong conclusions on the basis of the findings of one study, scientists focus on evaluating a body of research. Scientists evaluate theories not by waiting for the perfect experiment but by looking at the overall trends in a number of partially flawed studies. The idea of **converging evidence** tells us to examine the pattern of flaws running through the research literature because the nature of this pattern can either support or undermine the conclusions we wish to draw. Suppose the findings from a number of different studies were largely consistent in supporting a particular conclusion. If all of the studies were flawed in a similar way, for example, if all of the studies were correlational and contained the third variable problem and the directionality problem, this would undermine confidence in the conclusions drawn because the consistency of the outcome may simply have resulted from a particular flaw that all of the studies shared. On the other hand, if all of the studies were flawed in different ways and the weakness of some of the studies were the strength of others (the low external validity of a true experiment was balanced by the high external validity of a correlational study), then we could be more confident in our conclusions.

While there are fundamental tradeoffs in different research methods, the diverse set of approaches used by psychologists have complementary strengths that allow us to search for converging evidence. We can reach meaningful conclusions and come closer to understanding truth by examining a large number of different studies each with different strengths and weakness. If the result of a large number of studies all conducted using different designs converge on the same conclusion then our confidence in that conclusion can be increased dramatically. In science, we strive for progress, not perfection.

## Notes

1.  Danov, S. E., & Symons, F. E. (2008). A survey evaluation of the reliability of visual inspection and functional analysis

graphs. *Behavior Modification, 32,* 828–839.

2.  Scruggs, T. E., & Mastropieri, M. A. (2001). How to summarize single-participant research: Ideas and applications. *Exceptionality, 9,* 227–244.

3.  Shadish, W. R., Cook, T. D., & Campbell, D. T. (2002). *Experimental and quasi-experimental designs for generalized causal inference.* Boston, MA: Houghton Mifflin.

4.  Kazdin, A. E. (1982). *Single-case research designs: Methods for clinical and applied settings.* New York, NY: Oxford University Press.

5.  Dehaene, S. (2011). *The number sense: How the mind creates mathematics* (2nd ed.). New York, NY: Oxford.

# 47. Key Takeaways and Exercises

- Single-subject research—which involves testing a small number of participants and focusing intensively on the behavior of each individual—is an important alternative to group research in psychology.
- Single-subject studies must be distinguished from qualitative research on a single person or small number of individuals. Unlike more qualitative research, single-subject research focuses on understanding objective behavior through experimental manipulation and control, collecting highly structured data, and analyzing those data quantitatively.
- Single-subject research has been around since the beginning of the field of psychology. Today it is most strongly associated with the behavioral theoretical perspective, but it can in principle be used to study behavior from any perspective.
- Single-subject research designs typically involve measuring the dependent variable repeatedly over time and changing conditions (e.g., from baseline to treatment) when the dependent variable has reached a steady state. This approach allows the researcher to see whether changes in the independent variable are causing changes in the dependent variable.
- In a reversal design, the participant is tested in a baseline condition, then tested in a treatment condition, and then returned to baseline. If the dependent variable changes with the introduction of the treatment and then changes back with the return to baseline, this provides strong evidence of a treatment effect.
- In a multiple-baseline design, baselines are established for different participants, different dependent variables, or different settings—and the treatment is introduced at a different time on each baseline. If the introduction of the treatment is followed by a change in the dependent variable on each baseline, this provides strong evidence of a treatment effect.
- Single-subject researchers typically analyze their data by graphing them and making judgments about whether the independent variable is affecting the dependent variable based on level, trend, and latency.
- Differences between single-subject research and group research sometimes lead to disagreements between single-subject and group researchers. These disagreements center on the issues of data analysis and external validity (especially generalization to other people).
- Single-subject research and group research are probably best seen as complementary methods, with different strengths and weaknesses, that are appropriate for answering different kinds of research questions.

- Practice: Find and read a published article in psychology that reports new single-subject research. (An archive of articles published in the Journal of Applied Behavior Analysis can be found at http://www.ncbi.nlm.nih.gov/pmc/journals/309/) Write a short summary of the study.

- Practice: Design a simple single-subject study (using either a reversal or multiple-baseline design) to answer the following questions. Be sure to specify the treatment, operationally define the dependent variable, decide when and where the observations will be made, and so on.

  - Does positive attention from a parent increase a child's tooth-brushing behavior?
  - Does self-testing while studying improve a student's performance on weekly spelling tests?
  - Does regular exercise help relieve depression?

- Practice: Create a graph that displays the hypothetical results for the study you designed in Exercise 1. Write a paragraph in which you describe what the results show. Be sure to comment on level, trend, and latency.
- Discussion: Imagine you have conducted a single-subject study showing a positive effect of a treatment on the behavior of a man with social anxiety disorder. Your research has been criticized on the grounds that it cannot be generalized to others. How could you respond to this criticism?
- Discussion: Imagine you have conducted a group study showing a positive effect of a treatment on the behavior of a group of people with social anxiety disorder, but your research has been criticized on the grounds that "average" effects cannot be generalized to individuals. How could you respond to this criticism?
- Practice: Redesign as a group study the study by Hall and his colleagues described at the beginning of this chapter, and list the strengths and weaknesses of your new study compared with the original study.
- Practice: The generation effect refers to the fact that people who generate information as they are learning it (e.g., by self-testing) recall it better later than do people who simply review information. Design a single-subject study on the generation effect applied to university students learning brain anatomy.

# CHAPTER XI
# PRESENTING YOUR RESEARCH

Research is complete only when the results are shared with the scientific community.
-American Psychological Association

Imagine that you have identified an interesting research question, reviewed the relevant literature, designed and conducted an empirical study, analyzed the data, and drawn your conclusions. There is still one more step in the process of conducting scientific research. It is time to add your research to the literature so that others can learn from it and build on it. Remember that science is a social and cumulative process—a large-scale collaboration among many researchers distributed across space and time. For this reason, it could be argued that unless you make your research public in some form, you are not really engaged in science at all.

In this chapter, we look at how to present your research effectively. We begin with a discussion of American Psychological Association (APA) style—the primary approach to writing taken by researchers in psychology and related fields. Then we consider how to write an APA-style empirical research report. Finally, we look at some of the many other ways in which researchers present their work, including review and theoretical articles, theses and other student papers, and talks and posters at professional meetings.

# 48. American Psychological Association (APA) Style

*Learning Objectives*

1. Define APA style and list several of its most important characteristics.
2. Identify three levels of APA style and give examples of each.
3. Identify multiple sources of information about APA style.

## What Is APA Style?

APA style is a set of guidelines for writing in psychology and related fields. These guidelines are set down in the **Publication Manual of the American Psychological Association** (APA, 2010)[1]. The *Publication Manual* originated in 1929 as a short journal article that provided basic standards for preparing manuscripts to be submitted for publication (Bentley et al., 1929)[2]. It was later expanded and published as a book by the association and is now in its sixth edition. The primary purpose of APA style is to facilitate scientific communication by promoting clarity of expression and by standardizing the organization and content of research articles and book chapters. It is easier to write about research when you know what information to present, the order in which to present it, and even the style in which to present it. Likewise, it is easier to read about research when it is presented in familiar and expected ways.

APA style is best thought of as a "genre" of writing that is appropriate for presenting the results of psychological research—especially in academic and professional contexts. It is not synonymous with "good writing" in general. You would not write a literary analysis for an English class, even if it were based on psychoanalytic concepts, in APA style. You would write it in Modern Language Association (MLA) style instead. And you would not write a newspaper article, even if it were about a new breakthrough in behavioral neuroscience, in APA style. You would write it in Associated Press (AP) style instead. At the same time, you would not write an empirical research report in MLA style, in AP style, or in the style of a romance novel, an email to a friend, or a shopping list. You would write it in APA style. Part of being a good writer in general is adopting a style that is appropriate to the writing task at hand, and for writing about psychological research, this is APA style.

# The Levels of APA Style

Because APA style consists of a large number and variety of guidelines—the *Publication Manual* is nearly 300 pages long—it can be useful to think about it in terms of three basic levels. The first is the overall organization of an article (which is covered in Chapter 2 "Manuscript Structure and Content" of the *Publication Manual*). Empirical research reports, in particular, have several distinct sections that always appear in the same order:

- **Title page**. Presents the article title and author names and affiliations.
- **Abstract**. Summarizes the research.
- **Introduction**. Describes previous research and the rationale for the current study.
- **Method**. Describes how the study was conducted.
- **Results**. Describes the results of the study.
- **Discussion**. Summarizes the study and discusses its implications.
- **References**. Lists the references cited throughout the article.

The second level of APA style can be referred to as **high-level style** (covered in Chapter 3 "Writing Clearly and Concisely" of the *Publication Manual*), which includes guidelines for the clear expression of ideas. There are two important themes here. One is that APA-style writing is formal rather than informal. It adopts a tone that is appropriate for communicating with professional colleagues—other researchers and practitioners—who share an interest in the topic. Beyond this shared interest, however, these colleagues are not necessarily similar to the writer or to each other. A graduate student in British Columbia might be writing an article that will be read by a young psychotherapist in Toronto and a respected professor of psychology in Tokyo. Thus formal writing avoids slang, contractions, pop culture references, humor, and other elements that would be acceptable in talking with a friend or in writing informally.

The second theme of high-level APA style is that it is straightforward. This means that it communicates ideas as simply and clearly as possible, putting the focus on the ideas themselves and not on how they are communicated. Thus APA-style writing minimizes literary devices such as metaphor, imagery, irony, suspense, and so on. Again, humor is kept to a minimum. Sentences are short and direct. Technical terms must be used, but they are used to improve communication, not simply to make the writing sound more "scientific." For example, if participants immersed their hands in a bucket of ice water, it is better just to write this than to write that they "were subjected to a pain-inducement apparatus." At the same time, however, there is no better way to communicate that a between-subjects design was used than to use the term "between-subjects design."

## APA Style and the Values of Psychology

Robert Madigan and his colleagues have argued that APA style has a purpose that often goes unrecognized

(Madigan, Johnson, & Linton, 1995)[3]. Specifically, it promotes psychologists' scientific values and assumptions. From this perspective, many features of APA style that at first seem arbitrary actually make good sense. Following are several features of APA-style writing and the scientific values or assumptions they reflect.

| APA style feature | Scientific value or assumption |
| --- | --- |
| There are very few direct quotations of other researchers. | The phenomena and theories of psychology are objective and do not depend on the specific words a particular researcher used to describe them. |
| Criticisms are directed at other researchers' work but not at them personally. | The focus of scientific research is on drawing general conclusions about the world, not on the personalities of particular researchers. |
| There are many references and reference citations. | Scientific research is a large-scale collaboration among many researchers. |
| Empirical research reports are organized with specific sections in a fixed order. | There is an ideal approach to conducting empirical research in psychology (even if this ideal is not always achieved in actual research). |
| Researchers tend to "hedge" their conclusions, e.g., "The results *suggest that...*" | Scientific knowledge is tentative and always subject to revision based on new empirical results. |

Another important element of high-level APA style is the avoidance of language that is biased against particular groups. This is not only to avoid offending people—why would you want to offend people who are interested in your work?—but also for the sake of scientific objectivity and accuracy. For example, the term *sexual orientation* should be used instead of *sexual preference* because people do not generally experience their orientation as a "preference," nor is it as easily changeable as this term suggests (APA Committee on Lesbian, Gay, and Bisexual Concerns Joint Task Force on Guidelines for Psychotherapy With Lesbian, Gay, and Bisexual Clients, 2000)[4].

The general principles for avoiding biased language are fairly simple. First, be sensitive to labels by avoiding terms that are offensive or have negative connotations. This includes avoiding terms that identify people with a disorder or other problem they happen to have. Instead, refer to the individual, what the APA *Publication Manual* refers to as putting the "person first." For example, *people diagnosed with schizophrenia* is better than *schizophrenics*. Second, use more specific terms rather than more general ones. For example, *Chinese Americans* is better than *Asian Americans* if everyone in the group is, in fact, Chinese American. Third, avoid objectifying research participants. Instead, acknowledge their active contribution to the research. For example, "The *students completed* the questionnaire" is better than "The *subjects were administered* the questionnaire." Note that this principle also makes for clearer, more engaging writing. Table 11.1 shows several more examples that follow these general principles.

**Table 11.1 Examples of Avoiding Biased Language**

| Instead of... | Use... |
|---|---|
| man, men | men and women, people |
| firemen | firefighters |
| homosexuals, gays, bisexuals | lesbians, gay men, bisexual men, bisexual women |
| minority | specific group label (e.g., African American) |
| neurotics | people scoring high in neuroticism |
| special children | children with learning disabilities |

The previous edition of the *Publication Manual* strongly discouraged the use of the term *subjects* (except for nonhumans) and strongly encouraged the use of *participants* instead. The current edition, however, acknowledges that *subjects* can still be appropriate in referring to human participants in areas in which it has traditionally been used (e.g., basic memory research). But it also encourages the use of more specific terms when possible: *university students*, *children*, *respondents*, and so on.

The third level of APA style can be referred to as **low-level style** (which is covered in Chapter 4 "The Mechanics of Style" through Chapter 7 "Reference Examples" of the *Publication Manual*). Low-level style includes all the specific guidelines pertaining to spelling, grammar, references and reference citations, numbers and statistics, figures and tables, and so on. There are so many low-level guidelines that even experienced professionals need to consult the *Publication Manual* from time to time. Table 11.2 contains some of the most common types of APA style errors based on an analysis of manuscripts submitted to one professional journal over a 6-year period (Onwuegbuzie, Combs, Slate, & Frels, 2010)[5]. These errors were committed by professional researchers but are probably similar to those that students commit the most too. See also Note 11.8 "Online APA Style Resources" in this section and, of course, the *Publication Manual* itself.

**Table 11.2 Top 10 APA Style Errors**

| Error type | Example |
|---|---|
| 1. Use of numbers | Failing to use numerals for 10 and above |
| 2. Hyphenation | Failing to hyphenate compound adjectives that precede a noun (e.g., "role playing technique" should be "role-playing technique") |
| 3. Use of *et al.* | Failing to use it after a reference is cited for the first time |
| 4. Headings | Not capitalizing headings correctly |
| 5. Use of *since* | Using *since* to mean *because* |
| 6. Tables and figures | Not formatting them in APA style; repeating information that is already given in the text |
| 7. Use of commas | Failing to use a comma before *and* or *or* in a series of three or more elements |
| 8. Use of abbreviations | Failing to spell out a term completely before introducing an abbreviation for it |
| 9. Spacing | Not consistently double-spacing between lines |
| 10. Use of "&" in references | Using & in the text or *and* in parentheses |

# APA-Style References and Citations

Because science is a large-scale collaboration among researchers, references to the work of other researchers are extremely important. Their importance is reflected in the extensive and detailed set of rules for formatting and using them.

## References

At the end of an APA-style article or book chapter is a list that contains **references** to all the works cited in the text (and *only* the works cited in the text). The reference list begins on its own page, with the heading "References," centered in upper and lower case. The references themselves are then listed alphabetically according to the last names of the first named author for each citation. (As in the rest of an APA-style manuscript, *everything* is double-spaced.) Many different kinds of works might be cited in APA-style articles and book chapters, including magazine articles, websites, government documents, and even television shows. Of course, you should consult the *Publication Manual* or Online APA Style Resources for details on how to format them. Here we will focus on formatting references for the three most common kinds of works cited in APA style: journal articles, books, and book chapters.

## Journal Articles

For journal articles, the generic format for a reference is as follows:

Author, A. A., Author, B. B., & Author, C. C. (year). Title of article. *Title of Journal, volume*(issue), pp-pp. doi:xx.xxxxxxxxxx

Here is a concrete example:

Adair, J. G., & Vohra, N. (2003). The explosion of knowledge, references, and citations: Psychology's unique response to a crisis. *American Psychologist, 58*(1), 15–23. doi: 10.1037/0003-066X.58.1.15

There are several things to notice here. The reference includes a hanging indent. That is, the first line of the reference is not indented but all subsequent lines are. The authors' names appear in the same order as on the article, which reflects the authors' relative contributions to the research. Only the authors' last names and initials appear, and the names are separated by commas with an ampersand (&) between the last two. This is true even when there are only two authors. Only the first word of the article title is capitalized. The only exceptions are for words that are proper nouns or adjectives (e.g., "Freudian") or if there is a subtitle, in which case the first word of the subtitle is also capitalized. In the journal title, however, all the important words are capitalized. The journal title and volume number are italicized; however, the issue number (listed within parentheses) is not. At the very end of the reference is the digital object identifier (DOI), which provides a permanent link to the location of the article on the Internet. Include this if it is available. It can generally be found in the record for the item on an electronic database (e.g., PsycINFO) and is usually displayed on the first page of the published article.

## Books

For a book, the generic format and a concrete example are as follows:

Author, A. A. (year). *Title of book.* Location: Publisher.

Kashdan, T., & Biswas-Diener, R. (2014). *The upside of your dark side.* New York, NY: Hudson Street Press.

## Book Chapters

For a chapter in an edited book, the generic format and a concrete example are as follows:

> Author, A. A., Author, B. B., & Author, C. C. (year). Title of chapter. In A. A. Editor, B. B. Editor, & C. C. Editor (Eds.), *Title of book* (pp. xxx–xxx). Location: Publisher.

> Lilienfeld, S. O., & Lynn, S. J. (2003). Dissociative identity disorder: Multiple personalities, multiple controversies. In S. O. Lilienfeld, S. J. Lynn, & J. M. Lohr (Eds.), *Science and pseudoscience in clinical psychology* (pp. 109–142). New York, NY: Guilford Press.

Notice that references for books and book chapters are similar to those for journal articles, but there are several differences too. For an edited book, the names of the editors appear with their first and middle initials followed by their last names (not the other way around)—with the abbreviation "Eds." (or "Ed.," if there is only one) appearing in parentheses immediately after the final editor's name. Only the first word of a book title is capitalized (with the exceptions noted for article titles), and the entire title is italicized. For a chapter in an edited book, the page numbers of the chapter appear in parentheses after the book title with the abbreviation "pp." Finally, both formats end with the location of publication and the publisher, separated by a colon.

## Reference Citations

When you refer to another researcher's idea, you must include a **reference citation** (in the text) to the work in which that idea originally appeared and a full reference to that work in the reference list. What counts as an idea that must be cited? In general, this includes phenomena discovered by other researchers, theories they have developed, hypotheses they have derived, and specific methods they have used (e.g., specific questionnaires or stimulus materials). Citations should also appear for factual information that is not common knowledge so that other researchers can check that information for themselves. For example, in an article on the effect of cell phone usage on driving ability, the writer might cite official statistics on the number of cell phone–related accidents that occur each year. Among the ideas that do not need citations are widely shared methodological and statistical concepts (e.g., between-subjects design, *t* test) and statements that are so broad that they would be difficult for anyone to argue with (e.g., "Working memory plays a role in many daily activities."). Be careful, though, because "common knowledge" about human behavior is often incorrect. Therefore, when in doubt, find an appropriate reference to cite or remove the questionable assertion.

When you cite a work in the text of your manuscript, there are two ways to do it. Both include only the last names of the authors and the year of publication. The first method is to use the authors' last names in the sentence (with no first names or initials) followed immediately by the year of publication in parentheses. Here are some examples:

Burger (2008) conducted a replication of Milgram's (1963) original obedience study.

Although many people believe that women are more talkative than men, Mehl, Vazire, Ramirez-Esparza, Slatcher, and Pennebaker (2007) found essentially no difference in the number of words spoken by male and female college students.

Notice several things. First, the authors' names are treated grammatically as names of people, not as things. It is better to write "a replication of Milgram's (1963) study" than "a replication of Milgram (1963)." Second, when there are two authors the names are not separated by commas, but when there are three or more authors they are. Third, the word *and* (rather than an ampersand) is used to join the authors' names. Fourth, the year follows immediately after the final author's name. An additional point, which is not illustrated in these examples but is illustrated in the sample paper in Section 11.2 "Writing a Research Report in American Psychological Association (APA) Style", is that the year only needs to be included the first time a particular work is cited in the same paragraph.

The second way to cite an article or a book chapter is parenthetically—including the authors' last names and the year of publication in parentheses following the idea that is being credited. Here are some examples:

People can be surprisingly obedient to authority figures (Burger, 2008; Milgram, 1963).

Recent evidence suggests that men and women are similarly talkative (Mehl, Vazire, Ramirez-Esparza, Slatcher, & Pennebaker, 2007).

One thing to notice about such parenthetical citations is that they are often placed at the end of the sentence, which minimizes their disruption to the flow of that sentence. In contrast to the first way of citing a work, this way always includes the year—even when the citation is given multiple times in the same paragraph. Notice also that when there are multiple citations in the same set of parentheses, they are organized alphabetically by the name of the first author and separated by semicolons.

There are no strict rules for deciding which of the two citation styles to use. Most articles and book chapters contain a mixture of the two. In general, however, the first approach works well when you want to emphasize the person who conducted the research—for example, if you were comparing the theories of two prominent researchers. It also works well when you are describing a particular study in detail. The second approach works well when you are discussing a general idea and especially when you want to include multiple citations for the same idea.

The third most common error in Table 11.2 has to do with the use of *et al.* This is an abbreviation for the Latin term *et alia*, which means "and others." In APA style, if an article or a book chapter has *more than two authors but fewer than six*, you should include all their names when you first cite that work. After that, however, you should use the first author's name followed by "et al." If the article has only two authors then both should be included in every citation. If an article has six or more authors then you should only list the name of the first author followed by et al. each and every time you cite that work (even the first time). Here are some examples:

Recall that Mehl et al. (2007) found that women and men spoke about the same number of words per day on average.

There is a strong positive correlation between the number of daily hassles and the number of symptoms people experience (Kanner et al., 1981).

Notice that there is no comma between the first author's name and "et al." Notice also that there is no period after "et" but there is one after "al." This is because "et" is a complete word and "al." is an abbreviation for the word *alia*.

## Notes

1.  American Psychological Association. (2010). *Publication Manual of the American Psychological Association* (6th ed.). Washington, D.C.: American Psychological Association.
2.  Bentley, M., Peerenboom, C. A., Hodge, F. W., Passano, E. B., Warren, H. C., & Washburn, M. F. (1929). Instructions in regard to preparation of manuscript. *Psychological Bulletin, 26,* 57–63.
3.  Madigan, R., Johnson, S., & Linton, P. (1995). The language of psychology: APA style as epistemology. *American Psychologist, 50,* 428–436.
4.  American Psychological Association, Committee on Lesbian, Gay, and Bisexual Concerns Joint Task Force on Guidelines for Psychotherapy With Lesbian, Gay, and Bisexual Clients. (2000). *Guidelines for psychotherapy with lesbian, gay, and bisexual clients.* Retrieved from https://www.apa.org/pi/lgbt/resources/guidelines
5.  Onwuegbuzie, A. J., Combs, J. P., Slate, J. R., & Frels, R. K. (2010). Editorial: Evidence-based guidelines for avoiding the most common APA errors in journal article submissions. *Research in the Schools, 16,* ix–xxxvi.

# 49. Writing a Research Report in American Psychological Association (APA) Style

*Learning Objectives*

1. Identify the major sections of an APA-style research report and the basic contents of each section.
2. Plan and write an effective APA-style research report.

In this section, we look at how to write an APA-style **empirical research report**, an article that presents the results of one or more new studies. Recall that the standard sections of an empirical research report provide a kind of outline. Here we consider each of these sections in detail, including what information it contains, how that information is formatted and organized, and tips for writing each section. At the end of this section is a sample APA-style research report that illustrates many of these principles.

## Sections of a Research Report

## Title Page and Abstract

An APA-style research report begins with a **title page**. The title is centered in the upper half of the page, with each important word capitalized. The title should clearly and concisely (in about 12 words or fewer) communicate the primary variables and research questions. This sometimes requires a main title followed by a subtitle that elaborates on the main title, in which case the main title and subtitle are separated by a colon. Here are some titles from recent issues of professional journals published by the American Psychological Association.

- Sex Differences in Coping Styles and Implications for Depressed Mood
- Effects of Aging and Divided Attention on Memory for Items and Their Contexts
- Computer-Assisted Cognitive Behavioral Therapy for Child Anxiety: Results of a Randomized Clinical Trial
- Virtual Driving and Risk Taking: Do Racing Games Increase Risk-Taking Cognitions, Affect, and Behavior?

Below the title are the authors' names and, on the next line, their institutional affiliation—the university or other institution where the authors worked when they conducted the research. As we have already seen, the authors are listed in an order that reflects their contribution to the research. When multiple authors have made equal contributions to the research, they often list their names alphabetically or in a randomly determined order.

*It's Soooo Cute!* How Informal Should an Article Title Be?

In some areas of psychology, the titles of many empirical research reports are informal in a way that is perhaps best described as "cute." They usually take the form of a play on words or a well-known expression that relates to the topic under study. Here are some examples from recent issues of the Journal *Psychological Science*.

- "Smells Like Clean Spirit: Nonconscious Effects of Scent on Cognition and Behavior"
- "Time Crawls: The Temporal Resolution of Infants' Visual Attention"
- "Scent of a Woman: Men's Testosterone Responses to Olfactory Ovulation Cues"
- "Apocalypse Soon?: Dire Messages Reduce Belief in Global Warming by Contradicting Just-World Beliefs"
- "Serial vs. Parallel Processing: Sometimes They Look Like Tweedledum and Tweedledee but They Can (and Should) Be Distinguished"
- "How Do I Love Thee? Let Me Count the Words: The Social Effects of Expressive Writing"

Individual researchers differ quite a bit in their preference for such titles. Some use them regularly, while others never use them. What might be some of the pros and cons of using cute article titles?

For articles that are being submitted for publication, the title page also includes an author note that lists the authors' full institutional affiliations, any acknowledgments the authors wish to make to agencies that funded the research or to colleagues who commented on it, and contact information for the authors. For student papers that are not being submitted for publication—including theses—author notes are generally not necessary.

The **abstract** is a summary of the study. It is the second page of the manuscript and is headed with the word *Abstract*. The first line is not indented. The abstract presents the research question, a summary of the method, the basic results, and the most important conclusions. Because the abstract is usually limited to about 200 words, it can be a challenge to write a good one.

# Introduction

The **introduction** begins on the third page of the manuscript. The heading at the top of this page is the full title of the manuscript, with each important word capitalized as on the title page. The introduction includes three distinct subsections, although these are typically not identified by separate headings. The opening introduces the research question and explains why it is interesting, the literature review discusses relevant previous research, and the closing restates the research question and comments on the method used to answer it.

## The Opening

The **opening**, which is usually a paragraph or two in length, introduces the research question and explains why it is interesting. To capture the reader's attention, researcher Daryl Bem recommends starting with general observations about the topic under study, expressed in ordinary language (not technical jargon)—observations that are about people and their behavior (not about researchers or their research; Bem, 2003[1]). Concrete examples are often very useful here. According to Bem, this would be a poor way to begin a research report:

Festinger's theory of cognitive dissonance received a great deal of attention during the latter part of the 20th century (p. 191)

The following would be much better:

The individual who holds two beliefs that are inconsistent with one another may feel uncomfortable. For example, the person who knows that they enjoy smoking but believes it to be unhealthy may experience discomfort arising from the inconsistency or disharmony between these two thoughts or cognitions. This feeling of discomfort was called cognitive dissonance by social psychologist Leon Festinger (1957), who suggested that individuals will be motivated to remove this dissonance in whatever way they can (p. 191).

After capturing the reader's attention, the opening should go on to introduce the research question and explain why it is interesting. Will the answer fill a gap in the literature? Will it provide a test of an important theory? Does it have practical implications? Giving readers a clear sense of what the research is about and why they should care about it will motivate them to continue reading the literature review—and will help them make sense of it.

### Breaking the Rules

Researcher Larry Jacoby reported several studies showing that a word that people see or hear repeatedly can seem more familiar even when they do not recall the repetitions—and that this tendency is especially pronounced among older adults. He opened his article with the following humorous anecdote:

> A friend whose mother is suffering symptoms of Alzheimer's disease (AD) tells the story of taking her mother to visit a nursing home, preliminary to her mother's moving there. During an orientation meeting at the nursing home, the rules and regulations were explained, one of which regarded the dining room. The dining room was described as similar to a fine restaurant except that tipping was not required. The absence of tipping was a central theme in the orientation lecture, mentioned frequently to emphasize the quality of care along with the advantages of having paid in advance. At the end of the meeting, the friend's mother was asked whether she had any questions. She replied that she only had one question: "Should I tip?" (Jacoby, 1999, p. 3)

Although both humor and personal anecdotes are generally discouraged in APA-style writing, this example is a highly effective way to start because it both engages the reader and provides an excellent real-world example of the topic under study.

## The Literature Review

Immediately after the opening comes the **literature review**, which describes relevant previous research on the topic and can be anywhere from several paragraphs to several pages in length. However, the literature review is not simply a list of past studies. Instead, it constitutes a kind of argument for why the research question is worth addressing. By the end of the literature review, readers should be convinced that the research question makes sense and that the present study is a logical next step in the ongoing research process.

Like any effective argument, the literature review must have some kind of structure. For example, it might begin by describing a phenomenon in a general way along with several studies that demonstrate it, then describing two or more competing theories of the phenomenon, and finally presenting a hypothesis to test one or more of the theories. Or it might describe one phenomenon, then describe another phenomenon that seems inconsistent with the first one, then propose a theory that resolves the inconsistency, and finally present a hypothesis to test that theory. In applied research, it might describe a phenomenon or theory, then describe how that phenomenon or theory applies to some important real-world situation, and finally suggest a way to test whether it does, in fact, apply to that situation.

Looking at the literature review in this way emphasizes a few things. First, it is extremely important to start with an outline of the main points that you want to make, organized in the order that you want to make them. The basic structure of your argument, then, should be apparent from the outline itself. Second, it is important to emphasize the structure of your argument in your writing. One way to do this is to begin the literature review by summarizing your argument even before you begin to make it. "In this article, I will describe two apparently contradictory phenomena, present a new theory that has the potential to resolve the apparent contradiction, and finally present a novel hypothesis to test the theory." Another way is to open each paragraph with a sentence that summarizes the main point of the paragraph and links it to the preceding points. These opening sentences provide the "transitions" that many beginning researchers have difficulty with. Instead of beginning a paragraph by launching into a description of a previous study, such as "Williams (2004) found that...," it is better to start by indicating something about why you are describing this particular study. Here are some simple examples:

Another example of this phenomenon comes from the work of Williams (2004).

Williams (2004) offers one explanation of this phenomenon.

An alternative perspective has been provided by Williams (2004).

We used a method based on the one used by Williams (2004).

Finally, remember that your goal is to construct an argument for why your research question is interesting and worth addressing—not necessarily why your favorite answer to it is correct. In other words, your literature review must be balanced. If you want to emphasize the generality of a phenomenon, then of course you should discuss various studies that have demonstrated it. However, if there are other studies that have failed to demonstrate it, you should discuss them too. Or if you are proposing a new theory, then of course you should discuss findings that are consistent with that theory. However, if there are other findings that are inconsistent with it, again, you should discuss them too. It is acceptable to argue that the *balance* of the research supports the existence of a phenomenon or is consistent with a theory (and that is usually the best that researchers in psychology can hope for), but it is not acceptable to *ignore* contradictory evidence. Besides, a large part of what makes a research question interesting is uncertainty about its answer.

## The Closing

The **closing** of the introduction—typically the final paragraph or two—usually includes two important elements. The first is a clear statement of the main research question and hypothesis. This statement tends to be more formal and precise than in the opening and is often expressed in terms of operational definitions of the key variables. The second is a brief overview of the method and some comment on its appropriateness. Here, for example, is how Darley and Latané (1968)[2] concluded the introduction to their classic article on the bystander effect:

> These considerations lead to the hypothesis that the more bystanders to an emergency, the less likely, or the more slowly, any one bystander will intervene to provide aid. To test this proposition it would be necessary to create a situation in which a realistic "emergency" could plausibly occur. Each subject should also be blocked from communicating with others to prevent his getting information about their behavior during the emergency. Finally, the experimental situation should allow for the assessment of the speed and frequency of the subjects' reaction to the emergency. The experiment reported below attempted to fulfill these conditions. (p. 378)

Thus the introduction leads smoothly into the next major section of the article—the method section.

## Method

The **method section** is where you describe how you conducted your study. An important principle for writing a method section is that it should be clear and detailed enough that other researchers could replicate the study by following your "recipe." This means that it must describe all the important elements of the study—basic demographic characteristics of the participants, how they were recruited, whether they were randomly assigned to conditions, how the variables were manipulated or measured, how counterbalancing was accomplished, and so on. At the same time, it should avoid irrelevant details such as the fact that the study was conducted in Classroom 37B of the Industrial Technology Building or that the questionnaire was double-sided and completed using pencils.

The method section begins immediately after the introduction ends with the heading "Method" (not "Methods") centered on the page. Immediately after this is the subheading "Participants," left justified and in italics. The participants subsection indicates how many participants there were, the number of women and men, some indication of their age, other demographics that may be relevant to the study, and how they were recruited, including any incentives given for participation.

| Simple method | Typical method | Complex method |
|---|---|---|
| **Participants** | **Participants** | **Participants** |
| The participants were... | The participants were... | The participants were... |
| **Design and procedure** | **Design** | **Materials** |
| There were three conditions... | There were three conditions... | The stimuli were... |
| | **Procedure** | **Design** |
| | Participants viewed each stimulus on the computer screen... | There were three conditions... |
| | | **Procedure** |
| | | Participants viewed each stimulus on the computer screen... |

Figure 11.1 *Three Ways of Organizing an APA-Style Method*

After the participants section, the structure can vary a bit. Figure 11.1 shows three common approaches. In the first, the participants section is followed by a design and procedure subsection, which describes the rest of the method. This works well for methods that are relatively simple and can be described adequately in a few paragraphs. In the second approach, the participants section is followed by separate design and procedure subsections. This works well when both the design and the procedure are relatively complicated and each requires multiple paragraphs.

What is the difference between design and procedure? The design of a study is its overall structure. What were the independent and dependent variables? Was the independent variable manipulated, and if so, was it manipulated between or within subjects? How were the variables operationally defined? The procedure is how the study was carried out. It often works well to describe the procedure in terms of what the participants did rather than what the researchers did. For example, the participants gave their informed consent, read a set of instructions, completed a block of four practice trials, completed a block of 20 test trials, completed two questionnaires, and were debriefed and excused.

In the third basic way to organize a method section, the participants subsection is followed by a materials subsection before the design and procedure subsections. This works well when there are complicated materials to describe. This might mean multiple questionnaires, written vignettes that participants read and respond to, perceptual stimuli, and so on. The heading of this subsection can be modified to reflect its content. Instead of "Materials," it can be "Questionnaires," "Stimuli," and so on. The materials subsection is also a good place to refer to the reliability and/or validity of the measures. This is where you would present test-retest correlations, Cronbach's α, or other statistics to show that the measures are consistent across time and across items and that they accurately measure what they are intended to measure.

## Results

The **results section** is where you present the main results of the study, including the results of the statistical analyses. Although it does not include the raw data—individual participants' responses or scores—researchers should save their raw data and make them available to other researchers who request them. Many journals encourage the open sharing of raw data online, and some now require open data and materials before publication.

Although there are no standard subsections, it is still important for the results section to be logically organized. Typically it begins with certain preliminary issues. One is whether any participants or responses were excluded from the analyses and why. The rationale for excluding data should be described clearly so that other researchers can decide whether it is appropriate. A second preliminary issue is how multiple responses were combined to produce the primary variables in the analyses. For example, if participants rated the attractiveness of 20 stimulus people, you might have to explain that you began by computing the mean attractiveness rating for each participant. Or if they recalled as many items as they could from study list of 20 words, did you count the number correctly recalled, compute the percentage correctly recalled, or perhaps compute the number correct minus the number incorrect? A final preliminary issue is whether the manipulation was successful. This is where you would report the results of any manipulation checks.

The results section should then tackle the primary research questions, one at a time. Again, there should be a clear organization. One approach would be to answer the most general questions and then proceed to answer more specific ones. Another would be to answer the main question first and then to answer secondary ones. Regardless, Bem (2003)[3] suggests the following basic structure for discussing each new result:

- Remind the reader of the research question.
- Give the answer to the research question in words.
- Present the relevant statistics.
- Qualify the answer if necessary.

- Summarize the result.

Notice that only Step 3 necessarily involves numbers. The rest of the steps involve presenting the research question and the answer to it in words. In fact, the basic results should be clear even to a reader who skips over the numbers.

## Discussion

The **discussion** is the last major section of the research report. Discussions usually consist of some combination of the following elements:

- Summary of the research
- Theoretical implications
- Practical implications
- Limitations
- Suggestions for future research

The discussion typically begins with a summary of the study that provides a clear answer to the research question. In a short report with a single study, this might require no more than a sentence. In a longer report with multiple studies, it might require a paragraph or even two. The summary is often followed by a discussion of the theoretical implications of the research. Do the results provide support for any existing theories? If not, how *can* they be explained? Although you do not have to provide a definitive explanation or detailed theory for your results, you at least need to outline one or more possible explanations. In applied research—and often in basic research—there is also some discussion of the practical implications of the research. How can the results be used, and by whom, to accomplish some real-world goal?

The theoretical and practical implications are often followed by a discussion of the study's limitations. Perhaps there are problems with its internal or external validity. Perhaps the manipulation was not very effective or the measures not very reliable. Perhaps there is some evidence that participants did not fully understand their task or that they were suspicious of the intent of the researchers. Now is the time to discuss these issues and how they might have affected the results. But do not overdo it. All studies have limitations, and most readers will understand that a different sample or different measures might have produced different results. Unless there is good reason to think they *would* have, however, there is no reason to mention these routine issues. Instead, pick two or three limitations that seem like they could have influenced the results, explain how they could have influenced the results, and suggest ways to deal with them.

Most discussions end with some suggestions for future research. If the study did not satisfactorily answer the original research question, what will it take to do so? What *new* research questions has the study raised? This part of the discussion, however, is not just a list of new questions. It is a discussion of two or three of the most important unresolved issues. This means identifying and clarifying each question, suggesting some alternative answers, and even suggesting ways they could be studied.

Finally, some researchers are quite good at ending their articles with a sweeping or thought-provoking conclusion. Darley and Latané (1968)[4], for example, ended their article on the bystander effect by discussing the idea that whether people help others may depend more on the situation than on their personalities. Their final sentence is, "If people understand the situational forces that can make them hesitate to intervene, they may better overcome them" (p. 383). However, this kind of ending can be difficult to pull off. It can sound overreaching or just banal and end up detracting from the overall impact of the article. It is often better simply to end by returning to the problem or issue introduced in your opening paragraph and clearly stating how your research has addressed that issue or problem.

## References

The references section begins on a new page with the heading "References" centered at the top of the page. All references cited in the text are then listed in the format presented earlier. They are listed alphabetically by the last name of the first author. If two sources have the same first author, they are listed alphabetically by the last name of the second author. If all the authors are the same, then they are listed chronologically by the year of publication. Everything in the reference list is double-spaced both within and between references.

## Appendices, Tables, and Figures

Appendices, tables, and figures come after the references. An **appendix** is appropriate for supplemental material that would interrupt the flow of the research report if it were presented within any of the major sections. An appendix could be used to present lists of stimulus words, questionnaire items, detailed descriptions of special equipment or unusual statistical analyses, or references to the studies that are included in a meta-analysis. Each appendix begins on a new page. If there is only one, the heading is "Appendix," centered at the top of the page. If there is more than one, the headings are "Appendix A," "Appendix B," and so on, and they appear in the order they were first mentioned in the text of the report.

After any appendices come tables and then figures. Tables and figures are both used to present results. Figures can also be used to display graphs, illustrate theories (e.g., in the form of a flowchart), display stimuli, outline procedures, and present many other kinds of information. Each table and figure appears on its own page. Tables are numbered in the order that they are first mentioned in the text ("Table 1," "Table 2," and so on). Figures are numbered the same way ("Figure 1," "Figure 2," and so on). A brief explanatory title, with the important words capitalized, appears above each table. Each figure is given a brief explanatory caption, where (aside from proper nouns or names) only the first word of each sentence is capitalized. More details on preparing APA-style tables and figures are presented later in the book.

# Sample APA-Style Research Report

Figures 11.2, 11.3, 11.4, and 11.5 show some sample pages from an APA-style empirical research report originally written by undergraduate student Tomoe Suyama at California State University, Fresno. The main purpose of these figures is to illustrate the basic organization and formatting of an APA-style empirical research report, although many high-level and low-level style conventions can be seen here too.

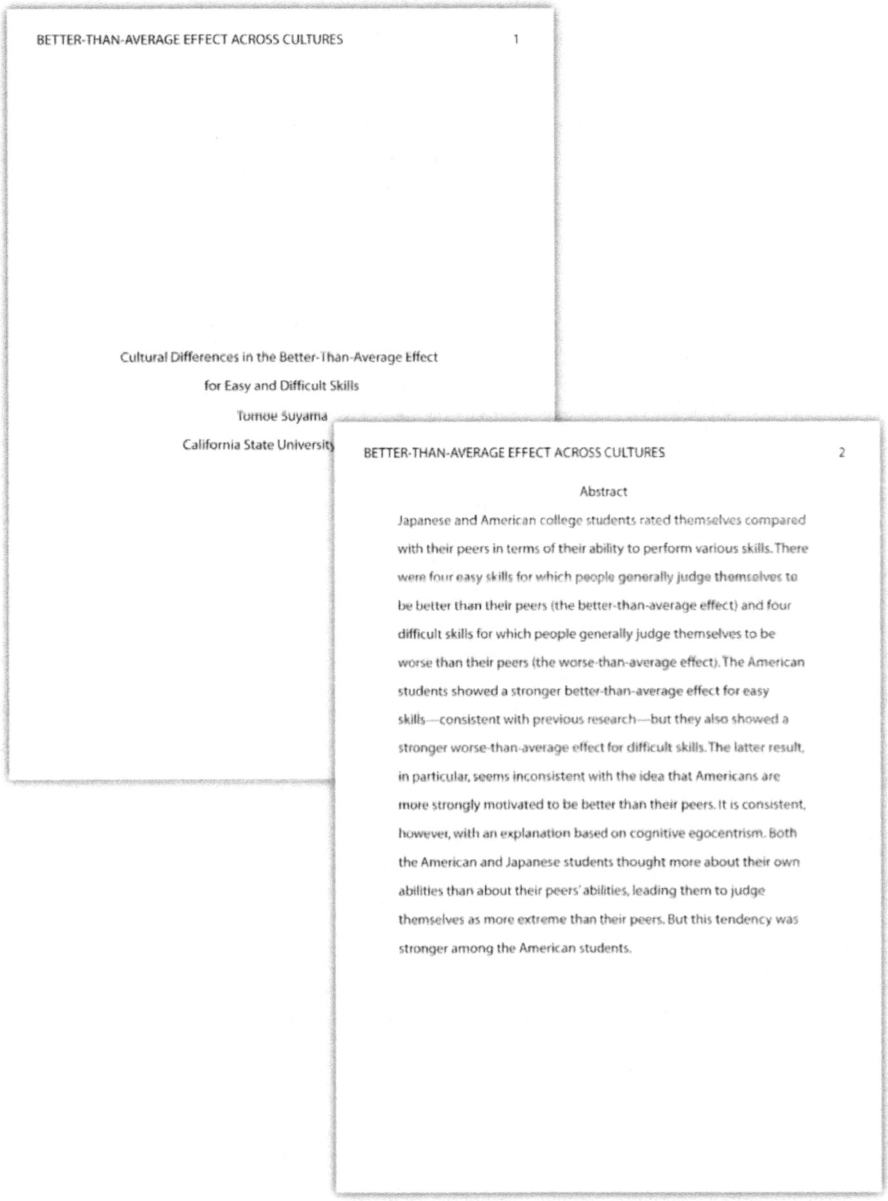
BETTER-THAN-AVERAGE EFFECT ACROSS CULTURES 1

Cultural Differences in the Better-Than-Average Effect
for Easy and Difficult Skills
Tomoe Suyama
California State University

BETTER-THAN-AVERAGE EFFECT ACROSS CULTURES 2

Abstract

Japanese and American college students rated themselves compared with their peers in terms of their ability to perform various skills. There were four easy skills for which people generally judge themselves to be better than their peers (the better-than-average effect) and four difficult skills for which people generally judge themselves to be worse than their peers (the worse-than-average effect). The American students showed a stronger better-than-average effect for easy skills—consistent with previous research—but they also showed a stronger worse-than-average effect for difficult skills. The latter result, in particular, seems inconsistent with the idea that Americans are more strongly motivated to be better than their peers. It is consistent, however, with an explanation based on cognitive egocentrism. Both the American and Japanese students thought more about their own abilities than about their peers' abilities, leading them to judge themselves as more extreme than their peers. But this tendency was stronger among the American students.

*Figure 11.2 Title Page and Abstract. This student paper does not include the author note on the title page. The abstract appears on its own page.*

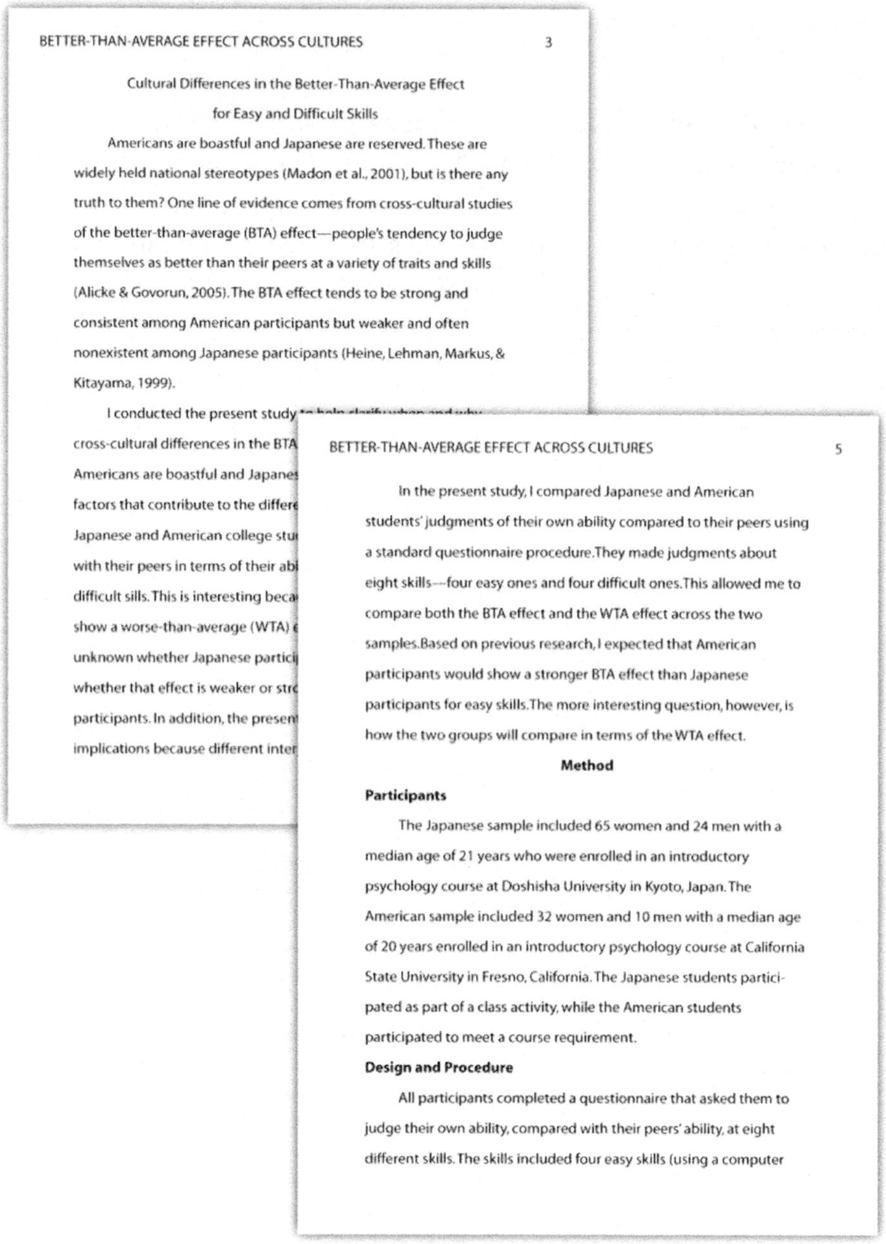

Cultural Differences in the Better-Than-Average Effect

for Easy and Difficult Skills

Americans are boastful and Japanese are reserved. These are widely held national stereotypes (Madon et al., 2001), but is there any truth to them? One line of evidence comes from cross-cultural studies of the better-than-average (BTA) effect—people's tendency to judge themselves as better than their peers at a variety of traits and skills (Alicke & Govorun, 2005). The BTA effect tends to be strong and consistent among American participants but weaker and often nonexistent among Japanese participants (Heine, Lehman, Markus, & Kitayama, 1999).

I conducted the present study to help clarify when and why cross-cultural differences in the BTA effect. Americans are boastful and Japanese factors that contribute to the differe Japanese and American college stu with their peers in terms of their abi difficult sills. This is interesting beca show a worse-than-average (WTA) unknown whether Japanese partici whether that effect is weaker or str participants. In addition, the presen implications because different inter

In the present study, I compared Japanese and American students' judgments of their own ability compared to their peers using a standard questionnaire procedure. They made judgments about eight skills—four easy ones and four difficult ones. This allowed me to compare both the BTA effect and the WTA effect across the two samples. Based on previous research, I expected that American participants would show a stronger BTA effect than Japanese participants for easy skills. The more interesting question, however, is how the two groups will compare in terms of the WTA effect.

**Method**

**Participants**

The Japanese sample included 65 women and 24 men with a median age of 21 years who were enrolled in an introductory psychology course at Doshisha University in Kyoto, Japan. The American sample included 32 women and 10 men with a median age of 20 years enrolled in an introductory psychology course at California State University in Fresno, California. The Japanese students participated as part of a class activity, while the American students participated to meet a course requirement.

**Design and Procedure**

All participants completed a questionnaire that asked them to judge their own ability, compared with their peers' ability, at eight different skills. The skills included four easy skills (using a computer

*Figure 11.3 Introduction and Method. Note that the introduction is headed with the full title, and the method section begins immediately after the introduction ends.*

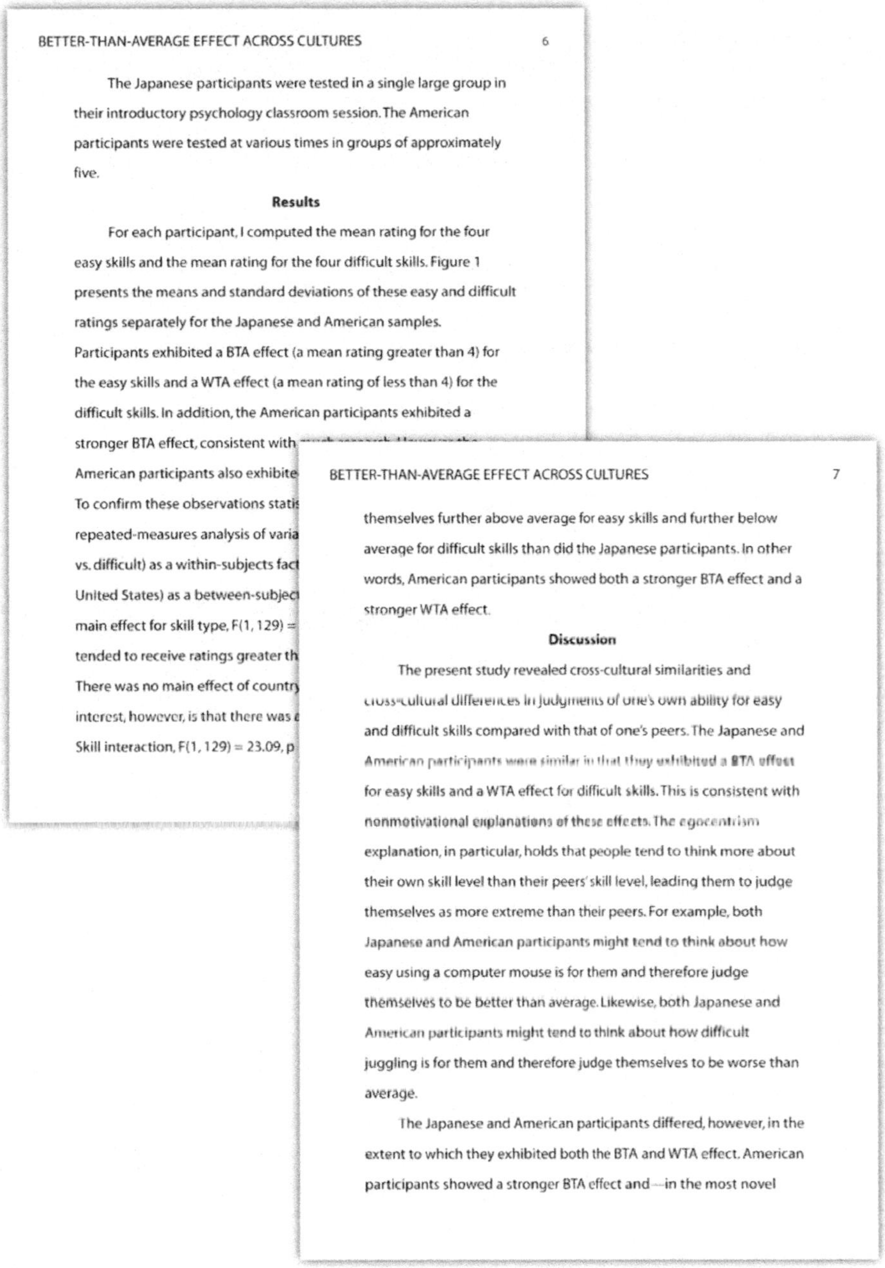

The Japanese participants were tested in a single large group in their introductory psychology classroom session. The American participants were tested at various times in groups of approximately five.

### Results

For each participant, I computed the mean rating for the four easy skills and the mean rating for the four difficult skills. Figure 1 presents the means and standard deviations of these easy and difficult ratings separately for the Japanese and American samples. Participants exhibited a BTA effect (a mean rating greater than 4) for the easy skills and a WTA effect (a mean rating of less than 4) for the difficult skills. In addition, the American participants exhibited a stronger BTA effect, consistent with ~~much research. However, the~~ American participants also exhibite~~d~~ To confirm these observations statis~~t~~ repeated-measures analysis of varia~~nce~~ vs. difficult) as a within-subjects fact~~or~~ United States) as a between-subjec~~t~~ main effect for skill type, F(1, 129) = tended to receive ratings greater th~~an~~ There was no main effect of countr~~y~~ interest, however, is that there was ~~a~~ Skill interaction, F(1, 129) = 23.09, p

themselves further above average for easy skills and further below average for difficult skills than did the Japanese participants. In other words, American participants showed both a stronger BTA effect and a stronger WTA effect.

### Discussion

The present study revealed cross-cultural similarities and cross-cultural differences in judgments of one's own ability for easy and difficult skills compared with that of one's peers. The Japanese and American participants were similar in that they exhibited a BTA effect for easy skills and a WTA effect for difficult skills. This is consistent with nonmotivational explanations of these effects. The egocentrism explanation, in particular, holds that people tend to think more about their own skill level than their peers' skill level, leading them to judge themselves as more extreme than their peers. For example, both Japanese and American participants might tend to think about how easy using a computer mouse is for them and therefore judge themselves to be better than average. Likewise, both Japanese and American participants might tend to think about how difficult juggling is for them and therefore judge themselves to be worse than average.

The Japanese and American participants differed, however, in the extent to which they exhibited both the BTA and WTA effect. American participants showed a stronger BTA effect and—in the most novel

*Figure 11.4 Results and Discussion The discussion begins immediately after the results section ends.*

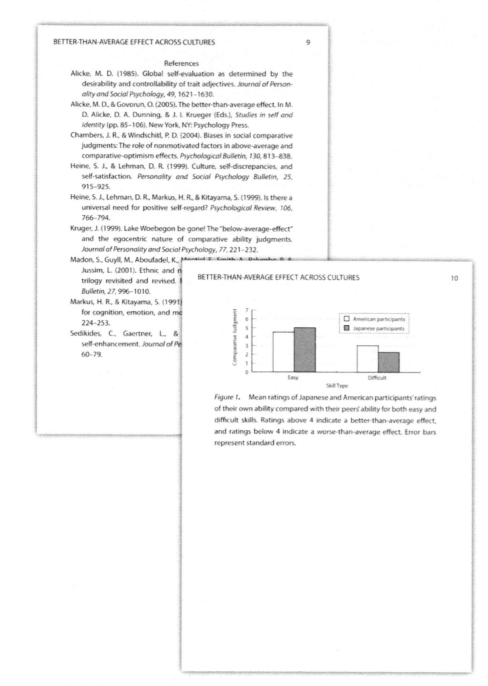

BETTER-THAN-AVERAGE EFFECT ACROSS CULTURES                    9

References

Alicke, M. D. (1985). Global self-evaluation as determined by the desirability and controllability of trait adjectives. *Journal of Personality and Social Psychology, 49,* 1621–1630.

Alicke, M. D., & Govorun, O. (2005). The better-than-average effect. In M. D. Alicke, D. A. Dunning, & J. I. Krueger (Eds.), *Studies in self and identity* (pp. 85–106). New York, NY: Psychology Press.

Chambers, J. R., & Windschitl, P. D. (2004). Biases in social comparative judgments: The role of nonmotivated factors in above-average and comparative-optimism effects. *Psychological Bulletin, 130,* 813–838.

Heine, S. J., & Lehman, D. R. (1999). Culture, self-discrepancies, and self-satisfaction. *Personality and Social Psychology Bulletin, 25,* 915–925.

Heine, S. J., Lehman, D. R., Markus, H. R., & Kitayama, S. (1999). Is there a universal need for positive self-regard? *Psychological Review, 106,* 766–794.

Kruger, J. (1999). Lake Woebegon be gone! The "below-average-effect" and the egocentric nature of comparative ability judgments. *Journal of Personality and Social Psychology, 77,* 221–232.

Madon, S., Guyll, M., Aboufadel, K., Montiel, E., Smith, A., Palumbo, P., & Jussim, L. (2001). Ethnic and n trilogy revisited and revised. F Bulletin, 27, 996–1010.

Markus, H. R., & Kitayama, S. (1991) for cognition, emotion, and mo 224–253.

Sedikides, C., Gaertner, L., & self-enhancement. Journal of Pe 60–79.

BETTER-THAN-AVERAGE EFFECT ACROSS CULTURES                    10

*Figure 1.* Mean ratings of Japanese and American participants' ratings of their own ability compared with their peers' ability for both easy and difficult skills. Ratings above 4 indicate a better-than-average effect, and ratings below 4 indicate a worse-than-average effect. Error bars represent standard errors.

*Figure 11.5 References and Figure. If there were appendices or tables, they would come before the figure.*

# Notes

1.  Bem, D. J. (2003). Writing the empirical journal article. In J. M. Darley, M. P. Zanna, & H. R. Roediger III (Eds.), *The complete academic: A practical guide for the beginning social scientist* (2nd ed.). Washington, DC: American Psychological Association.

2.  Darley, J. M., & Latané, B. (1968). Bystander intervention in emergencies: Diffusion of responsibility. *Journal of*

*Personality and Social Psychology, 4,* 377–383.

3.  Bem, D. J. (2003). Writing the empirical journal article. In J. M. Darley, M. P. Zanna, & H. R. Roediger III (Eds.), *The complete academic: A practical guide for the beginning social scientist* (2nd ed.). Washington, DC: American Psychological Association.

4.  Darley, J. M., & Latané, B. (1968). Bystander intervention in emergencies: Diffusion of responsibility. *Journal of Personality and Social Psychology, 4,* 377–383.

# 50. Other Presentation Formats

### Learning Objectives

1. List several ways that researchers in psychology can present their research and the situations in which they might use them.
2. Describe how final manuscripts differ from copy manuscripts in American Psychological Association (APA) style.
3. Describe the purpose of talks and posters at professional conferences.
4. Prepare a short conference-style talk and simple poster presentation.

Writing an empirical research report in American Psychological Association (APA) style is only one way to present new research in psychology. In this section, we look at several other important ways.

## Other Types of Manuscripts

The previous section focused on writing empirical research reports to be submitted for publication in a professional journal. However, there are other kinds of manuscripts that are written in APA style, many of which will not be submitted for publication elsewhere. Here we look at a few of them.

## Review and Theoretical Articles

Recall that **review articles** summarize research on a particular topic without presenting new empirical results. When these articles present a new theory, they are often called **theoretical articles**. Review and theoretical articles are structured much like empirical research reports, with a title page, an abstract, references, appendixes, tables, and figures, and they are written in the same high-level and low-level style. Because they do not report the results of new empirical research, however, there is no method or results section. Of course, the body of the manuscript should still have a logical organization and include an opening that identifies the topic and explains its importance, a literature review that organizes previous research (identifying important relationships among concepts or gaps in the literature), and a closing or conclusion that summarizes the main conclusions and suggests directions for further research or discusses theoretical and practical implications. In a theoretical article, of course, much of the body of the manuscript is devoted to presenting the new theory. Theoretical and review articles are usually divided into sections, each with a heading that is appropriate to that section. The sections and headings can vary considerably from article to article (unlike in an empirical research report). But whatever they are, they should help organize the manuscript and make the argument clear.

## Final Manuscripts

Until now, we have focused on the formatting of manuscripts that will be submitted to a professional journal for publication. In contrast, other types of manuscripts are prepared by the author in their final form with no intention of submitting them for publication elsewhere. These are called **final manuscripts** and include dissertations, theses, and other student papers. These manuscripts may look different from strictly APA style manuscripts in ways that make them easier to read, such as putting tables and figures close to where they are discussed so that the reader does not have to flip to the back of the manuscript to see them. If you read a dissertation or thesis, for example, you might notice it does not adhere strictly to APA style formatting. For student papers, it is important to check with the course instructor about formatting specifics. In a research methods course, papers are usually required to be written as though they were manuscripts being submitted for publication.

## Conference Presentations

One of the ways that researchers in psychology share their research with each other is by presenting it at **professional conferences**. (Although some professional conferences in psychology are devoted mainly to issues of clinical practice, we are concerned here with those that focus on research.) Professional conferences can range from small-scale events involving a dozen researchers who get together for an afternoon to large-scale events involving thousands of researchers who meet for several days. Although researchers attending a professional conference are likely to discuss their work with each other informally, there are two more formal types of presentation: oral presentations ("talks") and posters. Presenting a talk or poster at a conference usually requires submitting an abstract of the research to the conference organizers in advance and having it accepted for presentation—although the peer review process is typically not as rigorous as it is for manuscripts submitted to a professional journal.

## Oral Presentations

In an **oral presentation**, or "talk," the presenter stands in front of an audience of other researchers and tells them about their research—usually with the help of a slide show. Talks usually last from 10 to 20 minutes, with the last few minutes reserved for questions from the audience. At larger conferences, talks are typically grouped into sessions lasting an hour or two in which all the talks are on the same general topic.

In preparing a talk, presenters should keep several general principles in mind. The first is that the number of slides should be no more than about one per minute of the talk. The second is that talks are generally structured like an APA-style research report. There is a slide with the title and authors, a few slides to help provide the background, a few more to help describe the method, a few for the results, and a few for the conclusions. The third is that the presenter should look at the audience members and speak to them in a conversational tone that is less formal than APA-style writing but more formal than a conversation with a friend. The slides should not be the focus of the presentation; they should act as visual aids. As such, they should present the main points in bulleted lists or simple tables and figures.

## Posters

Another way to present research at a conference is in the form of a **poster**. A poster is typically presented during a one- to two-hour **poster session** that takes place in a large room at the conference site. Presenters set up their posters on bulletin boards arranged around the room and stand near them. Other researchers then circulate through the room, read the posters, and talk to the presenters. In essence, poster sessions are a grown-up version of the school science fair. But there is nothing childish about them. Posters are used by professional researchers in all scientific disciplines and they are becoming increasingly common. At a recent American Psychological Association Conference, nearly 2,000 posters were presented across 16 separate poster sessions. Among the reasons posters are so popular is that they encourage meaningful interaction among researchers.

Posters are typically a large size, maybe four feet wide and three feet high. The poster's information is organized into distinct sections, including a title, author names and affiliations, an introduction, a method section, a results section, a discussion or conclusions section, references, and acknowledgments. Although posters can include an abstract, this may not be necessary because the poster itself is already a brief summary of the research. Figure 11.6 shows two different ways that the information on a poster might be organized.

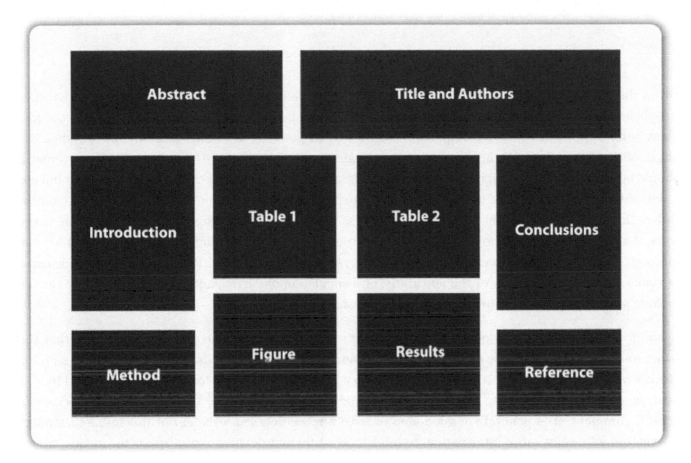

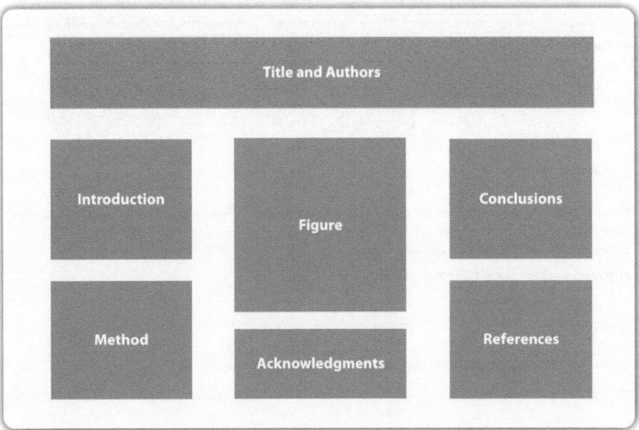

*Figure 11.6 Two Possible Ways to Organize the Information on a Poster*

Given the conditions under which posters are often presented—for example, in crowded ballrooms where people are also eating, drinking, and socializing—they should be constructed so that they present the main ideas behind the research in as simple and clear a way as possible. The font sizes on a poster should be large—perhaps 72 points for the title and authors' names and 28 points for the main text. The information should be organized into sections with clear headings, and text should be blocked into sentences or bulleted points rather than paragraphs. It is also better for it to be organized in columns and flow from top to bottom rather than to be organized in rows that flow across the poster. This makes it easier for multiple people to read at the same time without bumping into each other. Posters often include elements that add visual interest. Figures can be more colorful than those in an APA-style manuscript. Posters can also include copies of visual stimuli, photographs of the apparatus, or a simulation of participants being tested. They can also include purely decorative elements, although it is best not to overdo these.

Again, a primary reason that posters are becoming such a popular way to present research is that they facilitate interaction among researchers. Many presenters immediately offer to describe their research to visitors and use the poster as a visual aid. At the very least, it is important for presenters to stand by their posters, greet visitors, offer to answer questions, and be prepared for questions and even the occasional critical comment. It is generally a good idea to have a more detailed write-up of the research available for visitors who want more information, to offer to send them a detailed write-up, or to provide contact information so that they can request more information later.

For more information on preparing and presenting both talks and posters, see the website of the Undergraduate Advising and Research Office at Dartmouth College: http://www.dartmouth.edu/~ugar/undergrad/posterinstructions.html

## Professional Conferences

Following are links to the websites for several large national conferences in North America and also for several conferences that feature the work of undergraduate students. For a comprehensive list of psychology conferences worldwide, see the following website.

http://www.conferencealerts.com/psychology.htm

### Large Conferences

Canadian Psychological Association Convention: http://www.cpa.ca/convention

American Psychological Association Convention: http://www.apa.org/convention

Association for Psychological Science Conference: http://www.psychologicalscience.org/index.php/convention

Canadian Society for Brain, Behavior, and Cognitive Science Annual Meeting: https://www.csbbcs.org/meetings

Society for Personality and Social Psychology Conference: http://meeting.spsp.org/

Psychonomic Society Annual Meeting: http://www.psychonomic.org/annual-meeting

*U.S. Regional conferences where undergraduate researchers frequently present*

Eastern Psychological Association (EPA): http://www.easternpsychological.org

Midwestern Psychological Association (MPA): http://www.midwesternpsych.org/

New England Psychological Association (NEPA): http://www.newenglandpsychological.org/

Rocky Mountain Psychological Association (RMPA): http://www.rockymountainpsych.com/

Southeastern Psychological Association (SEPA): http://www.sepaonline.com/

Southwestern Psychological Association (SWPA): http://www.swpsych.org/

Western Psychological Association (WPA): http://westernpsych.org/

*Canadian Undergraduate Conferences*

Connecting Minds Undergraduate Research Conference: http://www.connectingminds.ca

Science Atlantic Psychology Conference: https://scienceatlantic.ca/conferences/

# 51. Key Takeaways and Exercises

## Key Takeaways

- APA style is a set of guidelines for writing in psychology. It is the genre of writing that psychologists use to communicate about their research with other researchers and practitioners.
- APA style can be seen as having three levels. There is the organization of a research article, the high-level style that includes writing in a formal and straightforward way, and the low-level style that consists of many specific rules of grammar, spelling, formatting of references, and so on.
- References and reference citations are an important part of APA style. There are specific rules for formatting references and for citing them in the text of an article.
- An APA-style empirical research report consists of several standard sections. The main ones are the abstract, introduction, method, results, discussion, and references.
- The introduction consists of an opening that presents the research question, a literature review that describes previous research on the topic, and a closing that restates the research question and comments on the method. The literature review constitutes an argument for why the current study is worth doing.
- The method section describes the method in enough detail that another researcher could replicate the study. At a minimum, it consists of a participants subsection and a design and procedure subsection.
- The results section describes the results in an organized fashion. Each primary result is presented in terms of statistical results but also explained in words.
- The discussion typically summarizes the study, discusses theoretical and practical implications and limitations of the study, and offers suggestions for further research.
- Research in psychology can be presented in several different formats. In addition to APA-style empirical research reports, there are theoretical and review articles; final manuscripts, including dissertations, theses, and student papers; and talks and posters at professional conferences.
- Talks and posters at professional conferences follow some APA style guidelines but are considerably less detailed than APA-style research reports. Their function is to present new research to interested researchers and facilitate further interaction among researchers.

## Exercises

- Practice: Find a description of a research study in a popular magazine, newspaper, blog, or website. Then identify five specific differences between how that description is written and how it would be written in APA style.
- Practice: Find and correct the errors in the following fictional APA-style references and citations.

    ◦ Walters, F. T., and DeLeon, M. (2010). Relationship Between Intrinsic Motivation and Accuracy of

Academic Self-Evaluations Among High School Students. Educational Psychology Quarterly, 23, 234–256.

- ○ Moore, Lilia S. (2007). Ethics in survey research. In M. Williams & P. L. Lee (eds.), Ethical Issues in Psychology (pp. 120–156), Boston, Psychological Research Press.
- ○ Vang, C., Dumont, L. S., and Prescott, M. P. found that left-handed people have a stronger preference for abstract art than right-handed people (2006).
- ○ This result has been replicated several times (Williamson, 1998; Pentecost & Garcia, 2006; Armbruster, 2011)

- Practice: Look through an issue of a general interest professional journal (e.g., *Psychological Science*). Read the opening of the first five articles and rate the effectiveness of each one from 1 (*very ineffective*) to 5 (*very effective*). Write a sentence or two explaining each rating.
- Practice: Find a recent article in a professional journal and identify where the opening, literature review, and closing of the introduction begin and end.
- Practice: Find a recent article in a professional journal and highlight in a different color each of the following elements in the discussion: summary, theoretical implications, practical implications, limitations, and suggestions for future research.
- Discussion: Do an Internet search using search terms such as *psychology* and *poster* to find three examples of posters that have been presented at conferences. Based on information in this chapter, what are the main strengths and main weaknesses of each poster?

# CHAPTER XII
# DESCRIPTIVE STATISTICS

At this point, we need to consider the basics of data analysis in psychological research in more detail. In this chapter, we focus on descriptive statistics—a set of techniques for summarizing and displaying the data from your sample. We look first at some of the most common techniques for describing single variables, followed by some of the most common techniques for describing statistical relationships between variables. We then look at how to present descriptive statistics in writing and also in the form of tables and graphs that would be appropriate for an American Psychological Association (APA)-style research report. We end with some practical advice for organizing and carrying out your analyses.

# 52. Describing Single Variables

1. Use frequency tables and histograms to display and interpret the distribution of a variable.
2. Compute and interpret the mean, median, and mode of a distribution and identify situations in which the mean, median, or mode is the most appropriate measure of central tendency.
3. Compute and interpret the range and standard deviation of a distribution.
4. Compute and interpret percentile ranks and z scores.

**Descriptive statistics** refers to a set of techniques for summarizing and displaying data. Let us assume here that the data are quantitative and consist of scores on one or more variables for each of several study participants. Although in most cases the primary research question will be about one or more statistical relationships between variables, it is also important to describe each variable individually. For this reason, we begin by looking at some of the most common techniques for describing single variables.

## The Distribution of a Variable

Every variable has a **distribution**, which is the way the scores are distributed across the levels of that variable. For example, in a sample of 100 university students, the distribution of the variable "number of siblings" might be such that 10 of them have no siblings, 30 have one sibling, 40 have two siblings, and so on. In the same sample, the distribution of the variable "sex" might be such that 44 have a score of "male" and 56 have a score of "female."

## Frequency Tables

One way to display the distribution of a variable is in a **frequency table.** Table 12.1, for example, is a frequency table showing a hypothetical distribution of scores on the Rosenberg Self-Esteem Scale for a sample of 40 college students. The first column lists the values of the variable—the possible scores on the Rosenberg scale—and the second column lists the frequency of each score. This table shows that there were three students who had self-esteem scores of 24, five who had self-esteem scores of 23, and so on. From a frequency table like this, one can quickly see several important aspects of a distribution, including the range of scores (from 15 to 24), the most and least common scores (22 and 17, respectively), and any extreme scores that stand out from the rest.

| Self-esteem | Frequency |
| --- | --- |
| 24 | 3 |
| 23 | 5 |
| 22 | 10 |
| 21 | 8 |
| 20 | 5 |
| 19 | 3 |
| 18 | 3 |
| 17 | 0 |
| 16 | 2 |
| 15 | 1 |

There are a few other points worth noting about frequency tables. First, the levels listed in the first column usually go from the highest at the top to the lowest at the bottom, and they usually do not extend beyond the highest and lowest scores in the data. For example, although scores on the Rosenberg scale can vary from a high of 30 to a low of 0, Table 12.1 only includes levels from 24 to 15 because that range includes all the scores in this particular data set. Second, when there are many different scores across a wide range of values, it is often better to create a grouped frequency table, in which the first column lists ranges of values and the second column lists the frequency of scores in each range. Table 12.2, for example, is a grouped frequency table showing a hypothetical distribution of simple reaction times for a sample of 20 participants. In a grouped frequency table, the ranges must all be of equal width, and there are usually between five and 15 of them. Finally, frequency tables can also be used for categorical variables, in which case the levels are category labels. The order of the category labels is somewhat arbitrary, but they are often listed from the most frequent at the top to the least frequent at the bottom.

Table 12.2 A Grouped Frequency
Table Showing a Hypothetical
Distribution of Reaction Times

| Reaction time (ms) | Frequency |
| --- | --- |
| 241–260 | 1 |
| 221–240 | 2 |
| 201–220 | 2 |
| 181–200 | 9 |
| 161–180 | 4 |
| 141–160 | 2 |

# Histograms

A **histogram** is a graphical display of a distribution. It presents the same information as a frequency table but in a way that is even quicker and easier to grasp. The histogram in Figure 12.1 presents the distribution of self-esteem scores in Table 12.1. The x-axis of the histogram represents the variable and the y-axis represents frequency. Above each level of the variable on the x-axis is a vertical bar that represents the number of individuals with that score. When the variable is quantitative, as in this example, there is usually no gap between the bars. When the variable is categorical, however, there is usually a small gap between them. (The gap at 17 in this histogram reflects the fact that there were no scores of 17 in this data set.)

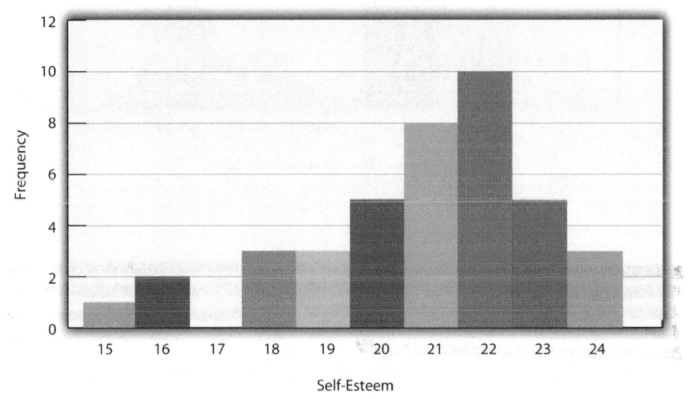

Figure 12.1 Histogram Showing the Distribution of Self-Esteem Scores Presented in Table 12.1

# Distribution Shapes

When the distribution of a quantitative variable is displayed in a histogram, it has a shape. The shape of the distribution of self-esteem scores in Figure 12.1 is typical. There is a peak somewhere near the middle of the distribution and "tails" that taper in either direction from the peak. The distribution of Figure 12.1 is unimodal, meaning it has one distinct peak, but distributions can also be bimodal, meaning they have two distinct peaks. Figure 12.2, for example, shows a hypothetical bimodal distribution of scores on the Beck Depression Inventory. Distributions can also have more than two distinct peaks, but these are relatively rare in psychological research.

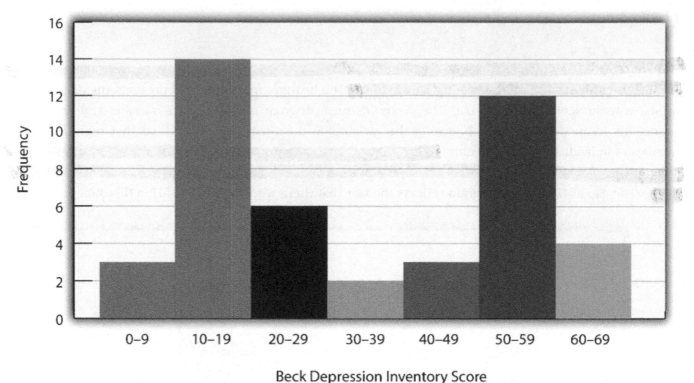

Figure 12.2 Histogram Showing a Hypothetical Bimodal Distribution of Scores on the Beck Depression Inventory

Another characteristic of the shape of a distribution is whether it is symmetrical or skewed. The distribution in the center of Figure 12.3 is **symmetrical**. Its left and right halves are mirror images of each other. The distribution on the left is negatively **skewed**, with its peak shifted toward the upper end of its range and a relatively long negative tail. The distribution on the right is positively skewed, with its peak toward the lower end of its range and a relatively long positive tail.

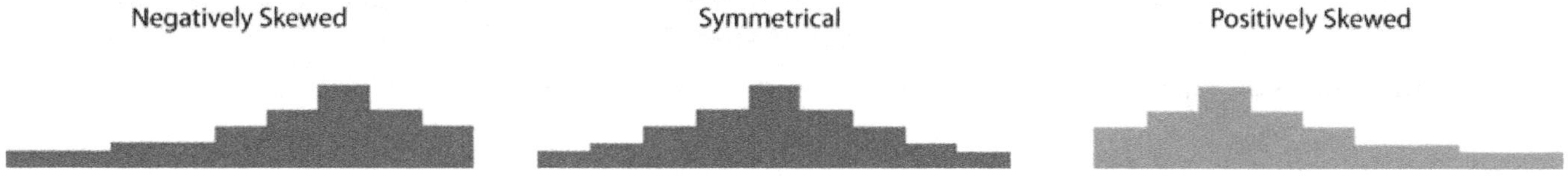

Negatively Skewed       Symmetrical       Positively Skewed

Figure 12.3 Histograms Showing Negatively Skewed, Symmetrical, and Positively Skewed Distributions

An **outlier** is an extreme score that is much higher or lower than the rest of the scores in the distribution. Sometimes outliers represent truly extreme scores on the variable of interest. For example, on the Beck Depression Inventory, a single clinically depressed person might be an outlier in a sample of otherwise happy and high-functioning peers. However, outliers can also represent errors or misunderstandings on the part of the researcher or participant, equipment malfunctions, or similar problems. We will say more about how to interpret outliers and what to do about them later in this chapter.

# Measures of Central Tendency and Variability

It is also useful to be able to describe the characteristics of a distribution more precisely. Here we look at how to do this in terms of two important characteristics: their central tendency and their variability.

## Central Tendency

The **central tendency** of a distribution is its middle—the point around which the scores in the distribution tend to cluster. (Another term for central tendency is *average*.) Looking back at Figure 12.1, for example, we can see that the self-esteem scores tend to cluster around the values of 20 to 22. Here we will consider the three most common measures of central tendency: the mean, the median, and the mode.

The **mean** of a distribution (symbolized M) is the sum of the scores divided by the number of scores. It is an average. As a formula, it looks like this:

$$M = \Sigma X / N$$

In this formula, the symbol $\Sigma$ (the Greek letter sigma) is the summation sign and means to sum across the values of the variable X. N represents the number of scores. The mean is by far the most common measure of central tendency, and there are some good reasons for this. It usually provides a good indication of the central tendency of a distribution, and it is easily understood by most people. In addition, the mean has statistical properties that make it especially useful in doing inferential statistics.

An alternative to the mean is the **median**. The median is the middle score in the sense that half the scores in the distribution are less than it and half are greater than it. The simplest way to find the median is to organize the scores from lowest to highest and locate the score in the middle. Consider, for example, the following set of seven scores:

8 4 12 14 3 2 3

To find the median, simply rearrange the scores from lowest to highest and locate the one in the middle.

2 3 3 **4** 8 12 14

In this case, the median is 4 because there are three scores lower than 4 and three scores higher than 4. When there is an even number of scores, there are two scores in the middle of the distribution, in which case the median is the value halfway between them. For example, if we were to add a score of 15 to the preceding data set, there would be two scores (both 4 and 8) in the middle of the distribution, and the median would be halfway between them (6).

One final measure of central tendency is the mode. The **mode** is the most frequent score in a distribution. In the self-esteem distribution presented in Table 12.1 and Figure 12.1, for example, the mode is 22. More students had that score than any other. The mode is the only measure of central tendency that can also be used for categorical variables.

In a distribution that is both unimodal and symmetrical, the mean, median, and mode will be very close to each other at the peak of the distribution. In a bimodal or asymmetrical distribution, the mean, median, and mode can be quite different. In a bimodal distribution, the mean and median will tend to be between the peaks, while the mode will be at the tallest peak. In a skewed distribution, the mean will differ from the median in the direction of the skew (i.e., the direction of the longer tail). For highly skewed distributions, the mean can be pulled so far in the direction of the skew that it is no longer a good measure of the central tendency of that distribution. Imagine, for example, a set of four simple reaction times of 200, 250, 280, and 250 milliseconds (ms). The mean is 245 ms. But the addition of one more score of 5,000 ms—perhaps because the participant was not paying attention—would raise the mean to 1,445 ms. Not only is this measure of central tendency greater than 80% of the scores in the distribution, but it also does not seem to represent the behavior of anyone in the distribution very well. This is why researchers often prefer the median for highly skewed distributions (such as distributions of reaction times).

Keep in mind, though, that you are not required to choose a single measure of central tendency in analyzing your data. Each one provides slightly different information, and all of them can be useful.

## Measures of Variability

The **variability** of a distribution is the extent to which the scores vary around their central tendency. Consider the two distributions in Figure 12.4, both of which have the same central tendency. The mean, median, and mode of each distribution are 10. Notice, however, that the two distributions differ in terms of their variability. The top one has relatively low variability, with all the scores relatively close to the center. The bottom one has relatively high variability, with the scores are spread across a much greater range.

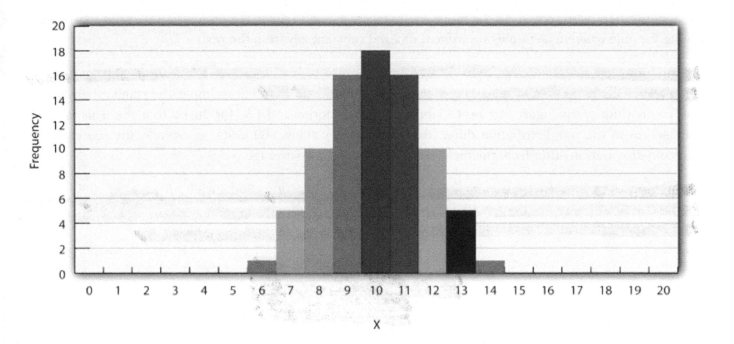

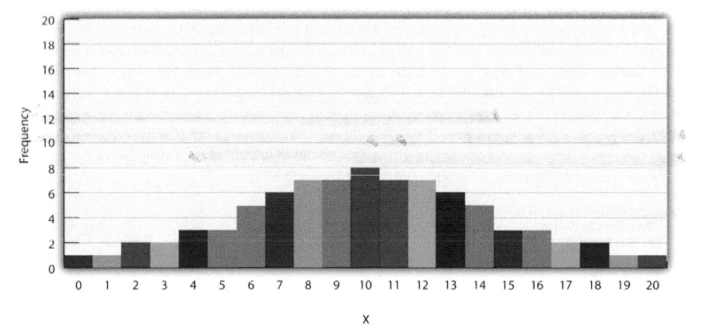

Figure 12.4 Histograms Showing Hypothetical Distributions With the Same Mean, Median, and Mode (10) but With Low Variability (Top) and High Variability (Bottom)

One simple measure of variability is the **range**, which is simply the difference between the highest and lowest scores in the distribution. The range of the self-esteem scores in Table 12.1, for example, is the difference between the highest score (24) and the lowest score (15). That is, the range is 24 – 15 = 9. Although the range is easy to compute and understand, it can be misleading when there are outliers. Imagine, for example, an exam on which all the students scored between 90 and 100. It has a range of 10. But if there was a single student who scored 20, the range would increase to 80—giving the impression that the scores were quite variable when in fact only one student differed substantially from the rest.

By far the most common measure of variability is the standard deviation. The **standard deviation** of a distribution is the average distance between the scores and the mean. For example, the standard deviations of the distributions in Figure 12.4 are 1.69 for the top distribution and 4.30 for the bottom one. That is, while the scores in the top distribution differ from the mean by about 1.69 units on average, the scores in the bottom distribution differ from the mean by about 4.30 units on average.

Computing the standard deviation involves a slight complication. Specifically, it involves finding the difference between each score and the mean, squaring each difference, finding the mean of these squared differences, and finally finding the square root of that mean. The formula looks like this:

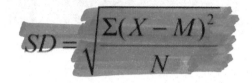

$$SD = \sqrt{\frac{\Sigma(X - M)^2}{N}}$$

The computations for the standard deviation are illustrated for a small set of data in Table 12.3. The first column is a set of eight scores that has a mean of 5. The second column is the difference between each score and the mean. The third column is the square of each of these differences. Notice that although the differences can be negative, the squared differences are always positive—meaning that the standard deviation is always positive. At the bottom of the third column is the mean of the squared differences, which is also called the **variance** (symbolized $SD^2$). Although the variance is itself a measure of variability, it generally plays a larger role in inferential statistics than in descriptive statistics. Finally, below the variance is the square root of the variance, which is the standard deviation.

**Table 12.3 Computations for the Standard Deviation**

| X | X - M | $(X - M)^2$ |
|---|-------|-------------|
| 3 | -2 | 4 |
| 5 | 0 | 0 |
| 4 | -1 | 1 |
| 2 | -3 | 9 |
| 7 | 2 | 4 |
| 6 | 1 | 1 |
| 5 | 0 | 0 |
| 8 | 3 | 9 |
| M = 5 | | $SD^2$=28/8=3.50 |
| | | $SD=\sqrt{3.50}$=1.87 |

### N or N − 1

If you have already taken a statistics course, you may have learned to divide the sum of the squared differences by N − 1 rather than by N when you compute the variance and standard deviation. Why is this?

By definition, the standard deviation is the square root of the mean of the squared differences. This implies dividing the sum of squared differences by N, as in the formula just presented. Computing the standard deviation this way is appropriate when your goal is simply to describe the variability in a sample. And learning it this way emphasizes that the variance is in fact the *mean* of the squared differences—and the standard deviation is the square root of this *mean*.

However, most calculators and software packages divide the sum of squared differences by N − 1. This is because the standard deviation of a sample tends to be a bit lower than the standard deviation of the population the sample was selected from. Dividing the sum of squares by N − 1 corrects for this tendency and results in a better estimate of the population standard deviation. Because researchers generally think of their data as representing a sample selected from a larger population—and because they are generally interested in drawing conclusions about the population—it makes sense to routinely apply this correction.

## Percentile Ranks and z Scores

In many situations, it is useful to have a way to describe the location of an individual score within its distribution. One approach is the percentile rank. The **percentile rank** of a score is the percentage of scores in the distribution that are lower than that score. Consider, for example, the distribution in Table 12.1. For any score in the distribution, we can find its percentile rank by counting the number of scores in the distribution that are lower than that score and converting that number to a percentage of the total number of scores. Notice, for example, that five of the students represented by the data in Table 12.1 had self-esteem scores of 23. In this distribution, 32 of the 40 scores (80%) are lower than 23. Thus each of these students has a percentile rank of 80. (It can also be said that they scored "at the 80th percentile.") Percentile ranks are often used to report the results of standardized tests of ability or achievement. If your percentile rank on a test of verbal ability were 40, for example, this would mean that you scored higher than 40% of the people who took the test.

Another approach is the z score. The **z score** for a particular individual is the difference between that individual's score and the mean of the distribution, divided by the standard deviation of the distribution:

$$z = (X-M)/SD$$

A z score indicates how far above or below the mean a raw score is, but it expresses this in terms of the standard deviation. For example, in a distribution of intelligence quotient (IQ) scores with a mean of 100 and a standard deviation of 15, an IQ score of 110 would have a z score of (110 − 100) / 15 = +0.67. In other words, a score of 110 is 0.67 standard deviations (approximately two thirds of a standard deviation) above the mean.

Similarly, a raw score of 85 would have a z score of (85 – 100) / 15 = –1.00. In other words, a score of 85 is one standard deviation below the mean.

There are several reasons that z scores are important. Again, they provide a way of describing where an individual's score is located within a distribution and are sometimes used to report the results of standardized tests. They also provide one way of defining outliers. For example, outliers are sometimes defined as scores that have z scores less than –3.00 or greater than +3.00. In other words, they are defined as scores that are more than three standard deviations from the mean. Finally, z scores play an important role in understanding and computing other statistics, as we will see shortly.

*Online Descriptive Statistics*

Although many researchers use commercially available software such as SPSS and Excel to analyze their data, there are several free online analysis tools that can also be extremely useful. Many allow you to enter or upload your data and then make one click to conduct several descriptive statistical analyses. Among them are the following.

Rice Virtual Lab in Statistics

http://onlinestatbook.com/stat_analysis/index.html

VassarStats

http://faculty.vassar.edu/lowry/VassarStats.html

Bright Stat

http://www.brightstat.com

For a more complete list, see http://statpages.org/index.html.

# 53. Describing Statistical Relationships

### Learning Objectives

1. Describe differences between groups in terms of their means and standard deviations, and in terms of Cohen's *d*.
2. Describe correlations between quantitative variables in terms of Pearson's *r*.

As we have seen throughout this book, most interesting research questions in psychology are about statistical relationships between variables. In this section, we revisit the two basic forms of statistical relationship introduced earlier in the book—differences between groups or conditions and relationships between quantitative variables—and we consider how to describe them in more detail.

## Differences Between Groups or Conditions

Differences between groups or conditions are usually described in terms of the mean and standard deviation of each group or condition. For example, Thomas Ollendick and his colleagues conducted a study in which they evaluated two one-session treatments for simple phobias in children (Ollendick et al., 2009)[1]. They randomly assigned children with an intense fear (e.g., to dogs) to one of three conditions. In the exposure condition, the children actually confronted the object of their fear under the guidance of a trained therapist. In the education condition, they learned about phobias and some strategies for coping with them. In the wait-list control condition, they were waiting to receive a treatment after the study was over. The severity of each child's phobia was then rated on a 1-to-8 scale by a clinician who did not know which treatment the child had received. (This was one of several dependent variables.) The mean fear rating in the education condition was 4.83 with a standard deviation of 1.52, while the mean fear rating in the exposure condition was 3.47 with a standard deviation of 1.77. The mean fear rating in the control condition was 5.56 with a standard deviation of 1.21. In other words, both treatments worked, but the exposure treatment worked better than the education treatment. As we have seen, differences between group or condition means can be presented in a bar graph like that in Figure 12.5, where the heights of the bars represent the group or condition means. We will look more closely at creating American Psychological Association (APA)-style bar graphs shortly.

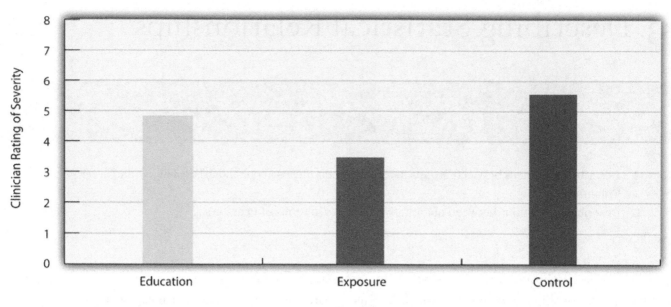

Figure 12.5 Bar Graph Showing Mean Clinician Phobia Ratings for Children in Two Treatment Conditions

It is also important to be able to describe the strength of a statistical relationship, which is often referred to as the **effect size**. The most widely used measure of effect size for differences between group or condition means is called **Cohen's d**, which is the difference between the two means divided by the standard deviation:

$$d = (M1 - M2)/SD$$

In this formula, it does not really matter which mean is M1 and which is M2. If there is a treatment group and a control group, the treatment group mean is usually M1 and the control group mean is M2. Otherwise, the larger mean is usually M1 and the smaller mean M2 so that Cohen's d turns out to be positive. Indeed Cohen's d values should always be positive so it is the absolute difference between the means that is considered in the numerator. The standard deviation in this formula is usually a kind of average of the two group standard deviations called the pooled-within groups standard deviation. To compute the pooled within-groups standard deviation, add the sum of the squared differences for Group 1 to the sum of squared differences for Group 2, divide this by the sum of the two sample sizes, and then take the square root of that. Informally, however, the standard deviation of either group can be used instead.

Conceptually, Cohen's d is the difference between the two means expressed in standard deviation units. (Notice its similarity to a z score, which expresses the difference between an individual score and a mean in standard deviation units.) A Cohen's d of 0.50 means that the two group means differ by 0.50 standard deviations (half a standard deviation). A Cohen's d of 1.20 means that they differ by 1.20 standard deviations. But how should we interpret these values in terms of the strength of the relationship or the size of the difference between the means? Table 12.4 presents some guidelines for interpreting Cohen's d values in psychological research (Cohen, 1992)[2]. Values near 0.20 are considered small, values near 0.50 are considered medium, and values near 0.80 are considered large. Thus a Cohen's d value of 0.50 represents a medium-sized difference between two means, and a Cohen's d value of 1.20 represents a very large difference in the context of psychological research. In the research by Ollendick and his colleagues, there was a large difference ($d = 0.82$) between the exposure and education conditions.

**Table 12.4 Guidelines for Referring to Cohen's d and Pearson's r Values as "Strong," "Medium," or "Weak"**

| Relationship strength | Cohen's $d$ | Pearson's $r$ |
|---|---|---|
| Strong/large | 0.80 | ± 0.50 |
| Medium | 0.50 | ± 0.30 |
| Weak/small | 0.20 | ± 0.10 |

Cohen's $d$ is useful because it has the same meaning regardless of the variable being compared or the scale it was measured on. A Cohen's $d$ of 0.20 means that the two group means differ by 0.20 standard deviations whether we are talking about scores on the Rosenberg Self-Esteem scale, reaction time measured in milliseconds, number of siblings, or diastolic blood pressure measured in millimeters of mercury. Not only does this make it easier for researchers to communicate with each other about their results, it also makes it possible to combine and compare results across different studies using different measures.

Be aware that the term *effect size* can be misleading because it suggests a causal relationship—that the difference between the two means is an "effect" of being in one group or condition as opposed to another. Imagine, for example, a study showing that a group of exercisers is happier on average than a group of nonexercisers, with an "effect size" of $d = 0.35$. If the study was an experiment—with participants randomly assigned to exercise and no-exercise conditions—then one could conclude that exercising caused a small to medium-sized increase in happiness. If the study was cross-sectional, however, then one could conclude only that the exercisers were happier than the nonexercisers by a small to medium-sized amount. In other words, simply calling the difference an "effect size" does not make the relationship a causal one.

## Sex Differences Expressed as Cohen's d

Researcher Janet Shibley Hyde has looked at the results of numerous studies on psychological sex differences and expressed the results in terms of Cohen's $d$ (Hyde, 2007)[3]. Following are a few of the values she has found, averaging across several studies in each case. (Note that because she always treats the mean for men as M1 and the mean for women as M2, positive values indicate that men score higher and negative values indicate that women score higher.)

| | |
|---|---|
| Mathematical problem solving | +0.08 |
| Reading comprehension | −0.09 |
| Smiling | −0.40 |
| Aggression | +0.50 |
| Attitudes toward casual sex | +0.81 |
| Leadership effectiveness | −0.02 |

Hyde points out that although men and women differ by a large amount on some variables (e.g., attitudes toward casual sex), they differ by only a small amount on the vast majority. In many cases, Cohen's $d$ is less than 0.10, which she terms a "trivial" difference. (The difference in talkativeness discussed in Chapter 1 was also trivial: $d = 0.06$.) Although researchers and non-researchers alike often emphasize sex *differences*, Hyde has argued that it makes at least as much sense to think of men and women as fundamentally *similar*. She refers to this as the "gender similarities hypothesis."

## Correlations Between Quantitative Variables

As we have seen throughout the book, many interesting statistical relationships take the form of correlations between quantitative variables. For example, researchers Kurt Carlson and Jacqueline Conard conducted a study on the relationship between the alphabetical position of the first letter of people's last names (from A = 1 to Z = 26) and how quickly those people responded to consumer appeals (Carlson & Conard, 2011)[4]. In one study, they sent emails to a large group of MBA students, offering free basketball tickets from a limited supply. The result was that the further toward the end of the alphabet students' last names were, the faster they tended to respond. These results are summarized in Figure 12.6.

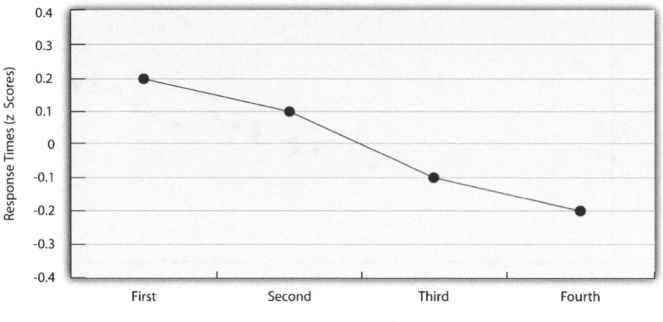

Figure 12.6 *Line Graph Showing the Relationship Between the Alphabetical Position of People's Last Names and How Quickly Those People Respond to Offers of Consumer Goods*

Such relationships are often presented using line graphs or scatterplots, which show how the level of one variable differs across the range of the other. In the line graph in Figure 12.6, for example, each point represents the mean response time for participants with last names in the first, second, third, and fourth quartiles (or quarters) of the name distribution. It clearly shows how response time tends to decline as people's last names get closer to the end of the alphabet. The scatterplot in Figure 12.7, shows the relationship between 25 research methods students' scores on the Rosenberg Self-Esteem Scale given on two occasions a week apart. Here the points represent individuals, and we can see that the higher students scored on the first occasion, the higher they tended to score on the second occasion. In general, line graphs are used when the variable on the $x$-axis has (or is organized into) a small number of distinct values, such as the four quartiles of the name distribution. Scatterplots are used when the variable on the $x$-axis has a large number of values, such as the different possible self-esteem scores.

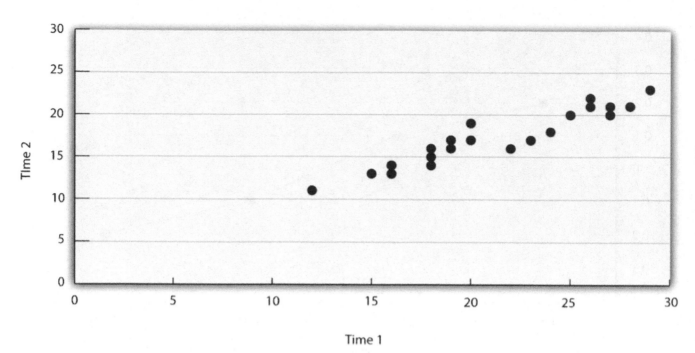

Figure 12.7 *Statistical Relationship Between Several University Students' Scores on the Rosenberg Self-Esteem Scale Given on Two Occasions a Week Apart*

The data presented in Figure 12.7 provide a good example of a positive relationship, in which higher scores on one variable tend to be associated with higher scores on the other (so that the points go from the lower left to the upper right of the graph). The data presented in Figure 12.6 provide a good example of a negative relationship, in which higher scores on one variable tend to be associated with lower scores on the other (so that the points go from the upper left to the lower right).

Both of these examples are also **linear relationships**, in which the points are reasonably well fit by a single straight line. **Nonlinear relationships** are those in which the points are better fit by a curved line. Figure 12.8, for example, shows a hypothetical relationship between the amount of sleep people get per night and their level of depression. In this example, the line that best fits the points is a curve—a kind of upside down "U"—because people who get about eight hours of sleep tend to be the least depressed, while those who get too little sleep and those who get too much sleep tend to be more depressed. Nonlinear relationships are not uncommon in psychology, but a detailed discussion of them is beyond the scope of this book.

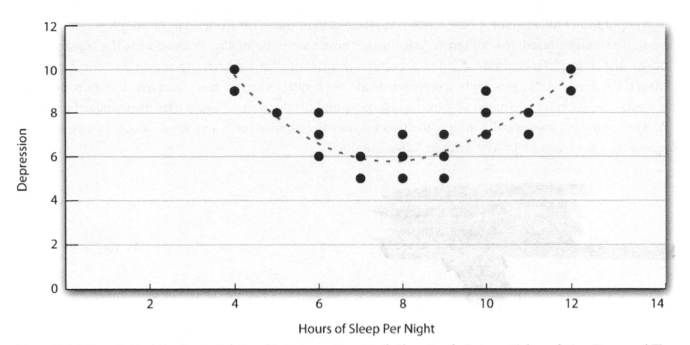

Figure 12.8 A Hypothetical Nonlinear Relationship Between How Much Sleep People Get per Night and How Depressed They Are

As we saw earlier in the book, the strength of a correlation between quantitative variables is typically measured using a statistic called Pearson's r. As Figure 12.9 shows, its possible values range from –1.00, through zero, to +1.00. A value of 0 means there is no relationship between the two variables. In addition to his guidelines for interpreting Cohen's d, Cohen offered guidelines for interpreting Pearson's r in psychological research (see Table 12.4). Values near ±.10 are considered small, values near ± .30 are considered medium, and values near ±.50 are considered large. Notice that the sign of Pearson's r is unrelated to its strength. Pearson's r values of +.30 and –.30, for example, are equally strong; it is just that one represents a moderate positive relationship and the other a moderate negative relationship. Like Cohen's d, Pearson's r is also referred to as a measure of "effect size" even though the relationship may not be a causal one.

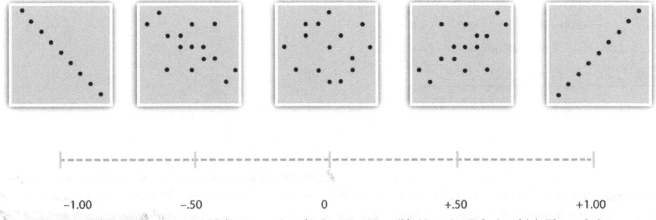

Figure 12.9 Pearson's r Ranges From –1.00 (Representing the Strongest Possible Negative Relationship), Through 0 (Representing No Relationship), to +1.00 (Representing the Strongest Possible Positive Relationship)

The computations for Pearson's r are more complicated than those for Cohen's d. Although you may never have to do them by hand, it is still instructive to see how. Computationally, Pearson's r is the "mean cross-product of z scores." To compute it, one starts by transforming all the scores to z scores. For the X variable, subtract the mean of X from each score and divide each difference by the standard deviation of X. For the Y variable, subtract the mean of Y from each score and divide each difference by the standard deviation of Y. Then, for each individual, multiply the two z scores together to form a cross-product. Finally, take the mean of the cross-products. The formula looks like this:

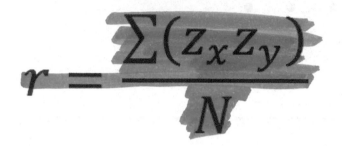

$$r = \frac{\sum (z_x z_y)}{N}$$

Table 12.5 illustrates these computations for a small set of data. The first column lists the scores for the X variable, which has a mean of 4.00 and a standard deviation of 1.90. The second column is the z-score for each of these raw scores. The third and fourth columns list the raw scores for the Y variable, which has a mean of 40 and a standard deviation of 11.78, and the corresponding z scores. The fifth column lists the cross-products. For example, the first one is 0.00 multiplied by –0.85, which is equal to 0.00. The second is 1.58 multiplied by 1.19, which is equal to 1.88. The mean of these cross-products, shown at the bottom of that column, is Pearson's r, which in this case is +.53. There are other formulas for computing Pearson's r by hand that may be quicker. This approach, however, is much clearer in terms of communicating conceptually what Pearson's r is.

Table 12.5 Sample Computations for Pearson's r

| X | $z_x$ | Y | $z_y$ | $z_x z_y$ |
|---|---|---|---|---|
| 4 | 0.00 | 30 | –0.85 | 0.00 |
| 7 | 1.58 | 54 | 1.19 | 1.88 |
| 2 | –1.05 | 23 | –1.44 | 1.52 |
| 5 | 0.53 | 43 | 0.26 | 0.13 |
| 2 | –1.05 | 50 | 0.85 | –0.89 |
| Mx = 4.00 | | My = 40.00 | | r = 0.53 |
| SDx = 1.90 | | SDy = 11.78 | | |

As we saw earlier, there are two common situations in which the value of Pearson's r can be misleading. One is when the relationship under study is nonlinear. Even though Figure 12.8 shows a fairly strong relationship between depression and sleep, Pearson's r would be close to zero because the points in the scatterplot are not well fit by a single straight line. This means that it is important to make a scatterplot and confirm that a relationship is approximately linear before using Pearson's r. The other is when one or both of the variables have a limited range in the sample relative to the population. This problem is referred to as **restriction of range.** Assume, for example, that there is a strong negative correlation between people's age and their enjoyment of hip hop music as shown by the scatterplot in Figure 12.10. Pearson's r here is −.77. However, if we were to collect data only from 18- to 24-year-olds–represented by the shaded area of Figure 12.11–then the relationship would seem to be quite weak. In fact, Pearson's r for this restricted range of ages is 0. It is a good idea, therefore, to design studies to avoid restriction of range. For example, if age is one of your primary variables, then you can plan to collect data from people of a wide range of ages. Because restriction of range is not always anticipated or easily avoidable, however, it is good practice to examine your data for possible restriction of range and to interpret Pearson's r in light of it. (There are also statistical methods to correct Pearson's r for restriction of range, but they are beyond the scope of this book).

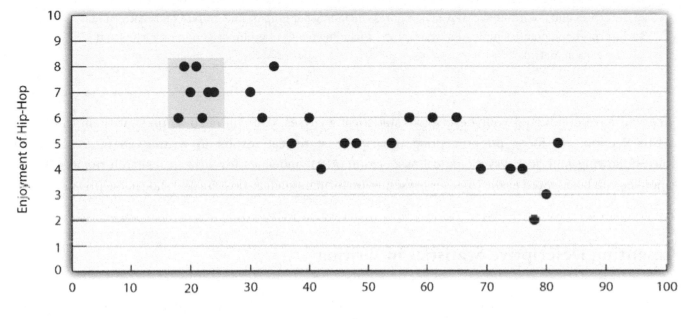

Figure 12.10 Hypothetical Data Showing How a Strong Overall Correlation Can Appear to Be Weak When One Variable Has a Restricted Range. The overall correlation here is −.77, but the correlation for the 18- to 24-year-olds (in the blue box) is 0.

# Notes

1.  Ollendick, T. H., Öst, L.-G., Reuterskiöld, L., Costa, N., Cederlund, R., Sirbu, C.,...Jarrett, M. A. (2009). One-session treatments of specific phobias in youth: A randomized clinical trial in the United States and Sweden. *Journal of Consulting and Clinical Psychology, 77,* 504–516.

2.  Cohen, J. (1992). A power primer. *Psychological Bulletin, 112,* 155–159.

3.  Hyde, J. S. (2007). New directions in the study of gender similarities and differences. *Current Directions in Psychological Science, 16,* 259–263.

4.  Carlson, K. A., & Conard, J. M. (2011). The last name effect: How last name influences acquisition timing. *Journal of Consumer Research, 38*(2), 300–307. doi: 10.1086/658470

# 54. Expressing Your Results

### Learning Objectives

1. Write out simple descriptive statistics in American Psychological Association (APA) style.
2. Interpret and create simple APA-style figures–including bar graphs, line graphs, and scatterplots.
3. Interpret and create simple APA-style tables–including tables of group or condition means and correlation matrices.

Once you have conducted your descriptive statistical analyses, you will need to present them to others. In this section, we focus on presenting descriptive statistical results in writing, in figures, and in tables–following American Psychological Association (APA) guidelines for written research reports. These principles can be adapted easily to other presentation formats such as posters and slide show presentations.

## Presenting Descriptive Statistics in Writing

Recall that APA style includes several rules for presenting numerical results in the text (see 4.31–4.34 in the APA *Publication Manual*) . These include using words only for numbers less than 10 that do not represent precise statistical results and using numerals for numbers 10 and higher. However, statistical results are always presented in the form of numerals rather than words and are usually rounded to two decimal places (e.g., "2.00" rather than "two" or "2"). They can be presented either in the narrative description of the results or parenthetically–much like reference citations. When you have a small number of results to report, it is often most efficient to write them out. Here are some examples:

The mean age of the participants was 22.43 years with a standard deviation of 2.34.

Among the participants with low self-esteem, those in a negative mood expressed stronger intentions to have unprotected sex ($M = 4.05$, $SD = 2.32$) than those in a positive mood ($M = 2.15$, $SD = 2.27$).

The treatment group had a mean of 23.40 ($SD = 9.33$), while the control group had a mean of 20.87 ($SD = 8.45$).

The test-retest correlation was .96.

There was a moderate negative correlation between the alphabetical position of respondents' last names and their response time ($r = -.27$).

Notice that when presented in the narrative, the terms *mean* and *standard deviation* are written out, but when presented parenthetically, the symbols M and *SD* are used instead. Notice also that it is especially important to use parallel construction to express similar or comparable results in similar ways. The third example is *much* better than the following nonparallel alternative:

The treatment group had a mean of 23.40 (SD = 9.33), while 20.87 was the mean of the control group, which had a standard deviation of 8.45.

## Presenting Descriptive Statistics in Figures

When you have a large number of results to report, you can often do it more clearly and efficiently with a graphical depiction of the data, such as pie charts, bar graphs, or scatterplots. In an APA style research report, these graphs are presented as **figures**. When you prepare figures for an APA-style research report, there are some general guidelines that you should keep in mind. First, the figure should always add important information rather than repeat information that already appears in the text or in a table (if a figure presents information more clearly or efficiently, then you should keep the figure and eliminate the text or table.) Second, figures should be as simple as possible. For example, the *Publication Manual* discourages the use of color unless it is absolutely necessary (although color can still be an effective element in posters, slide show presentations, or textbooks.) Third, figures should be interpretable on their own. A reader should be able to understand the basic result based only on the figure and its caption and should not have to refer to the text for an explanation.

There are also several more technical guidelines for presentation of figures that include the following (see the APA Publication Manual section 5.20 through 5.30):

- Layout of graphs

  - In general, scatterplots, bar graphs, and line graphs should be slightly wider than they are tall.
  - The independent variable should be plotted on the $x$-axis and the dependent variable on the $y$-axis.
  - Values should increase from left to right on the $x$-axis and from bottom to top on the $y$-axis.
  - The $x$-axis and $y$-axis should begin with the value zero.
- Axis Labels and Legends

  - Axis labels should be clear and concise and include the units of measurement if they do not appear in the caption.
  - Axis labels should be parallel to the axis.
  - Legends should appear within the figure.
  - Text should be in the same simple font throughout and no smaller than 8 point and no larger than 14 point.
- Captions

  - Captions are titled with the word "Figure", followed by the figure number in the order in which it appears in the text, and terminated with a period. This title is italicized.
  - After the title is a brief description of the figure terminated with a period (e.g., "Reaction times of the control versus experimental group.")

- Following the description, include any information needed to interpret the figure, such as any abbreviations, units of measurement (if not in the axis label), units of error bars, etc.

*"Convincing"* retrieved from http://imgs.xkcd.com/comics/convincing.png (CC-BY-NC 2.5)

# Bar Graphs

As we have seen throughout this book, **bar graphs** are generally used to present and compare the mean scores for two or more groups or conditions. The bar graph in Figure 12.11 is an APA-style version of Figure 12.4. Notice that it conforms to all the guidelines listed. A new element in Figure 12.11 is the smaller vertical bars that extend both upward and downward from the top of each main bar. These are **error bars**, and they represent the variability in each group or condition. Although they sometimes extend one standard *deviation* in each direction, they are more likely to extend one standard *error* in each direction (as in Figure 12.11). The **standard error** is the standard deviation of the group divided by the square root of the sample size of the group. The standard error is used because, in general, a difference between group means that is greater than two standard errors is statistically significant. Thus one can "see" whether a difference is statistically significant based on a bar graph with error bars.

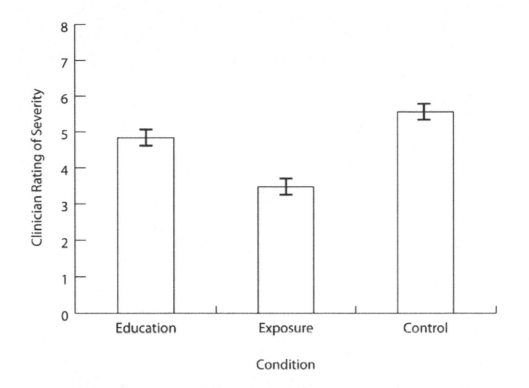

*Figure X.* Mean clinician's rating of phobia severity for participants receiving the education treatment and the exposure treatment. Error bars represent standard errors.

*Figure 12.11 Sample APA-Style Bar Graph, With Error Bars Representing the Standard Errors, Based on Research by Ollendick and Colleagues*

## Line Graphs

**Line graphs** are used when the independent variable is measured in a more continuous manner (e.g., time) or to present correlations between quantitative variables when the independent variable has, or is organized into, a relatively small number of distinct levels. Each point in a line graph represents the mean score on the dependent variable for participants at one level of the independent variable. Figure 12.12 is an APA-style version of the results of Carlson and Conard. Notice that it includes error bars representing the standard error and conforms to all the stated guidelines.

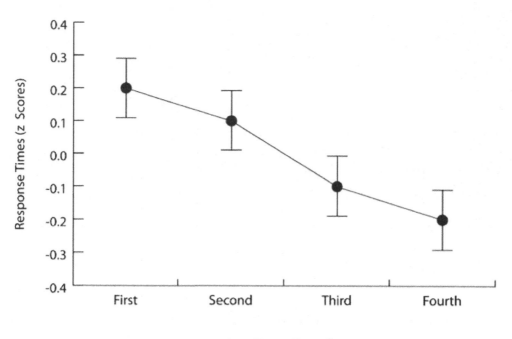

*Figure X.* Mean response time by the alphabetical position of respondents' names in the alphabet. Response times are expressed as **z** scores. Error bars represent standard errors.

*Figure 12.12 Sample APA-Style Line Graph Based on Research by Carlson and Conard*

In most cases, the information in a line graph could just as easily be presented in a bar graph. In Figure 12.12, for example, one could replace each point with a bar that reaches up to the same level and leave the error bars right where they are. This emphasizes the fundamental similarity of the two types of statistical relationship. Both are differences in the average score on one variable across levels of another. The convention followed by most researchers, however, is to use a bar graph when the variable plotted on the x-axis is categorical and a line graph when it is quantitative.

## Scatterplots

Scatterplots are used to present correlations and relationships between quantitative variables when the variable on the x-axis (typically the independent variable) has a large number of levels. Each point in a scatterplot represents an individual rather than the mean for a group of individuals, and there are no lines connecting the points. The graph in Figure 12.13 is an APA-style version of Figure 12.7, which illustrates a few additional points. First, when the variables on the x-axis and y-axis are conceptually similar and measured on the same scale—as here, where they are measures of the same variable on two different occasions—this can be emphasized by making the axes the same length. Second, when two or more individuals fall at exactly the same point on the graph, one way this can be indicated is by offsetting the points slightly along the x-axis. Other ways are by displaying the number of individuals in parentheses next to the point or by making the point larger or darker in proportion to the number of individuals. Finally, the straight line that best fits the points in the scatterplot, which is called the regression line, can also be included.

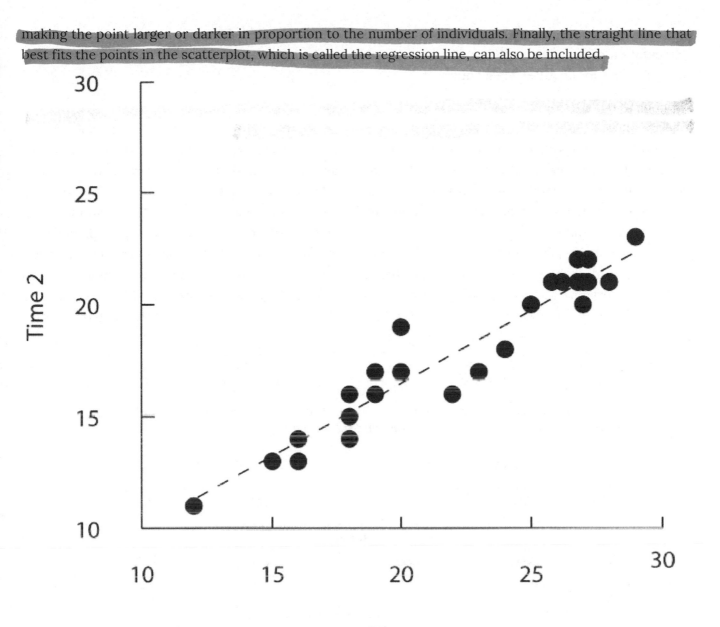

*Figure X.* Relationship between scores on the Rosenberg self-esteem scale taken by 25 research methods students on two occasions one week apart. Pearson's r =.96.

*Figure 12.13 Sample APA-Style Scatterplot*

## Expressing Descriptive Statistics in Tables

Like graphs, tables can be used to present large amounts of information clearly and efficiently. The same general principles apply to tables as apply to graphs. They should add important information to the presentation of your results, be as simple as possible, and be interpretable on their own. Again, we focus here on tables for an APA-style manuscript.

The most common use of tables is to present several means and standard deviations—usually for complex research designs with multiple independent and dependent variables. Figure 12.14, for example, shows the results of a hypothetical study similar to the one by MacDonald and Martineau (2002)[1] (The means in Figure 12.14 are the means reported by MacDonald and Martineau, but the standard errors are not). Recall that these researchers categorized participants as having low or high self-esteem, put them into a negative or positive mood, and measured their intentions to have unprotected sex. They also measured participants' attitudes toward unprotected sex. Notice that the table includes horizontal lines spanning the entire table at the top and bottom, and just beneath the column headings. Furthermore, every column has a heading—including the leftmost column—and there are additional headings that span two or more columns that help to organize the information and present it more efficiently. Finally, notice that APA-style tables are numbered consecutively starting at 1 (Table 1, Table 2, and so on) and given a brief but clear and descriptive title.

**Table X**

*Means and Standard Deviations of Intentions to Have Unprotected Sex and Attitudes Toward Unprotected Sex as a Function of Both Mood and Self-Esteem*

| Self-Esteem | Negative mood | | Positive mood | |
|---|---|---|---|---|
| | M | SD | M | SD |
| Intentions | | | | |
| High | 2.46 | 1.97 | 2.45 | 2.00 |
| Low | 4.05 | 2.32 | 2.15 | 2.27 |
| Attitudes | | | | |
| High | 1.65 | 2.23 | 1.82 | 2.32 |
| Low | 1.95 | 2.01 | 1.23 | 1.75 |

*Figure 12.14 Sample APA-Style Table Presenting Means and Standard Deviations*

Another common use of tables is to present correlations—usually measured by Pearson's r—among several variables. This kind of table is called a **correlation matrix**. Figure 12.15 is a correlation matrix based on a study by David McCabe and colleagues (McCabe, Roediger, McDaniel, Balota, & Hambrick, 2010)[2]. They were interested in the relationships between working memory and several other variables. We can see from the table that the correlation between working memory and executive function, for example, was an extremely strong .96, that the correlation between working memory and vocabulary was a medium .27, and that all the measures except vocabulary tend to decline with age. Notice here that only half the table is filled in because the other half would have identical values. For example, the Pearson's *r* value in the upper right corner (working memory and age) would be the same as the one in the lower left corner (age and working memory). The correlation of a variable with itself is always 1.00, so these values are replaced by dashes to make the table easier to read.

Table X

*Correlations Between Five Cognitive Variables and Age*

| Measure | 1 | 2 | 3 | 4 | 5 |
|---|---|---|---|---|---|
| 1. Working memory | — | | | | |
| 2. Executive function | .96 | — | | | |
| 3. Processing speed | .78 | .78 | — | | |
| 4. Vocabulary | .27 | .45 | .08 | — | |
| 5. Episodic memory | .73 | .75 | .52 | .38 | — |
| 6. Age | –.59 | –.56 | –.82 | .22 | –.41 |

Figure 12.15 Sample APA-Style Table (Correlation Matrix) Based on Research by McCabe and Colleagues

As with graphs, precise statistical results that appear in a table do not need to be repeated in the text. Instead, the writer can note major trends and alert the reader to details (e.g., specific correlations) that are of particular interest.

# Notes

1. MacDonald, T. K., & Martineau, A. M. (2002). Self-esteem, mood, and intentions to use condoms: When does low self-esteem lead to risky health behaviors? *Journal of Experimental Social Psychology, 38*, 299–306.

2. McCabe, D. P., Roediger, H. L., McDaniel, M. A., Balota, D. A., & Hambrick, D. Z. (2010). The relationship between working memory capacity and executive functioning. *Neuropsychology, 24*(2), 222–243. doi:10.1037/a0017619

# 55. Conducting Your Analyses

Even when you understand the statistics involved, analyzing data can be a complicated process. It is likely that for each of several participants, there are data for several different variables: demographics such as sex and age, one or more independent variables, one or more dependent variables, and perhaps a manipulation check. Furthermore, the "raw" (unanalyzed) data might take several different forms—completed paper-and-pencil questionnaires, computer files filled with numbers or text, videos, or written notes—and these may have to be organized, coded, or combined in some way. There might even be missing, incorrect, or just "suspicious" responses that must be dealt with. In this section, we consider some practical advice to make this process as organized and efficient as possible.

## Prepare Your Data for Analysis

Whether your raw data are on paper or in a computer file (or both), there are a few things you should do before you begin analyzing them. First, be sure they do not include any information that might identify individual participants and be sure that you have a secure location where you can store the data and a separate secure location where you can store any consent forms. Unless the data are highly sensitive, a locked room or password-protected computer is usually good enough. It is also a good idea to make photocopies or backup files of your data and store them in yet another secure location—at least until the project is complete. Professional researchers usually keep a copy of their raw data and consent forms for several years in case questions about the procedure, the data, or participant consent arise after the project is completed.

Next, you should check your **raw data** to make sure that they are complete and appear to have been accurately recorded (whether it was participants, yourself, or a computer program that did the recording). At this point, you might find that there are illegible or missing responses, or obvious misunderstandings (e.g., a response of "12" on a 1-to-10 rating scale). You will have to decide whether such problems are severe enough to make a participant's data unusable. If information about the main independent or dependent variable is missing, or if several responses are missing or suspicious, you may have to exclude that participant's data from the analyses. If you do decide to exclude any data, do not throw them away or delete them because you or another researcher might want to see them later. Instead, set them aside and keep notes about why you decided to exclude them because you will need to report this information.

Now you are ready to enter your data in a spreadsheet program or, if it is already in a computer file, to format it for analysis. You can use a general spreadsheet program like Microsoft Excel or a statistical analysis program like SPSS to create your **data file**. (Data files created in one program can usually be converted to work with other programs.) The most common format is for each row to represent a participant and for each column to represent a variable (with the variable name at the top of each column). A sample data file is shown in Table 12.6. The first column contains participant identification numbers. This is followed by columns containing demographic information (sex and age), independent variables (mood, four self-esteem items, and the total of the four self-esteem items), and finally dependent variables (intentions and attitudes). Categorical variables can usually be entered as category labels (e.g., "M" and "F" for male and female) or as numbers (e.g., "0" for negative mood and "1" for positive mood). Although category labels are often clearer, some analyses might require numbers. SPSS allows you to enter numbers but also attach a category label to each number.

**Table 12.6 Sample Data File**

| ID | SEX | AGE | MOOD | SE1 | SE2 | SE3 | SE4 | TOTAL | INT | ATT |
|----|-----|-----|------|-----|-----|-----|-----|-------|-----|-----|
| 1 | M | 20 | 1 | 2 | 3 | 2 | 3 | 10 | 6 | 5 |
| 2 | F | 22 | 1 | 1 | 0 | 2 | 1 | 4 | 4 | 4 |
| 3 | F | 19 | 0 | 2 | 2 | 2 | 2 | 8 | 2 | 3 |
| 4 | F | 24 | 0 | 3 | 3 | 3 | 3 | 11 | 0 | 0 |

If you have multiple-response measures—such as the self-esteem measure in Table 12.6—you could combine the items by hand and then enter the total score in your spreadsheet. However, it is much better to enter each response as a separate variable in the spreadsheet—as with the self-esteem measure in Table 12.6—and use the software to combine them (e.g., using the "AVERAGE" function in Excel or the "Compute" function in SPSS). Not only is this approach more accurate, but it allows you to detect and correct errors, to assess internal consistency, and to analyze individual responses if you decide to do so later.

# Preliminary Analyses

Before turning to your primary research questions, there are often several preliminary analyses to conduct. For multiple-response measures, you should assess the internal consistency of the measure. Statistical programs like SPSS will allow you to compute Cronbach's α or Cohen's κ. If this is beyond your comfort level, you can still compute and evaluate a split-half correlation.

Next, you should analyze each important variable separately. (This step is not necessary for manipulated independent variables, of course, because you as the researcher determined what the distribution would be.) Make histograms for each one, note their shapes, and compute the common measures of central tendency and variability. Be sure you understand what these statistics *mean* in terms of the variables you are interested in. For example, a distribution of self-report happiness ratings on a 1-to-10-point scale might be unimodal and negatively skewed with a mean of 8.25 and a standard deviation of 1.14. But what this *means* is that most participants rated themselves fairly high on the happiness scale, with a small number rating themselves noticeably lower.

Now is the time to identify outliers, examine them more closely, and decide what to do about them. You might discover that what at first appears to be an outlier is the result of a response being entered incorrectly in the data file, in which case you only need to correct the data file and move on. Alternatively, you might suspect that an outlier represents some other kind of error, misunderstanding, or lack of effort by a participant. For example, in a reaction time distribution in which most participants took only a few seconds to respond, a participant who took 3 minutes to respond would be an outlier. It seems likely that this participant did not understand the task (or at least was not paying very close attention). Also, including their reaction time would have a large impact on the mean and standard deviation for the sample. In situations like this, it can be justifiable to exclude the outlying response or participant from the analyses. If you do this, however, you should keep notes on which responses or participants you have excluded and why, and apply those same criteria consistently to every response and every participant. When you present your results, you should indicate how many responses or participants you excluded and the specific criteria that you used. And again, do not literally throw away or delete the data that you choose to exclude. Just set them aside because you or another researcher might want to see them later.

Keep in mind that outliers do not *necessarily* represent an error, misunderstanding, or lack of effort. They might represent truly extreme responses or participants. For example, in one large university student sample, the vast majority of participants reported having had fewer than 15 sexual partners, but there were also a few extreme scores of 60 or 70 (Brown & Sinclair, 1999)[1]. Although these scores might represent errors, misunderstandings, or even intentional exaggerations, it is also plausible that they represent honest and even accurate estimates. One strategy here would be to use the median and other statistics that are not strongly affected by the outliers. Another would be to analyze the data both including and excluding any outliers. If the results are essentially the same, which they often are, then it makes sense to leave the outliers. If the results differ depending on whether the outliers are included or excluded them, then both analyses can be reported and the differences between them discussed.

## Planned and Exploratory Analyses

Finally, you are ready to answer your primary research questions. When you designed your study, you might have had a hypothesis that a particular relationship might exist in the data. In this case, you would conduct a **planned analysis**, to test a relationship that you expected in your hypothesis. For example, if you expected a difference between group or condition means, you can compute the relevant group or condition means and standard deviations, make a bar graph to display the results, and compute Cohen's $d$. If you expected a correlation between quantitative variables, you can make a line graph or scatterplot (be sure to check for nonlinearity and restriction of range) and compute Pearson's $r$.

Once you have conducted your planned analyses, you can move on to examine the possibility there might be relationships in the data that you did not hypothesize. This would be an **exploratory analysis**, an analysis that you are undertaking without an existing hypothesis. These analyses will help you explore your data for other interesting results that might provide the basis for future research (and material for the discussion section of your paper). Daryl Bem (2003) suggests that you

[e]xamine [your data] from every angle. Analyze the sexes separately. Make up new composite indexes. If a datum suggests a new hypothesis, try to find additional evidence for it elsewhere in the data. If you see dim traces of interesting patterns, try to reorganize the data to bring them into bolder relief. If there are participants you don't like, or trials, observers, or interviewers who gave you anomalous results, drop them (temporarily). Go on a fishing expedition for something–anything–interesting. (p. 186–187)[2]

It is important to differentiate planned from exploratory analyses in writing your results and discussion sections of your report. This is because complex sets of data are likely to include "patterns" that occurred entirely by chance, and every time you do another unplanned analysis on these data, you increase the likelihood these chance patterns will appear to be real patterns, what is referred to as a "Type 1" error (see the chapter on Inferential Statistics). Thus results discovered while doing exploratory analyses (what Bem calls a "fishing expedition") should be viewed skeptically and replicated in at least one new study before being presented. But, if you do find interesting relationships you did not expect in the data, explain that they might be worthy of additional research.

## Understand Your Descriptive Statistics

In the next chapter, we will consider inferential statistics–a set of techniques for deciding whether the results for your sample are likely to apply to the population. Although inferential statistics are important for reasons that will be explained shortly, beginning researchers sometimes forget that their descriptive statistics really tell "what happened" in their study. For example, imagine that a treatment group of 50 participants has a mean score of 34.32 (SD = 10.45), a control group of 50 participants has a mean score of 21.45 (SD = 9.22), and Cohen's $d$ is an extremely strong 1.31. Although conducting and reporting inferential statistics (like a $t$ test) would certainly be a required part of any formal report on this study, it should be clear from the descriptive statistics alone that the treatment worked. Or imagine that a scatterplot shows an indistinct "cloud" of points and Pearson's $r$ is a trivial –.02. Again, although conducting and reporting inferential statistics would be a required part of any formal report on this study, it should be clear from the descriptive statistics alone that the variables are essentially unrelated. The point is that you should always be sure that you thoroughly understand your results at a descriptive level first, and then move on to the inferential statistics.

## Notes

1.  Brown, N. R., & Sinclair, R. C. (1999). Estimating number of lifetime sexual partners: Men and women do it differently. *The Journal of Sex Research, 36,* 292–297.

2.  Bem, D. J. (2003). Writing the empirical journal article. In J. M. Darley, M. P. Zanna, & H. L. Roediger III (Eds.), *The complete academic: A career guide* (2nd ed., pp. 185–219). Washington, DC: American Psychological Association.

# 56. Key Takeaways and Exercises

- Every variable has a distribution—a way that the scores are distributed across the levels. The distribution can be described using a frequency table and histogram. It can also be described in words in terms of its shape, including whether it is unimodal or bimodal, and whether it is symmetrical or skewed.
- The central tendency, or middle, of a distribution can be described precisely using three statistics—the mean, median, and mode. The mean is the sum of the scores divided by the number of scores, the median is the middle score, and the mode is the most common score.
- The variability, or spread, of a distribution can be described precisely using the range and standard deviation. The range is the difference between the highest and lowest scores, and the standard deviation is the average amount by which the scores differ from the mean.
- The location of a score within its distribution can be described using percentile ranks or z scores. The percentile rank of a score is the percentage of scores below that score, and the z score is the difference between the score and the mean divided by the standard deviation.
- Differences between groups or conditions are typically described in terms of the means and standard deviations of the groups or conditions or in terms of Cohen's *d* and are presented in bar graphs.
- Cohen's *d* is a measure of relationship strength (or effect size) for differences between two group or condition means. It is the difference of the means divided by the standard deviation. In general, values of ±0.20, ±0.50, and ±0.80 can be considered small, medium, and large, respectively.
- Correlations between quantitative variables are typically described in terms of Pearson's *r* and presented in line graphs or scatterplots.
- Pearson's *r* is a measure of relationship strength (or effect size) for relationships between quantitative variables. It is the mean cross-product of the two sets of z scores. In general, values of ±.10, ±.30, and ±.50 can be considered small, medium, and large, respectively.
- In an APA-style article, simple results are most efficiently presented in the text, while more complex results are most efficiently presented in graphs or tables.
- APA style includes several rules for presenting numerical results in the text. These include using words only for numbers less than 10 that do not represent precise statistical results, and rounding results to two decimal places, using words (e.g., "mean") in the text and symbols (e.g., "M") in parentheses.
- APA style includes several rules for presenting results in graphs and tables. Graphs and tables should add information rather than repeating information, be as simple as possible, and be interpretable on their own with a descriptive caption (for graphs) or a descriptive title (for tables).
- Raw data must be prepared for analysis by examining them for possible errors, organizing them, and entering them into a spreadsheet program.
- Preliminary analyses on any data set include checking the reliability of measures, evaluating the effectiveness of any manipulations, examining the distributions of individual variables, and identifying outliers.
- Outliers that appear to be the result of an error, a misunderstanding, or a lack of effort can be excluded from the analyses. The criteria for excluded responses or participants should be applied in the same way to all the data and described when you present your results. Excluded data should be set aside rather

than destroyed or deleted in case they are needed later.
- Descriptive statistics tell the story of what happened in a study. Although inferential statistics are also important, it is essential to understand the descriptive statistics first.

## Exercises

- Practice: Make a frequency table and histogram for the following data. Then write a short description of the shape of the distribution in words.

  ○ 11, 8, 9, 12, 9, 10, 12, 13, 11, 13, 12, 6, 10, 17, 13, 11, 12, 12, 14, 14

- Practice: For the data in Exercise 1, compute the mean, median, mode, standard deviation, and range.
- Practice: Using the data in Exercises 1 and 2, find

  ○ the percentile ranks for scores of 9 and 14
  ○ the z scores for scores of 8 and 12.

- Practice: The following data represent scores on the Rosenberg Self-Esteem Scale for a sample of 10 Japanese university students and 10 American university students. (Although hypothetical, these data are consistent with empirical findings [Schmitt & Allik, 2005][1].) Compute the means and standard deviations of the two groups, make a bar graph, compute Cohen's $d$, and describe the strength of the relationship in words.

| Japan | United States |
|-------|---------------|
| 25    | 27            |
| 20    | 30            |
| 24    | 34            |
| 28    | 37            |
| 30    | 26            |
| 32    | 24            |
| 21    | 28            |
| 24    | 35            |
| 20    | 33            |
| 26    | 36            |

- Practice: The hypothetical data that follow are extraversion scores and the number of Facebook friends for 15 university students. Make a scatterplot for these data, compute Pearson's $r$, and describe the relationship in words.

| Extraversion | Facebook Friends |
|---|---|
| 8 | 75 |
| 10 | 315 |
| 4 | 28 |
| 6 | 214 |
| 12 | 176 |
| 14 | 95 |
| 10 | 120 |
| 11 | 150 |
| 4 | 32 |
| 13 | 250 |
| 5 | 99 |
| 7 | 136 |
| 8 | 185 |
| 11 | 88 |
| 10 | 144 |

- Practice: In a classic study, men and women rated the importance of physical attractiveness in both a short-term mate and a long-term mate (Buss & Schmitt, 1993)[2]. The means and standard deviations are as follows. Men / Short Term: M = 5.67, SD = 2.34; Men / Long Term: M = 4.43, SD = 2.11; Women / Short Term: M = 5.67, SD = 2.48; Women / Long Term: M = 4.22, SD = 1.98. Present these results

  - in writing
  - in a figure
  - in a table

- Discussion: What are at least two reasonable ways to deal with each of the following outliers based on the discussion in this chapter? (a) A participant estimating ordinary people's heights estimates one woman's height to be "84 inches" tall. (b) In a study of memory for ordinary objects, one participant scores 0 out of 15. (c) In response to a question about how many "close friends" she has, one participant writes "32."

# Notes

1. Schmitt, D. P., & Allik, J. (2005). Simultaneous administration of the Rosenberg Self-Esteem Scale in 53 nations: Exploring the universal and culture-specific features of global self-esteem. *Journal of Personality and Social Psychology, 89*, 623–642.

2. Buss, D. M., & Schmitt, D. P. (1993). Sexual strategies theory: A contextual evolutionary analysis of human mating. *Psychological Review, 100,* 204–232.

# CHAPTER XIII
# INFERENTIAL STATISTICS

Recall that Matthias Mehl and his colleagues, in their study of sex differences in talkativeness, found that the women in their sample spoke a mean of 16,215 words per day and the men a mean of 15,669 words per day (Mehl, Vazire, Ramirez-Esparza, Slatcher, & Pennebaker, 2007)[1]. But despite this sex difference in their sample, they concluded that there was no evidence of a sex difference in talkativeness in the population. Recall also that Allen Kanner and his colleagues, in their study of the relationship between daily hassles and symptoms, found a correlation of +.60 in their sample (Kanner, Coyne, Schaefer, & Lazarus, 1981)[2]. But they concluded that this finding means there is a relationship between hassles and symptoms in the population. This assertion raises the question of how researchers can say whether their sample result reflects something that is true of the population.

The answer to this question is that they use a set of techniques called inferential statistics, which is what this chapter is about. We focus, in particular, on null hypothesis testing, the most common approach to inferential statistics in psychological research. We begin with a conceptual overview of null hypothesis testing, including its purpose and basic logic. Then we look at several null hypothesis testing techniques for drawing conclusions about differences between means and about correlations between quantitative variables. Finally, we consider a few other important ideas related to null hypothesis testing, including some that can be helpful in planning new studies and interpreting results. We also look at some long-standing criticisms of null hypothesis testing and some ways of dealing with these criticisms.

# 57. Understanding Null Hypothesis Testing

## The Purpose of Null Hypothesis Testing

As we have seen, psychological research typically involves measuring one or more variables in a sample and computing descriptive summary data (e.g., means, correlation coefficients) for those variables. These descriptive data for the sample are called **statistics**. In general, however, the researcher's goal is not to draw conclusions about that *sample* but to draw conclusions about the *population* that the sample was selected from. Thus researchers must use sample statistics to draw conclusions about the corresponding values in the population. These corresponding values in the population are called **parameters**. Imagine, for example, that a researcher measures the number of depressive symptoms exhibited by each of 50 adults with clinical depression and computes the mean number of symptoms. The researcher probably wants to use this sample statistic (the mean number of symptoms for the sample) to draw conclusions about the corresponding population parameter (the mean number of symptoms for adults with clinical depression).

Unfortunately, sample statistics are not perfect estimates of their corresponding population parameters. This is because there is a certain amount of random variability in any statistic from sample to sample. The mean number of depressive symptoms might be 8.73 in one sample of adults with clinical depression, 6.45 in a second sample, and 9.44 in a third—even though these samples are selected randomly from the same population. Similarly, the correlation (Pearson's $r$) between two variables might be +.24 in one sample, −.04 in a second sample, and +.15 in a third—again, even though these samples are selected randomly from the same population. This random variability in a statistic from sample to sample is called **sampling error**. (Note that the term *error* here refers to random variability and does not imply that anyone has made a mistake. No one "commits a sampling error.")

One implication of this is that when there is a statistical relationship in a sample, it is not always clear that there is a statistical relationship in the population. A small difference between two group means in a sample might indicate that there is a small difference between the two group means in the population. But it could also be that there is no difference between the means in the population and that the difference in the sample is just a matter of sampling error. Similarly, a Pearson's $r$ value of −.29 in a sample might mean that there is a negative relationship in the population. But it could also be that there is no relationship in the population and that the relationship in the sample is just a matter of sampling error.

In fact, any statistical relationship in a sample can be interpreted in two ways:

- There is a relationship in the population, and the relationship in the sample reflects this.
- There is no relationship in the population, and the relationship in the sample reflects only sampling error.

The purpose of null hypothesis testing is simply to help researchers decide between these two interpretations.

## The Logic of Null Hypothesis Testing

**Null hypothesis testing** (often called null hypothesis significance testing or NHST) is a formal approach to deciding between two interpretations of a statistical relationship in a sample. One interpretation is called the **null hypothesis** (often symbolized $H_0$ and read as "H-zero"). This is the idea that there is no relationship in the population and that the relationship in the sample reflects only sampling error. Informally, the null hypothesis is that the sample relationship "occurred by chance." The other interpretation is called the **alternative hypothesis** (often symbolized as $H_1$). This is the idea that there is a relationship in the population and that the relationship in the sample reflects this relationship in the population.

Again, every statistical relationship in a sample can be interpreted in either of these two ways: It might have occurred by chance, or it might reflect a relationship in the population. So researchers need a way to decide between them. Although there are many specific null hypothesis testing techniques, they are all based on the same general logic. The steps are as follows:

- Assume for the moment that the null hypothesis is true. There is no relationship between the variables in the population.
- Determine how likely the sample relationship would be if the null hypothesis were true.
- If the sample relationship would be extremely unlikely, then **reject the null hypothesis** in favor of the alternative hypothesis. If it would not be extremely unlikely, then **retain the null hypothesis**.

Following this logic, we can begin to understand why Mehl and his colleagues concluded that there is no difference in talkativeness between women and men in the population. In essence, they asked the following question: "If there were no difference in the population, how likely is it that we would find a small difference of $d = 0.06$ in our sample?" Their answer to this question was that this sample relationship would be fairly likely if the null hypothesis were true. Therefore, they retained the null hypothesis—concluding that there is no evidence of a sex difference in the population. We can also see why Kanner and his colleagues concluded that there is a correlation between hassles and symptoms in the population. They asked, "If the null hypothesis were true, how likely is it that we would find a strong correlation of +.60 in our sample?" Their answer to this question was that this sample relationship would be fairly unlikely if the null hypothesis were true. Therefore, they rejected the null hypothesis in favor of the alternative hypothesis—concluding that there is a positive correlation between these variables in the population.

A crucial step in null hypothesis testing is finding the probability of the sample result or a more extreme result if the null hypothesis were true (Lakens, 2017).[1] This probability is called the **p value**. A low $p$ value means that the sample or more extreme result would be unlikely if the null hypothesis were true and leads to the rejection of the null hypothesis. A $p$ value that is not low means that the sample or more extreme result would be likely if the null hypothesis were true and leads to the retention of the null hypothesis. But how low must the $p$ value criterion be before the sample result is considered unlikely enough to reject the null hypothesis? In null hypothesis testing, this criterion is called **α (alpha)** and is almost always set to .05. If there is a 5% chance or less of a result at least as extreme as the sample result if the null hypothesis were true, then the null hypothesis is rejected. When this happens, the result is said to be **statistically significant**. If there is greater than a 5% chance of a result as extreme as the sample result when the null hypothesis is true, then the null hypothesis is retained. This does not necessarily mean that the researcher *accepts* the null hypothesis as true—only that there is not *currently* enough evidence to reject it. Researchers often use the expression "fail to reject the null hypothesis" rather than "retain the null hypothesis," but they never use the expression "accept the null hypothesis."

## The Misunderstood p Value

The $p$ value is one of the most misunderstood quantities in psychological research (Cohen, 1994)[2]. Even professional researchers misinterpret it, and it is not unusual for such misinterpretations to appear in statistics textbooks!

The most common misinterpretation is that the $p$ value is the probability that the null hypothesis is true—that the sample result occurred by chance. For example, a misguided researcher might say that because the $p$ value is .02, there is only a 2% chance that the result is due to chance and a 98% chance that it reflects a real relationship in the population. But this is *incorrect*. The $p$ value is really the probability of a result at least as extreme as the sample result *if* the null hypothesis *were* true. So a $p$ value of .02 means that if the null hypothesis were true, a sample result this extreme would occur only 2% of the time.

You can avoid this misunderstanding by remembering that the $p$ value is not the probability that any particular *hypothesis* is true or false. Instead, it is the probability of obtaining the *sample result* if the null hypothesis were true.

*"Null Hypothesis" retrieved from http://imgs.xkcd.com/comics/null_hypothesis.png* (CC-BY-NC 2.5)

## Role of Sample Size and Relationship Strength

Recall that null hypothesis testing involves answering the question, "If the null hypothesis were true, what is the probability of a sample result as extreme as this one?" In other words, "What is the $p$ value?" It can be helpful to see that the answer to this question depends on just two considerations: the strength of the relationship and the size of the sample. Specifically, the stronger the sample relationship and the larger the sample, the less likely the result would be if the null hypothesis were true. That is, the lower the $p$ value. This should make sense. Imagine a study in which a sample of 500 women is compared with a sample of 500 men in terms of some psychological characteristic, and Cohen's $d$ is a strong 0.50. If there were really no sex difference in the population, then a result this strong based on such a large sample should seem highly unlikely. Now imagine a similar study in which a sample of three women is compared with a sample of three men, and Cohen's $d$ is a weak 0.10. If there were no sex difference in the population, then a relationship this weak based on such a small sample should seem likely. And this is precisely why the null hypothesis would be rejected in the first example and retained in the second.

Of course, sometimes the result can be weak and the sample large, or the result can be strong and the sample small. In these cases, the two considerations trade off against each other so that a weak result can be statistically significant if the sample is large enough and a strong relationship can be statistically significant even if the sample is small. Table 13.1 shows roughly how relationship strength and sample size combine to determine whether a sample result is statistically significant. The columns of the table represent the three levels of relationship strength: weak, medium, and strong. The rows represent four sample sizes that can be considered small, medium, large, and extra large in the context of psychological research. Thus each cell in the table represents a combination of relationship strength and sample size. If a cell contains the word *Yes*, then this combination would be statistically significant for both Cohen's *d* and Pearson's *r*. If it contains the word *No*, then it would not be statistically significant for either. There is one cell where the decision for *d* and *r* would be different and another where it might be different depending on some additional considerations, which are discussed in Section 13.2 "Some Basic Null Hypothesis Tests"

**Table 13.1 How Relationship Strength and Sample Size Combine to Determine Whether a Result Is Statistically Significant**

| Sample Size | Relationship strength | | |
|---|---|---|---|
| | Weak | Medium | Strong |
| Small (N = 20) | No | No | $d$ = Maybe<br>$r$ = Yes |
| Medium (N = 50) | No | Yes | Yes |
| Large (N = 100) | $d$ = Yes<br>$r$ = No | Yes | Yes |
| Extra large (N = 500) | Yes | Yes | Yes |

Although Table 13.1 provides only a rough guideline, it shows very clearly that weak relationships based on medium or small samples are never statistically significant and that strong relationships based on medium or larger samples are always statistically significant. If you keep this lesson in mind, you will often know whether a result is statistically significant based on the descriptive statistics alone. It is extremely useful to be able to develop this kind of intuitive judgment. One reason is that it allows you to develop expectations about how your formal null hypothesis tests are going to come out, which in turn allows you to detect problems in your analyses. For example, if your sample relationship is strong and your sample is medium, then you would expect to reject the null hypothesis. If for some reason your formal null hypothesis test indicates otherwise, then you need to double-check your computations and interpretations. A second reason is that the ability to make this kind of intuitive judgment is an indication that you understand the basic logic of this approach in addition to being able to do the computations.

## Statistical Significance Versus Practical Significance

Table 13.1 illustrates another extremely important point. A statistically significant result is not necessarily a strong one. Even a very weak result can be statistically significant if it is based on a large enough sample. This is closely related to Janet Shibley Hyde's argument about sex differences (Hyde, 2007)[3]. The differences between women and men in mathematical problem solving and leadership ability are statistically significant. But the word *significant* can cause people to interpret these differences as strong and important—perhaps even important enough to influence the college courses they take or even who they vote for. As we have seen, however, these statistically significant differences are actually quite weak—perhaps even "trivial."

This is why it is important to distinguish between the *statistical* significance of a result and the *practical* significance of that result. **Practical significance** refers to the importance or usefulness of the result in some real-world context. Many sex differences are statistically significant—and may even be interesting for purely scientific reasons—but they are not practically significant. In clinical practice, this same concept is often referred to as "clinical significance." For example, a study on a new treatment for social phobia might show that it produces a statistically significant positive effect. Yet this effect still might not be strong enough to justify the time, effort, and other costs of putting it into practice—especially if easier and cheaper treatments that work almost as well already exist. Although statistically significant, this result would be said to lack practical or clinical significance.

*"Conditional Risk" retrieved from http://imgs.xkcd.com/comics/conditional_risk.png (CC-BY-NC 2.5)*

# Notes

1. Lakens, D. (2017, December 25). About *p*-values: Understanding common misconceptions. [Blog post] Retrieved from https://correlaid.org/en/blog/understand-p-values/

2. Cohen, J. (1994). The world is round: *p* < .05. *American Psychologist, 49*, 997–1003.

3. Hyde, J. S. (2007). New directions in the study of gender similarities and differences. *Current Directions in Psychological Science, 16*, 259–263.

# 58. Some Basic Null Hypothesis Tests

### Learning Objectives

1. Conduct and interpret one-sample, dependent-samples, and independent-samples *t*- tests.
2. Interpret the results of one-way, repeated measures, and factorial ANOVAs.
3. Conduct and interpret null hypothesis tests of Pearson's *r*.

In this section, we look at several common null hypothesis testing procedures. The emphasis here is on providing enough information to allow you to conduct and interpret the most basic versions. In most cases, the online statistical analysis tools mentioned in Chapter 12 will handle the computations—as will programs such as Microsoft Excel and SPSS.

## The *t*-Test

As we have seen throughout this book, many studies in psychology focus on the difference between two means. The most common null hypothesis test for this type of statistical relationship is the **t- test**. In this section, we look at three types of *t* tests that are used for slightly different research designs: the one-sample *t*-test, the dependent-samples *t*- test, and the independent-samples *t*- test. You may have already taken a course in statistics, but we will refresh your statistical

## One-Sample *t*-Test

The **one-sample t-test** is used to compare a sample mean (M) with a hypothetical population mean ($\mu_0$) that provides some interesting standard of comparison. The null hypothesis is that the mean for the population ($\mu$) is equal to the hypothetical population mean: $\mu = \mu_0$. The alternative hypothesis is that the mean for the population is different from the hypothetical population mean: $\mu \neq \mu_0$. To decide between these two hypotheses, we need to find the probability of obtaining the sample mean (or one more extreme) if the null hypothesis were true. But finding this *p* value requires first computing a test statistic called *t*. (A **test statistic** is a statistic that is computed only to help find the *p* value.) The formula for *t* is as follows:

$$t = \frac{M - \mu_0}{\left(\dfrac{SD}{\sqrt{N}}\right)}$$

Again, M is the sample mean and $\mu_0$ is the hypothetical population mean of interest. SD is the sample standard deviation and N is the sample size.

The reason the t statistic (or any test statistic) is useful is that we know how it is distributed when the null hypothesis is true. As shown in Figure 13.1, this distribution is unimodal and symmetrical, and it has a mean of 0. Its precise shape depends on a statistical concept called the degrees of freedom, which for a one-sample t-test is N – 1. (There are 24 degrees of freedom for the distribution shown in Figure 13.1.) The important point is that knowing this distribution makes it possible to find the p value for any t score. Consider, for example, a t score of 1.50 based on a sample of 25. The probability of a t score at least this extreme is given by the proportion of t scores in the distribution that are at least this extreme. For now, let us define *extreme* as being far from zero in either direction. Thus the p value is the proportion of t scores that are 1.50 or above *or* that are –1.50 or below—a value that turns out to be .14.

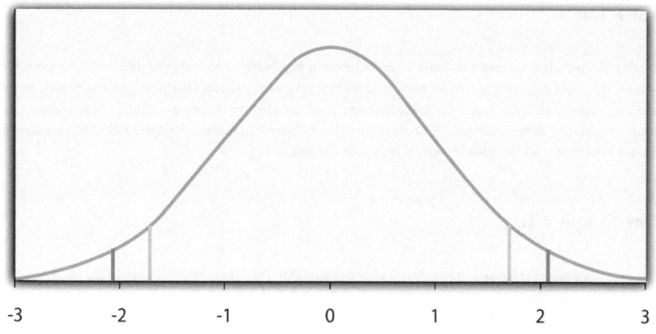

-3        -2        -1        0        1        2        3

Figure 13.1 Distribution of t Scores (With 24 Degrees of Freedom) When the Null Hypothesis Is True. *The red vertical lines represent the two-tailed critical values, and the green vertical lines the one-tailed critical values when α = .05.*

Fortunately, we do not have to deal directly with the distribution of t scores. If we were to enter our sample data and hypothetical mean of interest into one of the online statistical tools in Chapter 12 or into a program like SPSS (Excel does not have a one-sample t-test function), the output would include both the t score and the p value. At this point, the rest of the procedure is simple. If p is equal to or less than .05, we reject the null hypothesis and conclude that the population mean differs from the hypothetical mean of interest. If $p$ is greater than .05, we retain the null hypothesis and conclude that there is not enough evidence to say that the population mean differs from the hypothetical mean of interest. (Again, technically, we conclude only that we do not have enough evidence to conclude that it *does* differ.)

If we were to compute the $t$ score by hand, we could use a table like Table 13.2 to make the decision. This table does not provide actual $p$ values. Instead, it provides the **critical values** of $t$ for different degrees of freedom (*df*) when $\alpha$ is .05. For now, let us focus on the two-tailed critical values in the last column of the table. Each of these values should be interpreted as a pair of values: one positive and one negative. For example, the two-tailed critical values when there are 24 degrees of freedom are 2.064 and −2.064. These are represented by the red vertical lines in Figure 13.1. The idea is that any $t$ score below the lower critical value (the left-hand red line in Figure 13.1) is in the lowest 2.5% of the distribution, while any $t$ score above the upper critical value (the right-hand red line) is in the highest 2.5% of the distribution. Therefore any $t$ score beyond the critical value in *either* direction is in the most extreme 5% of $t$ scores when the null hypothesis is true and has a $p$ value less than .05. Thus if the $t$ score we compute is beyond the critical value in either direction, then we reject the null hypothesis. If the $t$ score we compute is between the upper and lower critical values, then we retain the null hypothesis.

**Table 13.2 Table of Critical Values of t When α = .05**

| df | Critical value One-tailed | Two-tailed |
|---|---|---|
| 3 | 2.353 | 3.182 |
| 4 | 2.132 | 2.776 |
| 5 | 2.015 | 2.571 |
| 6 | 1.943 | 2.447 |
| 7 | 1.895 | 2.365 |
| 8 | 1.860 | 2.306 |
| 9 | 1.833 | 2.262 |
| 10 | 1.812 | 2.228 |
| 11 | 1.796 | 2.201 |
| 12 | 1.782 | 2.179 |
| 13 | 1.771 | 2.160 |
| 14 | 1.761 | 2.145 |
| 15 | 1.753 | 2.131 |
| 16 | 1.746 | 2.120 |
| 17 | 1.740 | 2.110 |
| 18 | 1.734 | 2.101 |
| 19 | 1.729 | 2.093 |
| 20 | 1.725 | 2.086 |
| 21 | 1.721 | 2.080 |
| 22 | 1.717 | 2.074 |
| 23 | 1.714 | 2.069 |
| 24 | 1.711 | 2.064 |
| 25 | 1.708 | 2.060 |
| 30 | 1.697 | 2.042 |
| 35 | 1.690 | 2.030 |
| 40 | 1.684 | 2.021 |
| 45 | 1.679 | 2.014 |
| 50 | 1.676 | 2.009 |
| 60 | 1.671 | 2.000 |
| 70 | 1.667 | 1.994 |
| 80 | 1.664 | 1.990 |
| 90 | 1.662 | 1.987 |
| 100 | 1.660 | 1.984 |

Thus far, we have considered what is called a **two-tailed test**, where we reject the null hypothesis if the $t$ score for the sample is extreme in either direction. This test makes sense when we believe that the sample mean might differ from the hypothetical population mean but we do not have good reason to expect the difference to go in a particular direction. But it is also possible to do a **one-tailed test**, where we reject the null hypothesis only if the $t$ score for the sample is extreme in one direction that we specify before collecting the data. This test makes sense when we have good reason to expect the sample mean will differ from the hypothetical population mean in a particular direction.

Here is how it works. Each one-tailed critical value in Table 13.2 can again be interpreted as a pair of values: one positive and one negative. A $t$ score below the lower critical value is in the lowest 5% of the distribution, and a $t$ score above the upper critical value is in the highest 5% of the distribution. For 24 degrees of freedom, these values are –1.711 and 1.711. (These are represented by the green vertical lines in Figure 13.1.) However, for a one-tailed test, we must decide before collecting data whether we expect the sample mean to be lower than the hypothetical population mean, in which case we would use only the lower critical value, or we expect the sample mean to be greater than the hypothetical population mean, in which case we would use only the upper critical value. Notice that we still reject the null hypothesis when the $t$ score for our sample is in the most extreme 5% of the $t$ scores we would expect if the null hypothesis were true so $\alpha$ remains at .05. We have simply redefined extreme to refer only to one tail of the distribution. The advantage of the one-tailed test is that critical values are less extreme. If the sample mean differs from the hypothetical population mean in the expected direction, then we have a better chance of rejecting the null hypothesis. The disadvantage is that if the sample mean differs from the hypothetical population mean in the unexpected direction, then there is no chance at all of rejecting the null hypothesis.

## Example One-Sample $t$–Test

Imagine that a health psychologist is interested in the accuracy of university students' estimates of the number of calories in a chocolate chip cookie. He shows the cookie to a sample of 10 students and asks each one to estimate the number of calories in it. Because the actual number of calories in the cookie is 250, this is the hypothetical population mean of interest ($\mu_0$). The null hypothesis is that the mean estimate for the population ($\mu$) is 250. Because he has no real sense of whether the students will underestimate or overestimate the number of calories, he decides to do a two-tailed test. Now imagine further that the participants' actual estimates are as follows:

250, 280, 200, 150, 175, 200, 200, 220, 180, 250.

The mean estimate for the sample (M) is 212.00 calories and the standard deviation (SD) is 39.17. The health psychologist can now compute the $t$ score for his sample:

$$t = \frac{212 - 250}{\left(\dfrac{39.17}{\sqrt{10}}\right)} = -3.07$$

If he enters the data into one of the online analysis tools or uses SPSS, it would also tell him that the two-tailed $p$ value for this $t$ score (with 10 − 1 = 9 degrees of freedom) is .013. Because this is less than .05, the health psychologist would reject the null hypothesis and conclude that university students tend to underestimate the number of calories in a chocolate chip cookie. If he computes the $t$ score by hand, he could look at Table 13.2 and see that the critical value of $t$ for a two-tailed test with 9 degrees of freedom is ±2.262. The fact that his $t$ score was more extreme than this critical value would tell him that his $p$ value is less than .05 and that he should reject the null hypothesis. Using APA style, these results would be reported as follows: $t(9) = -3.07$, $p = .01$. Note that the $t$ and $p$ are italicized, the degrees of freedom appear in brackets with no decimal remainder, and the values of $t$ and $p$ are rounded to two decimal places.

Finally, if this researcher had gone into this study with good reason to expect that university students underestimate the number of calories, then he could have done a one-tailed test instead of a two-tailed test. The only thing this decision would change is the critical value, which would be −1.833. This slightly less extreme value would make it a bit easier to reject the null hypothesis. However, if it turned out that university students overestimate the number of calories—no matter how much they overestimate it—the researcher would not have been able to reject the null hypothesis.

## The Dependent-Samples $t$–Test

The **dependent-samples t-test** (sometimes called the paired-samples t-test) is used to compare two means for the same sample tested at two different times or under two different conditions. This comparison is appropriate for pretest-posttest designs or within-subjects experiments. The null hypothesis is that the means at the two times or under the two conditions are the same in the population. The alternative hypothesis is that they are not the same. This test can also be one-tailed if the researcher has good reason to expect the difference goes in a particular direction.

It helps to think of the dependent-samples t-test as a special case of the one-sample t-test. However, the first step in the dependent-samples t-test is to reduce the two scores for each participant to a single **difference score** by taking the difference between them. At this point, the dependent-samples t-test becomes a one-sample t-test on the difference scores. The hypothetical population mean ($\mu_0$) of interest is 0 because this is what the mean difference score would be if there were no difference on average between the two times or two conditions. We can now think of the null hypothesis as being that the mean difference score in the population is 0 ($\mu_0 = 0$) and the alternative hypothesis as being that the mean difference score in the population is not 0 ($\mu_0 \neq 0$).

# Example Dependent-Samples *t*–Test

Imagine that the health psychologist now knows that people tend to underestimate the number of calories in junk food and has developed a short training program to improve their estimates. To test the effectiveness of this program, he conducts a pretest-posttest study in which 10 participants estimate the number of calories in a chocolate chip cookie before the training program and then again afterward. Because he expects the program to increase the participants' estimates, he decides to do a one-tailed test. Now imagine further that the pretest estimates are

230, 250, 280, 175, 150, 200, 180, 210, 220, 190

and that the posttest estimates (for the same participants in the same order) are

250, 260, 250, 200, 160, 200, 200, 180, 230, 240.

The difference scores, then, are as follows:

20, 10, –30, 25, 10, 0, 20, –30, 10, 50.

Note that it does not matter whether the first set of scores is subtracted from the second or the second from the first as long as it is done the same way for all participants. In this example, it makes sense to subtract the pretest estimates from the posttest estimates so that positive difference scores mean that the estimates went up after the training and negative difference scores mean the estimates went down.

The mean of the difference scores is 8.50 with a standard deviation of 27.27. The health psychologist can now compute the t score for his sample as follows:

$$t = \frac{8.5 - 0}{\left(\frac{27.27}{\sqrt{10}}\right)} = 1.11$$

If he enters the data into one of the online analysis tools or uses Excel or SPSS, it would tell him that the one-tailed $p$ value for this t score (again with 10 – 1 = 9 degrees of freedom) is .148. Because this is greater than .05, he would retain the null hypothesis and conclude that the training program does not significantly increase people's calorie estimates. If he were to compute the t score by hand, he could look at Table 13.2 and see that the critical value of t for a one-tailed test with 9 degrees of freedom is 1.833. (It is positive this time because he was expecting a positive mean difference score.) The fact that his t score was less extreme than this critical value would tell him that his $p$ value is greater than .05 and that he should fail to reject the null hypothesis.

# The Independent-Samples $t$-Test

The **independent-samples $t$-test** is used to compare the means of two separate samples ($M_1$ and $M_2$). The two samples might have been tested under different conditions in a between-subjects experiment, or they could be pre-existing groups in a cross-sectional design (e.g., women and men, extraverts and introverts). The null hypothesis is that the means of the two populations are the same: $\mu_1 = \mu_2$. The alternative hypothesis is that they are not the same: $\mu_1 \neq \mu_2$. Again, the test can be one-tailed if the researcher has good reason to expect the difference goes in a particular direction.

The $t$ statistic here is a bit more complicated because it must take into account two sample means, two standard deviations, and two sample sizes. The formula is as follows:

$$t = \frac{M_1 - M_2}{\sqrt{\dfrac{SD_1^2}{n_1} + \dfrac{SD_2^2}{n_2}}}$$

Notice that this formula includes squared standard deviations (the variances) that appear inside the square root symbol. Also, lowercase $n_1$ and $n_2$ refer to the sample sizes in the two groups or condition (as opposed to capital N, which generally refers to the total sample size). The only additional thing to know here is that there are N – 2 degrees of freedom for the independent-samples t- test.

# Example Independent-Samples $t$–Test

Now the health psychologist wants to compare the calorie estimates of people who regularly eat junk food with the estimates of people who rarely eat junk food. He believes the difference could come out in either direction so he decides to conduct a two-tailed test. He collects data from a sample of eight participants who eat junk food regularly and seven participants who rarely eat junk food. The data are as follows:

Junk food eaters: 180, 220, 150, 85, 200, 170, 150, 190

Non–junk food eaters: 200, 240, 190, 175, 200, 300, 240

The mean for the non-junk food eaters is 220.71 with a standard deviation of 41.23. The mean for the junk food eaters is 168.12 with a standard deviation of 42.66. He can now compute his $t$ score as follows:

$$t = \frac{220.71 - 168.12}{\sqrt{\dfrac{41.23^2}{8} + \dfrac{42.66^2}{7}}} = 2.42$$

If he enters the data into one of the online analysis tools or uses Excel or SPSS, it would tell him that the two-tailed $p$ value for this $t$ score (with $15 - 2 = 13$ degrees of freedom) is .015. Because this $p$ value is less than .05, the health psychologist would reject the null hypothesis and conclude that people who eat junk food regularly make lower calorie estimates than people who eat it rarely. If he were to compute the $t$ score by hand, he could look at Table 13.2 and see that the critical value of $t$ for a two-tailed test with 13 degrees of freedom is ±2.160. The fact that his $t$ score was more extreme than this critical value would tell him that his $p$ value is less than .05 and that he should reject the null hypothesis.

## The Analysis of Variance

T-tests are used to compare two means (a sample mean with a population mean, the means of two conditions or two groups). When there are more than two groups or condition means to be compared, the most common null hypothesis test is the **analysis of variance (ANOVA)**. In this section, we look primarily at the **one-way ANOVA**, which is used for between-subjects designs with a single independent variable. We then briefly consider some other versions of the ANOVA that are used for within-subjects and factorial research designs.

## One-Way ANOVA

The one-way ANOVA is used to compare the means of more than two samples ($M_1$, $M_2$...$M_G$) in a between-subjects design. The null hypothesis is that all the means are equal in the population: $\mu_1- \mu_2 -...- \mu_G$. The alternative hypothesis is that not all the means in the population are equal.

The test statistic for the ANOVA is called F. It is a ratio of two estimates of the population variance based on the sample data. One estimate of the population variance is called the **mean squares between groups ($MS_B$)** and is based on the differences among the sample means. The other is called the **mean squares within groups ($MS_W$)** and is based on the differences among the scores within each group. The F statistic is the ratio of the $MS_B$ to the $MS_W$ and can, therefore, be expressed as follows:

$$F = MS_B/MS_W$$

Again, the reason that F is useful is that we know how it is distributed when the null hypothesis is true. As shown in Figure 13.2, this distribution is unimodal and positively skewed with values that cluster around 1. The precise shape of the distribution depends on both the number of groups and the sample size, and there are degrees of freedom values associated with each of these. The between-groups degrees of freedom is the number of groups minus one: $df_B = (G - 1)$. The within-groups degrees of freedom is the total sample size minus the number of groups: $df_W = N - G$. Again, knowing the distribution of F when the null hypothesis is true allows us to find the $p$ value.

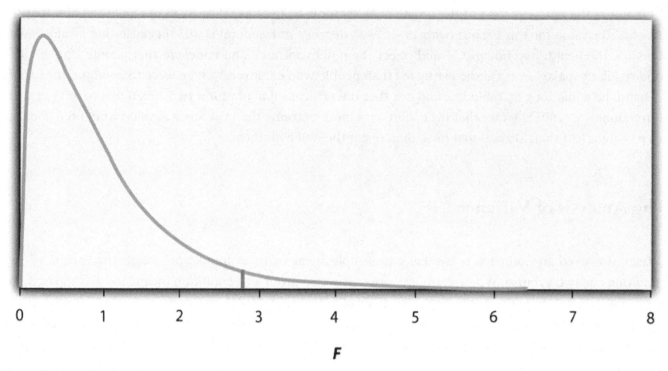

Figure 13.2 Distribution of the F Ratio With 2 and 37 Degrees of Freedom When the Null Hypothesis Is True. The red vertical line represents the critical value when α is .05.

The online tools in Chapter 12 and statistical software such as Excel and SPSS will compute F and find the $p$ value. If $p$ is equal to or less than .05, then we reject the null hypothesis and conclude that there are differences among the group means in the population. If $p$ is greater than .05, then we retain the null hypothesis and conclude that there is not enough evidence to say that there are differences. In the unlikely event that we would compute F by hand, we can use a table of critical values like Table 13.3 "Table of Critical Values of " to make the decision. The idea is that any F ratio greater than the critical value has a $p$ value of less than .05. Thus if the F ratio we compute is beyond the critical value, then we reject the null hypothesis. If the F ratio we compute is less than the critical value, then we retain the null hypothesis.

**Table 13.3 Table of Critical Values of F When α = .05**

| dfw | 2 | 3 | 4 |
|---|---|---|---|
| | | | $df_B$ |
| 8 | 4.459 | 4.066 | 3.838 |
| 9 | 4.256 | 3.863 | 3.633 |
| 10 | 4.103 | 3.708 | 3.478 |
| 11 | 3.982 | 3.587 | 3.357 |
| 12 | 3.885 | 3.490 | 3.259 |
| 13 | 3.806 | 3.411 | 3.179 |
| 14 | 3.739 | 3.344 | 3.112 |
| 15 | 3.682 | 3.287 | 3.056 |
| 16 | 3.634 | 3.239 | 3.007 |
| 17 | 3.592 | 3.197 | 2.965 |
| 18 | 3.555 | 3.160 | 2.928 |
| 19 | 3.522 | 3.127 | 2.895 |
| 20 | 3.493 | 3.098 | 2.866 |
| 21 | 3.467 | 3.072 | 2.840 |
| 22 | 3.443 | 3.049 | 2.817 |
| 23 | 3.422 | 3.028 | 2.796 |
| 24 | 3.403 | 3.009 | 2.776 |
| 25 | 3.385 | 2.991 | 2.759 |
| 30 | 3.316 | 2.922 | 2.690 |
| 35 | 3.267 | 2.874 | 2.641 |
| 40 | 3.232 | 2.839 | 2.606 |
| 45 | 3.204 | 2.812 | 2.579 |
| 50 | 3.183 | 2.790 | 2.557 |
| 55 | 3.165 | 2.773 | 2.540 |
| 60 | 3.150 | 2.758 | 2.525 |
| 65 | 3.138 | 2.746 | 2.513 |
| 70 | 3.128 | 2.736 | 2.503 |
| 75 | 3.119 | 2.727 | 2.494 |
| 80 | 3.111 | 2.719 | 2.486 |
| 85 | 3.104 | 2.712 | 2.479 |
| 90 | 3.098 | 2.706 | 2.473 |
| 95 | 3.092 | 2.700 | 2.467 |
| 100 | 3.087 | 2.696 | 2.463 |

# Example One-Way ANOVA

Imagine that the health psychologist wants to compare the calorie estimates of psychology majors, nutrition majors, and professional dieticians. He collects the following data:

Psych majors: 200, 180, 220, 160, 150, 200, 190, 200

Nutrition majors: 190, 220, 200, 230, 160, 150, 200, 210, 195

Dieticians: 220, 250, 240, 275, 250, 230, 200, 240

The means are 187.50 (SD = 23.14), 195.00 (SD = 27.77), and 238.13 (SD = 22.35), respectively. So it appears that dieticians made substantially more accurate estimates on average. The researcher would almost certainly enter these data into a program such as Excel or SPSS, which would compute F for him or her and find the $p$ value. Table 13.4 shows the output of the one-way ANOVA function in Excel for these data. This table is referred to as an ANOVA table. It shows that $MS_B$ is 5,971.88, $MS_W$ is 602.23, and their ratio, F, is 9.92. The $p$ value is .0009. Because this value is below .05, the researcher would reject the null hypothesis and conclude that the mean calorie estimates for the three groups are not the same in the population. Notice that the ANOVA table also includes the "sum of squares" (SS) for between groups and for within groups. These values are computed on the way to finding $MS_B$ and $MS_W$ but are not typically reported by the researcher. Finally, if the researcher were to compute the F ratio by hand, he could look at Table 13.3 and see that the critical value of F with 2 and 21 degrees of freedom is 3.467 (the same value in Table 13.4 under $F_{crit}$). The fact that his F score was more extreme than this critical value would tell him that his $p$ value is less than .05 and that he should reject the null hypothesis.

### Table 13.4 Typical One-Way ANOVA Output From Excel

**ANOVA**

| Source of variation | SS | df | MS | F | p-value | F_crit |
|---|---|---|---|---|---|---|
| Between groups | 11,943.75 | 2 | 5,971.875 | 9.916234 | 0.000928 | 3.4668 |
| Within groups | 12,646.88 | 21 | 602.2321 | | | |
| Total | 24,590.63 | 23 | | | | |

# ANOVA Elaborations

# Post Hoc Comparisons

When we reject the null hypothesis in a one-way ANOVA, we conclude that the group means are not all the same in the population. But this can indicate different things. With three groups, it can indicate that all three means are significantly different from each other. Or it can indicate that one of the means is significantly different from the other two, but the other two are not significantly different from each other. It could be, for example, that the mean calorie estimates of psychology majors, nutrition majors, and dieticians are all significantly different from each other. Or it could be that the mean for dieticians is significantly different from the means for psychology and nutrition majors, but the means for psychology and nutrition majors are not significantly different from each other. For this reason, statistically significant one-way ANOVA results are typically followed up with a series of **post hoc comparisons** of selected pairs of group means to determine which are different from which others.

One approach to post hoc comparisons would be to conduct a series of independent-samples *t*-tests comparing each group mean to each of the other group means. But there is a problem with this approach. In general, if we conduct a *t*-test when the null hypothesis is true, we have a 5% chance of mistakenly rejecting the null hypothesis (see Section 13.3 "Additional Considerations" for more on such Type I errors). If we conduct several *t*-tests when the null hypothesis is true, the chance of mistakenly rejecting *at least one* null hypothesis increases with each test we conduct. Thus researchers do not usually make post hoc comparisons using standard *t*-tests because there is too great a chance that they will mistakenly reject at least one null hypothesis. Instead, they use one of several modified *t*-test procedures—among them the Bonferonni procedure, Fisher's least significant difference (LSD) test, and Tukey's honestly significant difference (HSD) test. The details of these approaches are beyond the scope of this book, but it is important to understand their purpose. It is to keep the risk of mistakenly rejecting a true null hypothesis to an acceptable level (close to 5%).

## Repeated-Measures ANOVA

Recall that the one-way ANOVA is appropriate for between-subjects designs in which the means being compared come from separate groups of participants. It is not appropriate for within-subjects designs in which the means being compared come from the same participants tested under different conditions or at different times. This requires a slightly different approach, called the **repeated-measures ANOVA**. The basics of the repeated-measures ANOVA are the same as for the one-way ANOVA. The main difference is that measuring the dependent variable multiple times for each participant allows for a more refined measure of $MS_W$. Imagine, for example, that the dependent variable in a study is a measure of reaction time. Some participants will be faster or slower than others because of stable individual differences in their nervous systems, muscles, and other factors. In a between-subjects design, these stable individual differences would simply add to the variability within the groups and increase the value of $MS_W$ (which would, in turn, decrease the value of F). In a within-subjects design, however, these stable individual differences can be measured and subtracted from the value of $MS_W$. This lower value of $MS_W$ means a higher value of F and a more sensitive test.

## Factorial ANOVA

When more than one independent variable is included in a factorial design, the appropriate approach is the **factorial ANOVA**. Again, the basics of the factorial ANOVA are the same as for the one-way and repeated-measures ANOVAs. The main difference is that it produces an F ratio and $p$ value for each main effect and for each interaction. Returning to our calorie estimation example, imagine that the health psychologist tests the effect of participant major (psychology vs. nutrition) and food type (cookie vs. hamburger) in a factorial design. A factorial ANOVA would produce separate F ratios and $p$ values for the main effect of major, the main effect of food type, and the interaction between major and food. Appropriate modifications must be made depending on whether the design is between-subjects, within-subjects, or mixed.

## Testing Correlation Coefficients

For relationships between quantitative variables, where Pearson's $r$ (the correlation coefficient) is used to describe the strength of those relationships, the appropriate null hypothesis test is a test of the correlation coefficient. The basic logic is exactly the same as for other null hypothesis tests. In this case, the null hypothesis is that there is no relationship in the population. We can use the Greek lowercase rho ($\rho$) to represent the relevant parameter: $\rho = 0$. The alternative hypothesis is that there is a relationship in the population: $\rho \neq 0$. As with the t- test, this test can be two-tailed if the researcher has no expectation about the direction of the relationship or one-tailed if the researcher expects the relationship to go in a particular direction.

It is possible to use the correlation coefficient for the sample to compute a t score with $N - 2$ degrees of freedom and then to proceed as for a t-test. However, because of the way it is computed, the correlation coefficient can also be treated as its own test statistic. The online statistical tools and statistical software such as Excel and SPSS generally compute the correlation coefficient and provide the $p$ value associated with that value. As always, if the $p$ value is equal to or less than .05, we reject the null hypothesis and conclude that there is a relationship between the variables in the population. If the $p$ value is greater than .05, we retain the null hypothesis and conclude that there is not enough evidence to say there is a relationship in the population. If we compute the correlation coefficient by hand, we can use a table like Table 13.5, which shows the critical values of $r$ for various samples sizes when $\alpha$ is .05. A sample value of the correlation coefficient that is more extreme than the critical value is statistically significant.

**Table 13.5 Table of Critical Values of Pearson's r When α = .05**

| N | Critical value of r | |
| | One-tailed | Two-tailed |
|---|---|---|
| 5 | .805 | .878 |
| 10 | .549 | .632 |
| 15 | .441 | .514 |
| 20 | .378 | .444 |
| 25 | .337 | .396 |
| 30 | .306 | .361 |
| 35 | .283 | .334 |
| 40 | .264 | .312 |
| 45 | .248 | .294 |
| 50 | .235 | .279 |
| 55 | .224 | .266 |
| 60 | .214 | .254 |
| 65 | .206 | .244 |
| 70 | .198 | .235 |
| 75 | .191 | .227 |
| 80 | .185 | .220 |
| 85 | .180 | .213 |
| 90 | .174 | .207 |
| 95 | .170 | .202 |
| 100 | .165 | .197 |

# Example Test of a Correlation Coefficient

Imagine that the health psychologist is interested in the correlation between people's calorie estimates and their weight. She has no expectation about the direction of the relationship, so she decides to conduct a two-tailed test. She computes the correlation coefficient for a sample of 22 university students and finds that Pearson's $r$ is −.21. The statistical software she uses tells her that the $p$ value is .348. It is greater than .05, so she retains the null hypothesis and concludes that there is no relationship between people's calorie estimates and their weight. If she were to compute the correlation coefficient by hand, she could look at Table 13.5 and see that the critical value for 22 − 2 = 20 degrees of freedom is .444. The fact that the correlation coefficient for her sample is less extreme than this critical value tells her that the $p$ value is greater than .05 and that she should retain the null hypothesis.

# 59. Additional Considerations

*Learning Objectives*

1. Define Type I and Type II errors, explain why they occur, and identify some steps that can be taken to minimize their likelihood.
2. Define statistical power, explain its role in the planning of new studies, and use online tools to compute the statistical power of simple research designs.
3. List some criticisms of conventional null hypothesis testing, along with some ways of dealing with these criticisms.

In this section, we consider a few other issues related to null hypothesis testing, including some that are useful in planning studies and interpreting results. We even consider some long-standing criticisms of null hypothesis testing, along with some steps that researchers in psychology have taken to address them.

## Errors in Null Hypothesis Testing

In null hypothesis testing, the researcher tries to draw a reasonable conclusion about the population based on the sample. Unfortunately, this conclusion is not guaranteed to be correct. This discrepancy is illustrated by Figure 13.3. The rows of this table represent the two possible decisions that researchers can make in null hypothesis testing: to reject or retain the null hypothesis. The columns represent the two possible states of the world: the null hypothesis is false or it is true. The four cells of the table, then, represent the four distinct outcomes of a null hypothesis test. Two of the outcomes—rejecting the null hypothesis when it is false and retaining it when it is true—are correct decisions. The other two—rejecting the null hypothesis when it is true and retaining it when it is false—are errors.

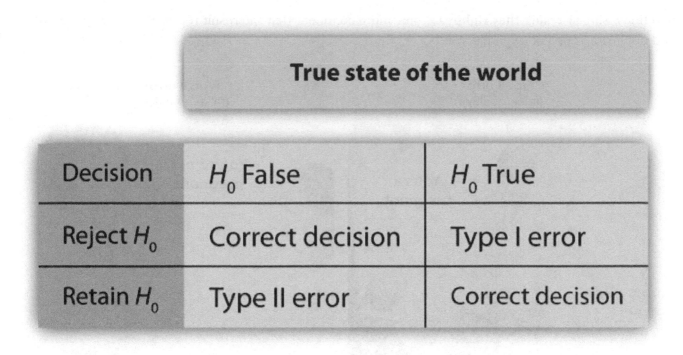

**True state of the world**

| Decision | $H_0$ False | $H_0$ True |
|---|---|---|
| Reject $H_0$ | Correct decision | Type I error |
| Retain $H_0$ | Type II error | Correct decision |

Figure 13.3 Two Types of Correct Decisions and Two Types of Errors in Null Hypothesis Testing

Rejecting the null hypothesis when it is true is called a **Type I error**. This error means that we have concluded that there is a relationship in the population when in fact there is not. Type I errors occur because even when there is no relationship in the population, sampling error alone will occasionally produce an extreme result. In fact, when the null hypothesis is true and α is .05, we will mistakenly reject the null hypothesis 5% of the time. (This possibility is why α is sometimes referred to as the "Type I error rate.") Retaining the null hypothesis when it is false is called a **Type II error**. This error means that we have concluded that there is no relationship in the population when in fact there is a relationship. In practice, Type II errors occur primarily because the research design lacks adequate statistical power to detect the relationship (e.g., the sample is too small). We will have more to say about statistical power shortly.

In principle, it is possible to reduce the chance of a Type I error by setting α to something less than .05. Setting it to .01, for example, would mean that if the null hypothesis is true, then there is only a 1% chance of mistakenly rejecting it. But making it harder to reject true null hypotheses also makes it harder to reject false ones and therefore increases the chance of a Type II error. Similarly, it is possible to reduce the chance of a Type II error by setting α to something greater than .05 (e.g., .10). But making it easier to reject false null hypotheses also makes it easier to reject true ones and therefore increases the chance of a Type I error. This provides some insight into why the convention is to set α to .05. There is some agreement among researchers that the .05 level of α keeps the rates of both Type I and Type II errors at acceptable levels.

The possibility of committing Type I and Type II errors has several important implications for interpreting the results of our own and others' research. One is that we should be cautious about interpreting the results of any individual study because there is a chance that it reflects a Type I or Type II error. This possibility is why researchers consider it important to replicate their studies. Each time researchers replicate a study and find a similar result, they rightly become more confident that the result represents a real phenomenon and not just a Type I or Type II error.

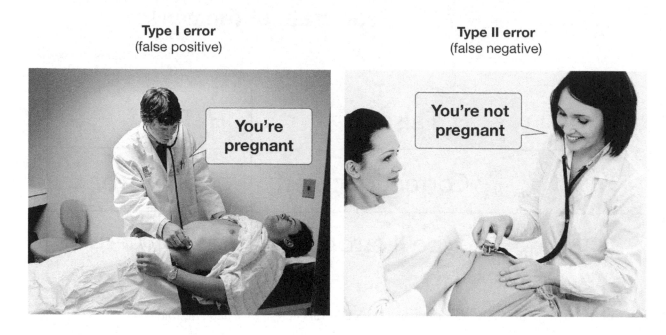

*Figure 13.4 A Humorous Example of How Type I and Type II Errors Could Play out in Pregnancy Exams.*

Another issue related to Type I errors is the so-called **file drawer problem** (Rosenthal, 1979)[1]. The idea is that when researchers obtain statistically significant results, they tend to submit them for publication, and journal editors and reviewers tend to accept them. But when researchers obtain non-significant results, they tend not to submit them for publication, or if they do submit them, journal editors and reviewers tend not to accept them. Researchers end up putting these non-significant results away in a file drawer (or nowadays, in a folder on their hard drive). One effect of this tendency is that the published literature probably contains a higher proportion of Type I errors than we might expect on the basis of statistical considerations alone. Even when there is a relationship between two variables in the population, the published research literature is likely to overstate the strength of that relationship. Imagine, for example, that the relationship between two variables in the population is positive but weak (e.g., $\rho$ = +.10). If several researchers conduct studies on this relationship, then sampling error is likely to produce results ranging from weak negative relationships (e.g., $r$ = −.10) to moderately strong positive ones (e.g., $r$ = +.40). But because of the file drawer problem, it is likely that only those studies producing moderate to strong positive relationships are published. The result is that the effect reported in the published literature tends to be stronger than it really is in the population.

The file drawer problem is a difficult one because it is a product of the way scientific research has traditionally been conducted and published. One solution is registered reports, whereby journal editors and reviewers evaluate research submitted for publication without knowing the results of that research (see https://cos.io/rr/). The idea is that if the research question is judged to be interesting and the method judged to be sound, then a non-significant result should be just as important and worthy of publication as a significant one. Short of such a radical change in how research is evaluated for publication, researchers can still take pains to keep their non-significant results and share them as widely as possible (e.g., in publicly available repositories and at professional conferences). Many scientific disciplines now have journals devoted to publishing non-significant results. In psychology, for example, there is the *Journal of Articles in Support of the Null Hypothesis* (http://www.jasnh.com).

In 2014, Uri Simonsohn, Leif Nelson, and Joseph Simmons published an article (Simonsohn, Nelson, & Simmons, 2014)[2] accusing psychology researchers of creating too many Type I errors in psychology by engaging in research practices they called **p-hacking**. Researchers who *p*-hack make various decisions in the research process to increase their chance of a statistically significant result (and type I error) by arbitrarily removing outliers, selectively choosing to report dependent variables, only presenting significant results, etc. until their results yield a desirable *p* value. Their groundbreaking paper contributed to a major conversation in the field about publishing standards and improving the reliability of our results that continues today.

# Statistical Power

The **statistical power** of a research design is the probability of rejecting the null hypothesis given the sample size and expected relationship strength. For example, the statistical power of a study with 50 participants and an expected Pearson's *r* of +.30 in the population is .59. That is, there is a 59% chance of rejecting the null hypothesis if indeed the population correlation is +.30. Statistical power is the complement of the probability of committing a Type II error. So in this example, the probability of committing a Type II error would be 1 − .59 = .41. Clearly, researchers should be interested in the power of their research designs if they want to avoid making Type II errors. In particular, they should make sure their research design has adequate power before collecting data. A common guideline is that a power of .80 is adequate. This guideline means that there is an 80% chance of rejecting the null hypothesis for the expected relationship strength.

The topic of how to compute power for various research designs and null hypothesis tests is beyond the scope of this book. However, there are online tools that allow you to do this by entering your sample size, expected relationship strength, and α level for various hypothesis tests (see "Computing Power Online"). In addition, Table 13.6 shows the sample size needed to achieve a power of .80 for weak, medium, and strong relationships for a two-tailed independent-samples *t*-test and for a two-tailed test of Pearson's *r*. Notice that this table amplifies the point made earlier about relationship strength, sample size, and statistical significance. In particular, weak relationships require very large samples to provide adequate statistical power.

**Table 13.6 Sample Sizes Needed to Achieve Statistical Power of .80 for Different Expected Relationship Strengths for an Independent-Samples t Test and a Test of Pearson's r**

**Null Hypothesis Test**

| Relationship Strength | Independent-Samples t-Test | Test of Pearson's r |
|---|---|---|
| Strong (d = .80, r = .50) | 52 | 28 |
| Medium (d = .50, r = .30) | 128 | 84 |
| Weak (d = .20, r = .10) | 788 | 782 |

What should you do if you discover that your research design does not have adequate power? Imagine, for example, that you are conducting a between-subjects experiment with 20 participants in each of two conditions and that you expect a medium difference ($d = .50$) in the population. The statistical power of this design is only .34. That is, even if there is a medium difference in the population, there is only about a one in three chance of rejecting the null hypothesis and about a two in three chance of committing a Type II error. Given the time and effort involved in conducting the study, this probably seems like an unacceptably low chance of rejecting the null hypothesis and an unacceptably high chance of committing a Type II error.

Given that statistical power depends primarily on relationship strength and sample size, there are essentially two steps you can take to increase statistical power: increase the strength of the relationship or increase the sample size. Increasing the strength of the relationship can sometimes be accomplished by using a stronger manipulation or by more carefully controlling extraneous variables to reduce the amount of noise in the data (e.g., by using a within-subjects design rather than a between-subjects design). The usual strategy, however, is to increase the sample size. For any expected relationship strength, there will always be some sample large enough to achieve adequate power.

*Computing Power Online*

The following links are to tools that allow you to compute statistical power for various research designs and null hypothesis tests by entering information about the expected relationship strength, the sample size, and the α level. They also allow you to compute the sample size necessary to achieve your desired level of power (e.g., .80). The first is an online tool. The second is a free downloadable program called G*Power.

- Russ Lenth's Power and Sample Size Page: http://www.stat.uiowa.edu/~rlenth/Power/index.html
- G*Power: http://www.gpower.hhu.de

# Problems With Null Hypothesis Testing, and Some Solutions

Again, null hypothesis testing is the most common approach to inferential statistics in psychology. It is not without its critics, however. In fact, in recent years the criticisms have become so prominent that the American Psychological Association convened a task force to make recommendations about how to deal with them (Wilkinson & Task Force on Statistical Inference, 1999)[3]. In this section, we consider some of the criticisms and some of the recommendations.

## Criticisms of Null Hypothesis Testing

Some criticisms of null hypothesis testing focus on researchers' misunderstanding of it. We have already seen, for example, that the $p$ value is widely misinterpreted as the probability that the null hypothesis is true. (Recall that it is really the probability of the sample result *if* the null hypothesis were true.) A closely related misinterpretation is that $1 - p$ equals the probability of replicating a statistically significant result. In one study, 60% of a sample of professional researchers thought that a $p$ value of .01—for an independent-samples $t$-test with 20 participants in each sample—meant there was a 99% chance of replicating the statistically significant result (Oakes, 1986)[4]. Our earlier discussion of power should make it clear that this figure is far too optimistic. As Table 13.5 shows, even if there were a large difference between means in the population, it would require 26 participants per sample to achieve a power of .80. And the program G*Power shows that it would require 59 participants per sample to achieve a power of .99.

Another set of criticisms focuses on the logic of null hypothesis testing. To many, the strict convention of rejecting the null hypothesis when $p$ is less than .05 and retaining it when $p$ is greater than .05 makes little sense. This criticism does not have to do with the specific value of .05 but with the idea that there should be any rigid dividing line between results that are considered significant and results that are not. Imagine two studies on the same statistical relationship with similar sample sizes. One has a $p$ value of .04 and the other a $p$ value of .06. Although the two studies have produced essentially the same result, the former is likely to be considered interesting and worthy of publication and the latter simply not significant. This convention is likely to prevent good research from being published and to contribute to the file drawer problem.

Yet another set of criticisms focus on the idea that null hypothesis testing—even when understood and carried out correctly—is simply not very informative. Recall that the null hypothesis is that there is no relationship between variables in the population (e.g., Cohen's $d$ or Pearson's $r$ is precisely 0). So to reject the null hypothesis is simply to say that there is *some* nonzero relationship in the population. But this assertion is not really saying very much. Imagine if chemistry could tell us only that there is *some* relationship between the temperature of a gas and its volume—as opposed to providing a precise equation to describe that relationship. Some critics even argue that the relationship between two variables in the population is never precisely 0 if it is carried out to enough decimal places. In other words, the null hypothesis is never literally true. So rejecting it does not tell us anything we did not already know!

To be fair, many researchers have come to the defense of null hypothesis testing. One of them, Robert Abelson, has argued that when it is correctly understood and carried out, null hypothesis testing does serve an important purpose (Abelson, 1995)[5]. Especially when dealing with new phenomena, it gives researchers a principled way to convince others that their results should not be dismissed as mere chance occurrences.

# What to Do?

Even those who defend null hypothesis testing recognize many of the problems with it. But what should be done? Some suggestions now appear in the APA *Publication Manual*. One is that each null hypothesis test should be accompanied by an effect size measure such as Cohen's $d$ or Pearson's $r$. By doing so, the researcher provides an estimate of how strong the relationship in the population is—not just whether there is one or not. (Remember that the $p$ value cannot substitute as a measure of relationship strength because it also depends on the sample size. Even a very weak result can be statistically significant if the sample is large enough.)

Another suggestion is to use **confidence intervals** rather than null hypothesis tests. A confidence interval around a statistic is a range of values that is computed in such a way that some percentage of the time (usually 95%) the population parameter will lie within that range. For example, a sample of 20 university students might have a mean calorie estimate for a chocolate chip cookie of 200 with a 95% confidence interval of 160 to 240. In other words, there is a very good (95%) chance that the mean calorie estimate for the population of university students lies between 160 and 240. Advocates of confidence intervals argue that they are much easier to interpret than null hypothesis tests. Another advantage of confidence intervals is that they provide the information necessary to do null hypothesis tests should anyone want to. In this example, the sample mean of 200 is significantly different at the .05 level from any hypothetical population mean that lies outside the confidence interval. So the confidence interval of 160 to 240 tells us that the sample mean is statistically significantly different from a hypothetical population mean of 250 (because the confidence interval does not include the value of 250).

Finally, there are more radical solutions to the problems of null hypothesis testing that involve using very different approaches to inferential statistics. **Bayesian statistics**, for example, is an approach in which the researcher specifies the probability that the null hypothesis and any important alternative hypotheses are true before conducting the study, conducts the study, and then updates the probabilities based on the data. It is too early to say whether this approach will become common in psychological research. For now, null hypothesis testing—supported by effect size measures and confidence intervals—remains the dominant approach.

## Notes

1. Rosenthal, R. (1979). The file drawer problem and tolerance for null results. *Psychological Bulletin, 83,* 638–641.

2. Simonsohn U., Nelson L. D., & Simmons J. P. (2014). P-Curve: a key to the file drawer. *Journal of Experimental Psychology: General, 143*(2), 534–547. doi: 10.1037/a0033242

3. Wilkinson, L., & Task Force on Statistical Inference. (1999). Statistical methods in psychology journals: Guidelines and explanations. *American Psychologist, 54,* 594–604.

4. Oakes, M. (1986). *Statistical inference: A commentary for the social and behavioral sciences.* Chichester, UK: Wiley.

5. Abelson, R. P. (1995). *Statistics as principled argument.* Mahwah, NJ: Erlbaum.

6. Tramimow, D. & Marks, M. (2015). Editorial. *Basic and Applied Social Psychology, 37,* 1–2. https://dx.doi.org/10.1080/01973533.2015.1012991

# 60. From the "Replicability Crisis" to Open Science Practices

*Learning Objectives*

1. Describe what is meant by the "replicability crisis" in psychology.
2. Describe some questionable research practices.
3. Identify some ways in which scientific rigor may be increased.
4. Understand the importance of openness in psychological science.

At the start of this book we discussed the "Many Labs Replication Project," which failed to replicate the original finding by Simone Schnall and her colleagues that washing one's hands leads people to view moral transgressions as less wrong (Schnall, Benton, & Harvey, 2008)[1]. Although this project is a good illustration of the collaborative and self-correcting nature of science, it also represents one specific response to psychology's recent **"replicability crisis,"** a phrase that refers to the inability of researchers to replicate earlier research findings. Consider for example the results of the Reproducibility Project, which involved over 270 psychologists around the world coordinating their efforts to test the reliability of 100 previously published psychological experiments (Aarts et al., 2015)[2]. Although 97 of the original 100 studies had found statistically significant effects, only 36 of the replications did! Moreover, even the effect sizes of the replications were, on average, half of those found in the original studies (see Figure 13.5). Of course, a failure to replicate a result by itself does not necessarily discredit the original study as differences in the statistical power, populations sampled, and procedures used, or even the effects of moderating variables could explain the different results (Yong, 2015)[3].

# RELIABILITY TEST

An effort to reproduce 100 psychology findings found that only 39 held up.* But some of the 61 non-replications reported similar findings to those of their original papers.

**Did replicate match original's results?**

**NO: 61**          **YES: 39**

**Replicator's opinion: How closely did findings resemble the original study:**

 Virtually identical    Extremely similar    Very similar
Moderately similar    Somewhat similar    Slightly similar
Not at all similar

\* based on criteria set at the start of each study

*Figure 13.5 Summary of the Results of the Reproducibility Project Reprinted by permission from Macmillan Publishers Ltd: Nature [Baker, M. (30 April, 2015). First results from psychology's largest reproducibility test. Nature News. Retrieved from http://www.nature.com/news/first-results-from-psychology-s-largest-reproducibility-test-1.17433], copyright 2015.*

Although many believe that the failure to replicate research results is an expected characteristic of cumulative scientific progress, others have interpreted this situation as evidence of systematic problems with conventional scholarship in psychology, including a publication bias that favors the discovery and publication of counter-intuitive but statistically significant findings instead of the duller (but incredibly vital) process of replicating previous findings to test their robustness (Aschwanden, 2015[4]; Frank, 2015[5]; Pashler & Harris, 2012[6]; Scherer, 2015[7]). Worse still is the suggestion that the low replicability of many studies is evidence of the widespread use of questionable research practices by psychological researchers. These may include:

1. The selective deletion of outliers in order to influence (usually by artificially inflating) statistical relationships among the measured variables.
2. The selective reporting of results, cherry-picking only those findings that support one's hypotheses.
3. Mining the data without an *a priori* hypothesis, only to claim that a statistically significant result had been originally predicted, a practice referred to as "**HARKing**" or hypothesizing after the results are known (Kerr, 1998[8]).
4. A practice colloquially known as "**p-hacking**" (briefly discussed in the previous section), in which a researcher might perform inferential statistical calculations to see if a result was significant before deciding whether to recruit additional participants and collect more data (Head, Holman, Lanfear, Kahn, & Jennions, 2015)[9]. As you have learned, the probability of finding a statistically significant result is influenced by the number of participants in the study.
5. Outright fabrication of data (as in the case of Diederik Stapel, described at the start of Chapter 3), although this would be a case of fraud rather than a "research practice."

It is important to shed light on these questionable research practices to ensure that current and future researchers (such as yourself) understand the damage they wreak to the integrity and reputation of our discipline (see, for example, the "Replication Index," a statistical "doping test" developed by Ulrich Schimmack in 2014 for estimating the replicability of studies, journals, and even specific researchers). However, in addition to highlighting *what not to do*, this so-called "crisis" has also highlighted the importance of enhancing scientific rigor by:

1. Designing and conducting studies that have sufficient statistical power, in order to increase the reliability of findings.
2. Publishing both null and significant findings (thereby counteracting the publication bias and reducing the file drawer problem).
3. Describing one's research designs in sufficient detail to enable other researchers to replicate your study using an identical or at least very similar procedure.
4. Conducting high-quality replications and publishing these results (Brandt et al., 2014)[10].

One particularly promising response to the replicability crisis has been the emergence of **open science practices** that increase the transparency and openness of the scientific enterprise. For example, *Psychological Science* (the flagship journal of the Association for Psychological Science) and other journals now issue digital badges to researchers who pre-registered their hypotheses and data analysis plans, openly shared their research materials with other researchers (e.g., to enable attempts at replication), or made available their raw data with other researchers (see Figure 13.6).

*Figure 13.6 Digital Badges from the Center for Open Science*

These initiatives, which have been spearheaded by the Center for Open Science, have led to the development of "Transparency and Openness Promotion guidelines" (see Table 13.7) that have since been formally adopted by more than 500 journals and 50 organizations, a list that grows each week. When you add to this the requirements recently imposed by federal funding agencies in Canada (the Tri-Council) and the United States (National Science Foundation) concerning the publication of publicly-funded research in open access journals, it certainly appears that the future of science and psychology will be one that embraces greater "openness" (Nosek et al., 2015)[11].

| | Level 0 | Level 1 | Level 2 | Level 3 |
|---|---|---|---|---|
| Citation Standards | Journal encourages citation of data, code, and materials, or says nothing | Journal describes citation of data in guidelines to authors with clear rules and examples. | Article provides appropriate citation for data and materials used consistent with journal's author guidelines. | Article is not published until providing appropriate citation for data and materials following journal's author guidelines. |
| Data Transparency | Journal encourages data sharing, or says nothing | Article states whether data are available, and, if so, where to access them. | Data must be posted to a trusted repository. Exceptions must be identified at article submission | Data must be posted to a trusted repository, and reported analyses will be reproduced independently prior to publication. |
| Analytic Methods (Code) Transparency | Journal encourages code sharing, or says nothing | Article states whether code is available, and, if so, where to access them. | Code must be posted to a trusted repository. Exceptions must be identified at article submission. | Code must be posted to a trusted repository, and reported analyses will be reproduced independently prior to publication. |
| Research Materials Transparency | Journal encourages materials sharing, or says nothing | Article states whether materials are available, and, if so, where to access them. | Materials must be posted to a trusted repository. Exceptions must be identified at article submission. | Materials must be posted to a trusted repository, and reported analyses will be reproduced independently prior to publication. |
| Design and Analysis Transparency | Journal encourages design and analysis transparency, or says nothing | Journal articulates design transparency standards | Journal requires adherence to design transparency standards for review and publication | Journal requires and enforces adherence to design transparency standards for review and publication |
| Preregistration of studies | Journal says nothing | Journal encourages preregistration of studies and provides link in article to preregistration if it exists | Journal encourages preregistration of studies and provides link in article and certification of meeting preregistration badge requirements | Journal requires preregistration of studies and provides link and badge in article to meeting requirements. |
| Preregistration of analysis plans | Journal says nothing | Journal encourages preanalysis plans and provides link in article to registered analysis plan if it exists | Journal encourages preanalysis plans and provides link in article and certification of meeting registered analysis plan badge requirements | Journal requires preregistration of studies with analysis plans and provides link and badge in article to meeting requirements. |
| Replication | Journal discourages submission of replication studies, or says nothing | Journal encourages submission of replication studies | Journal encourages submission of replication studies and conducts results blind review | Journal uses Registered Reports as a submission option for replication studies with peer review prior to observing the study outcomes. |

*Table 13.7 Transparency and Openness Promotion (TOP) Guidelines Reproduced with permission*

# Notes

1. Schnall, S., Benton, J., & Harvey, S. (2008). With a clean conscience: Cleanliness reduces the severity of moral judgments. *Psychological Science, 19*(12), 1219-1222. doi: 10.1111/j.1467-9280.2008.02227.x

2. Aarts, A. A., Anderson, C. J., Anderson, J., van Assen, M. A. L. M., Attridge, P. R., Attwood, A. S., ... Zuni, K. (2015, September 21). *Reproducibility Project: Psychology*. Retrieved from osf.io/ezcuj

3. Yong, E. (August 27, 2015). How reliable are psychology studies? Retrieved from http://www.theatlantic.com/science/archive/2015/08/psychology-studies-reliability-reproducability-nosek/402466/

4. Aschwanden, C. (2015, August 19). Science isn't broken: It's just a hell of a lot harder than we give it credit for. *Fivethirtyeight*. Retrieved from http://fivethirtyeight.com/features/science-isnt-broken/

5. Frank, M. (2015, August 31). *The slower, harder ways to increase reproducibility*. Retrieved from http://babieslearninglanguage.blogspot.ie/2015/08/the-slower-harder-ways-to-increase.html

6. Pashler, H., & Harris, C. R. (2012). Is the replicability crisis overblown? Three arguments explained. *Perspectives on Psychological Science, 7*(6), 531-536. doi:10.1177/1745691612463401

7. Scherer, L. (2015, September). *Guest post by Laura Scherer*. Retrieved from http://sometimesimwrong.typepad.com/wrong/2015/09/guest-post-by-laura-scherer.html

8. Kerr, N. L. (1998). HARKing: Hypothesizing after the results are known. *Personality and Social Psychology Review, 2*(3), 196-217. doi:10.1207/s15327957pspr0203_4

9. Head M. L., Holman, L., Lanfear, R., Kahn, A. T., & Jennions, M. D. (2015). The extent and consequences of p-hacking in science. *PLoS Biol, 13*(3): e1002106. doi:10.1371/journal.pbio.1002106

10. Brandt, M. J., IJzerman, H., Dijksterhuis, A., Farach, F. J., Geller, J., Giner-Sorolla, R., ... can't Veer, A. (2014). The replication recipe: What makes for a convincing replication? *Journal of Experimental Social Psychology, 50*, 217-224. doi:10.1016/j.jesp.2013.10.005

11. Nosek, B. A., Alter, G., Banks, G. C., Borsboom, D., Bowman, S. D., Breckler, S. J., ... Yarkoni, T. (2015). Promoting an open research culture. *Science, 348*(6242), 1422-1425. doi: 10.1126/science.aab2374

# 61. Key Takeaways and Exercises

- Null hypothesis testing is a formal approach to deciding whether a statistical relationship in a sample reflects a real relationship in the population or is just due to chance.
- The logic of null hypothesis testing involves assuming that the null hypothesis is true, finding how likely the sample result would be if this assumption were correct, and then making a decision. If the sample result would be unlikely if the null hypothesis were true, then it is rejected in favor of the alternative hypothesis. If it would not be unlikely, then the null hypothesis is retained.
- The probability of obtaining the sample result if the null hypothesis were true (the $p$ value) is based on two considerations: relationship strength and sample size. Reasonable judgments about whether a sample relationship is statistically significant can often be made by quickly considering these two factors.
- Statistical significance is not the same as relationship strength or importance. Even weak relationships can be statistically significant if the sample size is large enough. It is important to consider relationship strength and the practical significance of a result in addition to its statistical significance.
- To compare two means, the most common null hypothesis test is the $t$- test. The one-sample $t$-test is used for comparing one sample mean with a hypothetical population mean of interest, the dependent-samples $t$-test is used to compare two means in a within-subjects design, and the independent-samples $t$ test is used to compare two means in a between-subjects design.
- To compare more than two means, the most common null hypothesis test is the analysis of variance (ANOVA). The one-way ANOVA is used for between-subjects designs with one independent variable, the repeated-measures ANOVA is used for within-subjects designs, and the factorial ANOVA is used for factorial designs.
- A null hypothesis test of Pearson's $r$ is used to compare a sample value of Pearson's $r$ with a hypothetical population value of 0.
- The decision to reject or retain the null hypothesis is not guaranteed to be correct. A Type I error occurs when one rejects the null hypothesis when it is true. A Type II error occurs when one fails to reject the null hypothesis when it is false.
- The statistical power of a research design is the probability of rejecting the null hypothesis given the expected strength of the relationship in the population and the sample size. Researchers should make sure that their studies have adequate statistical power before conducting them.
- Null hypothesis testing has been criticized on the grounds that researchers misunderstand it, that it is illogical, and that it is uninformative. Others argue that it serves an important purpose—especially when used with effect size measures, confidence intervals, and other techniques. It remains the dominant approach to inferential statistics in psychology.
- In recent years psychology has grappled with a failure to replicate research findings. Some have interpreted this as a normal aspect of science but others have suggested that this is highlights problems stemming from questionable research practices.
- One response to this "replicability crisis" has been the emergence of open science practices, which increase the transparency and openness of the research process. These open practices include digital badges to encourage pre-registration of hypotheses and the sharing of raw data and research materials.

- Discussion: Imagine a study showing that people who eat more broccoli tend to be happier. Explain for someone who knows nothing about statistics why the researchers would conduct a null hypothesis test.
- Practice: Use Table 13.1 to decide whether each of the following results is statistically significant.

  - The correlation between two variables is $r = -.78$ based on a sample size of 137.
  - The mean score on a psychological characteristic for women is 25 (SD = 5) and the mean score for men is 24 (SD = 5). There were 12 women and 10 men in this study.
  - In a memory experiment, the mean number of items recalled by the 40 participants in Condition A was 0.50 standard deviations greater than the mean number recalled by the 40 participants in Condition B.
  - In another memory experiment, the mean scores for participants in Condition A and Condition B came out exactly the same!
  - A student finds a correlation of $r = .04$ between the number of units the students in his research methods class are taking and the students' level of stress.

- Practice: Use one of the online tools, Excel, or SPSS to reproduce the one-sample *t*-test, dependent-samples *t*-test, independent-samples *t*-test, and one-way ANOVA for the four sets of calorie estimation data presented in this section.
- Practice: A sample of 25 university students rated their friendliness on a scale of 1 (*Much Lower Than Average*) to 7 (*Much Higher Than Average*). Their mean rating was 5.30 with a standard deviation of 1.50. Conduct a one-sample *t*-test comparing their mean rating with a hypothetical mean rating of 4 (*Average*). The question is whether university students have a tendency to rate themselves as friendlier than average.
- Practice: Decide whether each of the following Pearson's *r* values is statistically significant for both a one-tailed and a two-tailed test.

  - The correlation between height and IQ is +.13 in a sample of 35.
  - For a sample of 88 university students, the correlation between how disgusted they felt and the harshness of their moral judgments was +.23.
  - The correlation between the number of daily hassles and positive mood is −.43 for a sample of 30 middle-aged adults.

- Discussion: A researcher compares the effectiveness of two forms of psychotherapy for social phobia using an independent-samples *t*-test.

  - Explain what it would mean for the researcher to commit a Type I error.
  - Explain what it would mean for the researcher to commit a Type II error.

- Discussion: Imagine that you conduct a *t*-test and the *p* value is .02. How could you explain what this *p* value means to someone who is not already familiar with null hypothesis testing? Be sure to avoid the common misinterpretations of the *p* value.
- For additional practice with Type I and Type II errors, try these problems from Carnegie Mellon's Open Learning Initiative.
- Discussion: What do you think are some of the key benefits of the adoption of open science practices

such as pre-registration and the sharing of raw data and research materials? Can you identify any drawbacks of these practices?

- Practice: Read the online article "Science isn't broken: It's just a hell of a lot harder than we give it credit for" and use the interactive tool entitled "Hack your way to scientific glory" in order to better understand the data malpractice of "$p$-hacking."

# Glossary

**α (alpha)**

The criterion that shows how low a p-value should be before the sample result is considered unlikely enough to reject the null hypothesis (Usually set to .05).

**ABA design**

Another term for reversal design.

**Abstract**

A brief summary of the study's research question, methods, results and conclusions.

**Alternating treatments design**

In this design two or more treatments are alternated relatively quickly on a regular schedule.

**Alternative hypothesis**

An alternative to the null hypothesis (often symbolized as H1), this hypothesis proposes that there **is** a relationship in the population and that the relationship in the sample reflects this relationship in the population.

**Analysis of variance (ANOVA)**

A statistical test used when there are more than two groups or condition means to be compared.

**Anonymity**

When a participants name and other personally identifiable information is not collected at all.

**APA Ethics Code**

Stands for the APA's Ethical Principles of Psychologists and Code of Conduct. It was first published in 1953 and includes about 150 specific ethical standards that psychologists and their students are expected to follow.

**APA style**

A set of guidelines for writing in psychology and related fields.

**Applied behavior analysis**

An application of the principles of experimental analysis of behavior that plays an important role in contemporary research on developmental disabilities, education, organizational behavior, and health, among many other applied areas.

**Applied research**

Research conducted primarily to address some practical problem.

**Autonomy**

A persons right to make their own choices and take their own actions free from coercion.

**Bar graphs**

A graphical presentation of data as bars of varying size, generally used to present and compare the mean scores for two or more groups or conditions.

**Baseline**

The beginning phase of an ABA design which acts as a kind of control condition in which the level of responding before any treatment is introduced.

**Basic research**

Research conducted primarily for the sake of achieving a more detailed and accurate understanding of human behavior, without necessarily trying to address any particular practical problem.

**Bayesian statistics**

An approach in which the researcher specifies the probability that the null hypothesis and any important alternative hypotheses are true before conducting the study, conducts the study, and then updates the probabilities based on the data.

**Behavioral measures**

Measures in which some other aspect of participants' behavior is observed and recorded.

**Belmont Report**

A set of federal guidelines written in 1978 as a response to the abuses of the Tuskegee study that recognize three important principles in research with humans: justice, respect for persons, and beneficience, and that formed the basis for federal regulations applied to research.

**Beneficence**

Underscores the importance of maximizing the benefits of research while minimizing harms to participants and society.

**Between-subjects experiment**

An experiment in which each participant is tested in only one condition.

**Between-subjects factorial design**

All of the independent variables are manipulated between subjects.

**Block randomization**

All the conditions occur once in the sequence before any of them is repeated.

**BRUSO**

An acronym that stands for "brief," "relevant," "unambiguous," "specific," and "objective," which is used to create effective questionnaire items that are brief and to the point.

**Carryover effect**

An effect of being tested in one condition on participants' behavior in later conditions.

**Case study**

An in-depth examination of an individual.

**Categorical variable**

A variable that represents a characteristic of an individual, such as chosen major, and is typically measured by assigning each individual's response to one of several categories (e.g., Psychology, English, Nursing, Engineering, etc.).

**Central tendency**

Is the middle of a distribution—the point around which the scores in the distribution tend to cluster. (Another term for central tendency is average.)

**Clinical practice of psychology**

The diagnosis and treatment of psychological disorders and related problems.

**Closed-ended items**

Questionnaire items that ask a question and provide a limited set of response options for participants to choose from.

**Cluster sampling**

A type of probability sampling in which larger clusters of individuals are randomly sampled and then individuals within each cluster are randomly sampled.

**Coding**

A part of structured observation whereby the observers use a clearly defined set of guidelines to "code" behaviors—assigning specific behaviors they are observing to a category—and count the number of times or the duration that the behavior occurs.

**Cohen's d**

The most widely used measure of effect size for differences between group or condition means, which is the difference between the two means divided by the standard deviation.

**Cohort effect**

Differences between the groups may reflect the generation that people come from rather than a direct effect of age.

**Complete counterbalancing**

A method in which an equal number of participants complete each possible order of conditions.

**Conceptual definition**

Describes the behaviors and internal processes that make up a psychological construct, along with how it relates to other variables.

**Concurrent validity**

A form of criterion validity, where the criterion is measured at the same time (concurrently) as the construct.

**Conditions**

The different levels of the independent variable to which participants are assigned.

**Confederate**

A helper who pretended to be a real participant in a study.

**Confidence intervals**

A range of values that is computed in such a way that some percentage of the time (usually 95%) the population parameter will lie within that range.

**Confidentiality**

An agreement not to disclose participants' personal information without their consent or some appropriate legal authorization.

**Confirmation bias**

Tendency to focus on cases that confirm our intuitive beliefs and to disregard cases that disconfirm our beliefs.

**Confounding variable**

An extraneous variable that varies systematically with the independent variable, and thus confuses the effect of the independent variable with the effect of the extraneous one.

**Confounds**

A specific type of extraneous variable that systematically varies along with the variables under investigation and therefore provides an alternative explanation for the results.

**Consent form**

The process of obtaining informed consent by having the participants read and sign the form.

**Construct validity**

One of the "big four" validities, whereby the research question is clearly operationalized by the study's methods.

**Constructs**

Psychological variables that represent an individual's mental state or experience, often not directly observable, such as personality traits, emotional states, attitudes, and abilities.

**Content analysis**

A family of systematic approaches to measurement using qualitative methods to analyze complex archival data.

**Content validity**

The extent to which a measure reflects all aspects of the construct of interest.

**Context effect (or contrast effect)**

Unintended influences on respondents' answers because they are not related to the content of the item but to the context in which the item appears.

**Control**

Holding extraneous variables constant in order to separate the effect of the independent variable from the effect of the extraneous variables.

**Control condition**

The condition in which participants do not receive the treatment.

**Convenience sampling**

A common method of non-probability sampling in which the sample consists of individuals who happen to be easily available and willing to participate (such as introductory psychology students).

**Convergent validity**

A form of criterion validity whereby new measures are correlated with existing established measures of the same construct.

**Converging evidence**

An idea that tells us to examine the pattern of flaws running through the research literature because the nature of this pattern can either support or undermine the conclusions we wish to draw.

**Converging operations**

When psychologists use multiple operational definitions of the same construct—either within a study or across studies.

**Correlation coefficient**

Describes the strength and direction of the relationship between two variables (often measured by Pearson's $r$).

**Correlation matrix**

Shows the correlation coefficient between pairs of variables in the study.

**Correlational research**

Research that is non-experimental because it focuses on the statistical relationship between two variables but does not include the manipulation of an independent variable.

**Counterbalancing**

Varying the order of the conditions in which participants are tested, to help solve the problem of order effects in within-subjects experiments.

**Criterion**

A variable that theoretically should be correlated with the construct being measured (plural: criteria).

**Criterion validity**

The extent to which people's scores on a measure are correlated with other variables (known as criteria) that one would expect them to be correlated with.

**Critical value**

The absolute value that a test statistic (e.g., F, t, etc.) must exceed to be considered statistically significant.

**Cronbach's α**

A statistic that measures internal consistency among items in a measure.

**Cross-over interaction**

Means the independent variable has an effect at both levels but the effects are in opposite directions.

**Cross-sectional studies**

Studies that involve comparing two or more pre-existing groups of people (e.g., children at different stages of development).

**Cross-sequential studies**

Studies in which researchers follow people in different age groups in a smaller period of time.

**Data file**

Data that has been entered into a spreadsheet and formatted in order to be analyzed.

**Debriefing**

This is the process of informing research participants as soon as possible of the purpose of the study, revealing any deception, and correcting any other misconceptions they might have as a result of participating.

**Deception**

Misinforming participants about the purpose of a study, using confederates, using phony equipment like Milgram's shock generator, and presenting participants with false feedback about their performance (e.g., telling them they did poorly on a test when they actually did well).

**Declaration of Helsinki**

An ethics code that was created by the World Medical Council in 1964.

**Demand characteristics**

Subtle cues that reveal to participants how the researcher expects them to respond in the experiment.

**Dependent variable**

The variable the experimenter measures (it is the presumed effect).

**Dependent-samples t-test**

Used to compare two means for the same sample tested at two different times or under two different conditions (sometimes called the paired-samples *t*-test).

**Descriptive statistics**

Refers to a set of techniques for summarizing and displaying data.

**Difference score**

A method to reduce pairs of scores (e.g., pre- and post-test) to a single score by calculating the difference between them.

**Directionality problem**

The problem where two variables, X and Y, are statistically related either because X causes Y, or because Y causes X, and thus the causal direction of the effect cannot be known.

**Discriminant validity**

The extent to which scores on a measure of a construct are **not** correlated with measures of other, conceptually distinct, constructs and thus discriminate between them.

**Disguised naturalistic observation**

When researchers engage in naturalistic observation by making their observations as unobtrusively as possible so that participants are not aware that they are being studied.

**Disguised participant observation**

Researchers pretend to be members of the social group they are observing and conceal their true identity as researchers.

**Disproportionate stratified random sampling**

Is used to sample extra respondents from particularly small subgroups—allowing valid conclusions to be drawn about those subgroups.

**Distribution**

The way scores are distributed across levels of a variable.

**Doctor of philosophy [Ph.D.]**

An academic degree earned through intensive study of a particular discipline and the completion of a set of research studies that contribute new knowledge to the academic literature.

**Double-blind peer review**

A process in which the reviewers of a research article do not know the identity of the researcher(s) and vice versa.

**Double-blind study**

A method to reduce experimenter bias, where neither the participant nor the experimenter is knowledgeable about the condition to which the participant is assigned.

**Edited volumes**

Books that are collections of chapters written by different authors on different aspects of the same topic, and overseen by one or more editors.

**Effect size**

Describes the strength of a statistical relationship.

**Empirical questions**

These are questions about the way the world actually is and, therefore, can be answered by systematically observing it.

**Empirical research report**

An article that presents the results of one or more new studies.

**Empirical research reports**

Research reports that describe one or more new empirical studies conducted by the authors.

**Empirically supported treatments**

A treatment that that has been shown through systematic observation to lead to better outcomes when compared to no-treatment or placebo control groups.

**Error bars**

Bars that represent the variability in each group or condition.

**Ethics**

The branch of philosophy that is concerned with morality—what it means to behave morally and how people can achieve that goal.

**Exempt research**

Research on the effectiveness of normal educational activities, the use of standard psychological measures and surveys of a nonsensitive nature that are administered in a way that maintains confidentiality, and research using existing data from public sources.

**Expedited research**

Research reviewed by the IRB that is not anonymous and/or may involve potentially stigmatizing information, or invasive or uncomfortable procedures, but exposes participants to risks that are no greater than minimal risk (risks encountered by healthy people in daily life or during routine physical or psychological examinations).

**Experiment**

A type of study designed specifically to answer the question of whether there is a causal relationship between two variables.

**Experimental analysis of behavior**

A subfield of psychology (behaviorism) that focuses exclusively on the effects of rewards, punishments, and other external factors on behavior.

**Experimenter expectancy effect**

When the experimenter's expectations about how participants "should" behave in the experiment affect how the participants behave.

**Exploratory analysis**

An analysis used to examine the possibility that there might be relationships in the data that you did not hypothesize.

**External validity**

Refers to the degree to which we can generalize the findings to other circumstances or settings, like the real-world environment.

**Extraneous variables**

Any variable other than the dependent and independent variable.

**Face validity**

The extent to which a measurement method appears, on superficial examination, to measure the construct of interest.

## Factor analysis

A complex statistical technique in which researchers study relationships among a large number of conceptually similar variables.

## Factorial ANOVA

A statistical method to detect differences in the means between conditions when there are two or more independent variables in a factorial design. It allows the detection of main effects and interaction effects.

## Factorial design table

Shows how each level of one independent variable is combined with each level of the others to produce all possible combinations in a factorial design.

## Factorial designs

Experiments that include more than one independent variable in which each level of one independent variable is combined with each level of the others to produce all possible combinations.

## Falsifiable

A scientific claim that must be expressed in such a way that there are observations that would—if they were made—count as evidence against the claim

## Fatigue effect

An effect where participants perform a task worse in later conditions because they become tired or bored.

## Feasibility

How likely is the research question going to be successfully answered depending on the amount of time, money, equipment and materials, technical knowledge and skill, and access to research participants there will be.

## Federal Policy for the Protection of Human Subjects

A set of laws based on the Belmont Report that apply to research conducted, supported, or regulated by the federal government.

## Field experiment

A type of field study where an independent variable is manipulated in a natural setting and extraneous variables are controlled as much as possible.

**Field study**

A study that is conducted in a "real world" environment outside the laboratory.

**Figures**

Graphical depictions of data, such as pie charts, bar graphs, or scatterplots used to clearly and efficiently report a number of results.

**File drawer problem**

The problem of research results not being published that fail to find a statistically significant result. As a consequence, the published literature fails to contain a full representation of the positive and negative findings about a research question.

**Final manuscripts**

Manuscripts that are prepared by the author in their final form and submitted for publication.

**Focus groups**

Used in qualitative research which involves small groups of people who participate together in interviews focused on a particular topic or issue.

**Folk psychology**

Intuitive beliefs about people's behavior, thoughts, and feelings.

**Frequency table**

A display of each value of a variable and the number of participants with that value.

**Greater than minimal risk research**

Research that poses greater than minimal risk to participants and must be reviewed by the full board of IRB members.

**Grounded theory**

Researchers start with the data and develop a theory or an interpretation that is "grounded in" those data.

**Group research**

Research that involves studying large numbers of participants and examining their behavior primarily in terms of group means, standard deviations, and so on.

**HARKing**

Hypothesizing After the Results are Known: A practice where researchers analyze data without an a priori hypothesis, claiming afterward that a statistically significant result had been originally predicted.

**Hawthorne effect**

In the case of undisguised naturalistic observation, it is a type of reactivity when people know they are being observed and studied, they may act differently than they normally would.

**Heuristics**

Mental shortcuts in forming and maintaining our beliefs.

**High-level style**

Guidelines in the APA Publication Manual for the clear expression of ideas, including writing that is formal, straightforward, and avoids biased language.

**Histogram**

A graphical display of a frequency distribution.

**History**

Events outside of the pretest-posttest research design that might have influenced many or all of the participants between the pretest and the posttest.

**Hypothesis**

A specific prediction about a new phenomenon that should be observed if a particular theory is accurate.

**Hypothetico-deductive method**

A cyclical process of theory development, starting with an observed phenomenon, then developing or using a theory to make a specific prediction of what should happen if that theory is correct, testing that prediction, refining the theory in light of the findings, and using that refined theory to develop new hypotheses, and so on.

**Independent variable**

The variable the experimenter manipulates.

**Independent-samples t-test**

Used to compare the means of two separate samples (M1 and M2).

**Inferential statistics**

A research method that allows researchers to draw conclusions or infer about a population based on data from a sample.

**Informed consent**

This means that researchers obtain and document people's agreement to participate in a study after having informed them of everything that might reasonably be expected to affect their decision.

**Institutional review board (IRB)**

A committee that is responsible for reviewing research protocols for potential ethical problems.

**Instrumentation**

A potential threat to internal validity when the basic characteristics of the measuring instrument change over the course of the study.

**Inter-rater reliability**

The extent to which different observers are consistent in their judgments.

**Interaction**

When the effect of one independent variable depends on the level of another.

**Interestingness**

How interesting the question is to people generally or the scientific community. Three things need to be considered: Is the answer in doubt, fills a gap in research literature, and has important practical implications.

**Internal consistency**

The consistency of people's responses across the items on a multiple-item measure.

**Internal validity**

Refers to the degree to which we can confidently infer a causal relationship between variables.

**Interrupted time-series desig**

A set of measurements taken at intervals over a period of time that is "interrupted" by a treatment.

**Interrupted time-series design with nonequivalent group**

Involves taking a set of measurements at intervals over a period of time both before and after an intervention of interest in two or more nonequivalent groups.

**Interval level**

A measurement that involves assigning scores using numerical scales in which intervals have the same interpretation throughout.

**Interviews**

A qualitative research method to collect lengthy and detailed information from participants using structured, semi-structured, or unstructured sets of open-ended questions.

**Item-order effect**

When the order in which the items are presented affects people's responses.

**Justice**

The importance of conducting research in a way that distributes risks and benefits fairly across different groups at the societal level.

**Laboratory study**

A study that is conducted in the laboratory environment.

**Levels of measurement**

Four categories, or scales, of measurement (i.e., nominal, ordinal, interval, and ratio) that specify the types of information that a set of scores can have, and the types of statistical procedures that can be used with the scores.

**Line graphs**

Graphs used when the independent variable is measured in a more continuous manner (e.g., time) or to present correlations between quantitative variables when the independent variable has, or is organized into, a relatively small number of distinct levels.

**Linear relationships**

Relationships between two variables whereby the points on a scatterplot fall close to a single straight line.

**Literature review**

Describes relevant previous research on the topic and can be anywhere from several paragraphs to several pages in length.

**Longitudinal studies**

Studies in which one group of people are followed over time as they age.

**Low-level style**

Is covered in Chapter 4 "The Mechanics of Style" through Chapter 7 "Reference Examples" of the Publication Manual, which includes all the specific guidelines pertaining to spelling, grammar, references and reference citations, numbers and statistics, figures and tables, and so on.

**Main effect**

The effect of one independent variable on the dependent variable—averaging across the levels of any other independent variable(s).

**Manipulate**

Changing the level, or condition, of the independent variable systematically so that different groups of participants are exposed to different levels of that variable, or the same group of participants is exposed to different levels at different times.

**Manipulation check**

Verifying the experimental manipulation worked by using a different measure of the construct the researcher is trying to manipulate.

**Matched-groups design**

An experiment design in which the participants in the various conditions are matched on the dependent variable or on some extraneous variable(s) prior the manipulation of the independent variable.

**Maturation**

Participants might have changed between the pretest and the posttest in ways that they were going to anyway because they are growing and learning.

**Mean**

The average of a distribution of scores (symbolized M) where the sum of the scores are divided by the number of scores.

**Mean squares between groups (MSB)**

An estimate of the population variance and is based on the differences among the sample means.

**Mean squares within groups (MSW)**

An estimate of the population variance and is based on the differences among the scores within each group.

**Measurement**

Is the assignment of scores to individuals so that the scores represent some characteristic of the individuals.

**Median**

The midpoint of a distribution of scores in the sense that half the scores in the distribution are less than it and half are greater than it.

**Meta-analysis**

A review article that provides a statistical summary of all of the previous results.

**Mixed factorial design**

A design which manipulates one independent variable between subjects and another within subjects.

**Mixed-methods research**

Research that combines both quantitative and qualitative approaches.

**Mode**

The most frequently occurring score in a distribution.

**Monograph**

A coherent written presentation of a topic much like an extended review article written by a single author or a small group of authors.

**Multiple regression**

Involves measuring several variables (X1, X2, X3,...Xi), and using them to predict some outcome variable (Y).

**Multiple-baseline design**

In this design, multiple baselines are either established for one participant or one baseline is established for many participants.

**Multiple-treatment reversal design**

In this design the baseline phase is followed by separate phases in which different treatments are introduced.

**Mundane realism**

When the participants and the situation studied are similar to those that the researchers want to generalize to and participants encounter every day.

**Naturalistic observation**

An observational method that involves observing people's behavior in the environment in which it typically occurs.

**Negative relationship**

A relationship in which higher scores on one variable tend to be associated with lower scores on the other.

**No-treatment control condition**

The condition in which participants receive no treatment whatsoever.

**Nominal level**

A measurement used for categorical variables and involves assigning scores that are category labels.

**Non-experimental research**

A research that lacks the manipulation of an independent variable.

**Non-manipulated independent variable**

An independent variable that is measured but is non-manipulated.

**Non-probability sampling**

Occurs when the researcher cannot specify the probability that each member of the population will be selected for the sample.

**Non-response bias**

Occurs when there is a systemic difference between survey non-responders from survey responders.

**Nonequivalent groups design**

A between-subjects design in which participants have not been randomly assigned to conditions.

**Nonlinear relationships**

Relationships between two variables in which the points on a scatterplot do not fall close to a single straight line, but often fall along a curved line.

**Null hypothesis**

The idea that there is no relationship in the population and that the relationship in the sample reflects only sampling error (often symbolized H0 and read as "H-zero").

**Null hypothesis testing**

A formal approach to deciding between two interpretations of a statistical relationship in a sample.

**Nuremberg Code**

A set of 10 ethical principles for research written in 1947 in conjunction with the Nuremberg trials of Nazi physicians accused of war crimes against prisoners in concentration camps.

**Observational research**

Research that is non-experimental because it focuses on recording systemic observations of behavior in a natural or laboratory setting without manipulating anything.

**One-group posttest only design**

A treatment is implemented (or an independent variable is manipulated) and then a dependent variable is measured once after the treatment is implemented.

**One-group pretest prottest design**

An experiment design in which the dependent variable is measured once before the treatment is implemented and once after it is implemented.

**One-sample t-test**

Used to compare a sample mean (M) with a hypothetical population mean ($\mu 0$) that provides some interesting standard of comparison.

**One-tailed test**

Where we reject the null hypothesis only if the t score for the sample is extreme in one direction that we specify before collecting the data.

**One-way ANOVA**

Used for between-subjects designs with a single independent variable.

**Open science practices**

A practice in which researchers openly share their research materials with other researchers in hopes of Increasing the transparency and openness of the scientific enterprise.

**Open-ended items**

Simply ask a question and allow participants to answer in whatever way they choose.

**Operational definition**

A definition of the variable in terms of precisely how it is to be measured.

**Operationalization**

The specification of exactly how the research question will be studied in the experiment design.

**Oral presentation**

The presenter stands in front of an audience of other researchers and tells them about their research—usually with the help of a slide show.

**Order effect**

An effect that occurs when participants' responses in the various conditions are affected by the order of conditions to which they were exposed.

**Ordinal level**

A measurement that involves assigning scores so that they represent the rank order of the individuals.

**Outcome variable or Criterion variable**

The variable that is being predicted by a predictor variable in a regression equation.

**Outlier**

An extreme score that is much higher or lower than the rest of the scores in the distribution.

**p value**

The probability of obtaining the sample result or a more extreme result if the null hypothesis were true.

**p-hacking**

When researchers make various decisions in the research process to increase their chance of a statistically significant result (and type I error) by arbitrarily removing outliers, selectively choosing to report dependent variables, only presenting significant results, etc. until their results yield a desirable $p$ value.

**Parameters**

Corresponding values in the population.

**Partial correlation**

A method of controlling extraneous variables by measuring them and including them in the statistical analysis.

**Participant observation**

Researchers become active participants in the group or situation they are studying.

**Pearson's Correlation Coefficient (or Pearson's r)**

A statistic that measures the strength of a correlation between quantitative variables.

**Percentage of non-overlapping data**

This is the percentage of responses in the treatment condition that are more extreme than the most extreme response in a relevant control condition.

**Percentile rank**

For any given score, the percentage of scores in the distribution that are lower than that score.

**Physiological measures**

Measures that involve recording any of a wide variety of physiological processes, including heart rate and blood pressure, galvanic skin response, hormone levels, and electrical activity and blood flow in the brain.

**Pilot test**

Is a small-scale study conducted to make sure that a new procedure works as planned.

**Placebo**

A simulated treatment that lacks any active ingredient or element that is hypothesized to make the treatment effective, but is otherwise identical to the treatment.

**Placebo control condition**

Condition in which the participants receive a placebo rather than the treatment.

**Placebo effect**

An effect that is due to the placebo rather than the treatment.

**Planned analysis**

Used to test a relationship that you expected in your hypothesis.

**Population**

A large group of people about whom researchers in psychology are usually interested in drawing conclusions, and from whom the sample is drawn.

**Positive relationship**

A relationship in which higher scores on one variable tend to be associated with higher scores on the other.

**Post hoc comparisons**

An unplanned (not hypothesized) test of which pairs of group mean scores are different from which others.

**Poster**

Another way to present research at a conference by using a large size board which demonstrates and summarizes the researchers study.

**Poster session**

A one- to two-hour session that takes place in a large room at an professional conference site where dozens of research posters are presented.

**Posttest only nonequivalent groups design**

Participants in one group are exposed to a treatment, a nonequivalent group is not exposed to the treatment, and then the two groups are compared.

**Practical significance**

Refers to the importance or usefulness of the result in some real-world context.

**Practice effect**

An effect where participants perform a task better in later conditions because they have had a chance to practice it.

**Pre-screening**

A way to minimize risks in a study and to identify and eliminate participants who are at high risk.

**Predictive validity**

A form of validity whereby the criterion is measured at some point in the future (after the construct has been measured), to determine that the construct "predicts" the criterion.

**Predictor variable**

A variable in a regression equation that is hypothesized to be related to ("predicts") the value of an outcome or criterion variable.

**Pretest-posttest design with switching replication design**

In this design nonequivalent groups are administered a pretest of the dependent variable, then one group receives a treatment while a nonequivalent control group does not receive a treatment, the dependent variable is assessed again, and then the treatment is added to the control group, and finally the dependent variable is assessed one last time.

**Pretest-posttest nonequivalent groups design**

In this design there is a treatment group that is given a pretest, receives a treatment, and then is given a posttest. Then, at the same time there is a nonequivalent control group that is given a pretest, does not receive the treatment, and then is given a posttest.

**Privacy**

A persons right to decide what information about them is shared with others.

**Probability sampling**

Occurs when the researcher can specify the probability that each member of the population will be selected for the sample.

**Professional conferences**

A conference that ranges from small- to large-scale events where researchers in psychology share their research with each other through presentations.

**Professional journals**

Are periodicals that publish original research articles.

**Proportionate stratified random sampling**

Is used to select a sample in which the proportion of respondents in each of various subgroups matches the proportion in the population.

**Protocol**

A detailed description of the research—that is reviewed by an independent committee.

**Pseudoscience**

Refers to activities and beliefs that are claimed to be scientific by their proponents—and may appear to be scientific at first glance—but are not.

**Psychological realism**

Where the same mental process is used in both the laboratory and in the real world.

**Psychometrics**

A subfield of psychology concerned with the theories and techniques of psychological measurement.

**PsycINFO**

A comprehensive electronic database covering thousands of professional journals and scholarly books going back more than 100 years—that for most purposes its content is synonymous with the research literature in psychology.

**Qualitative research**

Research that begins with a less focused research question, collects large amounts of relatively "unfiltered" data from a relatively small number of individuals, describes data using nonstatistical techniques, such as grounded theory, thematic analysis, critical discourse analysis, or interpretative phenomenological analysis and aims to understand in detail the experience of the research participants.

**Quantitative research**

Research that typically starts with a focused research question or hypothesis, collects a small amount of numerical data from a large number of individuals, describes the resulting data using statistical techniques, and draws general conclusions about some large population.

**Quantitative variable**

A quantity, such as height, that is typically measured by assigning a number to each individual.

**Quota sampling**

A form of non-probability sampling in which subgroups in the sample are recruited to be proportional to those subgroups in the population.

**Random assignment**

Means using a random process to decide which participants are tested in which conditions.

**Random counterbalancing**

A method in which the order of the conditions is randomly determined for each participant.

**Randomized clinical trial**

An experiment that researches the effectiveness of psychotherapies and medical treatments.

**Range**

A measure of dispersion that measures the distance between the highest and lowest scores in a distribution.

**Rating scale**

An ordered set of responses that participants must choose from.

**Ratio level**

A measurement that involves assigning scores in such a way that there is a true zero point that represents the complete absence of the quantity.

**Raw data**

Unanalyzed data that has several different forms—completed paper-and-pencil questionnaires, computer files filled with numbers or text, videos, or written notes which may have to be organized, coded, or combined in some way.

**Reactivity**

Refers to when a measure changes participants' behavior.

**Reference citation**

An in text citation to the work in which that idea originally appeared and a full reference to that work in the reference list.

**Regression**

A statistical technique that allows researchers to predict the value of one variable given another.

**Regression to the mean**

Refers to the statistical fact that an individual who scores extremely high or extremely low on a variable on one occasion will tend to score less extremely on the next occasion.

**Reject the null hypothesis**

A decision made by researchers using null hypothesis testing which occurs when the sample relationship would be extremely unlikely.

**Reliability**

Refers to the consistency of a measure.

**Repeated-measures ANOVA**

Compares the means from the same participants tested under different conditions or at different times in which the dependent variable is measured multiple times for each participant.

**Replicability crisis**

A phrase that refers to the inability of researchers to replicate earlier research findings.

**Research literature**

All the published research in that field.

**Respect for persons**

One of the Belmont report principles that emphasizes the need for participants to exercise autonomy and protection for those with reduced autonomy, often through informed consent.

**Respondents**

Participants in a survey or study.

**Restriction of Range**

When one or both variables have a limited range in the sample relative to the population, making the value of the correlation coefficient misleading.

**Results section**

Where you present the main results of the study, including the results of the statistical analyses.

**Retain the null hypothesis**

A decision made by researchers in null hypothesis testing which occurs when the sample relationship would not be extremely unlikely.

**Reversal design**

The most basic single-subject research design in which the researcher measures the dependent variable in three phases: Baseline, before a treatment is introduced (A); after the treatment is introduced (B); and then a return to baseline after removing the treatment (A). It is often called an ABA design.

**Review articles**

Articles that summarize previously published research on a topic and usually present new ways to organize or explain the results.

**Sample**

A smaller portion of the population the researcher would like to study.

**Sampling bias**

Occurs when a sample is selected in such a way that it is not representative of the entire population and therefore produces inaccurate results.

**Sampling error**

The random variability in a statistic from sample to sample.

**Sampling frame**

A list of all the members of the population from which to select the respondents.

**Scatterplot**

A graph that presents correlations between two quantitative variables, one on the x-axis and one on the y-axis. Scores are plotted at the intersection of the values on each axis.

**Scholarly books**

Books written by researchers and practitioners mainly for use by other researchers and practitioners.

**Science**

The systematic study of the structure and behaviour of the physical and natural world through observation and experiment.

**Scientific Method**

The scientific method is a process of systematically collecting and evaluating evidence to test ideas and answer questions.

**Self report measures**

Measures in which participants report on their own thoughts, feelings, and actions.

**Self-selection sampling**

A form of non-probability sampling in which individuals choose to take part in the research on their own accord, without being approached by the researcher directly.

**Simple effects**

Are a way of breaking down the interaction to figure out precisely what is going on.

**Simple random sampling**

A probability sampling method in which each individual in the population has an equal probability of being selected for the sample.

**Simple regression**

A statistical procedure which uses the value of one variable to predict another. Sometimes called "linear regression."

**Single factor multi level design**

When an experiment has one independent variable that is manipulated to produce more than two conditions.

**Single factor two-level design**

An experiment design involving a single independent variable with two conditions.

**Single-subject research**

A type of quantitative research that involves studying in detail the behavior of each of a small number of participants.

**Skepticism**

Pausing to consider alternatives and to search for evidence—especially systematically collected empirical evidence—when there is enough at stake to justify doing so.

**Skewed**

When a histogram's peak is either shifted toward the upper end of its range and has a relatively long negative tail (Negatively Skewed) or the peak is shifted toward the lower end of its range and has a relatively long positive tail (Positively Skewed).

**Snowball sampling**

A form of non-probability sampling in which existing research participants help recruit additional participants for the study.

**Social validity**

Referred to as treatments that have substantial effects on important behaviors and that can be implemented reliably in the real-world contexts in which they occur.

**Socially desirable responding**

When participants respond in ways that they think are socially acceptable.

**Split-half correlation**

A score that is derived by splitting the items into two sets and examining the relationship between the two sets of scores in order to assess the internal consistency of a measure.

**Spontaneous remission**

The tendency for many medical and psychological problems to improve over time without any form of treatment.

**Spreading interactions**

Means there is an effect of one independent variable at one level of the other independent variable and there is either a weak effect or no effect of that independent variable at the other level of the other independent variable.

**Spurious correlations**

Correlations that are a result not of the two variables being measured, but rather because of a third, unmeasured, variable that affects both of the measured variables.

**Standard deviation**

Is the average distance between the scores and the mean in a distribution.

**Standard error**

The standard deviation of the group divided by the square root of the sample size of the group.

**Statistical control**

Controlling potential third variables to rule out other plausible interpretations.

**Statistical power**

In research design, it means the probability of rejecting the null hypothesis given the sample size and expected relationship strength.

**Statistical validity**

Concerns the proper statistical treatment of data and the soundness of the researchers' statistical conclusions.

**Statistically significant**

An effect that is unlikely due to random chance and therefore likely represents a real effect in the population.

**Statistics**

Descriptive data that involves measuring one or more variables in a sample and computing descriptive summary data (e.g., means, correlation coefficients) for those variables.

**Steady state strategy**

When the researcher waits until the participant's behavior in one condition becomes fairly consistent from observation to observation before changing conditions.

**Stratified random sampling**

A common alternative to simple random sampling in which the population is divided into different subgroups or "strata" (usually based on demographic characteristics) and then a random sample is taken from each "stratum."

## Structured observation

When a researcher makes careful observations of one or more specific behaviors in a particular setting that is more structured than the settings used in naturalistic or participant observation.

## Subject pool

An established group of people who have agreed to be contacted about participating in research studies.

## Survey research

A quantitative and qualitative method with two important characteristics; variables are measured using self-reports and considerable attention is paid to the issue of sampling.

## Switching replication with treatment removal design

In this design the treatment is removed from the first group when it is added to the second group.

## Symmetrical

When a histogram's left and right halves are mirror images of each other.

## Systematic empiricism

Empiricism refers to learning based on observation, and scientists learn about the natural world systematically, by carefully planning, making, recording, and analyzing observations of it.

## t-test

A test that involves looking at the difference between two means.

## Test statistic

A statistic (e.g., F, t, etc.) that is computed to compare against what is expected in the null hypothesis, and thus helps find the p value.

## Test-retest reliability

When researchers measure a construct that they assume to be consistent across time, then the scores they obtain should also be consistent across time.

## Testable and falsifiable

The ability to test the hypothesis using the methods of science and the possibility to gather evidence that will disconfirm the hypothesis if it is indeed false.

## Testing

A threat to internal validity that occurs when when the measurement of the dependent variable during the pretest affects participants' responses at posttest.

**Theoretical article**

A review article that is devoted primarily to presenting a new theory.

**Theoretical narrative**

A qualitative research method that involves an interpretation of the data in terms of the themes a researcher has identified.

**Theory**

A coherent explanation or interpretation of one or more phenomena.

**Third-variable problem**

Two variables, X and Y, can be statistically related not because X causes Y, or because Y causes X, but because some third variable, Z, causes both X and Y.

**Tolerance for uncertainty**

Accepting that there are many things that we simply do not know.

**Treatment**

Any intervention meant to change people's behavior for the better.

**Treatment condition**

The condition in which participants receive the treatment.

**Triangulation**

The idea to use both quantitative and qualitative methods simultaneously to study the same general questions and to compare the results.

**Two-tailed test**

Where we reject the null hypothesis if the test statistic for the sample is extreme in either direction (+/-).

**Type I error**

A false positive in which the researcher concludes that their results are statistically significant when in reality there is no real effect in the population and the results are due to chance. In other words, rejecting the null hypothesis when it is true.

**Type II error**

A missed opportunity in which the researcher concludes that their results are not statistically significant when in reality there is a real effect in the population and they just missed detecting it. In other words, retaining the null hypothesis when it is false.

**Undisguised naturalistic observation**

Where the participants are made aware of the researcher presence and monitoring of their behavior.

**Undisguised participant observation**

Researchers become a part of the group they are studying and they disclose their true identity as researchers to the group under investigation.

**Validity**

The extent to which the scores from a measure represent the variable they are intended to.

**Variability**

The extent to which the scores vary around their central tendency in a distribution.

**Variable**

A quantity or quality that varies across people or situations.

**Variance**

A measurement of the average distance of scores from the mean.

**Visual inspection**

This means plotting individual participants' data, looking carefully at those plots, and making judgments about whether and to what extent the independent variable had an effect on the dependent variable.

**Wait-list control condition**

Condition in which participants are told that they will receive the treatment but must wait until the participants in the treatment condition have already received it.

**Within-subjects experiment**

An experiment in which each participant is tested under all conditions.

**Z score**

Is the difference between that individual's score and the mean of the distribution, divided by the standard deviation of the distribution. It represents the number of standard deviations the score is from the mean.

# References

## Chapter I

American Psychological Association. (2011). About APA. Retrieved from http://www.apa.org/about

Bushman, B. J. (2002). Does venting anger feed or extinguish the flame? Catharsis, rumination, distraction, anger, and aggressive responding. *Personality and Social Psychology Bulletin, 28*, 724–731.

Gilovich, T. (1991). *How we know what isn't so: The fallibility of human reason in everyday life*. New York, NY: Free Press.

Gladwell, M. E. (2005). *Blink: The power of thinking without thinking* (9th ed.). New York: Little, Brown & Co.

Hines, T. M. (1998). Comprehensive review of biorhythm theory. *Psychological Reports, 83*, 19–64.

Johnson, D. J., Cheung, F., & Donnellan, M. B. (2013). Does cleanliness influence moral judgments? A direct replication of Schnall, Benton, and Harvey (2008). *Social Psychology, 45*(3), 209-215. doi: 10.1027/1864-9335/a000186

Kassin, S. M., & Gudjonsson, G. H. (2004). The psychology of confession evidence: A review of the literature and issues. *Psychological Science in the Public Interest, 5*, 33–67.

Klein, R. A., Ratliff, K. A., Vianello, M., Adams, R. B., Bahník, S., Bernstein, M. J., . . . Nosek, B. A. (2013). Investigating variation in replicability: A "many labs" replication project. *Social Psychology, 45*(3), 142-152. doi: 10.1027/1864-9335/a000178

Lilienfeld, S. O., Lynn, S. J., Ruscio, J., & Beyerstein, B. L. (2010). *50 great myths of popular psychology*. Malden, MA: Wiley-Blackwell.

Mann, T., Tomiyama, A. J., Westling, E., Lew, A., Samuels, B., & Chatman, J. (2007). Medicare's search for effective obesity treatments: Diets are not the answer. *American Psychologist, 62*, 220-233.

Mehl, M. R., Vazire, S., Ramirez-Esparza, N., Slatcher, R. B., & Pennebaker, J. W. (2007). Are women really more talkative than men? *Science, 317*, 82.

Norcross, J. C., Beutler, L. E., & Levant, R. F. (Eds.). (2005). *Evidence-based practices in mental health: Debate and dialogue on the fundamental questions*. Washington, DC: American Psychological Association.

Popper, K. R. (2002). *Conjectures and refutations: The growth of scientific knowledge*. New York, NY: Routledge.

Schnall, S., Benton, J., & Harvey, S. (2008). With a clean conscience: Cleanliness reduces the severity of moral judgments. *Psychological Science, 19*(12), 1219-1222. doi: 10.1111/j.1467-9280.2008.02227.x

Sexton, M., Cuttler, C., Finnell, J., & Mischley, L (2016). A cross-sectional survey of medical cannabis users: Patterns of use and perceived efficacy. *Cannabis and Cannabinoid Research, 1*, 131-138. doi: 10.1089/can.2016.0007

Stanovich, K. E. (2010). *How to think straight about psychology* (9th ed.). Boston, MA: Allyn & Bacon.

# Chapter II

Adair, J. G., & Vohra, N. (2003). The explosion of knowledge, references, and citations: Psychology's unique response to a crisis. *American Psychologist, 58*, 15–23.

Collet, C., Guillot, A., & Petit, C. (2010). Phoning while driving I: A review of epidemiological, psychological, behavioral and physiological studies. *Ergonomics, 53*, 589–601.

Drews, F. A., Pasupathi, M., & Strayer, D. L. (2004). Passenger and cell-phone conversations in simulated driving. *Proceedings of the Human Factors and Ergonomics Society Annual Meeting, 48*, 2210–2212.

Milgram, S. (1963). Behavioral study of obedience. *Journal of Abnormal and Social Psychology, 67*, 371–378.

Mueller, P. A., & Oppenheimer, D. M. (2014). The pen is mightier than the keyboard: Advantages of longhand over laptop note taking. *Psychological Science, 25*(6), 1159–1168.

Schwarz, N., Bless, H., Strack, F., Klumpp, G., Rittenauer-Schatka, H., & Simons, A. (1991). Ease of retrieval as information: Another look at the availability heuristic. *Journal of Personality and Social Psychology, 61*, 195–202.

Weisberg, R. W. (1993). *Creativity: Beyond the myth of genius.* New York, NY: Freeman.

Zajonc, R. B., Heingartner, A., & Herman, E. M. (1969). Social enhancement and impairment of performance in the cockroach. *Journal of Personality and Social Psychology, 13*, 83–92.

Zajonc, R. B. (1965). Social facilitation. *Science, 149*, 269–274

Zajonc, R.B. & Sales, S.M. (1966). Social facilitation of dominant and subordinate responses. *Journal of Experimental Social Psychology, 2*, 160-168.

# Chapter III

Baumrind, D. (1985). Research using intentional deception: Ethical issues revisited. *American Psychologist, 40*, 165–174.

Bowd, A. D., & Shapiro, K. J. (1993). The case against animal laboratory research in psychology. *Journal of Social Issues, 49*, 133–142.

Burger, J. M. (2009). Replicating Milgram: Would people still obey today? *American Psychologist, 64*, 1–11.

Burns, J. F. (2010, May 24). British medical council bars doctor who linked vaccine to autism. *The New York Times.* Retrieved from:http://www.nytimes.com/2010/05/25/health/policy/25autism.html

Haidt, J., Koller, S. and Dias, M. (1993) Affect, culture, and morality, or is it wrong to eat your dog? *Journal of Personality and Social Psychology, 65*, 613-628. http://dx.doi.org/10.1037/0022-3514.65.4.613

Koocher, G. P. (1977). Bathroom behavior and human dignity. *Journal of Personality and Social Psychology, 35*, 120–121.

Mann, T. (1994). Informed consent for psychological research: Do subjects comprehend consent forms and understand their legal rights? *Psychological Science, 5,* 140–143.

Middlemist, R. D., Knowles, E. S., & Matter, C. F. (1976). Personal space invasions in the lavatory: Suggestive evidence for arousal. *Journal of Personality and Social Psychology, 33,* 541–546.

Middlemist, R. D., Knowles, E. S., & Matter, C. F. (1977). What to do and what to report: A reply to Koocher. *Journal of Personality and Social Psychology, 35,* 122–125.

Milgram, S. (1963). Behavioral study of obedience. *Journal of Abnormal and Social Psychology, 67,* 371–378.

Miller, N. E. (1985). The value of behavioral research on animals. *American Psychologist, 40,* 423–440.

Reverby, S. M. (2009). *Examining Tuskegee: The infamous syphilis study and its legacy.* Chapel Hill, NC: University of North Carolina Press.

Rosenthal, R. M. (1994). Science and ethics in conducting, analyzing, and reporting psychological research. *Psychological Science, 5,* 127–133.

Sieber, J. E., Iannuzzo, R., & Rodriguez, B. (1995). Deception methods in psychology: Have they changed in 23 years? *Ethics & Behavior, 5,* 67–85.

# Chapter IV

Amir, N., Freshman, M., & Foa, E. (2002). Enhanced Stroop interference for threat in social phobia. *Journal of Anxiety Disorders, 16,* 1–9.

Bandura, A., Ross, D., & Ross, S. A. (1961). Transmission of aggression through imitation of aggressive models. *Journal of Abnormal and Social Psychology, 63,* 575–582.

Cacioppo, J. T., & Petty, R. E. (1982). The need for cognition. *Journal of Personality and Social Psychology, 42,* 116–131.

Cohen, S., Kamarck, T., & Mermelstein, R. (1983). A global measure of perceived stress. *Journal of Health and Social Behavior, 24,* 386–396.

Costa, P. T., Jr., & McCrae, R. R. (1992). Normal personality assessment in clinical practice: The NEO Personality Inventory. *Psychological Assessment, 4,* 5–13.

Delongis, A., Coyne, J. C., Dakof, G., Folkman, S., & Lazarus, R. S. (1982). Relationships of daily hassles, uplifts, and major life events to health status. *Health Psychology, 1*(2), 119–136.

Gosling, S. D., Rentfrow, P. J., & Swann, W. B., Jr. (2003). A very brief measure of the Big Five personality domains. *Journal of Research in Personality, 37,* 504–528.

Holmes, T. H., & Rahe, R. H. (1967). The Social Readjustment Rating Scale. *Journal of Psychosomatic Research, 11*(2), 213–218.

Levels of Measurement. (2016, August 26). Retrieved from http://wikieducator.org/ Introduction_to_Research_Methods_In_Psychology/Theories_and_Measurement/Levels_of_Measurement

MacDonald, T. K., & Martineau, A. M. (2002). Self-esteem, mood, and intentions to use condoms: When does low self-esteem lead to risky health behaviors? *Journal of Experimental Social Psychology, 38*, 299–306.

Petty, R. E, Briñol, P., Loersch, C., & McCaslin, M. J. (2009). The need for cognition. In M. R. Leary & R. H. Hoyle (Eds.), *Handbook of individual differences in social behavior* (pp. 318–329). New York, NY: Guilford Press.

Rosenberg, M. (1965). *Society and the adolescent self-image.* Princeton, NJ: Princeton University Press

Rosenberg, M. (1989). *Society and the adolescent self-image* (rev. ed.). Middletown, CT: Wesleyan University Press.

Segerstrom, S. E., & Miller, G. E. (2004). Psychological stress and the human immune system: A meta-analytic study of 30 years of inquiry. *Psychological Bulletin, 130*, 601–630.

Stevens, S. S. (1946). On the theory of scales of measurement. *Science, 103*, 677–680.

Stroop, J. R. (1935). Studies of interference in serial verbal reactions. *Journal of Experimental Psychology, 18*, 643–662.

# Chapter V

Bauman, C.W., McGraw, A.P., Bartels, D.M., & Warren, C. (2014). Revisiting external validity: Concerns about trolley problems and other sacrificial dilemmas in moral psychology. *Social and Personality Psychology Compass, 8/9*, 536-554.

Birnbaum, M.H. (1999). How to show that 9>221: Collect judgments in a between-subjects design. *Psychological Methods, 4*(3), 243-249.

Cialdini, R. (2005, April). Don't throw in the towel: Use social influence research. APS *Observer.* Retrieved fromhttp://www.psychologicalscience.org/index.php/publications/observer/2005/april-05/dont-throw-in-the-towel-use-social-influence-research.html

Darley, J. M., & Latané, B. (1968). Bystander intervention in emergencies: Diffusion of responsibility. *Journal of Personality and Social Psychology, 4*, 377–383.

Fredrickson, B. L., Roberts, T.-A., Noll, S. M., Quinn, D. M., & Twenge, J. M. (1998). The swimsuit becomes you: Sex differences in self-objectification, restrained eating, and math performance. *Journal of Personality and Social Psychology, 75*, 269–284.

Goldstein, N. J., Cialdini, R. B., & Griskevicius, V. (2008). A room with a viewpoint: Using social norms to motivate environmental conservation in hotels. *Journal of Consumer Research, 35*, 472–482.

Guéguen, N., & de Gail, Marie-Agnès. (2003). The effect of smiling on helping behavior: Smiling and good Samaritan behavior. *Communication Reports, 16*, 133–140.

Ibolya, K., Brake, A., & Voss, U. (2004). The effect of experimenter characteristics on pain reports in women and men. *Pain, 112*, 142–147.

Judd, C.M. & Kenny, D.A. (1981). *Estimating the effects of social interventions*. Cambridge, MA: Cambridge University Press.

Knecht, S., Dräger, B., Deppe, M., Bobe, L., Lohmann, H., Flöel, A., . . . Henningsen, H. (2000). Handedness and hemispheric language dominance in healthy humans. *Brain: A Journal of Neurology, 123*(12), 2512-2518.http://dx.doi.org/10.1093/brain/123.12.2512

Manning, R., Levine, M., & Collins, A. (2007). The Kitty Genovese murder and the social psychology of helping: The parable of the 38 witnesses. *American Psychologist, 62*, 555–562.

Morling, B. (2014, April). Teach your students to be better consumers. APS *Observer*. Retrieved fromhttp://www.psychologicalscience.org/index.php/publications/observer/2014/april-14/teach-your-students-to-be-better-consumers.html

Moseley, J. B., O'Malley, K., Petersen, N. J., Menke, T. J., Brody, B. A., Kuykendall, D. H., ... Wray, N. P. (2002). A controlled trial of arthroscopic surgery for osteoarthritis of the knee. *The New England Journal of Medicine, 347*, 81–88.

Price, D. D., Finniss, D. G., & Benedetti, F. (2008). A comprehensive review of the placebo effect: Recent advances and current thought. *Annual Review of Psychology, 59*, 565–590.

Rosenthal, R., & Fode, K. (1963). The effect of experimenter bias on performance of the albino rat. *Behavioral Science, 8*, 183-189.

Rosenthal, R., & Rosnow, R. L. (1976). *The volunteer subject*. New York, NY: Wiley.

Rosenthal, R. (1976). *Experimenter effects in behavioral research* (enlarged ed.). New York, NY: Wiley.

Shapiro, A. K., & Shapiro, E. (1999). *The powerful placebo: From ancient priest to modern physician*. Baltimore, MD: Johns Hopkins University Press.

# Chapter VI

Abrams, L. S., & Curran, L. (2009). "And you're telling me not to stress?" A grounded theory study of postpartum depression symptoms among low-income mothers. *Psychology of Women Quarterly, 33*, 351–362.

Bryman, A. (2012). *Social Research Methods* (4th ed.). Oxford: Oxford University Press.

Bushman, B. J., & Huesmann, L. R. (2001). Effects of televised violence on aggression. In D. Singer & J. Singer (Eds.), *Handbook of children and the media* (pp. 223–254). Thousand Oaks, CA: Sage.

Cacioppo, J. T., & Petty, R. E. (1982). The need for cognition. *Journal of Personality and Social Psychology, 42*, 116–131.

Cohen, D., Nisbett, R. E., Bowdle, B. F., & Schwarz, N. (1996). Insult, aggression, and the southern culture of honor: An "experimental ethnography." *Journal of Personality and Social Psychology, 70*(5), 945-960.

Diener, E. (2000). Subjective well-being: The science of happiness, and a proposal for a national index. *American Psychologist, 55*, 34–43.

Festinger, L., Riecken, H., & Schachter, S. (1956). *When prophecy fails: A social and psychological study of a modern group that predicted the destruction of the world.* University of Minnesota Press.

Freud, S. (1961). *Five lectures on psycho-analysis.* New York, NY: Norton.

Geertz, C. (1973). *The interpretation of cultures.* New York, NY: Basic Books.

Glaser, B. G., & Strauss, A. L. (1967). *The discovery of grounded theory: Strategies for qualitative research.* Chicago, IL: Aldine.

Jouriles, E. N., Garrido, E., Rosenfield, D., & McDonald, R. (2009). Experiences of psychological and physical aggression in adolescent romantic relationships: Links to psychological distress. *Child Abuse & Neglect, 33*(7), 451–460.

Kraut, R. E., & Johnston, R. E. (1979). Social and emotional messages of smiling: An ethological approach. *Journal of Personality and Social Psychology, 37*, 1539–1553.

Levine, R. V., & Norenzayan, A. (1999). The pace of life in 31 countries. *Journal of Cross-Cultural Psychology, 30*, 178–205.

Lindqvist, P., Johansson, L., & Karlsson, U. (2008). In the aftermath of teenage suicide: A qualitative study of the psychosocial consequences for the surviving family members. *BMC Psychiatry, 8:26.* Retrieved from http://www.biomedcentral.com/1471-244X/8/26

Loftus, E. F., & Pickrell, J. E. (1995). The formation of false memories. *Psychiatric Annals, 25*, 720–725.

Messerli, F. H. (2012). Chocolate consumption, cognitive function, and Nobel laureates. *New England Journal of Medicine, 367*, 1562–1564.

Milgram, S. (1963). Behavioral study of obedience. *Journal of Abnormal and Social Psychology, 67*, 371–378.

Milgram, S. (1974). *Obedience to authority: An experimental view.* New York, NY: Harper & Row.

Pelham, B. W., Carvallo, M., & Jones, J. T. (2005). Implicit egotism. *Current Directions in Psychological Science, 14*, 106–110.

Peterson, C., Seligman, M. E. P., & Vaillant, G. E. (1988). Pessimistic explanatory style is a risk factor for physical illness: A thirty-five year longitudinal study. *Journal of Personality and Social Psychology, 55*, 23–27.

Plomin, R., DeFries, J. C., McClearn, G. E., & McGuffin, P. (2008). *Behavioral genetics* (5th ed.). New York, NY: Worth.

Radcliffe, N. M., & Klein, W. M. P. (2002). Dispositional, unrealistic, and comparative optimism: Differential relations with knowledge and processing of risk information and beliefs about personal risk. *Personality and Social Psychology Bulletin, 28*, 836–846.

Rentfrow, P. J., & Gosling, S. D. (2008). The do re mi's of everyday life: The structure and personality correlates of music preferences. *Journal of Personality and Social Psychology, 84*, 1236–1256.

Rosenhan, D. L. (1973). On being sane in insane places. *Science, 179*, 250–258.

Todd, Z., Nerlich, B., McKeown, S., & Clarke, D. D. (2004) *Mixing methods in psychology: The integration of qualitative and quantitative methods in theory and practice.* London, UK: Psychology Press.

Trenor, J.M., Yu, S.L., Waight, C.L., Zerda. K.S & Sha T.-L. (2008). The relations of ethnicity to female engineering students' educational experiences and college and career plans in an ethnically diverse learning environment. *Journal of Engineering Education,* 97(4), 449-465.

Watson, J. B., & Rayner, R. (1920). Conditioned emotional reactions. *Journal of Experimental Psychology,* 3, 1–14.

Wilkins, A. (2008). "Happier than Non-Christians": Collective emotions and symbolic boundaries among evangelical Christians. *Social Psychology Quarterly,* 71, 281–301.

# Chapter VII

Buhrmester, M., Kwang, T., & Gosling, S.D. (2011). Amazon's Mechanical Turk: A new source of inexpensive, yet high quality, data? *Perspectives on Psychological Science,* 6(1), 3-5.

Chang, L., & Krosnick, J.A. (2003). Measuring the frequency of regular behaviors: Comparing the 'typical week' to the 'past week'. *Sociological Methodology,* 33, 55-80.

Converse, J. M. (1987). *Survey research in the United States: Roots and emergence, 1890–1960.* Berkeley, CA: University of California Press.

Gosling, S. D., Vazire, S., Srivastava, S., & John, O. P. (2004). Should we trust web-based studies? A comparative analysis of six preconceptions about internet questionnaires. *American Psychologist,* 59(2), 93-104.

Groves, R. M., Fowler, F. J., Couper, M. P., Lepkowski, J. M., Singer, E., & Tourangeau, R. (2004). *Survey methodology.* Hoboken, NJ: Wiley.

Krosnick, J.A. & Berent, M.K. (1993). Comparisons of party identification and policy preferences: The impact of survey question format. *American Journal of Political Science,* 27(3), 941-964.

Lahaut, V. M. H. C. J., Jansen, H. A. M., van de Mheen, D., & Garretsen, H. F. L. (2002). Non-response bias in a sample survey on alcohol consumption. *Alcohol and Alcoholism,* 37, 256–260.

Lerner, J. S., Gonzalez, R. M., Small, D. A., & Fischhoff, B. (2003). Effects of fear and anger on perceived risks of terrorism: A national field experiment. *Psychological Science,* 14, 144–150.

Likert, R. (1932). A technique for the measurement of attitudes. *Archives of Psychology,* 140, 1–55.

Miller, J.M. & Krosnick, J.A. (1998). The impact of candidate name order on election outcomes. *Public Opinion Quarterly,* 62(3), 291-330.

Natala@aws. (2011, January 26). Re: MTurk CENSUS: About how many workers were on Mechanical Turk in 2010? Message posted to Amazon Web Services Discussion Forums. Retrieved from https://forums.aws.amazon.com/thread.jspa?threadID=58891

Peterson, R. A. (2000). *Constructing effective questionnaires*. Thousand Oaks, CA: Sage.

Schwarz, N., & Strack, F. (1990). Context effects in attitude surveys: Applying cognitive theory to social research. In W. Stroebe & M. Hewstone (Eds.), *European review of social psychology* (Vol. 2, pp. 31–50). Chichester, UK: Wiley.

Schwarz, N. (1999). Self-reports: How the questions shape the answers. *American Psychologist, 54*, 93–105.

Strack, F., Martin, L. L., & Schwarz, N. (1988). Priming and communication: The social determinants of information use in judgments of life satisfaction. *European Journal of Social Psychology, 18*, 429–442.

Sudman, S., Bradburn, N. M., & Schwarz, N. (1996). *Thinking about answers: The application of cognitive processes to survey methodology*. San Francisco, CA: Jossey-Bass.

# Chapter VIII

Cook, T. D., & Campbell, D. T. (1979). *Quasi-experimentation: Design & analysis issues in field settings*. Boston, MA: Houghton Mifflin.

Eysenck, H. J. (1952). The effects of psychotherapy: An evaluation. *Journal of Consulting Psychology, 16*, 319–324.

Posternak, M. A., & Miller, I. (2001). Untreated short-term course of major depression: A meta-analysis of studies using outcomes from studies using wait-list control groups. *Journal of Affective Disorders, 66*, 139–146.

Smith, M. L., Glass, G. V., & Miller, T. I. (1980). *The benefits of psychotherapy*. Baltimore, MD: Johns Hopkins University Press.

# Chapter IX

Brown, H. D., Kosslyn, S. M., Delamater, B., Fama, A., & Barsky, A. J. (1999). Perceptual and memory biases for health-related information in hypochondriacal individuals. *Journal of Psychosomatic Research, 47*, 67–78.

Gilliland, K. (1980). The interactive effect of introversion-extraversion with caffeine induced arousal on verbal performance. *Journal of Research in Personality, 14*, 482–492.

MacDonald, T. K., & Martineau, A. M. (2002). Self-esteem, mood, and intentions to use condoms: When does low self-esteem lead to risky health behaviors? *Journal of Experimental Social Psychology, 38*, 299–306.

Schnall, S., Benton, J., & Harvey, S. (2008). With a clean conscience: Cleanliness reduces the severity of moral judgments. *Psychological Science, 19*(12), 1219-1222. doi: 10.1111/j.1467-9280.2008.02227.x

Schnall, S., Haidt, J., Clore, G. L., & Jordan, A. H. (2008). Disgust as embodied moral judgment. *Personality and Social Psychology Bulletin, 34*, 1096–1109.

# Chapter X

Baer, D. M., Wolf, M. M., & Risley, T. R. (1968). Some current dimensions of applied behavior analysis. *Journal of Applied Behavior Analysis, 1,* 91–97.

Danov, S. E., & Symons, F. E. (2008). A survey evaluation of the reliability of visual inspection and functional analysis graphs. *Behavior Modification, 32,* 828–839.

Dehaene, S. (2011). *The number sense: How the mind creates mathematics* (2nd ed.). New York, NY: Oxford.

Fisch, G. S. (2001). Evaluating data from behavioral analysis: Visual inspection or statistical models. *Behavioral Processes, 54,* 137–154.

Hall, R. V., Lund, D., & Jackson, D. (1968). Effects of teacher attention on study behavior. *Journal of Applied Behavior Analysis, 1,* 1–12.

Kazdin, A. E. (1982). *Single-case research designs: Methods for clinical and applied settings.* New York, NY: Oxford University Press.

Ross, S. W., & Horner, R. H. (2009). Bully prevention in positive behavior support. *Journal of Applied Behavior Analysis, 42,* 747–759.

Scruggs, T. E., & Mastropieri, M. A. (2001). How to summarize single-participant research: Ideas and applications. *Exceptionality, 9,* 227–244.

Shadish, W. R., Cook, T. D., & Campbell, D. T. (2002). *Experimental and quasi-experimental designs for generalized causal inference.* Boston, MA: Houghton Mifflin.

Sidman, M. (1960). *Tactics of scientific research: Evaluating experimental data in psychology.* Boston, MA: Authors Cooperative.

Skinner, B. F. (1938). *The behavior of organisms: An experimental analysis.* New York, NY: Appleton-Century-Crofts.

Wolf, M. (1976). Social validity: The case for subjective measurement or how applied behavior analysis is finding its heart. *Journal of Applied Behavior Analysis, 11,* 203–214.

# Chapter XI

American Psychological Association, Committee on Lesbian, Gay, and Bisexual Concerns Joint Task Force on Guidelines for Psychotherapy With Lesbian, Gay, and Bisexual Clients. (2000). *Guidelines for psychotherapy with lesbian, gay, and bisexual clients.* Retrieved from https://www.apa.org/pi/lgbt/resources/guidelines

Bem, D. J. (2003). Writing the empirical journal article. In J. M. Darley, M. P. Zanna, & H. R. Roediger III (Eds.), *The complete academic: A practical guide for the beginning social scientist* (2nd ed.). Washington, DC: American Psychological Association.

Bentley, M., Peerenboom, C. A., Hodge, F. W., Passano, E. B., Warren, H. C., & Washburn, M. F. (1929). Instructions in regard to preparation of manuscript. *Psychological Bulletin, 26,* 57–63.

Darley, J. M., & Latané, B. (1968). Bystander intervention in emergencies: Diffusion of responsibility. *Journal of Personality and Social Psychology, 4,* 377–383.

Madigan, R., Johnson, S., & Linton, P. (1995). The language of psychology: APA style as epistemology. *American Psychologist, 50,* 428–436.

Onwuegbuzie, A. J., Combs, J. P., Slate, J. R., & Frels, R. K. (2010). Editorial: Evidence-based guidelines for avoiding the most common APA errors in journal article submissions. *Research in the Schools, 16,* ix–xxxvi.

American Psychological Association. (2010). *Publication Manual of the American Psychological Association* (6th ed.). Washington, D.C.: American Psychological Association.

# Chapter XII

Ollendick, T. H., Öst, L.-G., Reuterskiöld, L., Costa, N., Cederlund, R., Sirbu, C.,...Jarrett, M. A. (2009). One-session treatments of specific phobias in youth: A randomized clinical trial in the United States and Sweden. *Journal of Consulting and Clinical Psychology, 77,* 504–516.

Cohen, J. (1992). A power primer. *Psychological Bulletin, 112,* 155–159.

Hyde, J. S. (2007). New directions in the study of gender similarities and differences. *Current Directions in Psychological Science, 16,* 259–263.

Carlson, K. A., & Conard, J. M. (2011). The last name effect: How last name influences acquisition timing. *Journal of Consumer Research, 38*(2), 300-307. doi: 10.1086/658470

MacDonald, T. K., & Martineau, A. M. (2002). *Self-esteem, mood, and intentions to use condoms: When does low self-esteem lead to risky health behaviors? Journal of Experimental Social Psychology, 38,* 299–306.

McCabe, D. P., Roediger, H. L., McDaniel, M. A., Balota, D. A., & Hambrick, D. Z. (2010). *The relationship between working memory capacity and executive functioning. Neuropsychology, 24*(2), 222–243. doi:10.1037/a0017619

Brown, N. R., & Sinclair, R. C. (1999). Estimating number of lifetime sexual partners: Men and women do it differently. *The Journal of Sex Research, 36,* 292–297.

Bem, D. J. (2003). Writing the empirical journal article. In J. M. Darley, M. P. Zanna, & H. L. Roediger III (Eds.), *The complete academic: A career guide* (2nd ed., pp. 185–219). Washington, DC: American Psychological Association.

Schmitt, D. P., & Allik, J. (2005). Simultaneous administration of the Rosenberg Self-Esteem Scale in 53 nations: Exploring the universal and culture-specific features of global self-esteem. *Journal of Personality and Social Psychology, 89,* 623–642.

Buss, D. M., & Schmitt, D. P. (1993). Sexual strategies theory: A contextual evolutionary analysis of human mating. *Psychological Review, 100,* 204–232.

# Chapter XIII

Aarts, A. A., Anderson, C. J., Anderson, J., van Assen, M. A. L. M., Attridge, P. R., Attwood, A. S., ... Zuni, K. (2015, September 21). Reproducibility Project: Psychology. Retrieved from osf.io/ezcuj

Abelson, R. P. (1995). *Statistics as principled argument*. Mahwah, NJ: Erlbaum.

Aschwanden, C. (2015, August 19). Science isn't broken: It's just a hell of a lot harder than we give it credit for. Retrieved from http://fivethirtyeight.com/features/science-isnt-broken/

Brandt, M. J., IJzerman, H., Dijksterhuis, A., Farach, F. J., Geller, J., Giner-Sorolla, R., ... can't Veer, A. (2014). The replication recipe: What makes for a convincing replication? *Journal of Experimental Social Psychology, 50*, 217-224. doi:10.1016/j.jesp.2013.10.005

Cohen, J. (1994). The world is round: p < .05. *American Psychologist, 49*, 997-1003.

Frank, M. (2015, August 31). The slower, harder ways to increase reproducibility. Retrieved from http://babieslearninglanguage.blogspot.ie/2015/08/the-slower-harder-ways-to-increase.html

Head M. L., Holman, L., Lanfear, R., Kahn, A. T., & Jennions, M. D. (2015). The extent and consequences of p-hacking in science. *PLoS Biology, 13*(3): e1002106. doi:10.1371/journal.pbio.1002106

Hyde, J. S. (2007). New directions in the study of gender similarities and differences. *Current Directions in Psychological Science, 16*, 259–263.

Kanner, A. D., Coyne, J. C., Schaefer, C., & Lazarus, R. S. (1981). Comparison of two modes of stress measurement: Daily hassles and uplifts versus major life events. *Journal of Behavioral Medicine, 4*, 1–39.

Kerr, N. L. (1998). HARKing: Hypothesizing after the results are known. *Personality and Social Psychology Review, 2*(3), 196-217. doi:10.1207/s15327957pspr0203_4

Lakens, D. (2017, December 25). About p-values: Understanding common misconceptions. [Blog post] Retrieved from https://correlaid.org/en/blog/understand-p-values/

Mehl, M. R., Vazire, S., Ramirez-Esparza, N., Slatcher, R. B., & Pennebaker, J. W. (2007). Are women really more talkative than men? *Science, 317*, 82.

Nosek, B. A., Alter, G., Banks, G. C., Borsboom, D., Bowman, S. D., Breckler, S. J., ... Yarkoni, T. (2015). Promoting an open research culture. *Science, 348*(6242), 1422-1425. doi: 10.1126/science.aab2374

Oakes, M. (1986). *Statistical inference: A commentary for the social and behavioral sciences*. Chichester, UK: Wiley.

Pashler, H., & Harris, C. R. (2012). Is the replicability crisis overblown? Three arguments explained. *Perspectives on Psychological Science, 7*(6), 531-536. doi:10.1177/1745691612463401

Rosenthal, R. (1979). The file drawer problem and tolerance for null results. *Psychological Bulletin, 83*, 638–641.

Scherer, L. (2015, September). Guest post by Laura Scherer. Retrieved from http://sometimesimwrong.typepad.com/wrong/2015/09/guest-post-by-laura-scherer.html

Schnall, S., Benton, J., & Harvey, S. (2008). With a clean conscience: Cleanliness reduces the severity of moral judgments. *Psychological Science, 19*(12), 1219-1222. doi: 10.1111/j.1467-9280.2008.02227.x

Simonsohn U., Nelson L. D., & Simmons J. P. (2014). P-Curve: a key to the file drawer. *Journal of Experimental Psychology: General, 143*(2), 534-547. doi: 10.1037/a0033242

Tramimow, D. & Marks, M. (2015). Editorial. *Basic and Applied Social Psychology, 37*, 1-2. https://dx.doi.org/10.1080/01973533.2015.1012991

Wilkinson, L., & Task Force on Statistical Inference. (1999). Statistical methods in psychology journals: Guidelines and explanations. *American Psychologist, 54*, 594-604.

Yong, E. (August 27, 2015). How reliable are psychology studies? Retrieved from http://www.theatlantic.com/science/archive/2015/08/psychology-studies-reliability-reproducability-nosek/402466/

Made in the USA
Las Vegas, NV
08 January 2021